To Alice, for all the books

Why, soldiers, why
Should we be melancholy, boys?
Why, soldiers, why
Whose business 'tis to die!

General Wolfe's Song

Contents

CONTENTS

List of Illustrations

Picture research:
Laurie Platt Winfrey,
Carousel Research, Inc.

Acknowledgments

I would particularly like to thank Joanne Wood Ryan (later associate editor of the Public Papers of Aaron Burr), who was my advisor and assistant when I first began researching this book in the 1980s. Her help was invaluable. Equally important was counsel from John S. du Mont on the intricacies of duels and dueling pistols. Also helpful as a researcher was Anthony Chiafolo. My son, Richard Fleming, was equally important in my research efforts, especially on the Internet. The librarians at Yale University, where I did my early research, were invariably eager to cooperate with my requests. The same can be said of the staffs of The New York Historical Society, the New York Public Library, the New York Society Library and The Society of the Cincinnati Library in Washington, D.C., where Ellen McCallister Clark was especially helpful. Lewis Daniels of the Westbrook Public Library was indefatigable in obtaining interlibrary loans while I was working at my summer home in that charming Connecticut town. Finally I would like to thank my agent, Ted Chichak, for his constant counsel and assistance, as well as my wife, Alice, who read the manuscript from its earliest stages, and my editor, Don Fehr, who provided the ideal combination of personal friendship and wise advice.

CHAPTER 1

A General
Nurses His Wounds

*A*lexander Hamilton welcomed the year 1804 at his country estate, The Grange, seven miles north of New York City, on the two-hundred-foot-high ridge known as Harlem Heights. Not long after he arose, a bone-chilling rain began sluicing out of a gray sky.[1] The two-story house, with its high porches and four rectangular chimneys (two of them fakes, added for symmetry), had been designed by John McComb, creator of New York's City Hall and other distinguished buildings. From the front porch, which faced south, there was a magnificent view of New York City, its immense harbor, and the mighty Atlantic beyond Sandy Hook. Through the floor-to-ceiling bay windows of the elegant octagonal dining room there was an equally compelling view of the Harlem River valley, turbulent Hell Gate, and the swift-flowing East River. From similar windows on the other side of the parlor, Hamilton surveyed the broad Hudson River and its majestic western bluffs, the Palisades. Beyond stretched the vast American continent, peopled by a scant four million Americans and perhaps a million Indians.

These imperial views were not very entrancing on a rainy New Year's Day, of course. In fact, the stripped trees and the brown fields gave The Grange a forlorn, abandoned look. Someone with prophetic tendencies might have seen this gloom as a portent, but it is unlikely that Hamilton viewed it as anything more than a rainy winter morning. He did not know it was the last New Year's Day he would see.

1

Inside the house, which Hamilton had named after the ancestral estate of his Scottish grandfather, servants and perhaps Hamilton himself were soon busy keeping the numerous fireplaces blazing. Although The Grange's clapboard walls were lined with brick, the lofty site made it a target for icy winds. With seven children in the house, ranging in age from two to nineteen, it was impossible to warm only a few rooms. Since firewood was extremely expensive on Manhattan Island in 1804, each winter day Hamilton spent in The Grange literally burned a hole in his pocket.

The house and the surrounding thirty-two acres had cost him $22,220 (the equivalent in modern dollars of perhaps $300,000) and much of this remained borrowed money.[2] Furnishing The Grange and living in the style that such a fine mansion required, with servants, a cook, and a gardener, were also expensive burdens for a man who depended entirely on the cash he earned as a lawyer. One of the many ironies about Alexander Hamilton was the parlous state of his personal finances. The man who had resuscitated the expiring economy of the new nation frequently ran short of funds.

Hamilton averaged about $11,000 a year ($150,000 modern dollars) as one of the leading attorneys of the New York Bar. But his expenses constantly outran his income. When The Grange was nearing completion in 1802, he wrote to one client that it "would be amazingly convenient to me to touch your money as soon as possible."[3] Intermittently, Hamilton vowed to economize; at one point he considered leasing The Grange and reducing his expenses to $4,000 a year. But the house was linked too intimately with Hamilton's image of himself as a man of consequence. To abandon it would have been a psychic amputation he could never endure.

In 1804 everyone called Alexander Hamilton "General." He was even accorded the title in the New York City directory. A lieutenant colonel in the American Revolution, Hamilton had achieved this new rank in America's first undeclared war, the nasty brawl with revolutionary France that lasted from 1798 to 1800. All the shooting had been done at sea;

General Hamilton's army never fought a battle. But he was extremely proud of achieving this rank and virtually insisted on preserving it as a civilian.

This fondness for a title, military or otherwise, was not unusual. Foreign visitors noted that Americans of the early 1800s, while claiming to despise aristocracy and its artificial distinctions, constantly addressed one another as "Colonel," "Major," "Judge" long after the terms had an immediate application. The national passion for equality, another trait visitors noticed, apparently had its limits. But Hamilton's fondness for "General" meant far more than a mild desire for distinction among his peers. Like The Grange, the title had deep links with his innermost psychology.

Red-haired, large-headed, with deep blue, almost violet eyes and ruddy cheeks, Hamilton was short by modern standards—about five feet seven—but this was an average height in his era, when growth was sapped by numerous childhood diseases for which there were no vaccines. Hamilton's slim, sinewy frame, his vigorous manner, his erect carriage inevitably drew the adjectives "soldierly" and "martial" from many men who commented on his appearance. Some admirers called him "the little lion"—a tribute to his pugnacity.[4]

When Hamilton was building The Grange, he often came up from the city on weekends and lived with his three older sons in tents on the property. "He measured the distances as though marking the frontage of a (military) camp," his son John Church Hamilton later recalled. "When he walked along, his step seemed to fall naturally into the cadenced pace of practiced drill." John Church never forgot the way his father read the commentaries of Julius Caesar, translating the Latin as he went along: "With what emphasis and fervor did he read of battles . . . it would seem as though Caesar were present; for as much as any man that ever lived, he had the soldier's temperament."[5]

When he relaxed with his sons, Hamilton's favorite topic was stories from the American Revolution. The location of The Grange undoubtedly intensified these recollections. It was on Harlem Heights that nineteen-year-old Captain Alexander Hamilton first won the attention of the American army's high command. His artillery company was one of the few units in the ragtag assemblage of Continental regulars and state militia that retained its discipline and esprit de corps in the dolorous fall of 1776, when the Americans lost battle after battle to a resurgent British army. Early in the following year, Captain Hamilton was promoted to lieutenant colonel and became one of George Washington's aides, beginning his ascent to power and renown.

II

Later in the morning of New Year's Day, General Hamilton gathered his wife and seven children around him and read something very different from Caesar's commentaries—the Episcopal Church service. In his teens Hamilton had been intensely religious. Robert Troup, his roommate at New York's Kings College (which had changed its name to Columbia after the War for Independence), recalled that he had knelt to say his prayers every night and morning. A Presbyterian minister had been responsible for rescuing the illegitimate son of bankrupt James Hamilton and tempestuous Rachel Faucett Lavien from the West Indian backwater of St. Croix and sending him to America for an education. But Hamilton's adolescent piety had soon faded into the stoic creed that the leaders of the Revolution preferred to the complex theology of Christianity, with its belief in a crucified God and redemption through suffering.

Sometimes called Deism, the faith of the founding fathers replaced a personal God with an opaque Providence, whom George Washington once referred to as "it." Although the father of the country attended the Episcopal Church, Washington usually left before the communion service, pointedly if silently stating his disbelief in this central ceremony of the Christian faith. When Thomas Jefferson inveighed against "every form of tyranny over the mind of man," he was talking about organized Christianity. During the Constitutional Convention, when the delegates seemed deadlocked, Benjamin Franklin had suggested starting the day with a prayer to seek the help of divine wisdom. Hamilton had risen to oppose the idea, claiming it would be a confession of political disunity. He blithely added that he saw no need to seek "foreign aid."[6]

Deism had apparently seemed sufficient to the mature Hamilton, especially in the 1790s, when he had been President George Washington's secretary of the treasury, the young nation's most influential politician. Hamilton had taken a country floundering in a morass of $80 million in state and federal war debts (40 percent of the gross national product) and in a series of brilliant state papers, persuaded Congress to transform this demoralizing legacy of the Revolution into a national asset. Following England's example, Hamilton saw the debt could become "a blessing" if it was converted into liquid capital bonds backed by the full credit of the new federal government, which had the power to raise money by taxes and tariffs. To stabilize the new system and prime the national financial pump, Hamilton persuaded Congress to create the semipublic Bank of the United States. In five years, the United States had the highest credit rating in the world and a reliable money supply was fueling prosperity from Boston to Savannah.

In those heady days, Alexander Hamilton believed human intelligence was enough to shape a man's and a nation's destiny. But bitter personal and political experiences had altered this opinion. In recent years, intelligence seemed a frail safeguard against the onrush and inrush of passion, both personal and political. His view of mankind, never optimistic, had veered toward a belief in human depravity that could best be explained by another basic Christian concept, original sin.

General Hamilton read the Episcopal service with the sonorous sincerity of a man who genuinely wanted to inculcate religion in his seven children. Although he was something of an absentee father because of the demands of politics and the legal profession, Hamilton did his best to provide them with the happy family life he had seldom experienced as a boy in the West Indies. His dark-haired, attractive mother had never bothered to legitimize her common-law marriage to his financially inept father, James Hamilton, and she finally kicked him out of her bed to send him wandering through the islands like a pathetic, possibly alcoholic castaway. Before Hamilton was born, the headstrong Rachel had ended a legal marriage to John Michael Lavien (or Levine) by sleeping with other men so blatantly that her outraged husband had her jailed for "whoring with everyone." Although Hamilton sometimes mentioned "our dear father" in letters to his brother, James, there is no record of him ever having spoken or written affectionately of his mother.[7]

How seriously Hamilton regarded the sacred words of the Sunday service as food for his own soul is debatable. On January 11, 1804, he would be forty-seven, a fairly old age in an era when only a few people lived into their sixties and seventies. It would not be implausible to find him thinking about death and considering a return to the faith of his youth. Moreover, General Hamilton had experienced several varieties of suffering in the previous three years.

From the summit of political power on which he had stood in 1800, as the leader of the triumphant Federalist Party, he had been pitched into the pit of impotence when Thomas Jefferson won the presidency and Aaron Burr the vice presidency on the Republican ticket in November of that fateful year. In 1801 Hamilton's political humiliation was completed when he failed to elect his sister-in-law's husband, wealthy Stephen Van Rensselaer, governor of New York in a savage struggle with the state leader of the Republicans, a man the General detested, George Clinton.

In that contest, General Hamilton's political enemies had showered him with abuse. Robert Troup reported that at one polling place, Hamilton was "repeatedly called a thief; and at another . . . called a rascal, villain, and every thing else that is in famous [*sic*] in society."[8] For a man who saw himself as a patriot who had spent the previous fifteen years struggling selflessly for the good of his country, these insults were especially bitter.

In the circle of trusting faces around Hamilton there was evidence of another blow. His beautiful nineteen-year-old daughter Angelica listened to the stately prose of the Episcopal service with blank uncomprehending eyes. For the past two and one-half years, Angelica, who used to delight her father with her skill on the harp and pianoforte, had been insane. Her mental breakdown had been triggered by a tragedy that had almost driven General Hamilton and his wife, Elizabeth, berserk.

III

On November 20, 1801, the Hamiltons' handsome oldest son, nineteen-year-old Philip, recently graduated from Columbia College, had gotten into a quarrel with one of President Thomas Jefferson's supporters, a twenty-seven-year-old lawyer named George I. Eacker. Philip and his friend Richard Price had invaded Eacker's box at the Park Theater and taunted him about a speech he had made on July 4, 1801. Eacker had hailed President Thomas Jefferson as the rescuer of the Constitution and implied that General Hamilton was not averse to seizing power with a coup d'etat. Philip's hooliganish conduct suggests he and his friend Price were drunk. Realistic Robert Troup, belying his fond parents' view of Philip's talents and promise, described him as a "sad rake."

The infuriated Eacker called both young men "damned rascals"—an expression of contempt that left them with only one response, if they hoped to retain their standing in the masculine world of the time. They promptly challenged him to a duel.

This ritualized conflict was based on the assumption that a gentleman had to be prepared to defend his honor at all times. Inherited from the days of chivalry, in the sixteenth century dueling became popular among European aristocrats, army and naval officers, and politicians. It took root in America during the Revolution, when the officer corps of the Continental army strove to establish their status as gentlemen.[9]

During the 1790s, the American duel became a way to intimidate or humiliate a political opponent—and demonstrate a man's readiness to verify the sincerity of his opinions by risking his life. Frequently condemned by churchmen and banned by legislatures, it persisted because it was a way of acting out the fratricidal passions that the politics of the 1790s had evoked. Also, it was a chance for a man to display his courage without extreme risk, unless his opponent was a crack shot. In one study of dueling, fatalities were less than 20 percent. Another study found only one duelist in fourteen died. Most duelists escaped unscathed, or with minor wounds, at worst. It had become fashionable among some writers to portray these affairs as more farcical than fatal.[10]

Eacker and Richard Price met first. Because dueling was illegal in New York, they journeyed to Weehawken, on the New Jersey side of the Hudson River. The encounter seemed to confirm the impression that amateur duelists were not a serious threat to life or limb. Four shots were exchanged without a hit.

A Hamilton friend urged Philip to apologize to Eacker for his bad manners at the theater. That minimal courtesy might have persuaded Eacker to retract the insult, "rascal." Perhaps emboldened by Price's description of Eacker's poor aim, Philip declined, and insisted on an immediate "interview," as these affairs of honor were called.

General Hamilton, learning about the duel, advised Philip to fire his pistol into the air. Whether this advice was based on religious or tactical grounds is unclear. "Throwing away" one's fire—known as a *delope* by those who preferred French dueling terminology—was an accepted way of aborting a duel. The *deloper* had to let the other man fire at him first, giving no hint of what he was planning to do. If the other man insisted on another shot, he could be accused of bloodthirsty, even murderous intentions—a slur no gentleman wanted to incur. Often the duelists' seconds would declare that honor had been satisfied and ban another shot.

Hamilton may have been reluctant to see Philip wound or kill Eacker over a quarrel the young man had started—a motive that might have involved religious feelings, or simple common sense. Firing in the air was also a way to express a certain contempt for one's opponent, or a moral superiority. William Pitt, until recently prime minister of England, had chosen the *delope* when taunted into a duel by a parliamentary critic.[11]

Eacker and Philip Hamilton met on November 23, 1801. For a full minute, neither fired at the word "present." Eacker probably did not want to hurt Philip for a variety of reasons: the difference in their ages, the triviality of the quarrel, his father's influence and prestige. If Philip had offered an apology at this point, the dispute still could have been settled with a handshake.

Instead, Philip leveled his pistol. Perhaps the young man simply wanted to share bragging rights with his friend Price about hearing a bullet whistle. Or like most nineteen-year-olds, he considered himself indestructible. Eacker leveled and fired. His bullet struck Philip just above the hip, ripped through his body, and lodged in his arm. Philip's return shot went wild.

The young man died in agony twenty-four hours later, with his tormented mother and father beside him on the bed, frantically clutching him in their arms. At the funeral, General Hamilton almost collapsed. "Never did I see a man so completely overwhelmed with grief," wrote Robert Troup. Not long after the funeral, Angelica Hamilton drifted into a miasma of confusion and fear from which she never emerged for the rest of her long life. Over and over again she played on her piano and harp the songs of 1800–01 that had pleased her father—and presumably Philip—so much.[12]

IV

Those who have wanted to believe Alexander Hamilton experienced a profound change of heart as a result of these political disappointments and personal tragedies have combed his letters to find evidence of such a transformation. They have portrayed The Grange as a place where "his religious feelings grew with his growing intimacy with the marvellous works of nature."[13] But General Hamilton planned The Grange in 1798, when he was at the height of his political power. What he wanted was a country estate similar to those owned by other notable New Yorkers, such as Vice President Aaron Burr's elegant Richmond Hill, on the Hudson below present-day Fourteenth Street. Only in such a house could the General receive important visitors in a style that befitted a man who saw himself as the arbiter of the destiny of North America.

As for his growing intimacy with the works of nature, the General was a disaster as a farmer. Several times, he remarked wryly in letters that a garden was a "usual refuge of a disappointed politician." But he added late in 1802 that he was "as little fitted" to be a farmer "as Jefferson to guide the helm of the United States."[14] When he was planning The Grange, there was some heady talk of profits from the farm produce that could be raised on thirty-two acres. But that was just Hamilton's way of convincing himself that he could afford the house. In December of 1802, as they were moving in, Hamilton confided to a friend that "the greatest part of my little farm will be dedicated to grass." Whereupon he solicited advice on how to grow that plant successfully. Since they moved in, the Hamiltons' total profits from The Grange were $18.00 from the sale of some garden strawberries, cabbages, and asparagus.[15]

Further reason to doubt General Hamilton's conversion from politics to religion and domesticity was a letter to James A. Bayard, the influential Federalist congressman from Delaware, written not long after Philip Hamilton's death. The General proposed the creation of a "Christian Constitutional Society," which would be organized into local clubs, state councils, and a national council, consisting of a president and twelve members. Its purpose would be the defense of the Christian religion and the Constitution against the assaults of the Republicans, led by their purportedly atheistic leader, President Thomas Jefferson.

Hamilton told Bayard he feared the Federalist party was doomed unless it could "contrive to take hold of & carry along with us some strong feelings of the mind." In fact, he had begun to doubt whether it was possible for them to succeed "without in some degree employing the weapons which have been employed against us." By this he meant newspapers like Philadelphia's *Aurora* and New York's *American Citizen*, crammed with the sort of billingsgate the Republicans had used to demonize General Hamilton and the Federalists. At the same time Hamilton admitted he shuddered at "corrupting public opinion" until it became "fit for nothing but mischief."

The Christian Constitutional Society was his answer to this dilemma. Bayard rejected the idea, commenting that the notion was better suited to the Republicans. "We have the greater number of political Calculators and they of political fanaticks," he wrote.[16]

Manipulating religion for public purposes was not a new idea for General Hamilton. Ever since the French Revolution revealed its hatred of Christianity in the early 1790s, Hamilton had used piety to summon the Federalist faithful to the hustings. When he was preparing the country for war with France in 1797, he urged Congress to mobilize "the religious ideas of America." In 1798, excoriating Thomas Jefferson and other admirers of France, he accused them of "a conspiracy to establish atheism on the ruins of Christianity."[17] But for all his private and public displays of devotion to Christianity, General Hamilton had yet to join a church.

The reason for this hesitation was probably political. Hamilton was strongly attracted to the Episcopal church. But Episcopalians were not in good repute among most voters in New York, because so many of them had been loyalists during the Revolution. As members of the Church of England, they had tended to support their titular head, His Majesty, George III. Although the Episcopalians had redefined themselves as an American church and pledged their allegiance to the new nation, in the overheated politics of 1804, Hamilton's enemies were not above suggesting that joining them was further proof of his treasonous pro-British leanings.

Instead of scrutinizing General Hamilton's words and actions to indict him for religious hypocrisy or exonerate him as a genuine Christian, it might be wiser to regard him as a man in the middle of a spiritual journey, carrying with him all the baggage he had acquired from the previous forty-seven years of a crowded and tumultuous life. The ideas and ideals of Christianity had recently begun mingling with other core beliefs. But a man who toiled on dozens of complex cases in maritime and commercial law and simultaneously attempted to keep abreast of national and international politics did not have the time or the inclination to sort out the contradictions and inconsistencies.

V

There is some evidence that General Hamilton took more interest in his wife and family after his fall from power. "It will be more and more my endeavor to abstract myself from all pursuits which interfere with those of affection," he wrote.[18] But this statement was only a promise of future performance, about as convincing as his resolutions to economize. To Elizabeth Schuyler Hamilton, pregnant with their last child, the General wrote in 1801: "Indeed my Eliza, you are very essential to me. Your virtues more and more endear you to me and experience more and more convinces me that true happiness is only to be found in the bosom of one's own family."

This is a curious statement for a husband to make to a wife of twenty years. It suggests that only recently had Hamilton found Eliza endearing. Heretofore had he sought happiness in other bosoms? Or was there some other transformative experience that had captured the general's soul? The answer to both questions would seem to be: yes.

The words, and the realities behind them, explain the uncertainty that mars Elizabeth Hamilton's mouth in her 1787 portrait by Ralph Earl, the only likeness painted during her husband's lifetime. The mouth contributes to an overall impression of timidity, insecurity, even melancholy. She is a fairly attractive woman, with deep-set dark eyes beneath thick brows. But there is not an iota of the fire, the dash, the self-confidence that emanates from almost every portrait of her dynamic husband.

To be fair, Hamilton was not entirely to blame for inflicting these feelings of inadequacy on Elizabeth Hamilton. She grew up the daughter of

Hudson River lord Philip Schuyler, owner of vast upstate acreage, a major general in the Revolution, confidante of Washington. Schuyler's overbearing parental style goaded Elizabeth's four sisters into selecting husbands of whom their father disapproved—and three of them eloped. Only Elizabeth remained docile, choosing a man whose closeness to Washington guaranteed General Schuyler's blessing.

Another person who may have sown uncertainty in Elizabeth Hamilton's soul was her attractive oldest sister, Angelica. Witty, intelligent, rambunctious, in 1777 she eloped with John Barker Church, a wealthy Englishman who had fled to America under an assumed name, probably to escape jail for his gambling debts. Church eventually persuaded General Schuyler to help him obtain the post of commissary to the French army that came to America in 1780. The Englishman made a fortune, which he multiplied with shrewd investments in England and America. He spent it freely to give Angelica every imaginable luxury and let her roam high society in London, Paris, and New York as a flirtatious woman of fashion, while he concentrated on the one thing that seemed to interest him—making more money in business and at gaming tables.[19]

Betsy Hamilton seems to have worshiped Angelica almost as much as she adored her brilliant husband. But in 1804, many New Yorkers, including that constant Hamilton watcher, Robert Troup, suspected that Angelica and General Hamilton had resumed a torrid affair, suspended, with exquisite regret on both sides, in 1789, when she returned to England after a lengthy visit to New York without her husband. If Elizabeth Hamilton suspected anything about the General and Angelica, she suffered in silence. In their tormented letters to each other, the lovers constantly made it a point to include Betsy in their protestations of undying affection.[20]

It need hardly be added that this affair, for which circumstantial evidence is strong but absolute confirmation is elusive, did not exactly jibe with General Hamilton's newly discovered Christian inclinations. It is one more piece of evidence that the General's life had become very complicated—perhaps too complicated for him to comprehend.

VI

Compounding Elizabeth Hamilton's wifely melancholy in the years after Ralph Earl painted her portrait was Maria Reynolds, a dark-haired passionate woman-about-Philadelphia, with whom Hamilton became involved in 1791, when the Quaker City was the national capital. Although he was riding high as secretary of the treasury with President George Washington's firm backing for his determination to transform a mostly rural America into a financial and industrial powerhouse, Hamilton had recently experienced his first political defeat.

His father-in-law, General Philip Schuyler, had been serving as one of New York's senators in the new federal government. Hamilton had engineered his election by the state's legislature in 1789, cavalierly ignoring the expectations of the powerful Livingston family, who owned at least as much acreage in the Hudson River valley as Schuyler. In 1788, the eloquent leader of that family, Chancellor Robert R. Livingston, had warmly supported Hamilton in the ferocious struggle to persuade New Yorkers to ratify the Constitution in spite of Governor George Clinton's stubborn opposition. Underscoring his arrogance, Hamilton had vetoed the election of a Livingston in-law, New York Mayor James Duane, for the state's second senate seat and insisted on choosing Massachusetts-born Rufus King, who had only recently become a New York resident. This moment of hubris led to a Livingston alliance with Governor Clinton, with repercussions that still afflicted Hamilton.

When General Schuyler's name was placed in nomination for a second term in the U.S. Senate, the new allies flexed their political muscles. Another nominee came from nowhere to displace Schuyler: Aaron Burr. A fellow lawyer and veteran of the Revolution, Burr too had been a Hamilton ally against George Clinton for a while. But the short, affable New Jersey native had grown disillusioned with Hamilton's domineering leadership. Burr had been particularly irked by the way Hamilton had crammed Rufus King down New Yorkers' throats because the secretary of the treasury wanted to have this devoted follower in the U.S. Senate to support his financial program.

Hamilton's failure to deliver a coveted post for his father-in-law may have complicated his marriage to Elizabeth Schuyler—or his affair with Angelica Schuyler Church. The latter seems more likely. It is hard to imagine Betsy rebuking Hamilton for a political lapse. Angelica, on the other hand, savored mixing power and passion. Hamilton frequently wrote to her about his political travails and triumphs, and she seems to have been extremely disappointed by her father's humiliation. A rebuke from her could well have made Hamilton susceptible to Maria Reynolds, another woman of fashion who had no association with his defeat and who appealed to him as a man of power, capable of rescuing her from the grip of an abusive, unfaithful husband.

In no time Maria Reynold's husband, James, appeared, ready and eager to play the pimp, if Hamilton came through with enough cash. The bewitched Hamilton paid him over $1,000 for continuing access to Maria. Soon Reynolds was going around Philadelphia claiming that the secretary of the treasury was giving him inside tips to speculate in government securities. Accused of corruption by a delegation of congressmen led by Thomas Jefferson's close friend, Senator James Monroe of Virginia, Hamilton gave them copies of his love letters from Maria to prove his financial, if not his marital, integrity.

Five years later, in 1797, the letters surfaced in a pamphlet by a muckraking Scottish-born newspaperman, James Thomson Callender. The Scotsman accused Hamilton of faking the affair to cover up immense speculations based on his insider's knowledge of U.S. Treasury policies, enabling him and his friends to pocket millions of dollars. Hamilton responded by confessing the affair in a pamphlet that reaffirmed his financial integrity—and left the nation gasping with disbelief at his sexual candor.

In this confession, Hamilton displayed an almost breathtaking ability to see himself as blameless, even though he was admitting something that would make most men squirm. He claimed the entire scandal was a "conspiracy of vice against virtue"—the vice being all on the side of his political enemies—and even asserted he should be flattered to be the object of persecution by such a despicable faction. Seldom if ever, he declaimed, had any man been pursued with such rancor and venom for so little cause. Yet he was buoyed by his "proud consciousness of innocence" because he had not sullied his financial integrity, no matter how often he had sullied Maria Reynolds.[21]

Entwined as the statement was with politics, only a few biographers have noted that it included a passage in which Hamilton revealed an anguished, profoundly personal regret for his infidelity: "This confession is not made without a blush . . . I can never cease to condemn myself for the pang which it may inflict in a bosom eminently entitled to all my gratitude, fidelity, and love."[22] Unquestionably he was referring to Elizabeth Hamilton here.

Back in 1780, when Hamilton proposed to Betsy, his fellow aides on George Washington's staff called her "the little saint" and expressed amazement that Hamilton would select someone so devout for his wife. At army headquarters, Martha Washington, in one of her droller moments, had nicknamed the house pet, a bigheaded, extremely amorous tomcat, "Hamilton"—a glimpse of his reputation as a ladies man in those days.

Marrying Betsy did not turn Hamilton into a saint. In the heyday of his power, rumors swirled that he was constantly on the prowl for attractive women. One Federalist congressman from New England wrote home indignantly, telling a friend that he resented the way the secretary of the treasury, at a recent dinner in Philadelphia, had spent the evening casting "liquorish looks at my cara sposa."

Betsy's sisters seemed to have had no illusions about their brother-in-law. At another Philadelphia dinner party, Angelica Church lost a bow from her shoe. Her younger sister, Peggy Schuyler, described by one of the dinner guests as a "wild flirt," put the bow in the buttonhole of Hamilton's coat.

"There brother, I have made you a knight," she said.

"But of what order?" Angelica asked. "He can't be a knight of the garter in this country."

"True sister," replied Peggy Schuyler, "but he would be if you would let him."[23]

VII

Was Hamilton as financially pure as he claimed to be? The answer would seem to be yes. Charles Maurice de Talleyrand-Périgord, the wily thoroughly corrupt politician who served a half dozen French regimes, became a Hamilton admirer during the two years he spent in America to escape the guillotines of France's revolutionary wild men. In later years Talleyrand listed Hamilton with England's William Pitt and Napoléon Bonaparte as the three greatest men he had met in his lifetime. If he had to choose between the three, Talleyrand said he would have given Hamilton first place.[24]

One night in 1795, Talleyrand passed Hamilton's law office on his way to a party. He saw the former secretary of the treasury toiling over a brief by candlelight. At the party, the astounded Frenchman told everyone that he had just seen "a man who made the fortune of his country, but who is working all night in order to support his family." In France or England, a grateful government would have permitted a politician who handled millions in public funds with Hamilton's genius to get rich.[25]

An examination of Hamilton's account books reveals that he earned his $11,000 a year the hard way, handling scores of cases for mostly modest fees. Robert Troup often reproached Hamilton for his low fees, warning him that his friends would have to bury him at their expense. At one point, Troup got his own annual income up to $11,500 by working from dawn to midnight, seven days a week. The toll on the overweight attorney's health was horrendous. By 1804 he was suffering from recurrent asthma attacks and heart palpitations.[26]

In 1796, one of the big land speculators of the era, New York merchant James Greenleaf, asked Hamilton to help extricate him from a tangle of debt amounting to $1.2 million that he had accrued while buying some $5 million in land and stock. If Hamilton rescued him, his fee would be a third of Greenleaf's net worth. It was a chance to make perhaps a million dollars, but Hamilton turned him down. He feared Greenleaf was trying to trade on his influence as ex-secretary of the treasury.

Around the same time, Robert Troup, already weary of the legal grind, tried to inveigle Hamilton into joining him and another champion land speculator, ex-British army Captain Charles Williamson, in buying millions of acres of upstate New York for English investors. Williamson had become an American citizen, a legal fiction that would enable them to evade the state law against foreigners buying land. Hamilton and Troup would draw up covert agreements that would protect the English investors against fraud. Their reward would be a handsome slice of the action.

Troup offered to keep Hamilton's name secret, swearing on his honor that he would never reveal it. Hamilton turned down this deal too, because he was acutely sensitive to accusations by his political enemies that he was pro-British. "There must be some *public fools* who sacrifice private to public interest," Hamilton told Troup. It was his way of keeping himself "in a situation the best calculated to render service." [27]

VIII

Render service. By that phrase Hamilton meant public service. Underlying this seemingly mundane term was a far more powerful word that explained much of Hamilton's life: *fame*. This was the invisible mistress that he had pursued for two decades, repeatedly sacrificing the happiness offered to him by Elizabeth Schuyler Hamilton's bosom. In a letter to a Scottish uncle, written not long before he published the confession of his affair with Maria Reynolds, Hamilton discussed the "love of fame" as a "passion" that was the "spring of action." The pistol metaphor adds a heavy irony to these words. [28]

In the era of the American Revolution, fame had a very special meaning, which had little to do with being famous in the current celebrity sense of the word. For Hamilton and the other founders, fame was inextricably linked with honor and a special kind of achievement. Sir Francis Bacon, the English philosopher and organizer of knowledge, had popularized the concept. Bacon dismissed the praise of the common people as irrelevant to seekers after true fame. They had "no sense at all" of the higher virtues. Winning fame, Bacon maintained, meant winning the praise of persons of judgment and quality.

In Bacon's *Essays*, a book which the young Hamilton studied assiduously (as did Thomas Jefferson, John Adams, Aaron Burr, and many others), there is a five-stage classification of fame. On the bottom rung were fathers of the country, who "reign justly and make the times good wherein they live." Next came champions of empire, leaders who enlarge their country through conquest or defend her against invaders. Next came saviors of empire, who deliver their country from the miseries of tyrants or the chaos of civil wars. Next came the great lawgivers, such as Solon, Lycurgus, Justinian. Finally, at the summit, were founders of empires, such as Cyrus of Persia and Julius Caesar of Rome. These stellar heroes were both great generals and wise legislators.[29]

This passion for fame had deep roots in Hamilton's life. In 1778, as America's revolutionary fervor ebbed, he wrote a pamphlet attacking congressmen who were using their political power to get rich while the Continental army starved. Hamilton expressed amazement that a man could do such a thing, when he had a chance to be "THE FOUNDER OF AN EMPIRE." [These are Hamilton's capitals.] Such a man had an opportunity to "do good to all mankind." From such a "commanding eminence" he should look down "with contempt on every mean or interested pursuit."[30]

The imperatives of fame underlay Hamilton's decision to confess his sexual adventure with Maria Reynolds to prove his political and financial integrity. He was ready to sacrifice his marital happiness to keep his honor—and his eligibility as a candidate for fame—inviolate. Fame also explains why Hamilton's legal fees were notoriously low and he was still in debt. Making a lot of money was "a mean and interested pursuit"—unworthy of a pursuer of fame.

Hamilton's passion for fame was complicated by his rediscovery of his religious feelings. Christianity preached meekness, humility, almost a contempt for reputation, power, founding empires, and the other glories of this world. By 1804, General Hamilton was carrying more psychological baggage than even the most gifted man could handle without spiritual confusion.

IX

In another revealing comment in his letter to Robert Troup, rejecting a chance to make big money with Charles Williamson, Hamilton told his old friend they were playing a great game for the highest stakes: "nothing less than true liberty, property, order, religion and of course *heads*." The bloody excesses of the French Revolution had entwined death and politics to an unparalleled degree in many minds. The pugnacious Hamilton often demonstrated his readiness to put his life on the line in the swirling controversies that the French upheaval ignited in America, especially after war exploded between England and France in 1793.

In 1795, angry Republican mobs took to the streets protesting John Jay's commercial treaty with England, which defused a potential clash with the former mother country over their wholesale seizures of American ships trading with the French. Jay persuaded the British to pay for the seizures and also won most-favored-nation status for American ships carrying imports to England—an exemption that meant millions in profit for American merchants. But the Jeffersonian Republicans saw the agreement as a corrupt compromise that betrayed France, whose money and soldiers had supported America in her revolutionary struggle against England.

In New York, Hamilton defended Jay's treaty vigorously in the newspapers and met the protestors face to face in the streets. The mob was led by prominent Republicans such as Commodore James Nicholson, a veteran of the Revolutionary navy. A shouting match ensued in which Hamilton offered to fight "the whole *Detestable faction*" one by one. He emerged from the confrontation with two proffered duels, one with Nicholson and another with a member of the Livingston clan. Cooler heads intervened and both challenges were resolved short of gunfire.[31]

In the course of the Reynolds imbroglio, Hamilton came even closer to fighting a duel with ex-Senator James Monroe, who admitted he had kept copies of the incriminating letters and documents. Monroe had left the copies with one of Jefferson's most devoted followers, John Beckley, former clerk of the House of Representatives, who leaked them to James Thomson Callender. An infuriated Hamilton called Monroe a liar to his face when he denied any role in the revelations. This confrontation was followed by a stream of menacing letters from both men. Only the good offices of Aaron Burr, who served as Monroe's second in the affair, prevented immediate gunfire. Having read all the pertinent letters and documents, Burr said he was sure Monroe believed "as I do . . . that H. is innocent of the charge of any concern in speculation with Reynolds" and recommended saying so in a joint statement as "an act of magnanimity and justice." [32]

Monroe declined to make this gesture but Hamilton decided the confessional pamphlet was a better way to defend his honor. There was little visible evidence that it accomplished this goal. He was mocked unmercifully in the Republicans' newspapers for making his home "the rendezvous of whoredom." The former secretary of the treasury was told that he could claim no merit, except a dubious virility. In a letter to his mentor and hero, Thomas Jefferson, Callender gloated that Hamilton had done himself more damage than "fifty of the best pens in America could have said against him." Jefferson snidely commented that pleading guilty to one crime was not exactly de facto exoneration for another crime. Jefferson's closest friend, James Madison, called it "a curious specimen of the ingenious folly of its author."[33]

Most Federalists assumed the Reynolds' pamphlet finished Hamilton as a candidate for president or any other public office. But Judge

David Cobb of Massachusetts took a more realistic eighteenth-century view: "Hamilton is fallen for the present," he told ex-Secretary of War Henry Knox. "But if he fornicates with every woman in the cities of New York and Philadelphia, he will rise again." The American public, Cobb maintained, did not expect "purity of character" in their politicians.[34]

X

Perhaps the best proof of that debatable contention was Hamilton's close friend, fifty-two-year-old Gouverneur Morris, who lived on his splendid estate, Morrisania, across the Harlem River in what is now the southwest Bronx. Six feet tall, with a leonine head and commanding presence, Morris was known in France as "the great lover with the wooden leg," a tribute to the charm he inherited from his Huguenot mother.

In 1780, Morris had lost his leg in a Pennsylvania carriage accident, shortly after serving two distinguished years in the Continental Congress. Rumor—a rather strong one—had him fleeing an outraged husband. His sympathetic but straitlaced friend John Jay wrote to financier Robert Morris (no relation): "Gouverneur's leg has been a tax on my heart. I am almost tempted to wish he had lost *something else*."[35]

An aristocrat to his single set of toes, Morris had nonetheless supported the Revolution, doing everything in his power to rally New Yorkers in the long struggle. At the Constitutional Convention in 1787, he had been one of the primary speakers, fighting particularly hard for a strong presidency elected directly by the people. On June 18, 1787, he listened to Alexander Hamilton speak for five hours, proposing a federal government with a president and senate elected for life, and the power to appoint governors and otherwise reduce the states to mere shadows. Only thus could America guarantee the order and discipline needed to achieve greatness. No mean orator himself, Morris said it was the most impressive speech he had ever heard.

In 1792–94 Morris had been American ambassador to France at the height of the revolutionary terror. He rescued dozens of frantic noblemen and noblewomen from the guillotine by hiding them in the American embassy and smuggling them out of the tormented country. He saved many others, such as the marquis de Lafayette's wife, by loaning them money that preserved them from starvation. The experience only confirmed what Morris already felt deep in his aristocratic bones: The people were not to be trusted.

Throughout these turbulent times, Morris made love to many beautiful women with "good dispositions"—his euphemism for willing hearts. He carefully noted the results in his candid diary, and made shrewd and often prophetic observations on the politics of the era. Years before British member of Parliament Edmund Burke wrote his famous assault on the theory and practice of the French radicals, *Reflections on the Revolution in France (1789–1790)*, Morris predicted the great upheaval would end in military despotism.

Hamilton and Morris regularly exchanged letters about American politics. But they had very different attitudes toward public service and life in general. In 1802, shortly before Morris completed a truncated term in the U.S. Senate, Hamilton wrote him a letter that has convinced many historians and some biographers that the General had abandoned politics: "Mine is an odd destiny. Perhaps no man in the U[nited] States has sacrificed or done more for the present Constitution than myself—and contrary to all my anticipations of its fate, as you know from the very begginning (sic) I am still labouring to prop the frail and worthless fabric. Yet I have the murmurs of its friends no less than the curses of its foes for my rewards. Every day proves to me more and more that this American world was not made for me."[36]

Hamilton told Morris he was in the same position, but refused to admit it. Although Morris was by birth a native of America, "by *genius* [he was] an exotic." Morris was deluded if he fancied he was any more popular than Hamilton or "in any sort upon a theatre suited to you."[37]

Morris told Hamilton he was wrong: "Your talents, if not your virtue, entitle you to the rank of an American citizen . . ." But Morris put his finger on a major difference between them: "I wish to get out of this galley [the U.S. Senate] and live for myself. I shall then frequently laugh where now I must frown." Unlike Hamilton, Morris had no compulsion for public life and its harassments. His goal was serenity. Among his favorite mottos was: "The art of living consists . . . in some degree in knowing how to be cheated"—an idea the combative Hamilton would never endorse.[38]

Astutely, Morris advised Hamilton that it was just as well that he was in a position "not to take immediate part either way" by holding public office. He would be more free to react to new developments.[39] The man who had watched France form and discard a half dozen revolutionary governments was convinced that the Jefferson administration was heading for a smashup. "They know not how to govern, and cannot possibly last," he told Hamilton in 1802. By the autumn of 1803 Morris was saying: "The Constitution is . . . gone."[40]

XI

Robert Troup was another friend who frequently offered Hamilton advice. More than once, Troup tried to persuade the General to be more discreet in his attentions to Angelica Church—a good indication of how intimately this old friend and frequent legal colleague felt he could talk to his former college roommate. But Troup's influence with Hamilton—and probably with many other men on their level—had recently suffered a sharp reverse.

In early 1803, Troup got into an ugly argument with Colonel William Stephens Smith, surveyor of customs for the port of New York and ex-President John Adams's son-in-law. Troup accused Smith of trying to extort money from a merchant client who was having legal problems with a cargo. The accusation may have been true. Smith's money problems were notorious. Republican newspapers seized on the story as proof of Federalist corruption and Smith sent Troup a menacing letter. The overworked fat man, deeply in debt because of ill-advised land speculations, and with a devoted wife and six children to support, hastily withdrew his accusation.

In a triumphant letter to his friend Vice President Aaron Burr, Smith gloated: "You will observe he [Troup] takes the charges back, apologizes, and swallows the falsehood like a *biped*—his agitations you can better conceive than I describe—his reputation is blasted in society . . ." Noah Webster, author of America's first dictionary, defined *biped* as "an animal with two feet."

Writing as one soldier to another soldier, Smith boasted that Troup's humiliation would be a lesson to those who "presume to sport with the character of any of the few—the honorable few—the band of brothers." The latter was a term Washington often used to describe the officers of the Continental army. Even Hamilton had refused to assist Troup, Smith declared. The General had told his old friend that he would have to "grin and bear it," because there was "no milk and water in the composition of his antagonist."[41]

The impact of this experience on Troup is a veritable case history in psychosomatic medicine. The humiliated ex-soldier (he had achieved the rank of colonel in the Revolution) developed an ulcerated tongue and mouth that made speaking and eating agony. Combined with his other ailments, the condition led many people to think Troup was a dying man.[42]

XII

Death was often on General Hamilton's mind these days. His seventy-one-year-old father-in-law, Philip Schuyler, was bedridden for weeks at a time, his body racked by gout; Schuyler's lively wife, Catherine, had died in 1803 and so had his attractive daughter, Margarita, wife of Stephen Van Rennselaer. But one death loomed larger than all these losses, though it had occurred three years ago. Just before the century turned, George Washington had succumbed to a streptococcus infection of his throat (called "quinsy" by the doctors of the era) at Mount Vernon, after riding out in a winter rain not unlike the one drenching New York on this New Year's Day.

No one missed the greatest of the founding fathers more acutely than General Hamilton. The news, Hamilton told Tobias Lear, Washington's secretary, "filled my heart with bitterness. Perhaps no man in this community has equal cause with myself to deplore the loss. I have been much indebted to the kindness of the General, and he was an aegis very essential to me." Some people think those words meant that Hamilton saw Washington as a figurehead he could manipulate. But a more probable interpretation is the role Washington played as defender of Hamilton's financial system against repeated attacks by Thomas Jefferson and his followers. (The word *aegis* is from the Greek, meaning "shield.")

Washington shielded his brilliant protege in other ways. At the height of the uproar over Maria Reynolds in 1797, the ex-President had sent Hamilton and his wife a silver wine cooler as a gesture of support. When the undeclared war with France began in 1798, Congress called Washington out of retirement to lead the army. He in turn named Hamilton as his second in command. This elevation signaled to voters that the father of the country had absolved Hamilton of his Maria Reynolds sins—a political resurrection that put the New Yorker back in the center of the struggle for power again.

XIII

But this near-miraculous restoration had only led to more political heartbreak. The scene of this ultimate disaster was painfully visible to General Hamilton when he looked from a rain-streaked southern window of The Grange on the cluster of wood and brick houses at the bottom of Manhattan Island, where some sixty-five thousand New Yorkers lived and worked. New York had been Hamilton's personal political battlefield, the place where he exchanged verbal volleys with his enemies at election time and shivered them with devastating arguments in the newspapers. When he left the treasury to return to the city to resume the practice of law in 1795, the merchants and other leading citizens had welcomed him with a splendid banquet at which they toasted Hamilton as the creator of American prosperity.[43] They backed those wineglass salutes with vigorous support at the polls and generous contributions to the campaign coffers of the Federalist party.

But Hamilton's political enemies told New York's poor and middle class that the merchants backed Hamilton because his financial system was rigged to make the rich even richer. In 1800 those and other arguments came to a climactic boil. By a strange conjunction of population and geography, in 1800 New York City contained the swing votes that decided who was going to control the state legislature. That year, the legislature had the sole power to choose presidential electors. By an even stranger conjunction, New York's electoral votes were the decisive bloc in the race for the presidency between incumbent John Adams and challenger Thomas Jefferson. In May of 1800, Hamilton had seen these vital seats in the state legislature snatched from his grasp by the same politician who had humiliated him in 1791—Colonel Aaron Burr.

Hamilton's gloom could only have deepened if by this time he realized how he had contributed to this ruinous defeat. The undeclared war with France ignited violent emotions. The French were the aggressors, seizing or destroying hundreds of American ships in European ports and on the high seas in retaliation for what they deemed a pro-English tilt in America's foreign policy. When President Adams sent three envoys to France to negotiate peace or at least a truce, the French had demanded a huge bribe and an even larger government-to-government loan before they were willing to talk. "No, not a sixpence," was the American reply, which was later embellished to "millions for defense, not one cent for tribute!"

An inflamed Congress had voted a navy that eventually reached fifty-four warships and an army of ten thousand men. Washington had named

Hamilton to be the army's acting commander. But the new general could not contain the paranoid tendencies of President John Adams and the Federalist party.

Convinced that every Republican was a potential pro-French traitor, the Federalist-controlled Congress passed the Alien and Sedition Acts and President Adams signed them into law. The Alien Acts gave the government the power to expel any foreigner who was suspected of disloyalty. The Sedition Act empowered federal attorneys to arrest anyone who publicly criticized the president or any other official of the government and prosecute him for libel. Hamilton cautioned against these measures at first, but he was soon engulfed by the political passions they generated.

In almost every state in the Union, Republican newspaper editors were arraigned by federal prosecutors for disparaging the government. Jefferson and his friend James Madison, deeply alarmed by what they perceived as a large step toward federal tyranny, persuaded the Virginia and Kentucky legislatures to pass resolutions, declaring any state had the right to "nullify" an unjust law passed by Congress—an idea that would bear bitter fruit in subsequent decades, when it was reinterpreted by southerners determined to defend slavery.

For a while the country seemed to teeter on the brink of civil war. Republican militia began drilling from Massachusetts to Georgia, preparing to fight General Hamilton's army.[44] The General talked darkly of using his army to subdue "a refractory and powerful State."[45] He meant Virginia, which he thought was much too large for the nation's good. Among the General's thoughts for improving America's political health was a constitutional amendment that would enable one hundred thousand citizens of big states such as Virginia and Pennsylvania to form smaller states that would be easier for the federal government to manage.[46]

Meanwhile, the Republicans were skillfully converting the prosecuted critics into martyrs. In New York, when an assemblyman and former common pleas judge named Jedidiah Peck was arrested in Otsego County for circulating a petition to repeal the Alien and Sedition Acts, Jefferson's followers transformed Peck's two-hundred-mile trip from Cooperstown to New York City to stand trial into a political tour de force, with thousands surging onto the roads to cheer him. Republican newspapers described the Federal marshal manacling Peck and dragging him from his home at midnight. "The rule of George Third was gracious and loving compared to such tyranny," they cried.[47]

General Hamilton's pugnacious nature could not resist joining in these prosecutions. He was apparently oblivious to the way the Federalists were alienating thousands of voters. When the *New York Argus* reported that a Philadelphia doctor heard the General say he planned to run for president in 1800 using "the dollars I have heaped together whilst handling the government's cash," an infuriated Hamilton demanded that the Federalists indict the *Argus*'s owner, a widow, and her printer for libel.[48] The printer was found guilty in a sensational trial, in which Republican lawyers forced Hamilton to go over many of the facts of the Maria Reynolds scandal to prove, once more, that he was a confessed adulterer who had not embezzled any government money. Ignoring the jury's recommendation of clemency for the printer, who was the sole support of his wife and six children, the Federalist judge sentenced him to four months in jail and fined him $100. Two months later, New York City voters, galvanized by Aaron Burr, swept Hamilton and his party out of power.

XIV

For the past three years, General Hamilton had been a political spectator, reduced to commenting in letters and newspaper articles on the policies and decisions of men he regarded as detestable demagogues. Meanwhile his law practice continued to consume his days and nights with arguments over contracts, creditors' rights, marine insurance, admiralty jurisdiction, maritime liens. The cases were frequently complicated by tangled matters of fact and arcane legal precedents. Hamilton was among the leaders in an ongoing struggle to build a body of commercial law to handle the expanding business of the new nation.[49] For some time the General had been under the care of Dr. David Hosack, a faculty member of Columbia College's medical school, for a series of painful bowel and stomach complaints—probable evidence of psychological stress and overwork.[50]

But when Hamilton gazed down at the twisting streets of New York City from The Grange's southern windows, his insider's eyes saw signs and portents not visible to most people. His political enemies might be about to fall on their triumphant faces. In spite of his losses and disappointments, hope—and combative juices—stirred in General Hamilton's tired body and wounded soul.

CHAPTER 2

The Quarrelsome Men
of Gotham

Officials responsible for law and order in New York probably welcomed the downpour that began the New Year. Since 1768, New Year's Day had been a legal holiday, often celebrated in riotous fashion. Each year the Common Council ordered the city clerk to make "the usual publication in the news papers against the firing of guns &c on the approachg. season."[1] The city's daytime police force was minuscule and its members doubled as court officers and sanitary inspectors. The night police, known as The Watch, consisted of two captains, two deputies, and seventy-two men.[2] They were underpaid, poorly disciplined, and frequently demoralized by the lack of support they received from the courts.

The tradition of New Year's carousing had been inherited from the Dutch, who had made their own largely vain efforts to control it. As early as December 31, 1665, Governor Peter Stuyvesant had forbidden the firing of guns, beating of drums, or "treating with intoxicants" on the holiday. The ordinance was renewed repeatedly for the next ten years, suggesting the original ban had little impact on the burghers and their *goede vrouws*.[3]

New York's population of 65,000 may seem small to contemporary Americans. But almost all the commerce of New York State—$10 million in the previous year—flowed across its busy wharves, making the city the financial titan of the young nation. Even in 1804, when Gotham stretched only a mile up the Hudson and about two miles along the East River, and swarms of hogs ran wild in the streets, eating garbage, there was something imperial about New York. One English visitor said its watery vistas reminded him of Venice. Forests of masts loomed at the wharves; the marine lists printed the arrivals and departures of dozens of ships each day.

The city's polyglot population—already a volatile mixture of English, Dutch, German, Irish, Jewish, French, and African-American—made New York seem more European than any other port in America. The streets resounded with the curses of cart men and the cries of peddlers in a bewildering medley of accents. Simultaneously, the vast undeveloped reaches of northern New York State induced dreams of imperial grandeur in those who had the money and power to buy up those millions of fertile acres. Already, thanks to a letter in which George Washington referred to New York City as the seat of a new empire, New Yorkers were using the term "empire city" and "empire state."[4]

English visitors were usually surprised to discover New Year's Day was the most important day of the year.[5] They were especially struck by the custom of paying complimentary visits to friends and relations. This was almost a religious duty among the well-to-do New Yorkers who lived in the city's three lower wards, nearest to the Battery. One diarist noted it would have been an "unpardonable affront" to fail to call on an elderly friend, who regularly laid in "700 wt of cakes for his acquaintances."[6]

One English visitor noticed that "the mayor of the city and others of the constituted authorities advertise two or three days before that they will reciprocate the compliments of the season with the inhabitants." Trudging with a friend to the mayor's house on Water Street, the Englishman found "a crowded room, with gentlemen . . . coming in, going out and taking refreshments at a large table spread out with cakes, wine, punch." The visitor pronounced both the food and drink "excellent."[7]

To the Englishman, this was a passing bit of local color. But to Mayor DeWitt Clinton and his callers, a New Year's visit was a serious matter. In 1804, the thirty-four-year-old Clinton was the most powerful politician in the city and state of New York. Tall, handsome, with a violent temper and haughty manner, he was called "Magnus Apollo" behind his back. Those who came to shake his hand, drink his punch, and eat his cakes were pledging their political allegiance.

II

The mayor was the nephew of General Hamilton's foe Governor George Clinton, who was somewhat sarcastically called "the Old Incumbent." DeWitt had begun his political career as his uncle's secretary. The sixty-four-year-old governor's incumbency went back to 1777, when he was elected chief executive of a state in revolution, with Long Island and New York City in the hands of the British army and the northern border vulnerable to British and Indian incursions from Canada. Clinton had been an energetic war governor and on the basis of that youthful achievement and an ability to portray himself as the spokesman for the common man in a state where vast tracts were held by the very rich, he had occupied the gubernatorial chair for twenty-one of the next twenty-seven years. He had stepped aside only twice, in 1795 and 1798, when he foresaw he would lose.

Governor Clinton had survived several political debacles that would have ruined most men. In 1788, he had violently opposed the ratification of the federal constitution, mostly because he and New York were doing very well without it. The Empire State was briskly taxing everything imported from New Jersey or Connecticut, while simultaneously collecting customs duties on most of the foreign merchandise the two smaller states bought. Thirty-one-year-old Alexander Hamilton had almost single-handedly persuaded the Clinton-dominated ratifying convention to change their minds and accept the national charter. George Clinton never forgot or forgave that humiliation.

In 1792, Hamilton, now the leader of the emerging Federalist party in New York and the nation, had chosen as his candidate for governor John Jay, who had carved out a brilliant record as a diplomat during the

Revolution and had been appointed the first chief justice of the U.S. Supreme Court. The Old Incumbent had lost, but coolly stole the election by declaring the votes of three upstate counties invalid on technicalities and awarding himself three more years in Albany by a margin of eight votes. His followers in the legislature held their noses and approved this barefaced theft.[8]

The enraged Federalists had called on the state's two U.S. senators, Aaron Burr and Rufus King, to adjudicate the dispute. King brushed aside the technicalities and declared John Jay the winner. Burr came down on the side of the minutiae of the election laws.

Hamilton despised Clinton not only for playing this sort of corrupt politics, but also because he was a notorious cheapskate. Unlike George Washington, who spent money freely on dinners and receptions to create a bond between the new federal government and the people, the Old Incumbent seldom entertained, even when New York was both the state and the nation's capital from 1789–90. Clinton no doubt told himself this was good politics. Living too flashily could be interpreted as a dark tendency toward aristocratic Federalist habits. Hamilton thought it was unworthy of the leader of America's wealthiest state. Moreover, Clinton's version of "Republican simplicity" was a performance for the voters' benefit. Thanks to some shrewd speculations in upstate land, the Governor was worth about $250,000 (well over a million dollars in modern money).

III

Uncle George and nephew DeWitt and their outriding relatives, friends, and allies constituted America's first political machine—the virtual inventors of what came to be known as the spoils system. They had over fifteen thousand civil and military appointments to hand out and they seldom gave one to a man who was not a vociferous supporter. Many of these jobs sound innocuous to the modern ear: auctioneer, for instance. There were twenty-four of these licensed gentlemen in the New York City government in 1804. All took home a nice cut of what they sold to the public when property was condemned for debt. Notary Public was another plum. Today assistant bank managers and stationery store owners are notaries. In 1804 notaries were few and their fees were worth fighting for. One historian of the period has described the Clintonian apparatus as an army. The governor and his council of appointment, a four-man group selected from the state senate, named every district attorney and mayor in the state, every county clerk, surrogate, and sheriff and their staffs, and every justice of the peace. Then there were the coroners, inspectors of turnpike roads, and a dozen other commercial ventures plus a veritable horde of officers in the state militia.[9]

Along with an appetite for the spoils of office, the Clintonians brought to the political fray a fierce ideological hostility to their Federalist opponents. Not a little of this was left over from the bitter struggle over ratifying the Constitution. Many anti-Federalists, as they were called at that time, had an almost paranoid suspicion about the potential excesses of the federal government's power. They were bolstered in this attitude by their national leader, Thomas Jefferson, who was convinced that the Federalists were an evil conspiracy against the liberty won by the Revolution.

Like President Jefferson, the Clintonians called themselves Republicans—an attempt to link their party with the noble Romans of ancient Italy, before that complicated political system was overthrown by Julius Caesar. Their Federalist opponents called them democrats, a political smear word in 1804, when the French Revolution had made everyone starkly aware of the potential excesses of democracy. There was a futuristic truth to this Federalist gibe. The Jeffersonian Republicans are unquestionably the ancestors of the modern Democratic party.

The Republicans repaid the Federalists' insult by calling Hamilton and his followers monocrats, implying that they secretly hankered, if not plotted, to replace the presidency with a king—or at the very least failed to wish the French Revolution well, and even favored France's chief opponent, England. For a decade Republicans from Thomas Jefferson to the lowliest member of New York's Sons of St. Tammany had proclaimed the French struggle against aristocrats and kings the cause of mankind. In a moment of unrestrained passion, Jefferson had declared he would rather see the entire earth depopulated, until there was only a Republican Adam and Eve left, rather than see "this cause" fail.[10]

IV

That kind of enthusiasm disgusted General Hamilton, who was, like most of the Federalists, more inclined to play politics with a calculating mind—or so he told himself. The General accused Jefferson of a "womanish attachment to France and a womanish resentment" against England.[11] Hamilton had pushed for and largely achieved a diplomatic tilt toward England (exemplified by the Jay Treaty) because tariffs on her exports to America were crucial to his financial system. Jefferson and his followers rejected this motive as mercenary, and insisted America should support France. They argued that a majority of the American people shared this sentiment and that America was obligated to do so by the 1778 treaty of alliance signed with Louis XVI's France. Hamilton (and President Washington) replied that the royal government with whom America signed the treaty had ceased to exist.[12]

Jefferson expressed his personal opinion of this Hamiltonian diplomacy in a 1797 private letter to an Italian friend, Philip Mazzei, which got into the public prints. He maintained that most Americans still retained their revolutionary virtue. But there were many "apostates," men who had been "Samsons in the field and Solomons in the council, but who have had their heads shorn by the harlot England."[13]

The letter caused an enormous political uproar. The Federalists accused Jefferson of slandering ex-President Washington. Jefferson, who was vice president at the time, denied it, but the man from Mount Vernon never again communicated with his fellow Virginian after the publication of the Mazzei letter. Moreover, Washington soon expressed to others considerable personal enmity. Although the leader of America's revolution scrupulously avoided joining either political party, in his closing years he displayed a distinct Federalist tilt.[14]

V

No matter what the politicians called themselves or were called by their opponents, party politics was unquestionably becoming an integral part of the American system. The nation's founders had abhorred the idea of parties—they called them factions—and had written a constitution that presumed they would not exist. But the two parties soon took shape before the founders' somewhat dismayed eyes. Hamilton and his fellow Federalists bid for votes on the basis of their support for the Constitution, before, during, and after its ratification. They saw themselves as the party of "the wise and good," men of virtues, talents, and property best suited by birth and/or achievement to run the country. They pointed to the prosperity they had created as the best proof of their ability to govern.

The Republicans countered by styling themselves the party of the Declaration of Independence and its trumpet call for liberty and equality. They called themselves the spokesmen of the average man and insisted the will of the people was the final arbiter in matters political. In 1804, 83 percent of Americans were farmers. "Those who labor in the earth," declared Thomas Jefferson, "are the chosen people of God," the only sure guardians of American liberty. Combine this flattery with the indubitable fact that the Republicans could claim the author of the Declaration of Independence as their leader and the result was a powerful political message.

Moreover, the Republicans said the Federalists were a party of elite, money-grubbing merchants and lawyers who looked down on honest farmers and cheated them at every opportunity. They assailed Federalist prosperity as a scheme that, in Jefferson's words "filched . . . immense sums . . . from the poor and ignorant."[15] The Virginian and his followers still brooded over the way Hamilton had funded the nation's $80 million revolutionary war debt in 1790. Most people had given up getting full payment for the various debt certificates and promissory notes the bankrupt Continental Congress had issued to ex-soldiers and other supporters of the Revolution in lieu of cash. They had sold their claims to wealthy speculators for twenty or thirty cents on the dollar. Hamilton, insisting that a contract was sacred and only strict adherence to the law could restore the government's credit, resolved to pay the holders of these certificates their full value.

In New York, this delivered a bonanza into the hands of a relatively few individuals. Some seventy-eight New Yorkers, many of them friends of the secretary of the treasury, owned $2,717,754 in southern state debts, with eight accounting for more than $1.5 million of this cache. Add to this $4,949,253 in the federal debt, much of it held by this same group, and it is easy to see why Gotham's businessmen gave Hamilton a dinner when he resigned from the federal government.[16]

Hamilton defended this deliberate concentration of wealth in the hands of a few by arguing that without capital, America would never build a powerful economy. The Jeffersonians responded that Hamilton was trying to turn America into a mirror image of England, a country where financial speculation, political corruption, and mobs of disenfranchised factory workers required a standing army to keep the aristocrats in power. Hamilton's Bank of the United States and his toleration of a national debt were part of this nefarious plot.

In many minds—a majority in 1804—this political argument deified Thomas Jefferson and demonized General Hamilton. It did not seem to occur to this majority that Jefferson and his friends were defending a defunct status quo. They wanted to preserve the very role for which England had designed the colonies: suppliers of foodstuffs and other raw materials for the mother country's burgeoning factories. Hamilton wanted the United States to have banks, factories, a stock market—all things the Clintonians and Jeffersonians hated—because he saw a future in which an industrialized continental-sized America would reduce England to a mere appendage. Alas for Hamilton, it was a hard sell to farmers who were being told they were the chosen of the earth, and warned that Federalist policies favored businessmen and discriminated against honest tillers of the soil.

Now Jefferson was in the process of pulling off a political coup that seemed certain to skyrocket his popularity among this agrarian majority. He had agreed to buy New Orleans and the immense territory of Louisiana—virtually the entire middle of the continent from the Mississippi to the Rocky Mountains—from France, doubling the size of the United States. This 828,000-square-mile bonanza of open land was waiting for anyone with the money and courage to head west, so the Republicans crowed. How to counter this ultimate crowd pleaser had most Federalists, including General Hamilton, thinking long and hard—and often gloomily—about the future.

VI

Frequently in residence at the City Hotel on Varick Street was a living symbol of the previous decade's political ferocity: Thomas Paine. The author of *Common Sense*, the pamphlet that had played a dynamic role in persuading the Americans of 1776 to declare independence, had recently returned to the United States after fifteen years in Europe.[17]

Paine had welcomed the French Revolution and done his utmost to export it to his native England. His 1791 defense of the Revolution's early stages, *The Rights of Man*, was one of the most popular books ever published, selling an estimated two million copies in England, France, and America. Paine urged an end to the British monarchy and the creation of a democratic state that would promote the welfare of the masses through progressive taxation, retirement benefits, and public works projects for the unemployed. The British government responded with a warrant for Paine's arrest and he fled to France, where he soon became a member of the French revolutionary convention.

As the Revolution evolved in Paris, Paine found himself in the minority, urging the radicals not to execute Louis XVI. The king was guillotined in January 1793 and the so-called reign of terror erupted, during which as many as four hundred people a day were beheaded in Paris alone. Not even beautiful Austrian-born Queen Marie-Antoincttc was spared. Revulsion swept England and America and Paine's stock as an apologist for this blood-soaked eruption dropped to zero. Worse, in the paranoid frenzy created by the terror, Paine was soon in grave danger of losing his own head.

Perhaps trying to prove his revolutionary bona fides, Paine wrote an all-out attack on Christianity, *The Age of Reason,* which religious Americans found appalling. This did not prevent him from being arrested by the Parisian radicals, whom he antagonized by criciticizing their attempt to abolish Christianity in France. Paine thought it should be allowed to die a natural death. The book managed to infuriate everyone, including Jews, one of whom warned his fellow believers that they could not even touch it without committing a sin.[18]

After his release from prison, Paine decided President George Washington should have done more to liberate him. In fact, the president had exerted diplomatic pressure that probably saved Paine's life. But Paine was not satisfied and published *Letter to Washington,* a seventy-page diatribe denouncing the father of the country as a traitor to the cause of liberty for failing to support France in her war with England.[19]

In 1801, President Jefferson invited Paine to return to America aboard a U.S. frigate—a gesture he soon regretted, when Federalist newspapers opened their batteries on him. Over the years, a fondness for brandy had given Paine a bulbous red nose and an equally scarlet face. His clothes, never neat, were usually covered with snuff, which he inhaled in enormous quantities. The Federalists wanted to know how "so notorious and impious a buffoon" deserved free transportation to the United States.

When Jefferson invited Paine to dinner at the presidential "palace," in Washington, D.C. (the term "White House" had not yet been invented),

Federalist fury mounted. They declared the invitation proved that the president, like Paine, believed that the story of the birth of Jesus Christ was "AN OBSCENE BLASPHEMOUS FABLE." Paine did not help matters by blasting back in a series of public letters to "the citizens of the United States," comparing his services in the American Revolution to those of Washington, and concluding they were of equal importance.[20]

President Jefferson decided to put some distance between himself and Paine, and the old revolutionary had drifted to New York, where he was living off friends in his usual haphazard style. By 1804, Paine had gotten his liquor consumption under some control. The proprietor of the City Hotel claimed he imbibed less than any of his other tenants. Given the drinking habits of the era, this was not a testimonial to total reform.

The Federalists declined to abandon Paine as a target of opportunity. On January 5th, the *Evening Post* republished a poem from the *Connecticut Courant*, describing Paine and Jefferson celebrating their reunion.

> For tho when sober Tom is dull
> Stupid and filthy as a gull
> Yet give him brandy and the elf
> Will talk all night about himself.
> And whilst his patron stands amazed
> Waiting to hear himself be praised
> The drunken sot does naught but cry
> And sing and write of Mr. I.[21]

Reduced to an object of ridicule, Paine could find consolation in the more than one hundred disciples, most of them journalists like James Thomson Callender, who had embraced his radical ideas and had been forced to flee from England, Ireland, and Scotland to America. In their new country, almost all of them had become passionate advocates of the Republican cause, and their mastery of billingsgate had not a little to do with rendering General Hamilton and the Federalist party *hors de combat*.[22]

VII

Mayor Dewitt Clinton carefully noted the name of each New Year's visitor in his diary. Because January 1st fell on a Sunday in 1804, the visiting was extended to Monday, when the legal holiday was celebrated. The names took up four pages in the mayor's diary. Especially noteworthy was the number of Livingstons among them. The Clintons' alliance with this aristocratic family was the rock on which their political fortunes rested.

Nobody seemed bothered by this odd conjunction of wealth with the purported party of the people. Nor was anyone troubled by the lavish lifestyle of the head of the Republican party, President Jefferson, who lived in a magnificent brick mansion on a mountaintop in Virginia. The president's wealth rested on the labor of more than a hundred slaves, who had no hope of achieving liberty or equality from the man who had declared all men were entitled to these rights. The demonization of General Hamilton and the Federalists had been so successful, Republicans could ignore the inner contradictions of their party and convince themselves they were the deserving saviors of the nation.

In 1804, slavery was not a political issue that agitated many Americans. New York had over twenty thousand slaves and New Jersey twelve thousand.[23] Only a few Quakers were calling for the nationwide abolition of the ancient institution. General Hamilton was a founding member of the small New York Manumission Society and at one point proposed that the group free all their slaves. When the proposal was rejected, he dropped the idea and continued to own slaves. As recently as 1797, he paid his brother-in-law, John Barker Church, $225 for a "negro woman & child."[24]

Similarly, Vice President Aaron Burr once proposed in the New York legislature an immediate statewide abolition of slavery but the lawmakers said no and his Richmond Hill mansion remained staffed by slaves. [25] In the census of 1800, Massachusetts and Vermont were the only states without slaves.[26] But by 1804, all the Northern states had passed gradual manumission laws, which freed Africans born after a certain date when they reached maturity.

VIII

One aspect of slavery was an issue in the upcoming presidential election. In his book *Notes on Virginia* (1785) Jefferson had condemned the institution, remarking that it unleashed "the most boisterous passions" between master and slave. In 1802, the muckraking newspaper editor James Thomson Callender, who had exposed Hamilton's affair with Maria Reynolds in 1797, seemed to confirm this remark. Irked by the president's failure to give him a government job, Callender turned on Jefferson and declared the man from Monticello was the father of five children by one of his slaves, an attractive mulatto named Sally Hemings. In Callender's newspaper, the *Richmond* (Virginia) *Recorder,* he published a poem that savagely elaborated the accusation.

A Song
Supposed to have been written by the
SAGE OF MONTICELLO

Of all the damsels on the green
    On mountain or in valley
A lass so luscious neer was seen
    As the Monticellian Sally

(chorus) Yankee Doodle, who's the noodle?
    What wife were half so handy?
To breed a flock of slaves for stock
    A blackamoor's the dandy.

When pressed by loads of state affairs
    I seek to sport and dally

The sweetest solace of my cares
    Is in the lap of Sally.
She's black, you tell me—grant she be—
    Must colour always tally?
Black is love's proper hue for me
    And white's the hue for Sally.

What though she by the gland secretes
    Must I stand shill-I shall-I?
Tuck'd up between a pair of sheets
    There's no perfume like Sally.[27]

Federalist editors reprinted these and even more salacious verses around the nation. They also seized on another Callender charge: that Jefferson had tried to seduce Betsy Walker, wife of his friend and neighbor John Walker, during a tête-à-tête in the early 1770s. Finally, they accused Jefferson of paying Callender to slander President John Adams during the 1800 elections and to say some obnoxious things about George Washington in a pamphlet entitled *The Prospect Before Us*.

President Jefferson, the man who had frequently proclaimed a free press vital to the political health of the nation when Republican newspapers were assaulting the Federalists, had written to the Republican governor of Pennsylvania, Thomas McKean, suggesting that "a few prosecutions of the most prominent offenders" might make certain obnoxious editors behave. The word was swiftly passed to party leaders in other states.[28]

The Clinton-Livingston political machine targeted Harry Croswell, a young Federalist editor of a four-page paper, *The Wasp*, in the upriver town of Hudson, New York. Croswell had reprinted the charge that Jefferson had paid Callender to slander Washington and Adams. New York's attorney general, Ambrose Spencer, had indicted Croswell for seditious libel and prosecuted him personally, convicting him with the help of the Clinton-appointed chief justice of the state's Supreme Court, Morgan

Lewis, who presided at the trial. Lewis told the jury that the libel law of New York followed the common law of England, which made any criticism of the head of state a crime, whether or not it was true.

The Clintonians soon realized they had created a political time bomb. No less a personage than Alexander Hamilton agreed to argue before New York's Supreme Court that the young printer deserved a new trial. The case was on the court's docket for a February hearing. If Hamilton won, Croswell's accusations might be in the newspapers in the middle of Jefferson's run for a second term, next fall. Hamilton was telling people that he intended to subpoena the president to testify or at least give a deposition, stating whether or not he had paid Callender to slander Washington and Adams. It need hardly be added that reviving this charge would also enable Federalist editors to ruminate on Sally Hemings and Betsy Walker.

IX

Until the fall of 1803, the mayor of New York had been Edward Livingston, younger brother of the manor lord, Robert R. Livingston, who was in Paris as the United States ambassador—the juiciest political plum at President Thomas Jefferson's disposal. Further demonstrating the president's eagerness to please this powerful New York family, the younger Livingston was also the federal attorney for New York. Early in the summer of 1803 Livingston discovered that one of his clerks responsible for collecting federal taxes had embezzled $44,000.

Livingston tried to borrow money from New York's two banks or obtain a stay of judgment from the federal government. Neither was forthcoming. This particular Livingston was not in favor with President Jefferson. Edward was suspected of being too friendly with a man Jefferson no longer liked or trusted—Vice President Aaron Burr. Livingston had also outraged New York's Republicans by suggesting that the indigent tenants of the city poorhouse should do some productive work. In this first attempt to reform the welfare laws, the party of the people rose in wrath and denounced the idea, because it might impinge on the monopoly various artisans enjoyed.

Pledging all his property to cover the deficit, Livingston resigned and departed for New Orleans, followed by a chorus of Federalist hoots and jeers. In Paris, by ironic coincidence, Livingston's brother Robert was deep in the negotiations to purchase New Orleans and the immense territory of Louisiana from France. Edward Livingston's use of New Orleans as a refuge from prosecution only further darkened the Federalists' dislike of this stupendous real estate deal. Adding to the irony, President Jefferson was not much happier with the thought of this angry New York aristocrat in New Orleans, possibly arousing the already hostile populace against an American takeover.[29]

X

A fierce competition for the mayor's job had erupted within New York's Republican party, with a half dozen politicians in contention, including Attorney General Ambrose Spencer and Morgan Lewis, the chief justice of the Supreme Court, who was married to a Livingston. The mayor received no salary but he earned $10,000-$15,000 a year from various fees (the equivalent of $120,000-$180,000 late-twentieth-century dollars).[30] As chief judge of the mayor's court, he kept the fines he imposed on lawbreakers; as clerk of the city's five markets, he received a fee from every tradesman who sold food there. The hundreds of cart men who trundled goods through the city also coughed up to His Honor for annual licenses.[31] Considering the mayor's modest responsibilities, his take-home pay rivaled the $25,000 earned by the president of the United States. Vice President Aaron Burr earned a mere $5,000.[32]

DeWitt Clinton had watched the mayoral contest from the seemingly lofty realm of the U.S. Senate, to which his uncle had elevated him in 1802. Nepotism, in the literal meaning of the word (from the Italian *nepotismo*, "the favoring of nephews") was another issue that did not seem to trouble New York's Republicans. The Old Incumbent, still a covert antagonist to the Constitution, apparently saw nothing wrong with manipulating the state legislature's power to select senators. The founding fathers had written this proviso into the national charter because they did not want senators chosen by the people. Solons were supposed to be men of integrity and property, immune to thoughts of profit and loss and the other greedy passions of the masses. A senator's salary was commensurate with this noble ideal: $6 a day plus travel expenses, which came to about $800 in an average legislative year.[33]

On September 3, 1803, Senator Clinton wrote Governor Clinton a marvelously candid letter, dismissing the other contenders for the mayoralty as insatiable office seekers or untrustworthy politicians. He was particularly hard on Chief Justice Morgan Lewis, commenting that his two ruling passions were avarice and inordinate vanity. Moreover, as a politician, Lewis was not to be trusted; he was too likely to listen to "a little family junto." This was not a very nice way to refer to the Livingstons, the vital component in the Clinton machine.

Senator Clinton unabashedly recommended himself for the mayor's job. His "young and growing family" was one reason for this seemingly incongruous proposal. More important was the need for his presence in New York City to "detect and control conspiracies by busy and intriguing men." For a clincher, Clinton argued that from the viewpoint of the coming presidential election, the office of Mayor of New York was "among the most important positions in the U. States."[34] This was undoubtedly true, as Alexander Hamilton could bear rueful witness.

One of Clinton's fellow senators (a Federalist) commented that "not a single member of the Senate" was sorry to see Magnus Apollo depart. "He is a man of violent passions, of a bitter vindictive spirit—unfeeling—insolent—haughty & rough in his manners."[35] Clinton's reply to that denunciation might well have been a remark he made in another context: "The meekness of Quakerism will do in religion, but not in politics."[36]

In fact, Clinton had not wasted his time in Washington, D.C. In his brief senatorial tenure, he had demonstrated himself a down-the-line devotee of President Jefferson. At least one senator hated to see him go.

"Who is to supply the talents we have lost by your removal from the Senate and in whom shall we find the friend we have lost in you?" wrote Wilson Cary Nicholas of Virginia. He was one of President Jefferson's chief spokesmen in Congress and a frequent confidant. [37]

Conspicuous among the names missing from Mayor Clinton's diary checklist of New Year's visitors was New York's most prominent Republican, Vice President Aaron Burr, who was in Washington, D.C. But even if he had been occupying his New York mansion, it was extremely unlikely that the vice president would have gone to Mayor Clinton's house to shake his hand and wish him a happy and prosperous 1804. Burr wished the mayor and his uncle the governor the precise opposite, a feeling the Clintons heartily reciprocated. It was Burr, not Alexander Hamilton, who was foremost among the busy and intriguing men that Mayor Clinton had rushed to New York to detect and control during the upcoming presidential year.

XI

DeWitt Clinton had launched a political offensive against Vice President Burr a year before he took over the mayor's office. The issue was the oldest source of communal discord: power. Uncle George was declining into illness and desuetude. DeWitt decided there was only one way to prevent Burr from succeeding the Old Incumbent as the Republican leader of New York. The vice president had to be destroyed.

DeWitt soon discovered this could be dangerous work. In 1802, while Clinton was still a senator, he and his Livingston allies seized control of the bank known as the Manhattan Company and ousted Burr and his friends from the board of directors. Burr had founded the bank in 1799 to give the Republicans some crucial financial leverage against the Bank of New York, which was founded and controlled by General Hamilton. Clinton's move led to an exchange of insults with City Marshal John Swartout, a blond giant who was an ardent Burr supporter. Swartout accused Clinton of trying to ruin the vice president for his own personal advantage. DeWitt declared his opposition to Burr was based on the purest and most patriotic motives and called Swartout "a liar, a scoundrel and a villain" for impugning his integrity.

Swartout and Clinton exchanged angry letters, climaxed by Swartout's demand that Clinton sign a statement, admitting his expressions were "intemperate and unworthy" and humbly begging Swartout to accept his apology. Clinton refused, knowing such a confession would be his political death knell. Swartout promptly challenged him to pistols at ten paces.

With the usual pro forma obedience to New York's ban on such encounters, the antagonists had repaired to the New Jersey shore of the Hudson, on the peninsula known as Powles (Paulus) Hook, in contemporary Jersey City. Colonel William Stephens Smith, the combative Federalist son-in-law of ex-President John Adams, was Swartout's second—further evidence of the duel's political ramifications.

After taking a bullet through his coat, Clinton put two slugs into Swartout's left leg. Swartout, his boot filling with blood, insisted he was ready to exchange another round, but Clinton seized the high moral ground and refused to fire another shot at a wounded man. "I wish I had the *principal* here," Clinton had growled, while a doctor worked on Swartout. "I will meet him when he pleases." He was talking about Vice President Aaron Burr.

In the newspaper war that followed, Swartout claimed Clinton had shown the white feather by withdrawing from the fight. Clinton's backers accused Vice President Burr of cowardice by letting Swartout do his shooting for him.

Back in Washington, D.C., Clinton almost fought a duel with Senator Jonathan Dayton of New Jersey several months later. Although he was a Federalist, the contentious hawk-faced Dayton supported Burr when he ran for vice president in 1796. Their friendship went back to boyhood days in Elizabethtown, New Jersey. Dayton took a dim view of Clinton's hostility to his friend. In an argument over Jefferson's policy toward

Louisiana, Senator Dayton accused Senator Clinton of being more in‑
clined to "arraign a gentleman's motives than answer his arguments."
Clinton retorted that he had never arraigned the motives of any man.
Senator Dayton declared Clinton had called him a liar and soon acrid let‑
ters were being exchanged—the usual route to the nearest dueling
ground. But Clinton backed off and semiapologized, further impugning
his courage, in the opinion of the friends of Vice President Burr.

After those two close calls as a duelist, Clinton became more circum‑
spect in his offensive against the vice president. He persuaded the editor
of the *American Citizen*, an elongated Englishman named James
Cheetham, to turn against Burr. The vice president had been Cheetham's
original backer to head the paper, which was the lone Republican voice in
New York. Cheetham seldom let a day pass without publishing vicious at‑
tacks on Burr.

XII

Such graphic glimpses of deep divisions in the Republican party were
among the chief reasons why General Hamilton gazed down on New York
City with a mixture of melancholy and wary political hope on the first day
of 1804. In recent weeks, friends had sent him news of perturbing political
unrest elsewhere in the republic. None of these correspondents were under
the illusion that General Hamilton had retired from politics.

Timothy Pickering, the beaknosed, acerbic Federalist senator from
Massachusetts (and former secretary of state under Presidents Washing‑
ton and Adams) wanted to know how best to transmit to Hamilton "se‑
cret communications" from Washington, D.C. Among these was Senator
Pickering's opinion that the Louisiana Purchase made the secession of
the New England states and New York from the American union a polit‑
ical necessity.

Brigadier General James Wilkinson, commander of the American
army, wrote from Mobile, in the Mississippi Territory, to discuss the "Ac‑

quisition" of Spanish Florida. Practically smacking his lips, Wilkinson told Hamilton he had explored "with military Eyes . . . every critical pass, every direct route, & every devious way between the Mexican Gulph [the Gulf of Mexico] & the Tenessee River" but was growing weary of President Jefferson's perpetual pacifism and yearned for "Action."

From Perth Amboy, New Jersey, Commodore Thomas Truxtun, one of the heroes of the undeclared war with France, sent Hamilton a rueful growl about the way the Constitution was being "kicked about to answer the purposes of the ruleing [*sic*] faction." A thinker as well as a fighter (he had written important books on tactics and other naval matters), the forty-nine-year-old Truxtun was also disgusted with the way President Jefferson had virtually dismantled the U.S. Navy. The commodore told the General that he looked forward to a revision of the Constitution "to prevent such an abomniable [*sic*] Set from exclusively governing us a Second time."[38]

There is no record of General Hamilton disagreeing with this rather revolutionary suggestion. He undoubtedly filed it in his large head beside Gouverneur Morris's declaration that the Constitution was "gone" and Thomas Jefferson's administration was headed for an inevitable smashup.

CHAPTER 3

The New Caesar's
Long Shadow

*E*arly on January 2, 1804, General Hamilton hitched his favorite
horse, Riddle, to his buggy and drove into New York City, a one-
and-a-half–hour trip. Government servants had a holiday because New
Year's Day fell on Sunday. But the General was no longer a public man.
With his crowded casebook and ever mounting expenses, he could not afford to take an extra day off. Leaving Riddle in the stable of his town
house at 52 Cedar Street, Hamilton strolled around to his law office at 12
Garden Street. Along the way a half dozen friends greeted him with news
that had the city aflame with excitement: Napoléon Bonaparte had invaded Ireland with 180,000 men! The story was supposedly from the lips
of a man who had just debarked from an Irish ship.

The Irish had risen in revolt in 1798 and General Charles, Lord Corn-
wallis, the man whom the Americans had humbled at Yorktown in 1781,
had smashed the haphazard rebellion with ruthless efficiency. But the
Emerald Isle still seethed with anti-British fury. The story was more than
plausible. An Ireland under French control could wreak havoc on the
British merchant marine and drive England to her knees in a year's time.

By the end of the day, William Coleman, the energetic young editor of
the city's leading Federalist newspaper, the *New-York Evening Post*, had
done enough legwork to reduce the invasion story to "a bit of a bull."
Coleman had checked with sailors from other ships who had left England
or Ireland around the same time as the Irish vessel. They reported no sign

of a French army. Coleman also pointed out that 180,000 men would require 200 transports, far more than Napoléon's navy possessed.[1]

Napoléon Bonaparte's large shadow had already profoundly affected General Hamilton's politics. As early as 1798, when Napoléon first emerged from the chaos of the French Revolution, Hamilton called him "that unequalled conqueror from whom it is painful to detract, in whom one would wish to find virtues worthy of his shining talents." When Napoléon brushed aside the feeble five-man directory that was trying to rule France and made himself consul for ten years, with absolute power, Hamilton and his Federalist friends regarded the event with a nice mixture of admiration and cynicism. "After ten years of agitation, anarchy, proscription, murder, pillage and crimes of every degree and eight years of the must cruel and bloody wars," wrote one Federalist, the French were now subject to "the despotism of one man of sense, who may find it in his interest to govern well and in his power to govern with steadfastness. . . . General Bonaparte's government is for the best for France . . . and he deserves the thanks of the world for its establishment."[2]

President Jefferson and his fellow Republicans somewhat nervously tried to admire Bonaparte for a different reason: They hoped he was the savior of their beloved French Revolution, which had showed signs of imminent collapse under the combined assaults of the crowned heads of Europe. The Jeffersonians strained their brains and syntax to look favorably on Napoléon's emergence.

Jefferson piously announced he hoped it was really true that "Bonaparte had usurped the government with the intention of making it a free one."[3] When Napoléon forced Austria to sign the humiliating peace of Lunéville in 1801 and the battered British signed a similar semicapitulation at Amiens later in the year, leaving Napoléon master of Europe, the Republicans gloated and cheered. They maintained that the revolution that had begun in America had triumphed and even claimed that Napoléon had been fighting America's battle. If the English had beaten Bonaparte, the Republicans' reasoning went, London would have restored a king to the French throne and launched a war of annihilation against the United States.[4]

Within the year, Napoléon confounded President Jefferson's optimism by having himself elected first consul for life and restoring the Catholic church to all its ancient privileges in France. General Hamilton and his fellow Federalists lost no time in roasting the discomfited Republicans. The editorials in the *New-York Evening Post*, many of them dictated to William Coleman by Hamilton at the end of his long working day, were particularly savage: "Those who admired the French Revolution as a system of liberty are now put into the most ridiculous, whimsical and contemptible situation imaginable. Their great high priest Bonaparte has left them completely in the lurch . . . The First Consul has torn the mask from democracy and branded its forehead with infamy forever."[5]

Paradoxically, the *Evening Post* continued to praise the "tranquility and joy" that the elevation of Bonaparte had brought to France. The *Post* insisted, as General Hamilton often did in his letters, that it was not America's business to tell the people of France what kind of government they should choose. "A government must be fitted to a nation as much as a coat to an individual . . . What may be good at Philadelphia [the U.S. capital at the time] may be bad in Paris and ridiculous at Peterburgh"[St. Petersburg].[6]

II

In America, as in the rest of the world, Napoléon had become a subject of consuming interest. His taste in architecture, furniture, clothes, women, and food were reported in omnivorous detail. Newspapers devoted columns to telling their readers how fresh trout were caught in Lake Geneva and rushed to the first consul's table. For the Federalists, there was political capital in publicizing the new Caesar's imperial tastes. They were mocking Napoléon's indifference to the Republican simplicity that President Jefferson, his penny-pinching ally George Clinton, and their cohorts claimed was the epitome of revolutionary virtue.

Above all, Hamilton and the Federalists were pleased by the "emancipation of that ill-starred country from the ravages of Jacobinism." They did not mourn for French liberty because in their view, France had never been free. She had been ruled by a bloodthirsty atheistic mob, personified by Maximilien de Robespierre, the leader of the Jacobin Club. (The name derived from their original meeting place, a Dominican monastery; Jacobin was the French name for the religious order.) The Federalists hoped Napoléon's usurpation had put an end to the seductive menace of the Revolution's war cry: Liberty, Equality, Fraternity. "Every pious man rejoices at the restoration of Christianity," the *Evening Post* added.[7]

But General Hamilton did not stop worrying about France. "The spirit of Jacobinism which has almost desolated France and threatened the whole world [is] now held in chains by the power of one man . . . If the hand of the assassin [reached] Bonaparte, the monster [Jacobinism] would rage with more violence than ever," Hamilton declared at a meeting of the New York Federalists. This was the political equivalent of having your cake and eating it too. Hamilton pointed to the awesome power of France, supreme in Europe, with the fleets of Spain and Holland at her beck and call. There seemed to be no nation or combination of nations that could prevent her from achieving "universal empire."[8] What had President Jefferson done to meet this potential menace? He had virtually beached the U.S. Navy and dismantled the U.S. Army, and agreed to pay Napoléon $15 million for Louisiana. What could the President do if Napoléon changed his mind, or was assassinated, and France decided to take back Louisiana? Nothing.

In the spring of 1803, this unnerving idea had become more than a mere possibility when the two-year-old peace of Amiens collapsed. Napoléon announced he was going to invade England and dictate peace in St. James's Palace. Newspapers told how the so-called Man of Destiny was summoning reserves from Italy, Switzerland, and Germany to assemble an immense host, the Army of England, in the French channel ports and Holland. Many Americans predicted an internal revolution if Napoléon got his army ashore and the disenfranchised English masses started listening to the French siren song of "Liberty, Equality, and Fraternity."

Commodore Thomas Truxtun's letter to General Hamilton, deploring Jefferson's administration and calling for a revision of the Constitution, enclosed a copy of a long letter Truxtun had written to Senator Timothy Pickering, analyzing the chances of Napoléon successfully invading England. The commodore pointed out the various parts of the English coast where an army might land and what sort of naval support they would require. Truxtun thought Napoléon's army would take horrendous casualties at sea and the men who survived would be stopped on the beaches. But he was by no means certain the Corsican-born general could not succeed: "A Short time will make manifest Whether I have Judged correctly of the Subject," Truxtun wrote. At stake was nothing less than the "happiness of Nations."[9]

III

Hamilton and a group of moneyed Federalist friends had established the *Evening Post* late in 1801. Its fine white rag paper and clean type made it instantly superior to most of its cash-short rivals, who struggled along with cheap blue paper and battered fonts. A weekly edition, the *New York Herald*, circulated throughout the nation, giving General Hamilton's voice a continental dimension. Dapper Boston-born William Coleman, a graduate of Andover Academy, was a gentleman in an era when most editors were, in the words of Massachusetts Federalist Fisher Ames, "uneducated printers, shop boys and raw schoolmasters." Coleman specialized in satire and sarcasm, exemplifying the approach Ames had laid down for the Federalist press: to "whip the [American] Jacobins as a gentleman would a chimney sweeper, at arm's length, and keeping aloof from his soot."[10]

The chief New York rival of the short, delicately built Coleman was tall, swaggering James Cheetham, the DeWitt Clinton follower who edited the *American Citizen*. In 1803 Cheetham accused Coleman of fathering a mulatto child—a charge Coleman quickly refuted.[11] An exchange of insults between the two editors led to a challenge to a duel. New York Supreme Court Justice Brockholst Livingston, a Clinton ally, had the two men arrested to prevent bloodshed. This intervention had its ironic side. In 1798, Livingston, not yet a judge, had challenged and killed James (Jemmy) Jones for flinging insults at him about a skit he had published, satirizing the Federalists.[12]

Negotiations between the Coleman and Cheetham seconds produced a temporary peace. A few months later, one of Cheetham's friends, Captain Thompson, harbormaster of New York, accused Coleman of showing the white feather. Coleman immediately sent Thompson a challenge, which was carried by Washington Morton, husband of General Schuyler's youngest daughter. To avoid another encounter with Judge Livingston, the "meeting," as duels were sometimes called, was arranged with cloak-and-dagger secrecy.

On the appointed night, a prominent New York doctor was told to go to Bowling Green, at the tip of Manhattan, where he would find a horse and gig. He was directed to drive to Love Lane, now East Twenty-first Street, where his services might be needed. The doctor, who had no illusions about why he was being summoned, obeyed. As he arrived at Love Lane he heard two shots. The doctor found James Cheetham kneeling beside a prostrate Captain Thompson. "This gentleman requires your assistance," the editor said.

The doctor examined Thompson and told him the wound was mortal. The captain instructed the physician to carry him to his sister's house in the city and leave him on her doorstep. Thompson died the next day, refusing to name Coleman as his antagonist. It was an affair of honor, he said, and he had been honorably treated. He had no complaints. The next day William Coleman was back editing the *Evening Post* as if nothing in the least extraordinary had happened. Not a word of reproach was uttered against him. Thereafter, James Cheetham was notably more careful about using insulting words like *rascal* when he referred to his editorial rival.

IV

Later, on January 2nd, General Hamilton undoubtedly discussed another duel with Federalist friends at their favorite gathering place, the Tontine Coffee House, on the corner of Wall and Water Streets.[13] For a week New York had been agog with the rumor that Senator James Jackson of Georgia had exchanged shots with Vice President Aaron Burr and had severely wounded or killed him. It was plausible. As vice president, Burr presided in the Senate and frequently chided speakers who wandered from the point. Senator Jackson was fond of making windy speeches and took great exception to anyone who interrupted him.

A famous duelist, Jackson had killed the lieutenant governor of Georgia during the American Revolution. When DeWitt Clinton was in the Senate, he had made a speech criticizing Jackson. The Georgian asked for an *explanation*—a word that was frequently the prelude to a challenge. Clinton hastily apologized.

Senator Jackson was connected to another subject that intensely interested General Hamilton and his fellow Federalists—the Yazoo scandal. In 1796, the senator had browbeaten the state of Georgia into repudiating one of the biggest real estate deals in American history: the sale of 31 million acres watered by the Yazoo River—what is now the entire states of Alabama and Mississippi—to land speculators for between two cents and four cents an acre.

In engineering this legislative coup, Jackson had cavalierly ignored Article 1, Section 10, of the U.S. Constitution, which declared that no state shall pass a law ignoring the obligations of a contract. True, the Georgians who had pushed the Yazoo deal through the state's legislature in 1795 had bribed almost every member. But corruption was hardly unusual in land speculation; similar charges had swirled through the New York State legislature more than once when millions of upstate acres were sold to wealthy investors. Cynics opined that Senator Jackson, a major land speculator himself, had only gotten exercised about Yazoo because no one had offered him a piece of the action.

Hamilton's interest in the Yazoo mess had a personal dimension. William Coleman had lost almost every cent he possessed in the Georgia legislature's nullification of the deal. He had been forced to abandon a fine house he was building in Massachusetts and flee to New York to escape his creditors. New Englanders had invested heavily in the scheme—in the Boston area alone, people put up over $2 million.

Even more poignant was the story of Hamilton's friend and legal colleague Nathaniel Pendleton. From one of Virginia's prominent families, Pendleton had been aide-de-camp to Major General Nathanael Greene, the American commander in the South at the close of the revolutionary war, distinguishing himself in several battles. After the war Pendleton settled in Georgia and became a federal judge.

Although he was well aware of the corruption swirling through the Yazoo deal, Pendleton became one of its chief proponents. He lost a lot of money and not a little reputation in the ensuing scandal. Resigning his judgeship in semidisgrace, Pendleton moved to New York in 1796. The Virginian was also fleeing a disastrous affair with General Greene's bewitching widow, Catherine Littlefield Greene, which had threatened his marriage and his emotional stability.[14] A sympathetic Hamilton had helped Pendleton find a niche in the fiercely competitive New York legal world.

Pendleton provided Hamilton with an insider's view of the Yazoo affair, which had infuriated investors from New England and other states. They protested that they had known nothing about how the deal was arranged. The sale had been signed, sealed, and consented to by the legal officers of the state of Georgia. No doubt influenced by Pendleton and Coleman, the General had issued a resounding legal opinion in favor of repaying the investors.

The opinion may have been correct from a constitutional point of view. But from a political point of view it underscored Hamilton's alliance with men of wealth—and their tendency to do less than admirable things with their money. A great many New Yorkers had taken the windfall profits Hamilton handed them when he funded the Revolutionary debts at par and speculated recklessly in the nascent Wall Street stock market, bringing on America's first crash in the spring of 1792. More than a few prominent Federalists, most of them friends of Hamilton, wound up in debtor's prison and Thomas Jefferson promptly denounced a system that put so much money in the hands of "gambling scoundrels."

The Yazoo mess was a particularly reprehensible example of speculating in land. James Greenleaf, the financier whom Hamilton declined to rescue, was one of the chief crooks who sold millions of acres of land to gullible New Englanders. Greenleaf and Robert Morris of Pennsylvania, once the most reputable and wealthiest merchant in America, and another close Hamilton friend, were involved in an even more deplorable scheme to sell 2,314,796 acres in the Georgia Pine Barrens, a region of sandy, sterile soil and yellow pine trees, inhospitable to anyone but lumberjacks. Things got worse when the state surveyor general reported that speculators claimed 29,097,866 acres of Georgia, but there were only 8,717,960 acres in the state's twenty-four organized counties.[15] Soon Greenleaf, Morris, and many other land speculators were in debtor's prison, enabling the Jeffersonians to preach another sermon about gambling scoundrels. When Hamilton brooded about his "odd destiny," his disappointment in the behavior of these men almost certainly was an unspoken part of his lament.

Still refusing to admit any responsibility for the Yazoo investors' losses, the Jackson-controlled Georgia legislature had sold the disputed acres to the United States in 1802. In the agreement, 5 million acres were set aside to compensate anyone with prior claims to the land. New England's Yazoo investors, backed by a phalanx of Federalist congressmen, pressured the government to get their money back. They were opposed in the House of Representatives by Jefferson's floor leader, Virginian John Randolph, who turned the issue into a party as well as a sectional quarrel. Stirring the innate hostility of the agrarian South to Northern moneymen,

Randolph declared that it would be compounding a crime to give the investors a cent, no matter what the Constitution said about contracts. He was backed by the entire Georgia delegation in Congress, all of them faithful Republican followers of Senator Jackson, and by almost every other southern Republican in the House of Representatives.[16]

Yazoo's entanglement in party politics was another reason why many people thought Senator Jackson may have shot it out with Aaron Burr. Had the vice president aroused Jackson's wrath by backing the Yankees? Rumors had been drifting around New York for months about a growing rapport between Burr and the New England Federalists. No one listened to these reports with more concern than General Hamilton.

V

Senator Jackson and the Yazoo imbroglio may well have led to a larger and more alarming topic at the Tontine Coffee House. Some Republicans were asserting that legislatures, as bodies supposedly expressing the will of the people, should have the last word, not only on whether to honor a contract, but also on whether a judge's opinion had to be obeyed if the legislators differed with it. This was an idea easily linked to Jacobinism and upheaval.

The Jeffersonians in Congress had already taken a large step in this direction, from the Federalists' point of view. In 1802 they had repealed the Judiciary Act of 1801, abolishing twenty-six judgeships that the Federalist-controlled Congress had created in the closing weeks of its tenure. Outgoing President John Adams had appointed no one but Federalists to these jobs, of course. But if Congress could abolish a judge's job for political reasons, it seemed only a short step to removing him for any and every trumped up political charge.

Almost as alarming were developments in several states. In Kentucky, judges' salaries were kept at the starvation level—as little as $300 a year— and they were saddled with "assistants" who had no legal training but were free to give their opinions on cases. In Pennsylvania there was a movement afoot to abolish a whole range of state judgeships and replace them with referees who were equally devoid of legal degrees and would be chosen by popular vote. On January 3rd, the *Evening Post* ran a story about this referee bill, denouncing it as a scheme by "wretches" who wanted to destroy the jury system. The newspaper referred to Pennsylvania as a "degraded state"—meaning it was hopelessly in the grip of the Republicans—and gloomily predicted it would be the last to "come right." It was even worse than Virginia.[17]

VI

When General Hamilton conferred with William Coleman about the contents of the *Evening Post*'s upcoming issues, one topic transcended all others: Louisiana. Almost every day in this first week of the new year, the paper published letters from correspondents in the West, reporting on the political mood in New Orleans (calm) and the latest word on American preparations to occupy the city. No one knew whether the new rulers would be received with cheers—or with bullets.

Almost from the day Thomas Jefferson became president, the vast territory had roiled the nation. The French had ceded it to Spain in 1763 to compensate Madrid for its losses in the Seven Years War. As Jefferson took office, electrifying news swept the United States: Napoléon had combined threats and promises to persuade Spain to secretly return the huge domain to France.

A year later, angered by Napoléon's brutal tactics, the Spanish administrators of New Orleans had retaliated by revoking the "right of deposit," which George Washington's administration had negotiated in 1795. Under this agreement, Americans were entitled to export farm produce and other items of trade through New Orleans. When the right was revoked, an instant shout for war rose from the western states, led by warrior politicians such as Andrew Jackson of Tennessee. Kentucky alone had a half million dollars in goods and crops on the Mississippi when the news of the revocation arrived.

General Hamilton had warmly seconded this call for war in the pages of the *New-York Evening Post*. In private letters he gloated over the dilemma Jefferson confronted. He had been elected deploring the large army and navy the Federalists had raised for the undeclared war with France and the taxes that supported the new military establishment. He had repealed the taxes and reduced the armed forces to a shadow. Now he was faced with "the great embarrassment of how to carry on a war without taxes."

When Jefferson tried to defuse the situation by sending James Monroe to France as an envoy extraordinary, Hamilton, writing in the *Evening Post* as Pericles, ferociously attacked the move. Hamilton recommended going to war immediately, before the French had time to ship an army to New Orleans. He called on Jefferson to triple the size of the pathetic three-thousand-man regular army and muster a forty-thousand-man standby force of militia. The navy should be strengthened and negotiations opened with England to "cooperate with us at a moment's warning."

There was, Hamilton/Pericles declared, "not the remotest chance that the ambitious and aggrandizing views of Bonaparte will commute the territory for money." Within three months, this prophecy exploded in General Hamilton's face, demonstrating how difficult it was for even the most astute insider to read the political future. No one, including Thomas Jefferson, foresaw how soon a new war would erupt between England and France, putting Bonaparte in an acute financial squeeze.[18]

VII

Until that unexpected explosion of hostilities became imminent, France's first consul planned to do exactly what General Hamilton had predicted. Napoléon had gone to immense trouble to wangle Louisiana out of the grasp of his halfhearted Spanish ally. It was the first step to reestablishing

France's empire in North America. When the new war began, Napoléon had fifteen thousand men aboard troopships, ready to depart for New Orleans.

The new war—and the leak of the cession by Spain—made the mercurial first consul rethink his plans. He could never defend Louisiana against the British fleet, which might well seize New Orleans and claim the rest of the territory as a prize of war. Moreover, Napoléon's information led him to believe that if he sold Louisiana to the United States, the Americans would inevitably split into western and eastern confederacies and the warlike West could easily be seduced into becoming a French client state.

Both the Spanish and the French had spent thousands in secret service money to encourage this tendency. George Rogers Clark, conqueror of the Northwest Territory in the Revolution, was among the distinguished names on the French secret service payroll. Brigadier General James Wilkinson, the current commander in chief of the American army, got an equally secret annual stipend from Spain. Known to his Spanish handlers as Agent 13, Wilkinson had taken an oath swearing allegiance to Spain in 1787.

Early in April of 1803, Napoléon ordered his foreign minister, the same Maurice de Talleyrand-Périgord who admired Alexander Hamilton, to call in the American ambassador to France, Robert R. Livingston, and ask him how much he would pay for Louisiana. James Monroe arrived in time to help the astonished Livingston close the deal and enable the Jeffersonians to claim that sending the envoy extraordinary was a stroke of presidential genius. Thanks to the continuing vigor of Hamilton's financial system, the United States had no difficulty raising the $15 million. In December of 1803, the French commissioner in New Orleans, Pierre Clement Laussat, issued a proclamation informing the inhabitants that they were about to become citizens of the United States.

Textbook writers and Jefferson admirers have so regularly hailed the Louisiana Purchase as a diplomatic masterpiece that doubled the size of the United States, it is difficult for late-twentieth-century Americans to grasp the way General Hamilton and his followers saw it in 1804. They remained convinced that the Americans should have seized the territory by force, and they had no faith whatsoever in Napoléon's promise to honor the purchase.

Laussat's proclamation provided the Federalists with plenty of ammunition. Coleman and Hamilton thought it was so important, they reprinted it verbatim in the January 2, 1804, *Evening Post*. The Frenchman candidly admitted that the "advent of war" had been the only reason for Napoléon's decision to sell. (So much, sneered the *Evening Post*, for Jefferson's diplomatic genius.) Laussat also claimed the deal was a "pledge of friendship" between America and France. The *Evening Post* wondered if this meant Napoléon would feel free to abrogate the treaty if the friendship soured.

Laussat also claimed that the sale to the United States in no way lessened Napoléon's determination to "renew and perpetuate" the ties between Louisiana and France. "Your children will become our children and our children will become yours," he declared. He urged the Louisianians to make sure the United States listened to their "wise and impartial counsel," which he was sure would enable them to become a "preponderating influence" in the federal government.

"Is there one man with a single drop of American blood in his veins whose pride is not aroused, whose prudence is not alarmed, whose indignation is not fired at this triumphant display of French arrogance?" the *Evening Post* asked.[19] The paper also pointed out that the treaty called for giving France and Spain most-favored-nation-status for twelve years. This stipulation was certain to irritate the British, by far the largest exporters to America.

This pro-French tilt in America's supposedly neutral stance between the two superpowers was a grievous mistake, the *Evening Post* maintained, because the British fleet could do far more harm to America than Napoléon's armies. The paper urged readers to look at the treaty from the British point of view. The United States was giving Napoléon $15 million to make war on them. It was an equally bad deal from New York's and New England's point of view. Jefferson was going to finance the purchase out of import revenues, which meant that the commercial northern states, which did most of the importing, would pay for the new territory, while the agrarian South, which imported very little, would gain most of the benefits from Louisiana's proximity. The *Evening Post* denounced this policy as unfair and unwise, the product of Jefferson's pro-Southern, pro-French policy. The treaty, the paper warned, could become "the greatest curse which ever befell this country." Hamilton was almost certainly thinking about the letters he was getting from Senator Timothy Pickering of Massachusetts, arguing for New England's secession.

Other Federalist papers reminded readers of the treacherous undeclared war France had waged on America only six years ago, when Americans rejected a demand for a "loan" of $13 million. The editor of the *New England Palladium* asked if there was any difference between this extortion and the $15 million Jefferson was paying for the "wilderness of Louisiana." The difference was, George Washington would not pay tribute but "Thomas Jefferson would."[20]

General Hamilton and his editor also pointed out that the $15 million Jefferson paid for the territory would pay an army of twenty-five thousand men good wages for twenty-five years. If Napoléon succeded in invading and subduing England, Hamilton was convinced the United States was going to need an army to defend the Louisiana purchase. To raise and run an army required a government with energy, the quality that the pro-French politician in the presidential palace in Washington, D.C., conspicuously lacked.

VIII

Napoléon Bonaparte's role in the French Revolution was on many people's minds for another reason. Not a few Americans wondered if his ascension to power was a glimpse of what might happen in America. The *New-York Evening Post*'s reaction to a speech by James Jackson in the U.S. Senate was a good example of this train of thought. Jackson declared

President Jefferson no longer had to worry about Federalism. It was dead. If another political party succeeded Jefferson's Republicans, it would be organized by people who carried his ideas of liberty even farther than the author of the Declaration of Independence.

The *Evening Post* emphatically agreed with the Georgia Senator. "Judging from the lesson exhibited by France . . . one violent faction is destined to succeed another, even more violent than the former" until the agitation ends with "our usurper." If the Republicans' attack on the judiciary succeeded, "we make up our minds to be surprised at nothing that can follow." [21] Gouverneur Morris too foresaw a not too distant future when America's voyage on "the tempestuous sea of liberty" would require a "Cromwell or a Bonaparte" to restore order.

At least as intriguing was the question of who that usurper—the American Bonaparte—would be. Not a few people identified him as General Alexander Hamilton. This was the essence of the argument that had led to the duel between George Eacker and Philip Hamilton. In a letter to his son-in-law, Thomas Mann Randolph, written not long after Napoléon assumed power in France, President Jefferson concurred, describing Hamilton as "our Bonaparte," who was ready and eager to "step in and give us political salvation in his way."[22]

The man who offered the most pungent commentary on Hamilton as America's future Bonaparte was President George Washington's successor, John Adams. He and Hamilton had never been friendly and when Adams became president, they swiftly developed a loathing for each other that brought out the worst in both their personalities. Adams strongly opposed appointing Hamilton second in command of the army in the undeclared war with France. He yielded only when Washington threatened to resign if he did not get his way. By that time the cantankerous Adams despised Hamilton as a "foreigner" and "the greatest intriguant in the world—a man utterly devoid of moral principle."[23]

Ex-President John Adams was still very much alive in Quincy, Massachusetts, nursing with his wife's help a consuming hatred of General Hamilton. It would explode in conversation and correspondence with volcanic irregularity for the remaining twenty-two years of his life. As Adams saw it, Hamilton was the marplot who had destroyed his presidency and wrecked his campaign for a second term.

Adams had inherited his cabinet from President Washington and made the fatal mistake of hesitating to change it, lest he seem to be criticizing the Father of the Country. The four members were all handpicked by Hamilton and totally loyal to him rather than Adams. Five months after Washington's death, with the Hamiltonians still determined to fight the undeclared war with France to a finish, Adams revolted. He called in Secretary of War James McHenry and roared insults at him and General Hamilton.

"I . . . would rather be vice president under [Jefferson] than indebted to such a being as Hamilton for the presidency," bellowed old John Yankee, as Adams liked to call himself. He denounced McHenry for his subservience to Hamilton and threw in a blast at Washington, whom Hamilton had also "ruled." The first president had saddled him with secretaries who "would control me," he ranted. "But I shall take care of that."[24]

Adams fired McHenry and Secretary of State Timothy Pickering. But he made the mistake of keeping Oliver Wolcott Jr. as secretary of the treasury because he was good at the job. Wolcott was even more devoted to Hamilton than McHenry and kept "the Creole," as Adams called the General, informed of every move the president made.

When Adams backed away from the undeclared war with France and negotiated a truce, depriving the Federalist party of their best issue for the 1800 presidential race, General Hamilton decided John Yankee had to go. Further infuriating Hamilton was Adams's accusation that he headed a pro-British faction within the Federalist party. The General wrote a long supposedly secret letter to the party's leaders, ferociously attacking Adams as a mental case and an incompetent, and urging that he be dumped. He advised Federalist electors to vote instead for their vice presidential nominee, Charles Cotesworth Pinckney of South Carolina.

Hamilton's fifty-page screed on Adams was purloined from the printer by the man who was running for vice president on the Republican ticket,

Aaron Burr. Leaked to the newspapers, it tore the Federalist party apart. In South Carolina, General Pinckney, an extremely honorable if not especially intelligent man, announced that he would not accept any electoral vote that was not also pledged to President Adams. This noble stance put his would-be supporters in an impossible bind, and the South Carolina legislature, after ten days of wrangling, gave their electoral votes to Jefferson and Burr.

John Adams went home to Quincy convinced that General Hamilton was only a step removed from Satan. The ex-president held forth on Hamilton's "debaucheries in New York and Philadelphia," on "his audacious and unblushing attempts upon ladies of the highest rank and purest virtue." In another less genteel moment, Adams roared: "Hamilton couldn't cool his iron in his own trough!"[25]

Hamilton's private life was only a minor chord in old John Yankee's hymn of hatred of the Creole. He pointed even more vehemently to the striking resemblance between Hamilton and Napoléon. Both were born on an island off the continent; both were revolutionary soldiers with political ambitions. Hamilton, Adams maintained, "aimed at commanding the whole union." Although he was ready to tilt toward England in the war between the superpowers, he did not want an alliance. "If he could have made a tool of Adams as he did of Washington," John Yankee declared, "he hoped to erect such a government as he pleased over the whole union, and enter into alliance with France or England as would suit his convenience."[26] The ex-president's wife, Abigail, often described as "a compleat politician," totally agreed with her John. "That man [Hamilton] would become a second Bonaparty [*sic*] if he was possessed of equal power," she avowed.[27]

IX

The moonshine rantings of two embittered oldsters? Perhaps. But John Adams had been president of the United States. He had listened to the

Hamiltonians in his cabinet discuss their view of the world. He had heard them dismiss the Constitution of the United States as a botched document. Adams had served two terms as vice president under Washington with little to do but study the evolution of the republic's politics. By 1804, General Hamilton had spoken and written thousands of words about the American government. A surprising number of statements support the Adamses' fears.

From the start of his career, Hamilton was fascinated by the potential might of America. In *The Federalist*, the book of essays he wrote with James Madison and John Jay to promote the ratification of the Constitution, he declared: "Let the thirteen states concur in erecting one great American system, superior to the control of all transatlantic force or influence, and able to dictate the terms of the connection between the old and new world!" This system could never be established without giving the central government "plenary powers." Slipping unconsciously into a military metaphor, Hamilton continued: "Its policy must always be to increase its garrisons against . . . inevitable maladies like sedition and insurrection."

Power without limitation—that was what Hamilton recommended in his five-hour speech before the Constitutional Convention that had mesmerized Gouverneur Morris. When Hamilton found the majority were determined to limit the government's power by dividing it and checking it, he went home in disgust. Later he decided an unsatisfactory constitution was better than none and threw himself into the struggle to get the charter ratified. As President Washington's right-hand man, Hamilton soon advanced his theory of implied powers, which gave the federal government broad authority to found a Bank of the United States and to act in other areas not specifically discussed in the Constitution.

At the heart of General Hamilton's thinking about government was an army. In a letter to a Continental congressman in 1780, Hamilton wrote: "With me it is an axiom that . . . an army is essential to the American union." He never changed this opinion. Three years later, as the Revolution was ending, he urged Washington to use the Continental army to force Congress to establish a national taxation system that would fund the troops' long-overdue back pay and unite the country. When Washington refused to play such a dangerous political game, Hamilton concealed his role in the plot and helped the commander-in-chief to stifle the so-called Newburgh conspiracy. But Hamilton confided to another correspondent that he could still "almost wish to see force employed."[28]

In 1794, when Washington's second administration was confronted by a violent revolt in western Pennsylvania against Hamilton's tax on whiskey, the secretary of the treasury's reaction was ferociously military. He persuaded President Washington to raise a militia army and put him in command of it. The insurrection, an unstable mix of western bluster and class grievances, collapsed in the face of the show of federal force.

When General Hamilton commanded the provisional army in 1799, he spent many hours conferring with Brigadier James Wilkinson, discussing the possibility of taking both Florida and New Orleans from the Spanish by force. Hamilton appears to have known or suspected that Wilkinson was already a Spanish pensioner, but he apparently thought tempting him with the rewards of conquest would overcome his divided loyalty.

General Hamilton may have seen no great harm in Wilkinson's back-stairs dealings with Spain because he had done something similar himself when he was secretary of the treasury. He spent so much time talking to Major George Beckwith of the British secret service that he became "Number 7" in the major's reports to his superiors in London. Hamilton supplied him with thumbnail character sketches of Madison, Jefferson, and other leading American politicians, and was not above leaking information that enabled the British to anticipate if not sabotage Secretary of State Jefferson's pro-French policies.[29]

Hamilton's motive was not a retrograde penchant for monarchy, as his Jeffersonian enemies claimed. Throughout the early 1790s, he had worked hard to achieve a rapprochement with England to encourage British investment in America. As John Adams astutely discerned,

Hamilton was loyal only to his vision of an American empire, created by his foresight and daring. The rapprochement had long since collapsed, thanks to the shortsighted animosity of England's politicians and the hostility of the Jeffersonians.

Hamilton was soon pursuing other agendas. Ignoring the strenuous objections of his friend and devoted follower Secretary of War James McHenry, Hamilton recommended Brigadier Wilkinson's promotion to major general. He saw Wilkinson playing a part in his vision of an imperial America: "We ought certainly to look to the possession of the Floridas and Louisiana, and we ought to squint at South America," he told McHenry.[30]

In one of his more revealing remarks, General Hamilton declared Maurice de Talleyrand-Périgord the greatest statesman of his era, because he knew exactly when to look the other way while a government did "wrong," and also when to do "wrong" himself in the name of that iron law of power politics—necessity.

X

The roots of Hamilton's ideas ran deep into his American experience. As the revolutionary war ended, he confessed to a friend: "I have an indifferent opinion of the honesty of this country and ill-forebodings as to its future [political] system."[31] Hamilton acquired this skepticism of America's voters and the politicians they tended to elect during his four years as Washington's chief aide-de-camp. From that vantage point, he watched the atrocious performance of the Continental Congress during the Revolution, in particular its inability to summon the courage to tax the American people to pay for the war. The result was a ruinous inflation that turned the dollars Congress kept printing into wastepaper. Civilian morale plummeted, recruits shrank to the vanishing point, and three major mutinies shook the Continental army's ranks. In 1780, Hamilton told a congressman that the army was "a mob ... without clothing, without pay, without provisions, without morals, without discipline. We begin to hate the country for its neglect of us." To a fellow officer, he raged: "Our countrymen have all the folly of the ass and all the passiveness of the sheep in their compositions."[32]

This mixture of anger and distrust was never eliminated from Hamilton's psyche. He watched with dismay and disbelief the process by which most Americans congratulated themselves for winning the Revolution without admitting they had virtually abandoned the Continental army that had secured the victory. There was scarcely a quiver of the popular conscience when the soldiers went home mostly unpaid and the officers were denied the half pay for life that Congress had led them to expect.

"For my part," Hamilton wrote, while trying to persuade New Yorkers to ratify the Constitution, "I am not much attached to the majesty of the multitude. I consider them in general as very ill-qualified to judge for themselves what government will best suit their peculiar situations." By 1802, General Hamilton was describing the people as a huge, shapeless blind monster like the cyclops in Virgil's *Aeneid*.[33]

One of the ironies of this view, which was shared by many other Federalist leaders, was the way it became the Achilles heel of their party. Everywhere they resisted the idea of universal suffrage, repeatedly trying to limit the right to vote to property holders, on the theory that they would support good, wise, and virtuous leaders, i.e., Federalists. In New York City, 38 percent of the adult male population was barred from voting for any office. In elections for the Common Council, the barriers were even higher. Only 23 percent could vote, guaranteeing Federalist control, but at a destructive price. The Republicans skillfully exploited lower-middle-class resentment against Federalist distrust, easily convincing many people that the party was hostile to one of the fundamental ideals of the republic—equality.[34]

Nevertheless, Hamilton remained convinced that an America dependent on the popular will would always veer toward weakness and chaos. What was the answer? "There must be a systematic & persevering endeavor to establish the fortune of a great empire on foundations much firmer than have yet been devised," he told Delaware's Congressman James A. Bayard in 1802. America would never act with confidence and energy until "our National Edifice shall be such as naturally to control eccentric passions and views and to keep in check demagogues & knaves in the disguise of Patriots."[35]

At the same time, Hamilton frequently avowed that he "was as zealous an advocate for liberty as any man whatever." In spite of admitted doubts about the chances of success, he saw America as an ultimate test of the "fate of republican government." [36] As 1804 began Hamilton and his circle were growing extremely pessimistic about republicanism's future. But the General's endeavors to change the nation's political foundation were no longer systematic. Sporadic would be a more accurate description of Hamilton's political activity. The ailing, overworked lawyer simply did not have the time or energy for persevering effort.

XI

The first week of the new year saw General Hamilton in an approximation of his old aggressive mode, preparing for a major assault on Jefferson. At some point he conferred with Richard Harison, the attorney he had asked to assist him in the appeal for a new trial for the Hudson, New York, printer Harry Croswell. They were scheduled to appear in Albany before the full New York State Supreme Court on February 13th. It was time to decide how to divide the argument—and to speculate on the impact the case might have on Jefferson's run for a second term.

The General had chosen the scholarly Harison to serve as federal attorney for the southern district of New York from 1789 to 1801, which made him a devoted Hamilton man. Deepening Harison's attachment was his political background. During the American Revolution, he and his family had been loyalists. Hamilton had played a leading role in restoring respectability to such people in New York, arguing that the state needed their talents and influence. The Clintonians had preferred a vindictive policy of proscription and banishment.

Neither man was receiving a fee to represent Croswell. That meant work on the appeal had to be squeezed into their already crowded dockets. The renewed war between France and England was producing a flood of cases dealing with marine insurance, as privateers from both belligerents preyed on American merchant ships. General Hamilton regularly represented New York's two marine insurance companies as well as cases involving his brother-in-law, John Barker Church, who was active in this lucrative business—and was known for his reluctance to pay his losses.

Several times during the busy week, William Coleman, the editor of the *New-York Evening Post*, dropped into Hamilton's law office to discuss the latest news and make notes on the General's analyses of it. The editor and his chief backer maintained a delicate balance between taking orders and semi-independence. Hamilton did not have time to control every word in the *Evening Post* and Coleman would not have submitted to such bossism.

Between them, over the next several days, the Hamilton-Coleman team did a nice job of focusing public attention on the Croswell case. They opened the campaign with a sharp attack on Jefferson for removing a public servant like Harison, with an unimpeachable record, and replacing him with Edward Livingston. The bankrupt ex-mayor and former federal attorney had long since retreated to New Orleans, but he remained fair game for Federalist shafts.

Coleman followed this praise of Harison with a report that Croswell had become the sole owner of the Hudson, New York, newspaper, the *Balance* (parent publication of the *Wasp*, the paper in which Croswell had printed his supposed libels against President Jefferson) and would continue to publish it in spite of his persecution by the Clintonians. The story quoted a Washington *Federalist* claim that the Republican scheme to muzzle the press emanated from the presidential palace, following the principle of "concealing the hand that directs the blows."

Coleman pointed out that Croswell had been indicted and convicted for publishing stories that had also appeared in the *Evening Post*. But the Clintonians had not dared to attack the *Post* because they knew they could never get a New York jury to indict or convict a man without permitting him to present the truth in evidence.[37] The next day, the *Post* published a statement by Croswell in which he declared his faith in the independence of the state's supreme court. The printer was confident that the evil onward march of democracy in New York was about to falter. "The monster, Anarchy, is yet in chains."[38]

The time and attention Hamilton and his editor gave to this case underscored its importance to the General's political future. He was devoting a large amount of mental energy to defending this obscure country editor to prove Alexander Hamilton was still a committed Federalist, ready to serve the party gratis in this good cause.

XII

General Hamilton was well aware that his hope of regaining political power was endangered by the popularity of President Jefferson's Louisiana Purchase. He fought back in the pages of the *Evening Post* by praising the acquisition of New Orleans, damning the terms of the treaty, and denigrating the value of the rest of the territory. Abroad, he waited to see if Napoléon made a successful lunge across the English Channel. The General could not help hoping the first consul would smash England and turn his attention to the United States. Nothing else would more certainly guarantee Hamilton's return to power. Not even President Thomas Jefferson would dare to refuse the supreme command to the man whom George Washington had designated as his military heir apparent in 1798.

To take advantage of this opportunity, if it arose, one thing was absolutely essential. Hamilton had to retain control of the Federalist party. If war came, he would need a fierce outcry from the men of virtues and talents—and money—to overcome Jeffersonian resistance. Everything was in place to generate this political storm. The Federalists now had well-edited, aggressive newspapers throughout the United States. They never missed a chance to belabor the Jefferson administration.

But there were other factors in this whirlwind of history General Hamilton was trying to ride that threatened to undo his game plan. His control of the Federalist party was no longer absolute. Numerous moderates had lost confidence in him after his reckless attempt to eliminate John Adams in 1800. Even before that fiasco, his insistence on publishing the whole truth about himself and Maria Reynolds had caused many practical men to question his judgment.

Some prominent Federalists now talked back to General Hamilton. Noah Webster, who combined Federalism and lexicography, warned Hamilton after his attack on John Adams that his "ambition, pride and overbearing temper" were in danger of making him "the evil genius of this country."[39] Delaware's James Bayard dismissed the General's proposal for a Christian Constitutional Society so roundly, Hamilton never brought it up again. Even one of Hamilton's closest friends, Robert Troup, lamented that his character was *radically deficient in discretion.*[40]

In the 1802 congressional elections voters had deserted the party of virtues and talents in droves. There were now a mere 39 Federalists versus 103 Republicans in the House of Representatives and a paltry 9 Federalists versus 25 Republicans in the Senate. One Federalist lamented that they had become "a degraded minority."[41]

To revive the party, many Federalists were talking about the need for a new leader—a man who could appeal to moderate voters in both parties, someone who had also demonstrated ability as a vote getter. The chief contender for this role was the politician who had eviscerated General Hamilton's power in New York City and New York State, Vice President Aaron Burr.

CHAPTER 4

The Temptations
of a Vice President

"*M*r. Burr, the vice president, presides in the Senate with great ease, dignity & propriety."[1] This was the considered opinion of Senator William Plumer of New Hampshire, a crusty Federalist who seldom had anything good to say about Jeffersonian Republicans. From his seat on the elevated dais of the chamber, the forty-seven-year-old vice president bulked larger than his five feet six inches in height.[2] Burr was, according to the rules of the political game developed under Presidents Washington and Adams, the heir apparent to the presidency. That alone added several cubits to his stature. He also had what one friend called "a loftiness of mien" that usually impelled instant respect.

Burr had done far more than the two previous vice presidents, John Adams and Thomas Jefferson, to bring some order to the often chaotic proceedings of the U.S. Senate. An early British observer of Congress at work said it looked like London's Hyde Park (where speech makers, jugglers, Punch and Judy shows, and pleasure seekers haphazardly mingled) set down in the lobby of a hotel. Members chatted with lady friends on the floor and arrived or departed with yapping bird dogs; messengers wandered through, calling out legislators' names, distributing the mail while speakers rambled on without even trying to stick to the point. It was "Babeltown," one disillusioned congressman remarked.

In the Senate, Vice President Burr drastically reformed this exhibition of democracy at its most brainless. He insisted on "good order, silence & decorum" during debates. He frequently reprimanded wandering speakers and he barred all visitors from the chamber except members of the House of Representatives.

Succession and decorum aside, there were other reasons why a certified Yankee like Senator Plumer would regard Vice President Burr with respect. From a New England point of view, few men had a more impressive genealogy. The vice president was descended from a Burr who had arrived in Massachusetts in 1630 with Governor John Winthrop's Puritan fleet. His father, the Reverend Aaron Burr, had been born in Connecticut and migrated to become president of that Calvinist bastion, the College of New Jersey, which eventually changed its name to Princeton. On his mother's side, Burr was the grandson of Jonathan Edwards, the greatest name in New England churchdom, the kindler of the "Great Awakening" of 1735, which made the conversion experience central to American religion. Another grandson, Burr's first cousin, Timothy Dwight, was president of Yale.

Compared to Alexander Hamilton, and even to Thomas Jefferson, Aaron Burr was an American aristocrat. He shared with Hamilton a troubled childhood; in his case the woe was inflicted by the grim reaper, rather than the caprices of a weak father and a tempestuous mother. Both Burr's parents died before he was two and he and his older sister were raised by his mother's brother, Timothy Edwards.

"A grave animal," was how Aaron Burr once described himself. But he could be delightful company, witty, intelligent, thoughtful. His suave manners and stylish clothes prompted some people to call him "the American Chesterfield." The vice president did, in fact, subscribe to much of that English nobleman's hedonistic philosophy, which exempted gentlemen from conventional morality. But Burr did not flaunt his impiety. On the contrary, he frequently ended letters to close friends with "God bless thee."[3] From the start of his political career, he had striven to offend as few and charm as many as possible.

Burr had spent a year studying for the ministry before he decided that he lacked the fervent faith of his fathers. His reaction was typical of a general decline in theological fervor throughout America. The French Revolution's assault on religion as the bulwark of the ruling class accelerated this trend. In the Yale class of 1796, a poll revealed only one graduate who believed in God—a glimpse of why Federalists' attacks on Thomas Jefferson's supposed atheism went nowhere.

II

Impressive to men, Burr was even more fascinating to women. He was equally enthralled by their limitless variety. In the ten years since his wife's death in 1794, he had become famous in a clandestine way for his continentwide amours. During his vice-presidential years, he had mistresses in Philadelphia, New York, New Haven, and Boston. The latter two places were refuges to which he sent women to give birth discreetly. In New Haven lived his uncle, Pierpont Edwards, one of the great womanizers of the era, who was quick to understand such problems when they arose.

Among the American elite, there was nothing unusual about this pursuit of amorous pleasure. Although the nineteenth century had begun, Victorianism was four decades away. The less inhibited mores of the eighteenth century still prevailed. In his old age, Jefferson's secretary of the treasury, Albert Gallatin, remarked: "It would not be possible [today] to elect to high office men of such private morals" as several prominent politicians with whom he had served.[4]

But Vice President Burr seems to have carried sexual liberation to an extreme that troubled even his closest friends. Matthew Davis, the editor of his so-called memoirs (really a collection of letters with some commentary) was a lifelong admirer of Burr. Yet Davis felt compelled to admit "his intrigues were without number. His conduct most licentious [and] regardless of all ties which ought to control an honourable mind."[5]

According to Davis, Burr was at his best in a drawing room. His brilliant jet-black eyes, his polished courtly manner, his grace of movement and gesture created an aura that was "inconceivably fascinating." He operated on the assumption that all women were susceptible to flattery. But his great art was adapting his cajolery precisely to the intelligence of the woman he was pursuing. He was "excessively vain" about his conquests and saved every scrap of correspondence from his inamoratas. Davis added that he found all this incompatible with Burr's "elevated and towering mind."[6]

The vice president was also unique for his fascination with women's minds. He was one of the few Americans who believed in the education of women, an opinion he may have gotten by osmosis from his father, who urged his wife, Esther Burr, to learn Latin and French. Burr's enthusiasm for the female intellect had been deepened when he fell in love with Theodosia Prevost, widow of a British officer. Ten years his senior, she was an urbane well-read woman who incidentally did not approve of his enthusiasm for Lord Chesterfield, because of that nobleman's low opinion of the female sex.

Living proof of Vice President Burr's continuing fascination with women's minds was his daughter, Theodosia. Burr had supervised her education personally. Theodosia read Greek and Latin, spoke and read French fluently, and was well versed in English literature. Through her, he told his wife, he hoped "to convince the world what neither sex appear to believe—that women have souls!"[7]

An intensely paternal man, Burr took into his household a young refugee from Jacobinism, Nathalie Delage de Volude, to improve Theodosia's French. He was soon referring to Nathalie as his adopted daughter, adding that she was "the loveliest creature that I know in the world of her age (now in her 14th)."[8] He was also devoted to his wife's two sons by her first marriage, Frederick and Bartow Prevost. He fretted over shy withdrawn Fred, who retreated to a Westchester County farm. Bartow responded better to Burr's example, following him into the law and into New York politics.

Theodosia Burr was passionately devoted to her father's career. Some wondered if she accepted an offer of marriage from Joseph Alston, one of the richest—and homeliest—planters in South Carolina, because she would be in a position to enlist support for Burr in the Palmetto State, where the vice president was not well known.[9]

One New York woman, whose father was close to Burr, wrote to her sister: "Can it be that the father has sacrificed a daughter so lovely to affluence and influential connections?"[10] Another unromantic reason was her father's desperate need for cash to pay off his ever-mounting debts. Robert Troup, who cast his cold eye on Burr as often as he observed Hamilton (Troup and Burr had studied law together), told a mutual friend: "the marriage was an affair of Burr and not his daughter and the money in question was the predominating motive."[11]

Alston did, in fact, lend Burr money, and the marriage was somewhat unhappy. After giving birth to a son, Theodosia developed a debilitating and mysterious gynecological problem that apparently left her incapable of sexual relations with her husband. She hated South Carolina's climate and Alston's provincial relatives. At one point, traveling with two of them, she asked her father: "Pray teach me how to write two A's without producing something like an ass."[12]

If Theodosia's—or her father's—motives were impure, it was artfully concealed. In his letters to his gifted daughter, Burr seldom mentioned politics. But he often discussed this favorite subject with his son-in-law, who was serving in the South Carolina legislature. He urged Alston to attend faithfully and stay to the end of every session, and not to be shy about speaking out. He also encouraged the young man to buy land in northern Manhattan and begin building a handsome villa, christened Montalto.

III

Burr's pursuit of sexual pleasure at first seemed to have little or no effect on his political career. He was discreet, seldom mentioning his amours to anyone but a few close friends and his daughter, Theodosia. He had a strange compulsion to tell her almost everything about his love life. But in the compressed political and social world in which he moved, secrecy was impossible. In May of 1801, two months after he became vice president, Burr discovered this truth the hard way.

A handbill suddenly blossomed in New York City; it was passed from door to door and pinned on walls in taverns and coffeehouses. Entitled "Aaron Burr!" it suggested Federalist origins by claiming Burr was a "hater" of the Constitution. But its chief subject was sex. It accused Burr of "ABANDONED PROFLIGACY" and bemoaned "THE NUMEROUS UNHAPPY WRETCHES" who had fallen "VICTIMS" to this accomplished "DEBAUCHEE." The handbill went on to detail the story of a young woman Burr had seduced in Washington, D.C., and brought with him to New York, setting her up in rooms on Partition Street. She was the daughter of a "respectable tradesman" and her father was reportedly in New York, determined to shoot Burr on sight.[13]

Burr ruefully noted in a letter to a friend that "packages of [the handbill] were sent to various parts of the country." Pretending serenity, he said he presumed his friends would "treat as false, every thing said of me, which ought not to be true."[14] In a letter to the same friend, a month later, he tacitly admitted that the young lady in question was real, but lamented that she was "so surrounded & watched by every thing that hates and detests A. that all approach, without a sacrifice of dignity, seems to be barred."[15]

There are strong grounds for suspecting that the author or at least the sponsor of the handbill was DeWitt Clinton. Its appearance a few days after George Clinton was reelected governor of New York is more than a mere coincidence. The Old Incumbent's victory put the Clintons back into the game as contestants for federal patronage and the leadership of the Republican party in New York. It was the first shot in their undeclared war against the vice president.

IV

Burr's squared shoulders, his trim, erect carriage, conveyed an unmistakable military aura. He was proud of his service in the Revolution. In 1775, at the age of nineteen, he slogged through the Maine wilderness with a column led by Colonel Benedict Arnold to attack Quebec—one of the most horrendous forced marches in history. Appointed aide to Brigadier General Richard Montgomery, Burr was with the Irish-born soldier's force when he and Arnold assaulted the Canadian capital in a raging blizzard on New Year's Day 1776. They seemed on the brink of making Canada the fourteenth American state when a blast of grapeshot killed Montgomery and other men in the front ranks. Burr escaped unscathed and tried to rally the rest of the column, but the rattled soldiers fled. Burr tried to carry off the general's body. He finally had to abandon the task but his performance under fire made him an instant hero with his friend Jonathan Dayton (who also fought in Canada) and many other Americans.

After service as aide-de-camp to one of Washington's major generals, Burr was appointed lieutenant colonel and given command of a regiment at the age of twenty-one. He swiftly drilled and disciplined it into one of the best units in the American army. At the battle of Monmouth Court House in 1778, the "Malcolms," as they were called, after the wealthy New York businessman who had raised them, repeatedly distinguished themselves. But Burr emerged from this chaotic encounter, fought in 100-degree heat, with impaired health and a low opinion of George Washington as a general.

Washington court-martialed the army's second in command, General Charles Lee, for his conduct in the opening stage of the battle. The two generals had exchanged angry words when Lee ordered his men to retreat in the face of a British attack and Washington reprimanded him. Burr wrote the court-martial board a letter, strongly defending Lee—a gesture that was not appreciated by Washington and his admirers. (Hamilton, by contrast, encouraged his best friend and fellow aide, John Laurens, to challenge Lee to a duel for daring to insult the commander in chief and served as Laurens's second in the encounter.) Henceforth, Burr became associated with a minority of the army's officers who disliked and disparaged Washington's elevation to the status of a demigod.

Some think Washington or someone on his staff retaliated by giving Burr one of the most thankless jobs in the army—command of Westchester

County, just north of British-held New York. In this so-called neutral ground militia roamed, mostly looking for plunder, without loyalty to either side. Colonel Burr soon brought order to the chaotic situation. He banned plundering by the soldiers under his command and ordered them to return the stolen goods in which their camp abounded, whether the owners were loyalists or rebels. Militiamen caught with plunder were frequently dragged to the house they had robbed, given twenty-five and sometimes fifty lashes and forced to apologize to their victims. To his immediate commanding officer, Burr growled that the situation inclined him to "gibbet a half dozen good whigs [patriots]." He frequently rode twenty-four miles a night in brutal winter weather to make sure his outposts and pickets were on the alert.[16]

Still suffering from bouts of nausea and violent headaches that began after the Monmouth battle, Burr's health collapsed. In 1779, almost two years before the decisive victory at Yorktown, Lieutenant Colonel Burr resigned from the army. But when he had an opportunity, he remained ready to strike a blow at the enemy. In 1780, he happened to be in New Haven when the British raided the town. Burr took command of the local militia and had not a little to do with forcing the redcoats to make a hasty retreat.[17]

In 1798, during the undeclared war with France, Burr managed to get himself nominated as a brigadier general. President John Adams was inclined to appoint Burr, but George Washington rejected him, saying the ex-senator was too prone to "intrigue." Washington may have been thinking of Burr's support of Charles Lee after the battle of Monmouth. The commander in chief may also have heard rumors of Burr's private opinion of him as a "man of no talents" who "could not spell a sentence of common English." In spite of this rebuff, the vice president's ruling passion, according to one of his closest friends, remained "an ardent love of military glory."[18]

V

Like most ex-soldiers, Vice President Burr was sensitive about his honor, and not hesitant about defending it. That was one of the reasons why not a few New Yorkers were ready to believe he had shot it out with Senator James Jackson. In 1799, while Burr was a New York assemblyman, he heard that John Barker Church, Angelica Schuyler's husband, was telling friends that Burr had taken money under the table to help a group of European speculators known as the Holland Land Company obtain legal title to several million acres of upstate New York.

The charge was true, up to a point. The story was a good illustration of how speculators and their political spokesmen operated. The Dutchmen had first approached General Hamilton, who agreed to help them if they would loan his father-in-law, General Schuyler, $250,000 to complete a series of canals he was building to improve water transportation in upstate New York. Colonel Burr made a better offer. For a mere $5,000, which he distributed to key members of the New York legislature, Burr obtained a law waiving the ban on foreigners owning land. The colonel's fee was $5,500, disguised as a loan that was never repaid, and an opportunity to buy 100,000 acres of the speculators' land.

When Burr heard that Church was accusing him of fraud, the colonel sent him a challenge. Like all New York duelists, they met on the New Jersey side of the Hudson, either at Powles Hook or Weehawken, to evade the Empire State's ban. What everyone remembered was Burr's remarkable sang froid. The barrel of Burr's pistol required greasing before the bullet could be rammed home. His second forgot to bring the grease, and the bullet stuck halfway down. Nevertheless, Burr coolly stepped to the mark and exchanged a round with Church, although he had little chance of hitting him. Church's bullet passed through Burr's coat. As the seconds loaded the pistols for another round, Church apologized, admitting he had no proof for his assertion.[19]

VI

One of the secrets of Burr's success in politics was his ability to invest a political campaign with a military aura. In New York he had a group of dedicated followers, whom Theodosia dubbed "The Tenth Legion," recalling Julius Caesar's reliance on that ever-reliable body of shock troops when the fighting grew desperate. Burr demanded heroic exertions from these men as an election churned to a climax.

Nowhere was Burr's magnetic leadership better displayed than in his victory over General Hamilton and the Federalists in the New York elections of 1800—the triumph that broke Hamilton's power in New York and in the nation. Although many accounts have Burr energizing the social club known as the Tammany Society, he seems instead to have offered these gentlemen a model of how a big-city campaign should be run—a lesson they would put to dolorous use in New York for the next century and a half.

Burr took charge of the General Republican Committee and ordered them to compile an exhaustive list of every voter in the city. Beside each name was pertinent information about the voter's family, his political opinions, and how much money he was willing to contribute to the Republican cause. Next he assembled a slate of candidates for the legislature replete with famous names. He persuaded no less a personage than George Clinton, still in electoral purdah because of his 1792 theft of the governorship, to run and recruited revolutionary war general Horatio Gates, the victor at Saratoga, to join him. Other candidates were almost as distinguished. For a final touch, Burr kept all these names a profound secret.

General Hamilton, meanwhile, was having grave difficulty putting together a decent slate. In 1797, the state capital had been moved to Albany, and most leading New York City Federalists took a dim view of spending three or four months each year in that distant town, neglecting their businesses and law practices. Hamilton had to settle for two grocers, a baker, a potter, a mason, and a shoemaker.[20] Burr waited until Hamilton announced his lackluster slate, and two days later stunned him with his roster of big-name candidates.

As the campaign surged to a climax, Burr and his followers were everywhere, organizing rallies in the wards, canvasing voters house by house. In line with his party's policy, Burr conceded the Federalists the authorship of the Constitution, and told the voters the principles of the Declaration of Independence were at stake. That paean to equality was reinforced by enfranchising many New Yorkers who did not have the right to vote.

A citizen had to own property worth at least $50 (about $600 in modern currency) in order to vote for candidates for the state assembly.[21] Burr used an idea called the "tontine," whereby a dozen men bought a piece of property worth roughly $50, and each claimed it on election day. In the state legislature, Burr had also strongly endorsed giving free Negroes the vote—something many other states that had abolished slavery still declined to do. This won him the enthusiastic backing of that minority.

Hamilton flung himself into the struggle with desperate energy. More than once, Burr faced him at street corner rallies and challenged him to defend the Alien and Sedition Acts and the Federalist taxes for an army that had proved unnecessary. The ever-present Robert Troup, who lumbered through the streets beside Hamilton, complained to one correspondent that he had not eaten dinner for three days and had been on his feet from seven in the morning until seven at night.[22]

When the polls opened for the usual three days of balloting, Burr rode from ward to ward on horseback, urging voters to support his ticket. Hamilton also appeared on horseback and New Yorkers were treated to another verbal clash between the two men. It was as if opposing generals had met as a battle began to exchange a volley of rhetorical bullets. In the crucial seventh ward, where most of New York's artisans and workers lived, Burr stayed on duty for ten consecutive hours on the day the polls closed. A friend told James Monroe that the colonel had not slept or eaten for twenty-four hours.[23]

The result was a close but smashing citywide victory. By margins as small as one hundred votes, all thirteen of Burr's candidates were elected, guaranteeing a Republican legislature, which in turn guaranteed Republican electors and the presidency in November. Colonel Burr's "generalship, perseverance, industry and execution, exceeds all description," wrote Commodore James Nicholson to his son-in-law Albert Gallatin (soon to be Jefferson's secretary of the treasury). He was "as . . . superior to the Hambletonians [*sic*] as a man is to a boy." For Burr the most important word in that encomium was undoubtedly "generalship." [24]

VII

The vice president combined this talent for political leadership with a curious lack of interest in the theoretical and ideological side of politics. He did not play a leading part in the pamphlet wars that divided the Americans into Federalists and Republicans. It was Alexander Hamilton, writing under various pseudonyms, who made Thomas Jefferson and James Madison writhe as he beat down their objections to funding state as well as federal debts and launching the Bank of the United States. Shortly before Burr became a U.S. senator in 1791, he wrote to his friend, Federalist Congressman Theodore Sedgwick of Massachusetts, that everyone in New York was talking about the bank but he was "wholly incompetent to give an opinion of its merit" because his busy law practice did not give him time to read savants such as the philosopher David Hume, who had written extensively on the subject.[25]

On another aspect of political leadership, Burr was in complete agreement with General Hamilton—and out of step with New York's cheapskate Governor George Clinton. The vice president was convinced that a leader had to live in a style that befitted his large ambitions. His New York estate, Richmond Hill, had been the home of Vice President John Adams in 1790, when New York was briefly the nation's capital. George Washington had previously used it as a temporary headquarters. Its twenty-six verdant acres, at the intersection of what is now Charlton and Varick Streets, contained a lovely pond and a stately sixty-by-fifty-foot mansion with a handsome portico supported by Ionic columns.

The mansion's furniture included inlaid card tables, mahogany chairs, a "Turkey" carpet, and a library lined with hundreds of books that regularly arrived by the boatload from London. The vice president was always eager to be in touch with the latest poetry, fiction, and philosophy. He was especially fond of the philosopher Jeremy Bentham, whose utilitarian creed preached that moral judgments should be based on whatever produced the greatest happiness for the greatest number and that the chief goal of life was pleasure.

At least as important as Richmond Hill's library was its wine cellar, one of the best in New York. In the formal dining room on the second floor, overlooking the Hudson River (the Manhattan shore has been much extended by landfill since 1804), Senator—and more recently Vice President—Burr entertained distinguished visitors such as Maurice de Talleyrand-Périgord and Prince Louis-Philippe of France, as well as James Madison, Alexander Hamilton, and numerous Livingstons.

All this cost money, but the need for this fundamental source of pleasure and happiness, which induced palpitations in his friend Robert Troup and stomach and bowel spasms in General Hamilton, never seemed to worry Vice President Burr. His financial affairs were an incredible tangle of promissory notes, mortgages, options, bank stock, and deeds to thousands of acres of upstate New York lands that might or might not be worth a fortune some day.

In October 1802, a Gargantua of debt seemed about to devour the vice president. To escape he concocted an ingenious scheme. He divided the twenty-six acres of his Richmond Hill estate into building lots which well-to-do friends purchased, then mortgaged back to him. Armed with these documents, Burr was able to persuade the Manhattan Company Bank to loan him $112,407 (the equivalent of at least $1 million today). It no doubt helped that Burr was a director of the bank at the time. While such maneuvers did not make him solvent, they contributed to his reputation for legerdemain, especially in the ranks of the Tenth Legion.[26]

VIII

Since Christmas Day 1803, Vice President Burr had been in Maryland, visiting two politicians whom he had met when he was a U.S. senator:

Charles Carroll and his son-in-law, Robert Goodloe Harper. Both were prominent Federalists, and the Baltimore and Washington newspapers buzzed with the possible significance of the Republican vice president's decision to spend the holidays with them.

The sixty-seven-year-old Carroll retained some of the aura of a folk hero for his role in the American Revolution. As "First Citizen" he had written newspaper essays that persuaded Maryland to revolt, and had risked his life and large fortune—he was the richest man in Maryland and possibly in the nation—by signing the Declaration of Independence. As a devout Roman Catholic, Carroll had been repelled by the atheism and bloody excesses of the French Revolution, and made no secret of his antipathy for its leading American proponent, President Thomas Jefferson.

Affable and eloquent, thirty-nine-year-old Robert Goodloe Harper began his career as a congressman from South Carolina. In 1800, he had dismissed Jefferson's candidacy for president as a ridiculous venture. He called the man from Monticello an indecisive visionary fit to be "a professor in a college or president of a philosophical society . . . but certainly not the first magistrate of a great nation." Harper had badly misjudged what his constituents thought about Jefferson and as a result faced certain defeat in the next congressional elections. He had withdrawn to Baltimore, where he married Carroll's daughter, Catherine, and began making a very good living as a lawyer.[27]

Harper did not cease being a Federalist, and an influential one, once he persuaded Charles Carroll to accept him as a son-in-law. Their meeting with Burr caused the *Fredericksburg Republican Advocate* to bristle with alarm. "Every movement of the Vice President of the United States ought to be watched," the editor averred. "The good of the republic demands such vigilance." The editor accused Burr of plotting to win Maryland's electoral votes in the next presidential election. As evidence of the "perfect understanding" between Burr and Harper, the editor pointed to material in the *Baltimore Anti-Democrat*, a paper recently founded with Harper's backing, that "abused the Hon. DeWitt Clinton, whose mortal enemy Mr. Burr is."[28]

IX

Whatever their plans for the future, Robert Goodloe Harper connected Vice President Burr to the most controversial episode in his political past: the six weeks in 1801 when the national victory Burr had helped to win for himself and Thomas Jefferson in the fall of the previous year turned into a nightmare. In those early days of the Republic, the president was not sworn in until March 4th of the year following his election, and the Congress that assembled in December sat until that date, although many of them were lame ducks. This was especially true in 1800. The Republican sweep had scythed down a veritable host of Federalist congressmen and senators.

When the politicians gathered in Washington under the baleful eye of the lame-duck president, John Adams, they made the stunning discovery that the Republican presidential candidate, Thomas Jefferson, had seventy-three electoral votes—and so did the party's vice presidential candidate, Aaron Burr. (Runner-up Adams received sixty-five.) The cause of the deadlock was rooted in the founders' determination to ignore the possibility of political parties. They envisioned the electors as high-minded patriots who would select the two best men for president and vice president.

Loath to start amending the Constitution, the politicians of both parties had tried to steer around the dilemma by having electors drop one or two votes for the vice presidential candidate, thus enabling the man at the head of the ticket to become the legal winner. The initial result was only more confusion. In 1796, so many electors dropped vice presidential votes that Thomas Jefferson, running against Adams for president, wound up as vice president. Burr, the Republican nominee, and Thomas Pinckney, the Federalist nominee for the lesser office, finished out of the race.

To avoid this humiliation in 1800, Burr had secured a promise from Jefferson's campaign manager, James Madison, that no southern elector would drop his Burr vote. In turn, Burr promised to arrange for someone in the North, from a safe Jeffersonian state like Rhode Island, to do the deed. But the Federalists carried Rhode Island, and all the Republican electors, north and south, voted unanimously for Jefferson and Burr. The Constitution decreed that this deadlock threw the election into the House of Representatives.

The Federalists, ignoring the lame-duck status of their majority, decided to support Burr for president, on the unflattering assumption that anyone was better than Jefferson. Hatred for the Virginian had become ingrained in Federalist hearts. It coincided with a growing resentment of the power of Virginia, the largest state, with her phalanx of congressman and her readiness to act as the voice of the South.

The Federalists controlled six states, the Republicans eight. Only a few defections from the Republican ranks would give the Federalists the nine states the Constitution required to elect a president. Among the identified waverers were Congressmen Edward Livingston of New York, Samuel Smith of Maryland, and James Linn of New Jersey. Each held a swing vote that could throw his state either way. All were friends of Burr.

Soon threats and counterthreats of violence swirled through the nation. The Republican governors of Virginia and Pennsylvania vowed to call out their militia to make Jefferson president. The Federalist *Gazette of the United States* declared this would mean civil war.

Throughout the furor, Colonel Burr remained in Albany, New York, serving in the state legislature (he had been elected in his coup d'etat of 1800) and purportedly fussing over the details of his daughter Theodosia's imminent wedding to Joseph Alston. Here he received a letter from his good friend Albert Gallatin of Pennsylvania, urging Burr to come to Washington, D.C, immediately. Gallatin was convinced that Jefferson was unelectable. He felt if Burr exercised his formidable powers of persuasion on the three waverers, he would become president—an outcome Gallatin felt was far better than letting the Federalists declare an interregnum and chose one of their own as acting president.

Burr conferred with two of his lieutenants, Peter Townsend, proprietor of the Sterling Iron Works in Orange County, New York, and John

Swartout, soon to be the target of DeWitt Clinton's pistol. They urged him to take Gallatin's advice and head for Washington immediately. Burr seemed to agree with them. He packed his bags. But doubts accumulated as he thought about Gallatin's letter and others he was receiving, urging him to declare that he would not accept the Federalist deal under any circumstances. "His heart failed him," Townsend said, recounting the story years later.[29]

While rumors abounded about Burr's attempts to suborn the swing congressmen, the colonel steadfastly insisted he was loyal to Thomas Jefferson. But he never declared that if the Federalists elected him, he would refuse to serve. Pro-Jefferson historians assert this proved Burr's perfidy. But as Gallatin's letter made clear, there were good grounds for thinking it would be better for someone to claim the Republican victory.

Burr could not make this argument publicly, of course. Avowing a father's concern for a daughter's happiness, he refused to come to Washington, where Federalist and Republican congressmen voted in menacing deadlock for seven tense days, while various people made often harsh judgments about the colonel's studied silence.

X

Alexander Hamilton, watching the proceedings with growing alarm from New York, was appalled at the thought of Burr becoming president. To Oliver Wolcott Jr., his successor as secretary of the treasury, he wrote: "There is no doubt that upon every virtuous and prudent calculation Jefferson is to be preferred. He is by far not so dangerous a man and he has pretensions to character.

"As to *Burr* there is nothing in his favour. His private character is not defended by his most partial friends. He is bankrupt beyond redemption except by the plunder of his country . . . If he can, he will certainly disturb our institutions to secure himself *permanent power* and with it *wealth*." Hamilton closed by calling Burr "the Catiline of America," comparing him to the nobleman who stirred popular unrest against the Roman Republic and earned historic infamy thanks to Cicero's vehement attacks on him.[30]

If Wolcott showed this ferocious blast to other Federalists in Washington, it did not do much good. Hamilton was soon receiving letters from numerous members of the party of virtues and talents who were inclined to vote for Burr. Senator Gouverneur Morris explained that many felt Burr was preferable because the country was likely to be fighting a war against France or England soon and Burr was "a vigorous practical man."[31]

To Harrison Gray Otis of Massachusetts, a by-now splenetic Hamilton wrote: "Burr loves nothing but himself; thinks of nothing but his own aggrandizement, and will be content with nothing, short of permanent power in his own hands." To Gouverneur Morris went a similar denunciation: Burr had "no principle public or private—could be bound by no agreement—will listen to no monitor but his ambition . . . He is sanguine enough to hope every thing—daring enough to attempt every thing—wicked enough to scruple nothing."[32]

Hamilton wrote similar letters to many other Federalist congressman, often using the same harsh phrases. As an alternative to choosing Burr, Hamilton urged a backstairs negotiation with Jefferson to get some important promises from him: (1) He would not meddle with the financial system. (2) America's foreign policy would remain neutral. (3) The Navy would be preserved and gradually increased. (4) There would be no wholesale removal of Federalists from public offices.

On January 1, 1801, Hamilton got a stunning reply from John Marshall, the new chief justice of the Supreme Court and a cousin of Thomas Jefferson. Although he no longer had a vote in the House of Representatives, Marshall's influence in Washington was large. He bluntly told Hamilton that he had "insuperable objections" to Jefferson. Marshall feared Jefferson would collude with the House of Representatives to overthrow the independent judiciary and increase his personal power. The chief justice admitted he was impressed by Hamilton's objections to Burr, "believing that you know him well & are impartial" but he could not bring himself to recommend Jefferson. "The morals of the Author of the letter to Mazzei cannot be pure," Marshall wrote.[33]

Hamilton only redoubled his attacks. Writing to John Rutledge Jr. of South Carolina, he called Burr "one of the most unprincipled men in the UStates." By this time the General had drawn up a thousand-word character sketch of Burr that he enclosed with his letters. In it Hamilton called Burr "a profligate; a voluptuary in the extreme." He accused the colonel of resigning his commission during the revolutionary war at "a critical period" by pleading ill health. He asserted Burr owed one creditor "about 80,000 dollars" and claimed there were many others waiting with similar demands. He declared Burr would make "a bargain and sale" with some foreign power—in a word, commit treason. At his dinner table Burr regularly toasted "The French Republic" and *Buonaparte*. Finally, "though possessing infinite art cunning and address" Burr had yet to give proofs of "great or solid abilities."[34]

A few days later, in a letter to Gouverneur Morris, Hamilton added an even more serious charge: "Mr. Burr is in frequent & close conference with a Frenchman who is suspected of being an agent of the French government." To James Bayard he added still another slur, the worst, in Hamilton's lexicon: "Mr. Burr has never appeared solicitous for fame . . . great Ambition unchecked by principle, or the love of Glory, is an unruly Tyrant."[35] Underscoring his desperation as well as his loathing of Burr, Hamilton added that if the Federalist party adopted Burr he would consider himself "an isolated man." He would withdraw from a party that had "degraded itself & the country."[36]

XI

Were any of the General's charges true? Was Burr "bankrupt beyond redemption?" In 1800 the colonel owed a lot of money but he was no more bankrupt beyond redemption than General Hamilton, who also owed some very large sums to banks and wealthy friends and relations such as John

Barker Church. As we have already seen, in 1802, the vice president used the Manhattan Company Bank to leverage himself from the putative hell of bankruptcy into something approximating temporary financial redemption.

The worst of Burr's debts came from unwise investments in land speculation—a temptation to which virtually every third American with money in his pocket had succumbed in the heady early years of the Republic. Philadelphia's Robert Morris, the greatest merchant in the nation; William Duer, Hamilton's first assistant secretary of the treasury; and James Wilson, associate justice of the Supreme Court, were among the notable men who had already gone bankrupt.

Beyond the settled portions of America lay millions of forested acres of public domain, purchasable for next to nothing an acre, to be resold to the eager millions of European immigrants who seemed certain to cascade into the new promised land. Alas, when France and England went to war in 1793, this cascade became a trickle, and thousands of dollars in borrowed money had to be repaid to bankers and other lenders.

The $80,000 Burr owed to a single creditor was probably a reference to a lawsuit against Burr by a London merchant, one John Julius Angerstein. (The sum was actually $90,000.) He had sold Burr and super speculator James Greenleaf a huge tract in northern New York for that round sum, when the Londoner found out that the New York legislature refused to let him hold the title because he was a foreigner. Greenleaf defaulted on his share of the debt, leaving Burr liable for the whole amount.

In 1804, there were many ways to reduce if not eliminate a man's debts, especially if he retained political power and influence. Cooperative judges could persuade contentious creditors to settle for fifty or even twenty-five cents on the dollar. A lawyer as skillful as Burr could do some deft negotiating on his own. In 1802, Hamilton, representing John Julius Angerstein, agreed to settle that $90,000 debt for $25,000. Beyond these routes was the equally acceptable subscription method. A circle of wealthy friends could join forces and relieve a popular—and powerful—public servant of his financial woes. A group of Federalists in Massachusetts recently solved Senator Timothy Pickering's acute cash shortage this way, enabling him to stay in public life. [37]

General Hamilton's attitude toward bankruptcy depended a good deal on whether the bankrupt was a Federalist or a Republican. When the attorney general of New York State, Josiah Ogden Hoffman, suffered a financial collapse in 1798 and was caught dipping into public funds, Hamilton did everything in his power to prevent Governor John Jay from removing him. A "merely temporary embarrassment" did not justify dismissing Hoffman, General Hamilton told Jay. The governor replied with some exasperation that Hoffman's affairs were not merely embarrassed but "utterly irretrievable." To the considerable mortification of the Federalist party, Attorney General Hoffman wound up in debtor's prison.[38]

As for Hamilton's charge that Burr was a *profligate*—a word that American dictionary writer Noah Webster defined in his first edition (1806) as a *"debauchee"*—the evidence is simply not there. The vice president was fond of willing women, but so was Hamilton's close friend, Gouverneur Morris, and Hamilton himself was hardly sinless in this department. Burr's affairs were undoubtedly more numerous than most men's, but he showed no sign of the orgiastic drinking and sex addiction that "debauchee" suggests. He drank no more wine than President Jefferson—or General Hamilton. As for Burr toasting the French Republic and Bonaparte, Jefferson and the rest of the Republican party were doing the same thing in 1800.

The accusation that Burr left the revolutionary army at a critical time was a particularly vicious slander, which Hamilton must—or should—have known was grossly untrue. In 1791, writing to his friend Theodore Sedgwick, Burr described how his health had collapsed in 1779 from "fatiguing and hazardous" duty in Westchester's Neutral Ground. By the time the army responded to his plea to be allowed to resign, he was "so low as to be unable to walk fifty yds." For the next two years he was "wavering between life and death."[39]

As for Hamilton's assertion that Burr had never been solicitous for fame, the accusation is based on a highly selective reading of Burr's career. Burr charged far higher fees than Hamilton, but so did almost every other lawyer on their level in New York. Burr did not issue manifestos about the nature of government or identify his ambitions with the future of the Republic, but he saw himself as more than qualified to be a contestant in this race for earthly immortality.

This was obviously the opinion of one of Burr's more sophisticated women admirers, known only as "Mrs. Z."

> Tell me how you do and how you pass your time . . . Flying after the Atalantas of Virginia, more swift than their celebrated racers? Or more probably, poring over musty records; offering your time, your pleasures, your health at the shrine of Fame . . . pursuing a chimera which ever has and ever will mock the grasp . . . [40]

What was the real reason for General Hamilton's frenzied hostility to Aaron Burr? The answer to that question is visible in the General's threat to withdraw from the Federalists and consider himself an "isolated man" if the party's congressmen supported Burr for president. Burr was threatening to take over the party that the General considered his political property.

Whenever Colonel Burr threatened Hamilton's power, the General discovered "a religious duty to oppose his career."[41] As early as 1792, when there was talk of making Burr, then a U.S. senator, the Federalist candidate for vice president, Hamilton wrote private letters claiming, among other things, "his integrity as an individual is not unimpeached . . . as a public man he is of the worst sort."[42] When Burr lobbied to succeed Gouverneur Morris as ambassador to France in 1794, Hamilton warned President Washington against appointing him, using similar animadversions on his character. Only when Burr tried to become a brigadier general in 1798 did Hamilton tolerate him because he needed some Republican officers in his army, and Burr's political career seemed to be going nowhere at that point.

Until 1800, there is no evidence that Burr was aware of Hamilton's concealed assaults. Face to face they maintained fairly cordial relations. They worked together on law cases and Theodosia had been friendly with Hamilton's daughter, Angelica. Burr had been the General's partner in one of the most important cases of the day, an enormously complicated suit for fraud on behalf of a Frenchman named Louis Le Guen against two New York merchants. The Hamilton-Burr team won the biggest judgment awarded by an American court up to that time. But when politics intruded, Hamilton's fear of Burr's ability to appeal to Federalists as well as Republicans stirred the General to rancorous—and extremely unchristian—slander.

XII

Ironically, historians now discount Hamilton's role in the eventual failure of the Federalist scheme to make Burr the third president of the United States. At the end of January, after almost six weeks of Hamiltonian missives to Washington, D.C., Congressman Theodore Sedgwick told his son "the disposition to prefer Mr. Burr to Mr. Jefferson has been increasing [among the Federalists] until it has become nearly unanimous."[43] Most Federalists, including Robert Goodloe Harper, went on stubbornly voting for Burr until the opposition to Jefferson collapsed.

Burr's refusal to cut a deal had far more influence with James Bayard, Delaware's lone congressman, who had the power to decide the issue single-handedly by giving the Jeffersonians the one additional state they needed. Bayard threw in his cards expressing his disgust at Burr's timidity. All he had to do, Bayard said, was reach agreements with the three men who were swing votes in their states and he would have been president. Bayard added that the "little use" Burr made of his chance to win the highest office "gives me but a humble opinion of the talents of an unprincipled man."[44]

By attempting to remain loyal to the Republicans without quite alienating the Federalists, Burr had infuriated the ultras of both parties. Realistically, the Federalist scheme was a fantasy. If Burr had switched parties at such a moment, he would have been branded as a traitor by almost every Republican in the country. Yet in the context of the bitter deadlock, he was apparently able to convince himself that accepting the presidency from the Federalists while insisting he was still a Republican was a better alternative than civil war.

XIII

Once the crisis was resolved by Delaware's James Bayard's decision to vote for Jefferson (after a covert agreement on Jefferson's part, negotiated through third parties, to accept Hamilton's four negotiating points), the new chief executive and his vice president exchanged cordial notes, assuring each other that their friendship was undamaged, their mutual confidence undimmed by the nasty episode. Both vowed they would pay no attention to the slanderers and rumormongers who were attempting to make trouble between them. But Jefferson began filling pages of the journal he called his *Anas* with reports of Burr's double-dealing. As for many Federalists, they began to think Colonel Burr, having once been tempted, could be tempted again.

CHAPTER 5

Politicians in
the Wilderness

*C*omplicating Vice President Burr's situation was his relative isolation in Washington, D.C. Cut off from his New York power base, he was both literally and figuratively a politician in the wilderness. Occasionally the sound of gunfire penetrated the lofty semicircular Senate chamber, with its red morocco leather chairs and comfortable lounge, warmed by two massive fireplaces. There was nothing martial, or unusual, about the gunplay. Hunters regularly shot grouse and other game birds within a few hundred yards of the Capitol.

If anything, the pops and bangs underscored the anomaly of Aaron Burr's position as the second highest officer in the administration of the man who had persuaded the federal government to move the nation's capital to the District of Columbia. In the opinion of John Adams, the vice presidency was the most insignificant office "that ever the invention of man contrived or his imagination conceived." Enduring the vice presidency in Washington, D.C., could only increase an ambitious politician's feelings of insignificance.

The federal government was a puny affair in 1804. Excluding 6,479 sailors, soldiers, and marines, it numbered only 2,267 employees. Most of these worked as postmasters and collectors of customs in distant cities and towns. Congress, the Supreme Court, the president and his cabinet, and their employees numbered only 293 people. When this tiny band migrated to the Federal District in 1800, they virtually vanished from the national consciousness.

By almost any standard, the nation's new Capitol was a political, socio-logical, and commercial disaster. One shocked congressman called it "a city in ruins." Launched with the hope that land speculation would pro-duce most of its income, the district had lurched into permanent bank-ruptcy almost immediately.

Not even real estate ballyhoo led by George Washington personally, backed by two brass bands, brought out any buyers. Talk of a city of 160,000 springing up in a decade soon faded into the woods and swamps that covered most of the district's ten square miles. Instead of increasing, commerce dwindled to half of what it had been in 1791, when the district was created. Speculators such as Robert Morris and James Greenleaf at one point owned as many as 7,234 lots, averaging 5,000 square feet each, on which they had recklessly contracted to build 20 brick houses a year. Morris made a profit of 300 percent on his first purchases by selling to other true believers, but by 1797 he, Greenleaf, and everyone else who put money into the district had abandoned the place.[1]

Almost every private business except a brewery failed. The only com-pleted block of buildings stood empty and crumbling. Similar fates befell projected hotels and other housing sites. One visitor described Green-leaf's Point, another large cluster of buildings, as looking like "a consider-able town which has been destroyed by some unusual calamity." On Anacostia Creek, Secretary of the Treasury Albert Gallatin found "a very large but perfectly empty warehouse and a wharf graced by not a single vessel." On Rock Creek a bridge that was supposed to connect the federal metropolis to the rest of the nation (it had been built with symbolic stones from the thirteen original states) had collapsed.[2]

II

In the first years of Thomas Jefferson's administration, the politicians dis-covered that Washington, D.C., not only failed to attract land buyers and businessmen, it had a special appeal for the mentally ill, the criminal, the indigent, and the lazy; people who thought Napoléon or General Hamilton was persecuting them; who wanted pardons, reprieves, or pensions; or who connected the pursuit of happiness to a government job. In 1802, only 233 males in the local population of 4,000 had more than $100 in cash or property to their names. Welfare, called Poor Relief in 1803, consumed 42 percent of the district's revenue. A census could only find 15 "gentlemen" in the whole city.[3]

"Strangers, after viewing the edifices of state, are apt to enquire for the city," wrote one visitor, "while they are in its very centre."[4] A group of congressmen returning from a dinner party got lost and spent the entire night in their carriage, negotiating bogs and gullies in search of their boardinghouse. "In the heart of the city," wrote another visitor, "not a sound is to be heard," even by day. "Every thing here seems in a dead calm," reported another newly arrived Congressman. "An absolute supineness overwhelms all."

On Jenkins Hill, renamed Capitoline, as Goose Creek was renamed Tiber when the district's planners saw a new Rome rising around them, the principal edifice of the federal government, the capitol, squatted on a shrubless plateau looking like an architectural abortion. Thanks to Jefferson's abandonment of the Federalists' internal taxes, the U.S. Treasury lacked the cash to erect the central hall and dome; the two wings were connected by a crude covered boardwalk. Around it clustered seven or eight boarding houses and a few shops.

To the west, a gash through the alderbushes was named Pennsylvania Avenue. Most of the year it was a morass in which carriages sank to their axletrees. Congress appropriated $10,000 to build a sidewalk on its north side. Made of chips from the stone used for the Capitol, it sliced open soles when it was dry; rain turned it into an oozy glue that pulled shoes off the unwary walker's feet.

The census head count of fifteen gentlemen did not include the nation's federal politicians. They were considered transients, and that is how they lived in the "federal village." Few brought their wives or children with them. They stayed in boardinghouses with congressmen from their state or neighboring states. Privacy was impossible. "They live two or three to a room, even senators," wrote one observer. Guests had to be entertained in a common parlor, "a hot oven abounding with noise and confusion."[5]

"Friendships . . . we had few and limited opportunities to cultivate [them]," recalled one Congressman. The fellow politicians whom they got to know, they often did not like. The boardinghouse syndrome only accentuated sharp regional antagonisms. New Englanders recoiled from southerners "accustomed to speak in tones of masters" to their slaves. The Yankees were equally displeased by the men of Kentucky, Tennessee, and western Pennsylvania, with their "license of tongue incident to a wild and uncultivated state of society." Southerners concluded after meeting the dry, cool men of New England that there was "not one who possesses the slightest tie of common interest or of common feeling with us."[6]

All this led to a phenomenal congressional turnover. Senators and congressmen by the dozens abandoned the federal government for jobs in their home states. In the same year that DeWitt Clinton quit the Senate to become Gotham's mayor, New York Congressman Theodorus Bailey resigned to become the city's postmaster. Clinton's replacement as senator, John Armstrong, told his old revolutionary war commander, General Horatio Gates, that "a banishment of six months to Siberia would not be more disagreeable" than a sojourn in the nation's capital.[7]

By 1804 Washington, D.C.—and, by implication, the national government—had become a joke, particularly to Federalists. It exemplified the maxim laid down by Hamilton in an essay he contributed to *The Federalist*, the book he wrote with James Madison and John Jay, defending the Constitution: "a government continually at a distance and out of sight can hardly be expected to interest the sensations of the people."[8] Federalist newspapers ridiculed the district as a Capitoline Hill without a Cicero, a Tiber without a Rome. Others compared it to a country estate, where "state sportsmen may . . . shoot public service flying." In the midst of this desuetude sat the author of it all, President Thomas Jefferson.

III

The widower president lived in the only other District of Columbia public edifice worthy of comment, the "palace" at the end of Pennsylvania Avenue, a mile from the Capitol. The building made him "an object of ridicule with some and of pity with others," one visitor said. The staircase to the second floor remained unbuilt. The ceiling in one of the principal rooms had collapsed and a half dozen other rooms were unfinished. The grounds were still cluttered with workmen's shanties and privies, with stagnant pools of water used for mixing mortar and with the ruins of brick kilns. On a dark night, wrote one congressman, "instead of finding your way to the house, you were likely to fall into a pit or stumble over a pile of rubbish." Around the house was a fence "of the meanest sort: a common post and rail enclosure."[9]

A foreign diplomat described the sixty-one-year-old Jefferson in 1804: "He is a tall man with a very red freckled face and grey neglected hair, his manners goodnatured, frank and rather friendly, though he [has] somewhat of a cynical expression on his face." The president received the startled diplomat in a costume that was as haphazard as his palace: "He wore a blue coat and a thick grey-colored hairy waistcoat and a red under waistcoat lapped over it, green velveteen breeches with pearl buttons, yarn stockings and slippers down at the heel."[10]

Jefferson, the diplomat reported, refused to see anything wrong with Washington, D.C. Through his lieutenants in Congress he covertly squelched attempts to move the government back to Philadelphia. The president maintained that reopening the question would arouse dangerous disputes between the states. The diplomat was more inclined to think Jefferson preferred the District of Columbia because only there could he play the game of Republican simplicity, which his rural followers loved. In a major city, the president of the United States could never have ridden out alone to do his shopping or received visitors in yarn stockings and slippers.

Also, in Washington, D.C., Jefferson's "palace" was one of the few places where congressmen and senators could find some civilization. Although Jefferson did not bother to finish the stairs to the second floor, he excavated a sixteen-foot-deep cellar to store his wines. Dinner at the president's house was often the only alternative to living in congressional boardinghouses "like bears . . . brutalized and stupefied by hearing nothing but politics from morning until night." The only other public amusements in the district were a racetrack, which Congress frequently adjourned to attend, and a theater, where a troupe of actors starved for a season before fleeing to Richmond, Virginia.[11]

IV

The diplomat was right about the president's passion for public simplicity. But the wine cellar betrayed the contradiction between the performance and the real man, who was mired in debt at least as deep as General Hamilton and Vice President Burr, thanks to his expensive tastes in architecture, furniture, wine, food, and the other good things of life. But the reason for Jefferson's public style—and his fondness for Washington, D.C.—was more complex than General Hamilton's explanation: that he was a "contemptible hypocrite."

In 1785, when Jefferson was ambassador to France, he wrote James Madison a revealing letter from the royal palace of Fontainebleau, where the king and queen were enjoying the hunting season. Jefferson told Madison how, while strolling in the countryside, he had met a ragged woman who had two children to feed and no bread. Jefferson described the vast acreage of the king's demesne and told Madison he thought the grossly unequal division of property that prevailed in aristocratic Europe was a curse. They must see to it that it never happened in America. The earth was given as "a common stock for men to labour & live on," Jefferson declared. The future happiness of America depended on giving as many people as possible at least "a little portion" of land.

"The small landholders," Jefferson wrote, "are the most precious part of a state."[12]

This vision of an America of small farms tells us a good deal about Thomas Jefferson's psyche. He was a romantic with an almost bewildering inability to see the gap between his political ideas and American realities. In his own Virginia, the happy, independent, small farmer was a down-at-the-heel-myth in a state dominated by large slaveholders like Jefferson. But this psychological gap does not mean Jefferson's loathing for the kind of society that Alexander Hamilton was trying to create in the North was insincere. On the contrary, Jefferson was passionately convinced that the Federalist party was an incubus on the American body politic. He was sure that their leaders, at least, were planning to betray the basic principles of the American Revolution, with its call for liberty and equality for all.

The creation of Washington, D.C., was part of Jefferson's attempt to delay and even to frustrate this supposed Hamiltonian plot. Back in 1790, with James Madison's help, Jefferson had blocked Hamilton's plan to assume the states' revolutionary war debts because it seemed to him one more dangerous step toward giving the federal government too much power, and it was an even more outrageous act of Hamiltonian favoritism for the rich. State debts had seemed an even worse bet for future collection than the federal debt. When Hamilton insiders leaked the news that he was going to include the state debts in his funding system, one speculator immediately chartered two ships and sent them to South Carolina loaded with cash to buy up every state certificate in sight for a few cents on the dollar. While Congress debated the funding bill in New York's Federal Hall, the galleries were packed with Gotham speculators who made no secret of which orators they favored. The speculators had seen to it that not a few members of Congress were holders of the about to be magically multiplied paper. This experience convinced Jefferson and his colleague James Madison that if the American capital remained New York, the government would soon be owned by men of wealth, led by their hero, Secretary of the Treasury Alexander Hamilton.[13]

At a dinner meeting Jefferson had offered Secretary Hamilton a deal. The South would vote for assumption of state debts if Hamilton agreed to shift the capital to the District of Columbia in ten years. For the interim capital Jefferson chose Philadelphia, which seemed to him less prone to speculative passions than New York. Hamilton had acquiesced, never foreseeing that if Jefferson became president, a city that was closer to a rural village would be the ideal stage on which the Sage of Monticello might perform. Nor did the usually astute Hamilton realize that the South would swiftly acquire a predominant influence in a capital below the Mason-Dixon line.

V

As 1804 began, President Jefferson seemed to have fulfilled one of the Federalists' prophecies by picking a fight with the British ambassador. Anthony Merry and his large formidable wife had arrived in Washington, D.C., in the fall of 1803. Merry was the first diplomat to establish a full legation in the federal district. The other diplomats were mere chargés d'affaires, with no special claim to respect.

Merry, who liked to style himself "an old diplomat," did everything "au fait"—by the book. For his first meeting with the president, he decked himself out in full dress: a deep blue coat with black velvet trim and gold braid, white breeches, silk stockings and ornate buckled shoes, plumed hat and sword. Jefferson greeted him in pantaloons and slippers, which the outraged Merry saw as "utter slovenliness . . . a state of negligence carefully studied."

Merry's conviction that Jefferson was trying to insult him and Britain's honor deepened after a disastrous dinner party at the presidential palace. Merry thought the dinner was in his honor. When he and his wife arrived, once more in full regalia, they found the French chargé d'affaires, Louis André Pichon, and the Spanish ambassador, the marqués de Casa Yrujo, already in attendance. Pichon's presence was a special shock. Normally, diplomats from countries at war were not invited to break bread with each other, lest they begin breaking heads.

The real trouble began when dinner was announced. Instead of giving Mrs. Merry his arm, the president escorted Dolley Madison, buxom wife of Secretary of State James Madison, to the table and sat her in the place of honor on his right. The politically astute Dolley knew this was a blunder and vainly whispered in Jefferson's ear, "Take Mrs. Merry." Sally McKean Yrujo, the American-born wife of the Spanish ambassador, was aghast. "This will be a cause of war," she exclaimed.

Secretary of State Madison tried to make amends by escorting Mrs. Merry to the table. But Merry's rage was redoubled when he was elbowed aside by a congressman as he was about to sit down beside pretty Mrs. Yrujo. Jefferson sat at the head of the table, smiling at the ambassador's discomfiture. The seething Merrys departed the moment they finished their dinners.

A few days later, Secretary of State Madison invited the Merrys to dinner and repeated the insult, offering his arm to the wife of Secretary of the Treasury Albert Gallatin. This time Merry seized his wife's arm and marched her to the head of the table, where he insisted she be seated on Madison's right. Hannah Gallatin hastily withdrew, but Mrs. Merry, unmollified, proceeded to make nasty remarks about each course that was served.

The next day, in a choleric dispatch to his government, Merry maintained these slights were "evidently from design and not from ignorance and awkwardness." Jefferson had, after all, been U.S. ambassador to France and knew diplomatic etiquette. Merry also filled the ears of Federalist senators and congressmen with his umbrage. They wrote to their local newspaper editors and the country was soon buzzing with the story. Philadelphia's Federalist *Gazette of the United States* attributed Jefferson's "unaccountable conduct" to "pride, whim, weakness and malignant revenge." At the very least, the president seemed to be confirming Hamilton's claim that he had a "womanish resentment" against England.[14]

For the growing number of Americans who saw England as the champion of freedom in her war with Napoléon, this apparently gratuitous insult to the British ambassador and his wife meant Jefferson was worse than an incompetent president. He was dangerous.

V

Vice President Aaron Burr's approach to the surly Merry was markedly different. Late in December, he had to tell the ambassador that henceforth, diplomats would no longer enjoy the courtesy of chairs on the floor of the Senate. The vice president went out of his way to explain that the prohibition had nothing to do with Great Britain or Mr. Merry. The marqués de Yrujo had abused the privilege by indiscreetly trying to influence certain senators. Merry's report to the foreign secretary about this slight loss of privilege had none of the rancor of his account of his introduction to Jeffersonian etiquette at the presidential palace.[15]

Other diplomats were also watching Vice President Burr closely. When Spain closed the Mississippi in 1802 and the western country and the Federalists called for war, and Jefferson had temporized by sending James Monroe to France, Louis Pichon, the French chargé d'affaires, wrote to Paris that if the president's policy failed, "then it would be time for Vice President Burr to show himself to advantage."[16] Like General Hamilton, Colonel Burr had long been a proponent of "energy" in government. It was easy to see why Burr's ability to position himself between the two parties had long unnerved the Federalist leader.

VI

As 1804 began, the vice president was an equally unnerving entity to President Jefferson. Burr personified a problem with which Jefferson had been wrestling since he took office. Victory, far from solidifying and harmonizing his party, threatened to splinter it. Many of his more fanatic followers were outraged by Jefferson's declaration in his inaugural address, "We are all Republicans, we are all Federalists." For those who styled themselves Old Republicans, the statement was tantamount to saying "We are all Protestants, we are all Catholics." It was either heresy or betrayal, depending on one's mood and ideological tendencies.

Most of the Old Republicans were unreconstructed anti-Federalists who had fought the ratification of the Constitution and regarded the decade covered by the presidencies of George Washington and John Adams as a vile conspiracy to undo the pristine right to life, liberty, and the pursuit of happiness won by the revolt against George III. "In our Virginia quarter," wrote John Randolph, leader of the Old Republicans in Congress, shortly after Jefferson's triumph, "we think the great work is only begun; and that without *substantial reform*, we shall have little reason to congratulate ourselves on a mere change of men."[17]

Jefferson was fond of calling his electoral victory "the revolution of 1800." But he soon discovered that a gift for resounding phrases, while a priceless asset for a writer of declarations of independence, got a president in trouble. In later years, James Madison tried to defend his best friend by claiming that "allowances ought to be made" for the Jeffersonian tendency to express "in strong and round terms the impressions of the moment." The Old Republicans were not inclined to make any allowances. They seized on the revolution of 1800 as a call for a thorough overhaul of the Constitution and the American government.

In the fall of 1801, a Virginia Old Republican published an article, "The Danger Not Over," which was endorsed by the state's legislature as a perfect expression of what they felt the president should do. The author called for limiting the president to a single term, reducing senatorial terms to four years, and placing strict checks on the spending powers of the executive branch. The wording of the Constitution was to be made more precise and its interpretation rigidly limited, ending once and for all talk of broad federal powers.

Most drastic was the Old Republicans' demand to give Congress the power to remove federal judges by a majority vote. Almost all the judges on the bench when Jefferson came to power were Federalists. The Old Republicans wanted them discarded wholesale and they wanted Congress, not the president, to have the power to appoint new ones. Only then would the United States have a government that was responsive to the will of the people. Virginian William Branch Giles, one of the radicals' leaders in Congress, summed up their attitude toward the judiciary in a letter to Jefferson: "The Revolution [of 1800] is incomplete as long as that strong fortress is in possession of the enemy."[18]

The Old Republicans were opposed inside the Republican party by moderate or "National" Republicans led by Secretary of State James Madison. They supported the federal government and the Constitution as they existed and were critical only of what they deemed Hamiltonian excesses in the use of federal power, such as crushing Pennsylvania's whiskey rebels with an army. The National Republicans were anxious to conciliate as many moderate Federalists as possible. "Otherwise," wrote Vice President Burr's good friend Alexander J. Dallas of Pennsylvania, "the parties will continue always equally to divide the nation; every Federalist will become a conspirator . . . and each general election will involve the hazard of a civil war."

The moderates were more than a little uneasy about the unnerving number of radicals in Jefferson's party. These men, warned Senator Wilson Cary Nicholas of Virginia, Jefferson's spokesman in the Senate, had a "bias . . . strongly against those who rule." Treasury Secretary Albert Gallatin told Jefferson it would be better to lose these "political friends" and ingratiate the moderate Federalists.[19]

Jefferson's call for reconciliation in his inaugural address was not what hungry patronage seekers like DeWitt Clinton wanted to hear. As one Federalist newspaper put it, "the thorough going Jacobins are much disappointed in the President's speech . . . Their joy is only teeth outwards." Jefferson was soon being pounded by the radicals. John Randolph began firing letters in all directions, recalling his prediction that the "dissolution of the party would commence with its elevation to power." Others warned Jefferson against "favors conferred on your enemies."

Jefferson found it hard to ignore these shafts. There was a streak of radicalism in his own personality, exemplified by remarks such as "the earth belongs to the living" (which meant each generation could cancel all the debts of the previous generation) and "the tree of liberty must be refreshed from time to time by the blood of martyrs and patriots." But he was primarily a verbal extremist. His intellect, bolstered by the cool common sense of James Madison, usually enabled him to refrain from radical actions.

The Federalists did not make it easy for this reluctant moderate to stay in the middle of the road. The Judiciary Act of 1801 not only created twenty-six new Federalist judges. The legislation made it easier to move litigation from state to federal courts and gave these courts almost complete jurisdiction over cases involving land titles. This provision alone made the act anathema to westerners, who were constantly in conflict with speculators who had bought up huge chunks of the West. It delivered them into the hands of eastern lawyers like Alexander Hamilton. The New England claimants in the Yazoo scandal rubbed their hands in greedy anticipation.

Moreover, Jefferson's policy of removing as few Federalists as possible from office did not seem to conciliate his foes. Writhing under the lash of Federalist newspapers such as the *New-York Evening Post*, Jefferson began to wonder how much longer he should "push the patience of our friends to the utmost."[20] He decided to pacify the radicals and defy the Federalists by repealing the Judiciary Act of 1801.

The Federalist press fired predictable salvos calling the move an attack on the independence of the judiciary. More surprising was Vice President Burr's reaction. He did not think highly of this shift in policy. He told several Federalist congressmen that he opposed it. During a visit to the rooms of Federalist Senator Gouverneur Morris, he was even more outspoken, telling Morris he disliked the bill but was reluctant to break with his party over it. In a letter to his son-in-law, Joseph Alston, Burr described himself as doubting the "equity . . . of depriving the twenty-six judges of office and pay" when the Constitution clearly stated that federal judges would serve for life and their pay could not be reduced. To another correspondent, he wondered if the bill was "constitutionally moral."[21]

In the Senate, enough Republicans had similar doubts to threaten the passage of the repeal. Many showed their reluctance by absenting themselves when key votes loomed. On January 26, 1802, the bill came up for a second reading in the Senate. Fifteen Federalists opposed and fifteen Republicans favored the motion to proceed. The vice president had the casting vote. Although a reading was not a final vote, more than one piece of legislation has been killed by refusing to let it proceed. The Federalists held their collective breaths and exhaled with a muted groan when Burr said "yea."

That night, Gouverneur Morris confided to his diary the conviction that if Burr had said "nay" he would have instantly become the Federalist candidate for president in 1804, no matter what Alexander Hamilton said about it. "But there is a tide in the affairs of men which he suffered to go by."[22] Like many men caught in the middle of two warring political parties, Aaron Burr found it hard to decide which way to go. Instead, he tilted left and right, and waited to see the reaction from both sides.

The story of Burr and the Judiciary Act was not over. At a crucial moment in the debate on the bill a few days later, Burr's old friend Federalist Senator Jonathan Dayton of New Jersey, suggested that instead of repealing the act, it ought to be "revised and amended." The motion lost by a bare two votes. The radicals hastily called for a vote on the bill. On its third reading, Dayton again called for returning the bill to a special committee which the Federalists controlled, because a South Carolina Senator had switched sides. This time the Senate tied, 15 to 15, and the vice president had another casting vote.

Now it was the turn of the Republicans to hold their collective breaths. A vote to recommit would be an act of hostility to President Jefferson and the Republican party. Burr voted to recommit and then serenely denied any intention of breaking with the President. He claimed he only wanted to give proponents of a compromise, like Dayton, a fair hearing. Before the special committee could produce agreement, an absent Republican Senator turned up and the bill was resubmitted and passed, 16 to 15. In the House, it passed with three Republicans bolting. One, William Eustis of Massachusetts, was a close friend of the vice president.

President Jefferson gleefully signed the bill, dismissing moderates and their talk of a compromise as "wayward freaks which now and then disturb operations." Federalist Congressman James A. Bayard reported Republican moderates "openly cursed the measure."[23] Another moderate Republican said if the vote had been taken by secret ballot, the bill would have certainly been rejected. Others began talking about a third party. "Cannot good moderate men," asked a disenchanted Jeffersonian, "form a party of constitutionalists composed of true patriots which will avoid extremes?"[24]

Such remarks only made President Jefferson even more nervous about his vice president.

VII

Another reason Burr made Jefferson uneasy was the vice president's popularity with the military. They responded warmly to "Colonel" Burr, the title he preferred. His war record won every military man's respect. Jefferson had nothing on his military escutcheon but a disastrous term as wartime governor of Virginia, in which he had been unable to rally his populous state to repel raids by a few thousand British soldiers, and twice had to flee when the Royal Army rampaged in his direction. At the close of his term, the disgusted state legislature passed a vote of censure on his performance.

Through his Philadelphia friend Charles Biddle, Burr had become a warm friend of Brigadier General James Wilkinson, the much suspected commander in chief of the American army. Wilkinson was married to Biddle's first cousin, Ann. Through Biddle, Burr had also made numerous friends in the U.S. Navy. Thomas Truxtun, the hero of the undeclared war with France, wrote to the vice president as often as he wrote to General Hamilton.

The navy was where Jefferson was most vulnerable, as 1804 began. Early in his administration he had talked of eliminating it entirely. Changing his mind, he launched an undeclared war against the Moslem pirates of Tripoli, who preyed on U.S. merchant ships in the Mediterranean. This conflict had been dribbling on for three years with no appreciable success, because the tiny squadron Jefferson sent to the theater of war lacked the firepower to make a serious impact on the formidable forts that guarded Tripoli's harbor.

Instead of building new frigates to meet the threat to the American merchant marine created by the renewal of war between England and France, the president was pushing for dozens—eventually as many as 180—cheaply built gunboats. Equipped with one or two cannon, these small craft were supposed to protect American ports and shoreline against enemy bombardment. Jefferson argued gunboats were more in keeping with the purely defensive posture America should espouse and were cheaper than building elaborate forts—or men of war. Again revealing his isolationist streak, Jefferson declared a seagoing fleet would involve us in "eternal wars"—a statement that blithely ignored the inept one he was fighting in the Mediterranean.[25]

Unfortunately, Jefferson's gunboats could do nothing to stop British frigates from cruising outside New York and other harbors, inspecting any and every American ship that sailed out, boarding them to search for any cargo designated as contraband if they were heading for non-English ports—and frequently kidnapping a half dozen of their crews, claiming they were English not American citizens. This often dubious conclusion gave His Majesty's men the right to drag these hapless sailors into their ranks in the same brutal style that press gangs recruited unlucky civilians in British ports. This policy alone was enough to make Mr. Jefferson unpopular in New England, home of most of America's merchant marine.

VIII

The president occasionally invited the vice president to his palace for dinner. But there was a perfunctory quality to Jefferson's politeness, and even something demeaning in the way Burr was commingled with random congressmen and senators. In a town where politics was discussed from morning until midnight, many people noticed the second citizen of the republic was being ignored by the administration in other ways. Burr was never invited to a cabinet meeting. His requests for political jobs for his followers in New York were largely dismissed.

Burr's chief lieutenant in New York, Matthew Davis, became so annoyed by Jefferson's refusal to appoint him naval officer of the port that he trekked all the way to Monticello to confront the president in person. The job, one of the juicer on the patronage list, paid $7,000 a year. The secretary of the treasury, Albert Gallatin, was in close touch with New York politics thanks to his combative father-in-law, Commodore James Nicholson, the man who had almost fought a duel with Hamilton in 1795 and extravagantly praised Burr's "generalship" in 1800. Gallatin rushed a letter to Jefferson while Davis was enroute, warning the president that the way he handled the uninvited visitor would have important implications for his reelection and the future of the party.

Gallatin was very much afraid that the resurgent Federalists, with their well-edited papers and Hamilton's reviving leadership, could take New York away from them. The secretary suggested it was time Jefferson and the rest of the party made up their minds about Vice President Burr: "Do they eventually mean not to support Burr as your successor, when you shall see fit to retire? Do they mean not to support him at the next election for vice president? These are important questions." If Jefferson persisted in refusing Davis the job, Gallatin warned, it would be regarded by Burr and his followers as "a declaration of war."[26]

Gallatin may have been speaking in his timorous way on Burr's behalf. In 1794, when Burr was a senator from New York, he had vigorously opposed the Federalist decision to expel the Swiss-born Gallatin from the Senate because he had not been an American citizen for nine years, as required by the Constitution. Later Burr circulated Gallatin's ideas about political economy among influential northern Republicans, helping him become secretary of the treasury.[27]

At Monticello, Matthew Davis met the man whom he and Aaron Burr had schemed and sweated to make president in 1800 by eking 500 extra votes out of New York's lower-class wards. The Republican leader sat in the book-lined library of his hilltop mansion and listened to the hard-eyed politician, who was known as Little Mercury for his slam-bang speeches to the dockers and carters of New York. Davis's theme was how much Jefferson owed to Aaron Burr. He was not only asking for the job for himself. He was demanding it as a show of faith in "the Colonel."

The president talked and talked of his esteem for Colonel Burr. He talked at even more length about how badly he wanted to give Davis the job. But the Federalist who held it was extremely well qualified. True, he had been a loyalist during the Revolution but most Federalists were monarchists of one kind or another. To bring them into the Republican camp, he was trying to avoid "wholesale removals" from office.

As Davis started to answer these circumlocutions, the president plucked from the air a lazy fly that had been droning around his head. Jefferson's long slender fingers seized it by one leg and held it up in front of the baffled Davis. "Note," the president said, "the remarkable dispropor-tion between one part of the insect and its entire body."[28]

Was Jefferson suggesting there was a similar disproportion between Vice President Aaron Burr and his small number of followers in the Re-publican party? Davis went back to New York and the Federalist naval of-ficer remained in his job until the spring of 1803, when he was replaced by Samuel Osgood, stepfather of Mayor DeWitt Clinton's wife.

IX

To the distress of his followers, Vice President Burr refused to declare war. He thought he was better off remaining ostensibly loyal to Jefferson, while sending signals to the moderates in both parties who were growing disenchanted with the President's tilt toward the radicals.

On Washington's Birthday in 1802, the Federalists held a sumptuous feast in the capital, hoping to wrap their party in the mantle of the great man's fame. They invited the vice president to join them. Burr arrived after the prescribed toasts to the late and lamented *pater patriae*, the army, the navy, and other Federalist-revered institutions had been drunk. It was time for impromptu toasts from men at the head table. The vice president raised his glass and said: "To the union of all honest men."

The words reverberated through the federal district—and the nation. A union of honest men was in sharp contrast to Jefferson's soothing inaugural bromide, "We are all federalists, we are all republicans." Burr's toast was far more in touch with political realities. A growing number of Americans were tired of the ideological war between the so-called high Federalists led by General Hamilton, with their aggressive demands for an ever more powerful federal government, and the radical Republicans, sometimes if not always led by President Jefferson, determined to shrink the central government to the vanishing point and make the judiciary an appendage of the legislature.

In many ways the call for a union of honest men was the most significant political comment Aaron Burr ever made. It revealed him to be something new and important in American life, a professional politician. Americans, with their perpetual suspicions of political power, which they have inherited from the anti-Federalists and the Jeffersonians, have never completely accepted the legitimacy of such a calling. But the development of political parties made such men inevitable and even valuable, because they devoted themselves to making the system work and had only a minimal interest in ideology.

In contrast to Jefferson, who seldom stopped bemoaning the vexations of public service, and Hamilton, who decorated his pursuit of power with apocalyptic pessimism and a hunger for ultimate fame, Burr enjoyed politics. He once described it as a way of life that provided "fun, profit and honor." He liked the camaraderie with men like Matt Davis and John Swartout, the battle of wits and issues with opponents such as Hamilton. He preferred politics to a lawyer's life, which he called "druggery [*sic*]."

At the same time, like the professional politicians who have followed him, Burr had opinions. He was not a mere technician. He was genuinely disturbed by the tendencies of the radical Jeffersonians. He viewed the Federalist attempt to govern as an elite of wealth and talents as tantamount to political suicide in postrevolutionary America. Burr could see the flaws in both the Jeffersonian and Hamiltonian positions. But how to exploit these insights was an excruciating problem in a political atmosphere that was rancid with hostility and even hatred on both sides. As a professional who had no other source of income but his political salary, Burr had to think seriously about the problem of getting elected. He was keenly aware that challenging a Jefferson who had pulled off the Louisiana Purchase was not a wise move.

This understandable caution explains why Colonel Burr started backing away from his call for a union of honest men almost the moment he said it. He disingenuously claimed he had been joking. He said he had come to the dinner in search of entertainment, which was all too scarce in the federal district. The temptation to indulge in a little harmless political humor had been irresistible.

Ever watchful of Burr's moves, Alexander Hamilton soon had a letter in the mail to his friend Senator Gouverneur Morris. Wryly commenting on "the strange apparition which was taken for the V.P." at the Federalist fête and the even stranger toast, Hamilton advised Morris that on the whole he considered Burr's foray good news "if we use it well." Hamilton wanted the Federalists to manipulate Burr as an "instrument" to sow discord among the Republicans. But if they embraced him he would "disgrace and destroy the party."[29] Once more the General was reacting to the threat of a Burr takeover with rancorous extremism.

X

Inside the presidential palace, a worried Thomas Jefferson became even more susceptible to anti-Burr reports from New York. All these bulletins emanated from DeWitt Clinton, who had already decided there was room for only one leader of the democratic forces of the empire state. Jefferson was also corresponding with James Cheetham, editor of the *American Citizen*, who provided him with a bundle of documentation to prove that Burr was a traitor to the party and to Jefferson.[30]

The president told the newspaperman his information was "pregnant with considerations" and added he would "be glad hereafter to receive your daily paper by post." In an era when every paper had a fixed political orientation, this was tantamount to saying "I agree with you." When a president said it to an editor, and added he was sending the letter without using his franking signature, to make sure it traveled anonymously, the meaning was even clearer.

Jefferson was soon reading things in Cheetham's paper that could not have increased his fondness for Colonel Burr. The most serious salvo was *A View of the Political Conduct of Aaron Burr, Esq., Vice-President of the United States*. The Englishman accused Burr of trying to steal the presidency in 1800–01 and plotting to run against Jefferson with Federalist support in 1804. Less meaningful to modern readers but damning to readers of 1803 was a convoluted charge that Burr had attempted to suppress a highly critical history of the Adams administration by buying up all its copies, supposedly proving he was a secret Federalist. These accusations were intermixed with epithets and insulting phrases that held Burr up to ridicule as well as contempt. He was "habituated to intrigue," "cunning," "wicked," the perpetrator of "an evil of great magnitude."[31]

There was nothing vague about Cheetham's accusations in regard to Burr's supposed attempt to steal the presidency. The editor accused the vice president of plotting to create the tie vote long before election day. He tracked Burr's trips to Connecticut and New Jersey and identified by name the men he saw there, supposedly trying to persuade them to switch their electoral votes to him. Cheetham even declared he had in hand the receipts for the stagecoach tickets to New Jersey that Burr and a Federalist lawyer, David A. Ogden, had bought at the time of the 1801 deadlock. During the ride they supposedly conferred on the terms Burr demanded if he switched parties, and when Ogden reached Washington he attempted to negotiate on Burr's behalf.[32] Cheetham also claimed that Burr had described the president as "a plodding mechanical person, of little activity of mind and possessed of judgment not very discriminating."

Everyone in New York knew that behind this barrage of accusations and billingsgate stood the part owner of James Cheetham's *American Citizen*, DeWitt Clinton. Robert Troup told one of his many correspondents that the Clintonians now hated Burr "as much as the Jacobins in France hate Bonaparte."[33] Ironically, a Burr defender emerged from a totally unexpected corner: William Coleman, editor of the *New-York Evening Post*. Coleman had practiced law with Burr and did not share Hamilton's extreme animosity toward the vice president. Under the name "Fair Play" he published a vigorous reply to Cheetham's assault.

Burr's friends soon decided the *Evening Post* was not a suitable venue for their responses. They urged him to set up a rival newspaper to answer Cheetham on a regular basis. Burr's son-in-law, Joseph Alston, warned that he was being damaged even in distant South Carolina. Burr persisted in ignoring the attacks. "It will in due time be known what they are, and what is DeWitt Clinton . . . their instigator," he told Alston.[34]

The *Philadelphia Aurora*, voice of the Republican left wing, began reprinting Cheetham's accusations. Soon they were appearing in the *Albany Register*, one of New York's most influential papers, and other Republican journals around the nation. Still Burr remained silent, letting his supporters defend him in the columns of Federalist papers. Not until Cheetham had gone unanswered for six months did the vice president, in response to frantic pleas from his New York supporters, set up a paper to fire back at him.

The *Morning Chronicle* was edited by Dr. Peter Irving, called "Miss Irving" by Matthew Davis and other more rough-and-ready types. Dr. Irving's talented younger brother, Washington Irving, wrote graceful essays for the paper under the pen name Jonathan Oldstyle. No doubt with Burr's approval, the two Irvings refused to get down in the gutter with Cheetham. They relied on satire and on dignified arguments on behalf of their backer.

Some of Burr's supporters chose direct action to silence Cheetham and Clinton. After one particularly nasty blast, Matthew Davis roamed the downtown streets with a pistol, vowing to shoot Cheetham on sight. Another Burr loyalist, Robert Swartout, brother of the man who shot it out with DeWitt Clinton, exchanged insults with the mayor's district attorney, Robert Riker. The two resorted to pistols at ten paces across the Hudson in Weehawken and Riker emerged with a flesh wound.

Perhaps it was this whiff of distant gunpowder that made Colonel Burr decide to escalate hostilities. To his son-in-law, Joseph Alston, he wrote on December 7, 1803: "In New York . . . great pains have been taken to acquire information . . . Many base acts and machinations of the C. [Clinton] banditti are daily coming to light." Whereupon Mr. Burr unmasked his heavy artillery. His gunner was a young lawyer named William P. Van Ness. Ruddy cheeked, with blond curling hair and a pointed nose that might have sprung from a Frans Hals painting, Van Ness was a passionate believer in Aaron Burr. At a nod from the colonel, he put a match to the touchhole of his cannon. From it hurtled: *An Examination of the Various Charges Exhibited Against Aaron Burr . . . And A Development of the Character and Views of His Political Opponents.*

XI

Van Ness signed this missile "Aristides," suggesting that justice was his goal. He achieved a good deal of that scarce commodity, from the vice president's point of view. The *Examination* became the hottest-selling pamphlet in America since Tom Paine's *Common Sense*. Buttressing his case with letters and depositions from key witnesses, Van Ness demolished Cheetham's claim that Burr had tried to steal the presidency in 1800. That muddy shoe was on the other foot. It was Jefferson's friends who had wooed the Federalists during the crisis, guaranteeing them that there would be no wholesale removals from office and even promising specific jobs to swing congressmen. For proof Van Ness cited a speech by

Hamilton's friend James Bayard of Delaware, in which he named names and jobs; Jefferson had never tried to answer it.

People read Aristides not only for the skill with which he marshalled his arguments but for the way he lashed Colonel Burr's enemies. His invective, said one breathless reader, was "like a whip of scorpions." James Cheetham was "an open blasphemer of his God, a reviler of the Savior and a conspirator against the religious establishments of this country." DeWitt Clinton, named as Cheetham's backer, was "cruel by nature . . . an adept in moral turpitude, skilled in all combinations of treachery and fraud." His uncle, the governor, was a hypocrite who pretended to support Jefferson while whispering he was "an accommodating trimmer." Aristides also detailed DeWitt Clinton's flirtations with the Federalists in 1797–98, when they looked unbeatable, and accused him of sabotaging Robert R. Livingston when he ran for governor against John Jay in 1798.

Lesser lights in the Clinton-Livingston machine were flayed with equal savagery. Attorney General Ambrose Spencer, the prosecutor of the printer Harry Croswell, for libeling Jefferson, was "an inflexible professor of virtuous cowardice." Tunis Wortman, Mayor DeWitt Clinton's city clerk, was "the lowest class of creatures recognized as rational." Nor were the Livingstons spared. Brockholst Livingston, recently appointed to New York's Supreme Court, was asked how he managed to settle a staggering load of debts for about ten cents on the dollar, thanks to the benevolence of certain judges. Thomas Tillotson, married to another Livingston, was described as going about "begging for offices like a spaniel." Doubling back on DeWitt Clinton, Aristides described how Magnus Apollo got himself into the U.S. Senate by making Tillotson New York's secretary of state and thereby winning his support.[35]

At least as fascinating for readers who did not live in New York was a direct attack on Thomas Jefferson, portraying him as a weak and fickle visionary, unable to control "the excesses of democracy." This blast sent an unmistakable signal to Federalist readers that Aaron Burr did not consider the president a worthy candidate for his union of honest men.

The vice president had finally declared war.

XII

It was a war conducted with the most exquisite politeness. Colonel Burr's name was not on the pamphlet by Aristides. He gave no outward sign that he approved Van Ness's fusillade. Any more than DeWitt Clinton acknowledged backing the *American Citizen* or Thomas Jefferson admitted that he had given his covert blessing to its editor, James Cheetham.

But behind the scenes, the president was demonstrating his intense interest in the vice president's political maneuvers. On December 31, 1803, he wrote a soothing letter to George Clinton, assuring him that he considered Aristides' assault a tissue of libels and lies. "Little squibs in certain papers had long ago apprized me of a design to sow tares between particular Republican characters," he added. "But to divide those by lying tales whom truth cannot divide, is the hackneyed policy of the gossips of every society."[36] This comment was one of the more remarkable examples of Jefferson's ability to stand the truth on its head when his political blood was up. It was the Clintons and the president, not Burr, who had started the slander game, sowing enough tares to divide the vice president out of the Republican party.

The president was also busy at his *Anas*, inscribing damning gossip against Vice President Burr. Almost three years into his presidency, Jefferson was still exercised about the deadlock of 1801 and Burr's role in the crisis.

December 31 [1803] After dinner today, the pamphlet on the conduct of Colonel Burr being the subject of conversation, Matthew Lyon [Kentucky congressman and ultraradical noticed the insinuations against the Republicans in Washington pending the presidential election [of 1800] and expressed his wish that everything was spoken out which was known; that it would appear on which side there was a bidding for votes, and he declared that John Brown of Rhode Island, urging him to vote for Colonel Burr, used these words: "What is it you want, Colonel Lyon? Is it office, is it money? Only say what you want, and you shall have it."

Jan 2nd 1804 Colonel Hitchburn of Massachusetts says . . . he was in company at Philadelphia with Colonel Burr and Gen. Smith [of Maryland] (when the latter took his trip there to meet Burr) . . . that in the course of the conversation on the election, Colonel Burr said, "We must have a president and a constitutional one, in some way." "How is it be done?" says Mr. Hitchburn; "Mr. Jefferson's friends will not quit him and his enemies are not strong enough to carry another." "Why," says Burr, "Our friends must join the Federalists and give the President." The next morning at breakfast, Mr. Burr repeated nearly the same, saying: "We cannot be without a president, our friends must join the Federal vote." "But," says Hitchburn, "We shall then be without a vice president; who is to be our Vice President?" Colonel Burr answered: "Mr. Jefferson."[37]

A few days after writing this, Jefferson sent a note to Colonel Burr that underscored his nervousness—or deviousness—or both.

Th. Jefferson presents his respects to the vice president and is sorry that an error of his Secretary mentioning Thursday the 17th in his note of invitation should have occasioned a miscomprehension of the day. Mr. Harvie wrote a note correcting his error to the v. president; but lest it should not have been delivered, Th. J. asks leave to expect the pleasure of his company to dinner on Tuesday, the 17th inst.[38]

XIII

Early in 1804, Senator William Plumer of New Hampshire and other Federalist legislators discovered the existence of an alternative to dinner at the presidential palace. The Second Citizen of the District, Mr. Burr, was sending messengers ranging through the woods and swamps to invite gentlemen to dine with him in a comfortable house near Capitol Hill. Even more significant than Senator Plumer was another New England guest, John Quincy Adams, the senator from Massachusetts, son of the defeated president, who was as ready to damn Alexander Hamilton as he was to criticize

Jefferson. Federalist congressmen came in a steady stream. Also among the guests were congressmen and senators from Kentucky and Tennessee. Colonel Burr had a surprisingly strong following among westerners. As a senator, he had led the fight to make Tennessee the sixteenth state.

By this time, newspapers were reporting every move the vice president made. One noticed Burr studiously rejected "all invitations to drink toddy and play cards . . . with the Virginians." His Christmas holiday trip to Maryland was described in detail. To editors and politicians, he was acting more and more like a presidential candidate. Thomas Jefferson may have remembered a sentence in Albert Gallatin's letter about the danger of refusing Matthew Davis a job: "We run the risk of the Federal Party making Burr President."

XIV

There was little evidence of this political uproar in Burr's letters to his daughter, Theodosia. On January 3rd, he scotched the rumor that he had fought a duel with Senator Jackson of Georgia: "I am in perfect health . . . General Jackson is my good friend . . . I have had no duel or quarrel with anybody," he assured her.[39]

Of his visit to Annapolis, he wrote almost nothing. "I find the newspapers have anticipated me. They will tell you where I dined and supped and whom I saw." Of Mrs. Merry, whom Jefferson was now calling "a virago," the vice president wrote: "Tall, fair, fat—pas trop, however. No more than a desirable embonpoint. Much of grace and dignity, ease and sprightliness; full of intelligence. An English-woman who has lived much in Paris, and has all that could be wished of the manners of both countries. An amiable and interesting companion."[40]

Theodosia had also asked about another woman who was very much in the news. Auburn-haired Betsy Patterson, daughter of a wealthy Marylander, had just married Jerome Bonaparte, youngest brother of France's first consul. Archbishop John Carroll, titular head of the Roman Catholic church in America, had officiated. The vice president liked Betsy too: "A charming little woman; just the size and nearly the figure of Theodosia Burr Alston; by some thought a little like her; perhaps not so well in the shoulders; dresses with taste and simplicity (by some thought too free); has sense and spirit and sprightliness."[41]

Betsy was a bit more than sprightly. She later said she married Jerome Bonaparte because he represented her one hope of getting out of Baltimore. The thought of spending her life there had several times caused her to consider suicide. Warned by the French chargé, Louis Pichon, that the marriage was illegal under French law and Napoléon was certain to oppose it, Betsy replied, "I would rather be the wife of Jerome Bonaparte for an hour than any other man for life."

During her stay in the federal district, swarms of oglers followed Betsy everywhere. They came, one acerbic commentator wrote, "to see a naked woman." Perhaps to please Jerome, who had a boyish nostalgia for the way women dressed (or undressed) in the early frenzy of the French Revolution, Betsy's outfits revealed almost everything. She disdained petticoats, so the outline of the little that remained covered was delightfully visible. At her wedding, a guest said: "Whatever clothes worn by the bride could have been put in my pocket."[42]

A lieutenant in the French navy, Jerome had been serving in the West Indies when England and France went to war again in the spring of 1803. The British devoted a squadron of ships to capturing him, foreseeing that he would make a valuable hostage. He had come to United States in the hope of getting back to France incognito on an American ship. Nevertheless Federalists and their wives saw ominous portents in this appearance of Napoléon's brother in America. Betsy's revolutionary nakedness only added to their dudgeon. Rumors swirled that Jerome was going to become the first consul's ambassador to the United States and his mission was the negotiation of a new treaty of alliance. This only fueled Federalist anxiety about the Louisiana Purchase and the transfer of 15 million American dollars to Napoléon's war machine.

Virtually confirming these rumors, President Jefferson, petulant over Ambassador Merry's umbrage, invited Betsy and Jerome Bonaparte to dinner at the palace. When dinner was served, Jefferson offered his arm to the scantily clad Mrs. Bonaparte and led her to the place of honor at the dinner table. What were already hostile Federalists to think of such behavior? The rumors of a sellout to France multiplied.

Vice President Burr did not join the suspicious chorus. He told Theodosia that he had also entertained the Bonapartes at a "breakfast á la François, at twelve o'clock." But the suspicious might have been fascinated to learn that Burr wanted Theodosia to translate the U.S. Constitution into French for Jerome's benefit. "I cannot get it done here," he wrote, "and it may not be useless to you to burnish up your French a little."[43]

Equally important as international politics to the vice president was the education of his grandson, Aaron Burr Alston, aged one and a half. "Of the boy you can never say enough," he told Theodosia. "I hope you talk to him much in French . . . You do not say whether [he] knows his letters. I am sure he may be taught them, and then put a pen into his hand and set him to imitate them. He may read and write before he is three years old. This, with speaking French, would make him a tolerably accomplished lad of that age and worthy of his blood." [44]

Sometimes, when the vice president and Theodosia discussed the boy, they called him "the heir apparent."

CHAPTER 6

A Wary Candidate
Tests the Waters

*I*n the Senate, on January 3, 1804, Vice President Burr presided over a scene that could not fail to interest him—a debate on how to impeach a federal judge. In the context of Burr's doubts about the legality of Jefferson's decision to repeal the Judiciary Act, this move became one more piece of evidence that the president was drifting into the arms of his party's extremists—a trend that could only enhance Colonel Burr's appeal to Republican moderates.

The debate was complicated by the judge's insanity. A Harvard graduate, John Pickering had been a revolutionary leader in New Hampshire and author of the state's constitution. For a while he had been a distinguished judge, first in the state's courts, then on the federal bench. But a fondness for strong drink and consequent brain damage reduced him to a maniac who shouted obscenities, insulted attorneys, and handed down decisions without bothering to listen to the evidence. A strong streak of Federalism in his rants did nothing to endear him to his political enemies.

Under the Judiciary Act, which the Jeffersonians had repealed, an incapacitated judge could be replaced on a temporary basis. Pickering had been semiretired and another judge appointed to hear cases in his district. By returning all judges to their previous status, the Republicans forced Pickering to resume the bench, where his antics soon attracted national attention. When Jefferson sent a message to the House of Representatives, calling for Pickering's impeachment, the Federalists were infuriated. They saw it as another step in the radicals' assault on an independent judiciary.

Particularly ominous was the alacrity with which the House of Representatives, led by John Randolph, voted to impeach Pickering, ignoring arguments that an insane man could not be found guilty of "treason, bribery, or other high crimes and misdemeanors"—the only grounds for impeachment in the Constitution. Federalists saw the Republican haste as an attempt to render these words meaningless. They thought the Jeffersonians were moving toward a policy of impeaching any and all Federalist judges on a straight party vote.

As far as Randolph and his fellow radicals were concerned, the Federalists were right. Dour Senator Timothy Pickering of Massachusetts (no relation to the impeached judge) reported that Randolph was saying the provision in the Constitution that judges shall hold office during good behavior, that is, for life, was intended "to guard them against the executive alone and not by any means to control the power of Congress."[1] Randolph was demonstrating at this early stage of the Republic the danger that had worried James Madison most when he contemplated his handiwork, the U.S. Constitution—the legislature's tendency to encroach on the other two branches of the government.

President Jefferson, at best a lukewarm friend of the Constitution, seemed unconcerned about this threat. He told Senator William Plumer that impeachment was an unsatisfactory way to remove a judge. "A President ought to be authorized to remove a judge on the address of the two houses of Congress," Jefferson said.[2] These remarks aroused the specter of the unchecked French assembly, with its blood-soaked claim to personify the will of the people.

With the House vote in effect indicting Judge Pickering, it was now up to the Senate to form a Court of Impeachment and decide whether the charges could withstand legal scrutiny. Burr, almost but not quite at war with Jefferson, would preside over this process, as president of the Senate. He would be in a position to issue rulings that could have a large impact on the outcome. Many saw significance in the selection of Robert Goodloe Harper, the man whom Burr had visited over the Christmas holidays, as Pickering's defense attorney. For the time being these questions remained in the realm of speculation. A subpoena was issued, ordering Judge Pickering to appear for his trial on March 2.

II

The vice president had other things on his mind besides Judge Pickering. A week before Christmas, Burr had gathered a group of his leading New York supporters in Washington. They included Dr. Peter Irving, the editor of the *Morning Chronicle*, and William P. Van Ness, the author of the ferocious reply to James Cheetham and his backer, DeWitt Clinton, *An Examination of the Various Charges Exhibited Against Aaron Burr.*

These loyalists brought with them dismaying, even infuriating news of another Clinton slander. The Old Incumbent, George Clinton, was accusing Burr of maneuvering him out of the vice presidency in 1800, after the colonel's victory over General Hamilton in the New York City elections. The governor claimed that Burr had conned the New York Republicans' spokesman, Commodore James Nicholson, into believing Clinton did not want the job. Reneging on his lavish praise of Burr's achievement in letters at the time, Nicholson was confirming the accusation.

There was little doubt that the purpose of this sudden about-face was to make George Clinton the president's running mate in 1804. The Burrites may also have learned of another even more outrageous (to them) political move. There was talk of Clinton running for governor and vice president simultaneously. When elected, he would resign the governorship and the legislature would appoint Ambassador Robert R. Livingston, who was planning an early departure from France.[3]

This news raised the question of whether Burr should run for governor of New York in the spring. No final decision was reached, but most of these confidential friends thought the colonel should chance it. DeWitt Clinton's arrogant style was already alienating many Republicans. Numerous New York Federalists were whispering they would welcome a

Burr candidacy. If he won, he might be in a position to challenge Jefferson as the moderate presidential candidate in the fall. At the very least, a gubernatorial victory would be exquisite revenge on the Clintons.

The Burr lieutenants seemed to have traveled from New York and back by various routes, spreading the gospel of a union of honest men. The by now thoroughly hostile Philadelphia *Aurora* noted that the vice president's "satellites" had "lately been scattered in various parts and . . . it has been insinuated that some of them have been treated with cordiality on their excursion through Trenton, Philadelphia, Wilmington, Baltimore &c." The *Aurora* blandly denied this report, claiming that "as the agents of Mr. Burr they gained no respect." [4]

This canard was demolished by a January 3rd letter from Dr. John Vaughan, one of Delaware's prominent Republicans, in which he told the vice president how much he had enjoyed a visit from Dr. Peter Irving and another devoted Burrite, Abraham Bishop of Connecticut. Bishop's slashing attack on Federalism in his Phi Beta Kappa address at Yale in 1800 had created a national sensation. [5] Dr. Vaughan reported that "some wicked man" had sent him a copy of "a pamphlet entitled *An Examination &c, by Aristides.*" Another copy had gone to the state's revolutionary icon, John Dickinson, whose *Letters From a Farmer (1767–68)* had made him one of the early spokesmen against British imperialism. Like Burr, Dickinson had begun as a Federalist and switched to Republicanism in the 1790s. The old man had authorized Vaughan to say that he was "never prejudiced" (against Burr) and is now "highly gratified." Dickinson's opinion of the vice president was "untarnished by the malignant clamour of demagogues."

After reading Aristides with "equal pleasure and avidity," Dr. Vaughan wrote, he was more than ever convinced that the Republic was drifting toward either oligarchy or anarchy. America's one hope was a "firm union of honest men." He closed by wishing Burr "complete retribution for the past." [6] Here was impressive proof that Burr's toast at the Federalist banquet was far more than a casual remark. It was taking root among the electorate.

A day later, John Dickinson wrote Burr to tell him how much he enjoyed a visit from Abraham Bishop: "I rejoice at the prospect he opened to me of the advancement of Republican principles and measures, to the eastward," the patriarch said. The eastward reference usually meant New England, but it could easily include New York and a Burr run for the governorship. Dickinson closed by assuring Burr: "I am thy sincere friend."[7]

Burr's political strategy was becoming clear. He was trying to marshal the kind of big-name support he had concocted when he took New York away from Alexander Hamilton in 1800. Endorsements from Charles Carroll and John Dickinson were exactly the sort of thing he needed to refute the slanders being flung at him by the Clintonians and their allies. They could even be a counterweight to the animus emanating from that other revolutionary icon, Thomas Jefferson.

Early in 1804, a southern edition of Aristides's pamphlet was printed in Virginia, with an appendix by "A gentleman of North Carolina" offering proof that "GEN. HAMILTON AT THE LAST PRESIDENTIAL ELECTION, EXERTED ALL HIS INFLUENCE TO SUPPORT MR. JEFFERSON IN OPPOSITION TO MR. BURR."[8] Since Hamilton's name was anathema to Republicans, this constituted a nasty inferential dig at Jefferson. Maybe the president's political principles were not so pure after all. How else could he have attracted Hamilton's support? If the arch-Satan of Federalism opposed Burr, did not that suggest a certain purity on the vice president's part?

III

In the Senate, meanwhile, the latest news from the House of Representatives stirred fresh alarm among moderate men. The same committee headed by John Randolph that had indicted Judge Pickering was preparing to impeach a sitting justice of the U.S. Supreme Court, Samuel Chase of Maryland, and the federal district judge for Pennsylvania, Richard Peters. Chase had attracted Republican ire by his outspoken denunciations of errant editors who came before him during the Sedition Act furor. More recently he had condemned the repeal of the Judiciary Act and declared the country was heading for "mobocracy." Peters was on the bench with Chase during one of his more incendiary fusillades, and radical Republicans from Pennsylvania demanded his impeachment too.[9]

Chase's Federalist rants infuriated many Republicans. But were they treason, high crimes, or misdemeanors? Again, the Federalists began to dread, with apparently good reason, this latest revelation of the Jefferson administration's intentions. More and more it seemed to them that Jefferson was abandoning the backstairs promises he had made during the electoral college deadlock with Burr. He seemed to be moving toward a populist tyranny sanctified by his overwhelming majorities in Congress. Here was the heart of the reason why Gouverneur Morris told General Hamilton that the Constitution was "gone."

IV

The Senate also began debating another issue that was troubling many moderate Republicans and most Federalists—Jefferson's handling of the takeover of Louisiana. The Federalists were keenly aware that only three months before, on September 27, 1803, the Spanish Ambassador, the marqués de Casa Yrujo, had written to Secretary of State James Madison, informing him that Spain violently disapproved of Napoléon's sale of Louisiana to the United States. Yrujo claimed it contravened "the most solemn assurances given in writing" to the king of Spain that France would never sell Louisiana to anyone. Yrujo, with his American wife, was an intriguer of the first order. Vice President Burr had demonstrated his Republican bona fides when he barred him from the Senate floor.[10]

Jefferson and Madison had brushed aside Yrujo's protest and submitted the treaty to the Senate in the fall of 1803 with orders to their legislative leaders to ratify it as soon as possible. They carefully concealed the reason for this haste: letters from their diplomats in Paris, Ambassador Robert

R. Livingston and special envoy James Monroe, warning that First Consul Napoléon Bonaparte was having second thoughts about the sale and had hinted he would renege on it if the Americans hesitated too long or tried to change the terms of the treaty in any way. Overriding Federalist objections and stifling their strong opinion that an amendment to the Constitution was necessary (at one point Jefferson had even drafted a proposed text), the congressional Republicans obeyed orders from their chief and rammed the treaty through Congress in four days.[11]

The moment it was passed, clerks worked day and night to prepare the documents for a takeover. Included was a proclamation that warned the inhabitants of the territory that the "incivility" of Spain would not deter America. "We shall retain our rights. But it belongs to you to decide whether you are disposed to share in them or attack them."[12] This testy language underscored the extreme nervousness of the administration that their marvelous deal might unravel if the Spanish on the ground in New Orleans proved intransigent. Napoléon might find local resistance an even better excuse than American foot-dragging to repudiate the sale.

By presidential order, Postmaster Gideon Granger arranged for an 1803 version of express mail to rush the documents to American officials at Natchez in the Mississippi Territory just north of Louisiana at a breakneck day and night pace. Fresh horses were stationed every thirty miles and fresh riders were ready every hundred miles to make sure not a minute was lost.[13]

Everyone in Washington was in a state of suspense, waiting to hear if the Spanish had decided to resist the paltry 450 U.S. troops that Jefferson had ordered to New Orleans under the command of Brigadier General James Wilkinson. There was talk of raising six thousand militia from Tennessee and Kentucky, but these fighting men had not materialized.[14] The handful of regulars was all Jefferson could muster to escort the acting governor, twenty-eight-year-old William C. C. Claiborne. There were only 300 Spanish troops in New Orleans but Spain could easily ship formidable numbers from Havana. Everyone knew it was a test of Jefferson's decision to virtually demobilize General Hamilton's regular army.

General Hamilton, obviously hoping something would go wrong, solemnly warned in the *New-York Evening Post* that if the Spanish resisted, the bloodshed "would be on the heads of those who have resorted to arms to enforce injustice." By this the General presumably meant Napoléon's violation of his agreement with Spain to keep Louisiana forever French. General Hamilton's alter ego, editor William Coleman, intoned: "In our view, nothing can be more critical than the present state of our public affairs."[15]

President Jefferson—and everyone else in Washington, D.C.—would have been more than a little nonplused if they had known that General James Wilkinson, commander of the U.S. Army, had been on the Spanish secret service payroll since 1787. The beefy hard-drinking brigadier was looking forward to this trip to New Orleans. He hoped to use his new power to collect $20,000 in arrears payments from Havana. Wilkinson was fond of describing himself as the man "whose head directed & whose hand signed the Convention of Saratoga." As deputy adjutant general of the American Northern army, he had helped negotiate the 1777 surrender of the British army led by General John Burgoyne—the turning point of the Revolutionary War. [16]

Thanks to their mutual friendship with Charles Biddle, General Wilkinson was a friend and frequent correspondent of Vice President Aaron Burr. The vice president and Biddle were among the few people who knew Wilkinson detested President Jefferson and his administration. In 1802, Jefferson had given the Republican cost cutters in Congress permission to go to work on the U.S. Army. At one point they abolished Wilkinson's rank of brigadier general. One congressman had sneered that Wilkinson was a mere "sinecure officer." Vice President Burr had used his influence to persuade a congressional committee to restore Wilkinson's brigadiership.

In May of 1802, Wilkinson had written Burr a bitter letter from the Georgia backcountry. He told the vice president his experience with Congress had "awakened me as from a dream." After eleven years of hardship and low pay on the frontier, he had to watch his salary reduced and his rank almost abolished by "a set of prating puppies and coxcombs." Only the "derangement" of his private affairs prevented him from resigning his commission.[17]

This disillusioned cash-hungry soldier did not have a moral bone in his body. He was a wild card that might not be played for the moment. But he was in the political deck, waiting for someone to draw him.

V

While Washington, D.C., waited to hear if Louisiana was going to resist President Jefferson's minimal force majeure, the politicians debated the government Jefferson had created for the territory's fifty thousand new citizens. Introduced in the Senate by John Breckinridge of Kentucky, the bill was drafted by the president, working the way he frequently preferred, in deep background.[18] The plan was totally undemocratic. The new governor—and the president—were given the power to rule by executive order. There were no voters and no legislature. Judges and a council of advisors were to be appointed by the president. Most shocking of all, there was no provision for trial by jury, and the inhabitants were going to be taxed by the American government without their consent.

Federalist Senator William Plumer of New Hampshire furiously declared that if his party had sponsored such a bill, they would have been denounced as monarchists. Another Federalist said it made Jefferson "as despotic as the Grand Turk." Not a few Republicans assailed the bill on similar grounds, unaware that Jefferson was its secret author. Matthew Lyon of Kentucky called it "probationary slavery."[19]

At least as heated was the question of whether to tolerate slavery in the new territory and whether Louisianians should be permitted to import slaves directly from Africa. Every state except South Carolina had passed laws banning the importation of slaves; under the compromise that won southern ratification of the Constitution, all states would be prohibited by federal law to import them after 1808. Most New Englanders favored a total ban on the dubious institution. Some even wanted to free or remove the thousands of slaves already in the territory. Not a single senator tried to defend slavery, but the Jeffersonian majority decided the "faith of the nation" was pledged in the treaty to permit Louisianians all the rights enjoyed by Americans—and one of these was the right to own slaves. But they forbade their new subjects to import any blacks from Africa.[20]

These objections coalesced with a far more serious Federalist demurral: They were convinced that Jefferson could not incorporate Louisiana into the Union without consulting the already existing states. Senator Plumer went so far as to contend that the consent of every state in the present union was necessary before this could be done. Here the New Hampshireman was voicing the intense hostility New Englanders felt toward the Louisiana Purchase. They were refusing, in Plumer's words, to "tamely . . . shrink into a state of insignificance."[21]

The Yankees violently objected to the third section of the treaty with Napoléon, where Jefferson promised to give Louisiana the same rights and privileges as American citizens. Not only did this permit slavery to flourish, it meant Louisiana would eventually send representatives to Congress. Gouverneur Morris, who had written the final draft of the Constitution in 1787, flatly declared that the document required Louisiana to be ruled as an external province, the way the British ruled Canada, with "no voice in our councils."[22] With such an expert in their corner, the mostly Federalist New Englanders were beginning to say if the Republicans could violate the Constitution with impunity, so could they. Their answer to Virginian hegemony was "disunion." That idea made them look with renewed interest to that son of New England, Vice President Aaron Burr.

VI

For the moment, these dire thoughts were overshadowed by a message from President Thomas Jefferson, which reached the Senate on Monday,

January 16th. The president reported that General Wilkinson and Governor Claiborne and the military escort had reached New Orleans without incident and taken possession of Louisiana in the name of the United States on December 20, 1803. The message ended in a Jeffersonian paean: "On this important acquisition, so favorable to the immediate interests of our western citizens, so auspicious to the peace and security of the nation in general, which adds to our country territories so extensive and fertile . . . I offer to Congress and our country my sincere congratulations."[23]

The Republicans lost no time in utilizing to the fullest the political implications of this success. "Never have mankind contemplated so vast and important an accession of empire by means so pacific and just," gushed Washington, D.C.'s, *National Intelligencer*, whose publisher and wife were close friends of the president. Ignored were the cries of euchred Spain, the heated debate in the Senate about the "oppressed" people of Louisiana, sold like a slave coffle to the Jefferson-created nonrepresentative government. Totally evaporated was the debate over permitting slavery in the new territory.

The *National Intelligencer* was soon publishing ecstatic reports of the celebration by the citizens of Louisiana, expressing their joy at becoming Americans. More accurate was an eyewitness account from a Parisian traveler, who watched the French flag come down and the American flag go up at New Orleans. "An anxious silence reigned among all the spectators who flooded the plaza," he wrote. When the flag reached the top of the pole, a cheer burst from a small group of Americans in the crowd. "These cries . . . made more gloomy the silence and quietness of the rest of the crowd" who were all French and Spanish.[24]

On Friday, January 27th, the federal district's Republicans gave a dinner at Stelle's Hotel for over one hundred members of Congress. President Jefferson and his cabinet and Vice President Burr were among the honored guests. Three pieces of cannon were dragged from the navy yard and discharged on Capitol Hill before and after the festivities. An ode, supposedly translated from the Latin, was sung by several voices accompanied by instrumental music. Among its stanzas were:

> To Jefferson, belov'd of Heav'n
> May golden peace be ever given

After the president and the vice president retired from the scene, a toast was offered: "The President of the United States." It was drunk with three cheers. Someone else proposed a toast to the vice president. "Few cheered him and many declined drinking it," Senator Plumer reported to his journal. Then Congressman Joseph B. Varnum of Massachusetts rose to volunteer: "The Union of All Parties." This less than subtle tribute to Burr was "ill-received," Plumer reported. "Some refused to drink it." The celebrators also rejected an offering from a radical Republican: "The tempestuous sea of liberty—may it never be calm." The politicians were obviously trying to avoid looking committed to either side of this mounting quarrel. Instead, they settled down to serious drinking. By the time they reeled home, many of them were so drunk they forgot their hats.[25]

A few days later, the Republicans sobered up enough to give a ball at an assembly room in Georgetown. A reported five hundred people trekked through snowy streets to dance beneath festoons of laurel. On a rear wall hung an illuminated portrait of President Jefferson surrounded by military banners. These festivities seemed to collide somewhat with the ideals of Republican simplicity, but the *National Intelligencer* met that issue head on, praising "the plain unembellished walls" of the assembly room and contrasting the display to "the spectacles that celebrate the achievements of warriors."[26]

Unquestionably, President Jefferson and his friends had one eye on General Hamilton and the other one on Colonel Burr. They were also working hard to elevate Jefferson to par value in the American pantheon with George Washington.

VII

There was no longer any question that being a friend of Mr. Burr meant you were not a friend of Thomas Jefferson. The hostility came out in small ways—and large ones. When Burr became ill in mid-January, someone proposed his friend, Senator John Brown of Kentucky, as president pro-tem of the Senate. [27] Senator Plumer noted in his journal that "the senators from Virginia . . . set up Mr. [Jesse] Franklin from North Carolina." It took seven tries to get Brown elected, and he only made it with the help of the Federalists. Plumer watched the brawl with barely concealed satisfaction, commenting that "every such event tends to weaken and divide" the Republicans. [28]

Another instance of Jeffersonian hostility was a House bill presented to the Senate to reduce the Marine Corps to near invisibility. For a year, Jefferson had refused to fill any vacancies in the corps. In his journal, Senator Plumer explained why. The commandant of the corps, Lieutenant Colonel William Ward Burrows, was a "favorite" of Vice President Burr and was suspected of federalism—"crimes that appear of a deep dye in the mind of Jefferson." In spite of what Plumer called "the meanness of the President," he had been unable to get rid of Burrows and several other officers. This attempt also ended in utter failure. The bill lost by a vote of 18 to 8—a shock that caused one of Jefferson's frequent spokesmen, Senator John Breckinridge of Kentucky, to "turn pale." [29]

Further evidence of Jefferson-Burr hostilities was the presence of William Duane, editor of the Philadelphia *Aurora*, on the Senate floor. When Burr left the Senate for a trip to New York, Duane began showing up each day, chatting with friendly senators and otherwise acting as an honored guest. Sharp-eyed Senator Plumer noticed that "no other person had been admitted as a spectator" except members of the House of Representatives. This unusual hospitality to a Burr enemy and an inveterate spokesman for the radical wing of Jefferson's party was an undoubted signal of which way the wind was blowing from the presidential palace. [30]

Vice President Burr left no doubt that he knew what was happening. When he returned from New York later in February, he directed the Senate doorkeeper to order Duane to stay at the stenographer's table or leave the chamber instantly. Duane "reluctantly" complied, Senator Plumer noted.

Burr was sending as many signals as Jefferson, and a group of Federalists decided to see how far he was ready to go. Senator Timothy Pickering of Massachusetts, Senator James Hillhouse of Connecticut, and Senator William Plumer of New Hampshire had dinner with the vice president. Senator Hillhouse, who was passionately opposed to Jefferson's handling of the Louisiana Purchase, especially the Republican decision to allow slavery in the new possession, opined to the vice president that there would soon be two governments in the United States. He was talking about the secession of New England. Colonel Burr did not show the least sign of disapproval. "The impression made on my mind," Senator Plumer told his journal later that night, "was that he not only thought such an event would take place, but that it was necessary that it should . . ."

But when Plumer thought over the conversation, he added a postscript: "After critically analyzing his [Burr's] words, there was nothing in them that necessarily implied his approbation of Hillhouse's observations. Perhaps no man's language was ever so apparently explicit, and, at the same time, so covert and indefinite."[31] Here was a prima facie example of Burr the professional politician at work. One of the cardinal rules of the species is a profound wariness to a premature commitment to an idea or program.

In 1804, the idea of secession was not as heinous as Americans have come to regard it as a result of the Civil War, when it became entangled with the abolitionist crusade against slavery. In spite of George Washington's perception of the Union's importance, people's chief allegiance remained to their home states or regions. The Constitution and its assertions of federal power were still regarded as an experiment.

As early as 1792, Secretary of State Jefferson had warned President George Washington that the South was likely to secede because of southern dissatisfaction with Hamilton's financial system.[32] Two years later,

Senators Rufus King of New York and Oliver Ellsworth of Connecticut approached Senator John Taylor of Virginia to discuss ways to arrange a peaceable separation of the Union, because "the southern and eastern [New England and New York] people thought quite differently."[33]

When the Senate debated whether or not to ratify the Louisiana Purchase, Senator John Breckinridge of Kentucky bluntly declared that if they rejected it, the western states would immediately secede from the union and form a separate country.[34] President Jefferson, writing about Louisiana to the English scientist Joseph Priestly on January 29, 1804, was unbothered by this idea: "Whether we remain in one confederacy or form into Atlantic and Mississippi confederacies, I believe not very important to the happiness of either part. Those of the western confederacy will be as much our children and descendants as those of the eastern . . . "[35]

Put in this Jeffersonian context, Vice President Burr's semiapproval of New England's secession was neither surprising nor treasonous. It was one among several options that this somewhat beleagured but still formidable politician was considering.

CHAPTER 7

From Migraine to Miracle

*F*rom Vice President Burr's point of view, embarking on a secessionist plot with the New Englanders was chancy at best. It was difficult if not impossible to discover how much backing the Yankee politicians who approached Burr in Washington, D.C., had among average voters. Running for governor of New York was an equally risky venture. A great deal depended on how well his counterattack against the DeWitt Clinton–Cheetham slanders was working. To win, Burr would need Federalist support, and blocking that possibility was his enemy, General Alexander Hamilton.

Yet Burr's followers, the Swartouts, William P. Van Ness, and Matthew Davis, were imploring him to run. It was their only hope of payback for the humiliations to which the Clinton-Jefferson alliance had subjected them. On a man-to-man basis, Burr owed it to them to make the race. But if he lost, what was his political future? Perhaps it would be better to retire to the sidelines for a while and await developments, as General Hamilton was doing.

Burr hinted of his irresolution in a January 17, 1804, letter to Theodosia. "Of my plans for the spring," he wrote, "nothing can be said, for nothing is resolved." He concealed his feelings behind banter about forgetting to wish Theodosia a happy New Year in a previous letter. "My heart is full of good wishes for you every day of the calendar," he quipped. "Yet I like to see attention paid to all *les jours de fête.*"[1]

Behind his cool demeanor, the vice president was human. As he pondered his alternatives, his head began to throb. Like his enemy, Mr. Jefferson, who also affected a debonair manner, Burr was subject to migraine attacks—an illness with psychosomatic overtones. The violent headaches and nausea he experienced after the battle of Monmouth in 1778 were probably the onset of the disease. Usually, the "torment," as Burr called it, lasted only twenty-four hours (whereas Jefferson's attacks seldom lasted less than a week). As Burr told his friend Charles Biddle in a letter on January 23rd, this attack turned out to be much more severe:. "I have undergone cathartic, emetic and phlebotomy (bloodletting), operations not experienced by me in twenty years, and all to no purpose. The pain continues."

On the day he wrote this letter, Burr was able to get out of bed only for about an hour. In a postscript added to the Biddle letter the next day, the vice president reported he was much better: "Yet my head [is] too weak to bear the least motion, and [I] fear it will not allow me to travel for several days."[2]

II

In the midst of this migraine attack, Burr made one of the strangest moves of his life. He asked President Thomas Jefferson for a private meeting to discuss his political future. Here, once more, we see evidence of a man who had become, without acknowledging the term, a professional politician. On one level at least, it seemed logical for him to sit down with the head of his party for a candid conversation.

Jefferson's habit of operating in deep background, behind a screen of followers, made it difficult for Burr to see that the president was up to his hips in the plot to destroy him. Burr was unaware that Jefferson had given James Cheetham his covert blessing and was reading every issue of the *American Citizen*. The hostility emanating from the Republicans in the Senate and the House was not visibly endorsed by the president. Burr could—and seemingly did—attribute it to the Clinton-Cheetham slanders.

Burr may also have reasoned that Jefferson, having negotiated the final step in the Louisiana Purchase, would be in a generous mood. He had pulled off the greatest political coup since George Washington won the Revolution. A man on the threshold of such immense fame should be willing to share his good fortune. Burr may also have read Jefferson as a man who hated confrontations and could be intimidated. Hamilton had driven him out of George Washington's cabinet with his headlong attacks, in person and in print. In the deadlock for the presidency in 1801, Jefferson had retreated, agreeing sotto voce to Hamilton's negotiating points while giving himself ample latitude to deny he had made a deal. Burr might have been trying to do something similar in this meeting in the presidential palace, which took place on the evening of January 26, 1804—three days after Burr described himself as a semi-invalid, too weak to travel.

Unfortunately, we have only Jefferson's version of their conversation. He thought it was so important, he filled a half dozen pages of his *Anas* with the account. According to the president, Burr began with a backward look at his early days in politics. He had come to New York as a stranger and found two wealthy families, the Livingstons and the Clintons, in control of the state. He had "meddled not" in their domain until the crisis of 1800, when they "solicited his aid with the people." He had given them his help "without any views of promotion" and had never expected to be named vice president.

If this is what Burr said, it was pathetically far from the truth—and extremely unlikely to have impressed Jefferson. As a fellow insider, Jefferson knew that Burr had eagerly accepted a veritable raft of political offices, from state assemblyman to attorney general of New York to U.S. senator and had sought several others such as governor of New York and ambassador to France.

Next, in Jefferson's *Anas* record, was an even more dubious statement. Burr supposedly said that he had only accepted the vice presidency "with a view to promote" my [Jefferson's] fame & advancement and from a de-

151

sire to be with me, whose company & conversation had always been fascinating to him." This from a man who had just published a pamphlet by
his literary lieutenant, William P. Van Ness, describing Jefferson as a
fickle visionary!

One begins to suspect that Jefferson's record of this conversation is
somewhat less than reliable. Continuing Burr's self-pitying narration, the
president reported the colonel saw himself as a victim of "those great families" of New York, the Clintons and the Livingstons. They had become
hostile to him, and "excited the calumnies" that were damaging him politically. Burr supposedly claimed Hamilton had joined in this target practice on his reputation.

Yet, Burr was said to avow, "his attachment" to Jefferson had been "sincere and was still unchanged" in spite of "little stories" that had been carried to him about the president's hostility. Burr assumed similar things
had been carried to the president; he hoped Jefferson despised them as
much as he did. But attachments were not a one-way street. They must be
"reciprocal" or they "cease to exist." Burr wanted to know, face to face and
man to man, if Jefferson's attitude toward him had changed.

Burr reminded Jefferson of a letter the president had written to him in
1801 after the ugly business of the electoral college deadlock had ended.
Jefferson had lamented that the colonel was now vice president because it
had left "a chasm in my arrangements," meaning he had looked forward
to giving him a major appointment in his administration. Burr went on to
admit "it would be for the interest of the republican cause for him to retire" from politics. "A disadvantageous schism would otherwise take
place." But he disliked the idea of retiring as if he "shrunk from the public
sentence." Since his enemies were using Jefferson's name to destroy him,
"some mark of favor" from the president was necessary to "deprive them
of that weapon." In short, he wanted to be able to offer the world clearcut
evidence that he retired with Jefferson's "confidence."

At this point in Jefferson's account, a ring of truth begins to occur. We
can see the small, compact, elegantly dressed vice president, erect in his

chair with shoulders braced in his best military manner, leaning toward the tall, angular president in his down-at-the-heel slippers, farmer's breeches, and tattered red waistcoat. Jefferson slouched in his chair, one leg slung over the other in his usual style, listening to the colonel's ultimatum.

Burr was asking Jefferson to appoint him ambassador to France. He knew—and Jefferson undoubtedly also knew—that Robert R. Livingston had announced a desire to return to New York, possibly to run for governor. The vice president probably would have settled for ambassador to England—a post that had recently been vacated by General Hamilton's friend and follower Rufus King. Either assignment would take Burr out of American politics for a while, but the seething global conflict between France and England might enable him to play a role in the unpredictable future. Special Envoy James Monroe had won more than a little acclaim for his part in closing the deal for the Louisiana Purchase, although Monroe had gone out of his way to give the president all the glory. An ambassadorship would also put Colonel Burr beyond the reach of his creditors for a few years, and reassure them about his ability to pay them eventually.

Jefferson's answer was a torrent of circumlocutions and evasions, similar to the monologue that Matthew Davis had gotten when he trekked to Monticello in search of his federal job. The president "recapitulated" the election of 1800, claiming he had never "interfered directly or indirectly" to influence the choice of either Burr or himself, except that in Virginia he had taken some pains to make sure no one dropped any electoral votes for Burr, lest it be imputed to personal jealousy or ambition.

In the presidential election "now coming on" Jefferson blandly declared he was pursuing the same conduct. He had talked to no one about it and at this very moment had no idea "who were to be proposed as the candidates for the public choice." This lie was almost an insult to the vice president's intelligence. If Burr knew the Clintons and their coterie were writing letters to Jefferson, advertising the Old Incumbent for vice president, surely the president knew it.

Jefferson plunged on, claiming that he had noticed the attacks on Burr in the newspapers "but as the passing wind." Exhibiting a twinge of conscience, the president admitted he had seen complaints by some Republicans against James Cheetham, who was given the business of printing the latest federal laws in his newspaper, thus being permitted to "eat the publick bread & abuse its second officer." But Jefferson said he had nothing to do with that incongruity. The publishers were selected by the secretary of state, making it sound like this gentleman was someone from another planet, instead of James Madison, the president's closest friend and constant confidant.

As for the letter Burr mentioned, Jefferson corrected him on the date: It was written before the deadlock, when he thought all was well in the electoral college. Was Jefferson telling Burr that prior to the deadlock they had been friends but not afterward? Before the colonel could react to that implication, Jefferson plunged into a veritable disquisition on precedents set by Presidents Washington and Adams that made it impossible for him to give Vice President Burr any kind of federal appointment, such as an ambassadorship.

Jefferson thought his monologue was "indirectly an answer to [Burr's] present hints." He apparently was right, because Burr left his request for a mark of favor for Jefferson's future "consideration" and the two men conversed on "indifferent subjects" until Burr departed. The president proceeded to round out his report by stating his contempt for Vice President Burr. He "must have thot [sic] I could swallow strong things in my own favor," Jefferson wrote, dismissing Burr's claim to have taken the vice presidency only to promote the president's honor.

"I had never seen Colo. B till he came as a member of the Senate," the president continued. "his conduct very soon inspired me with distrust. I habitually cautioned Mr. Madison against trusting him too much." Jefferson added that during the Washington and Adams administrations, whenever an important military or diplomatic appointment was pending, Burr was "always at market." By way of final dismissal, Jefferson declared "there never had been an intimacy between us, and but little association."[3]

This snide comment ignores the fact that Jefferson had run for the presidency in 1796 with Burr as his vice president—surely a sign of some degree of trust. The president had also apparently forgotten the long letter he had written to Burr in 1797, after the colonel had left the Senate, giving him an inside report on the ongoing struggle with the Federalists. Proving he could flatter as assiduously as Burr when he was in the asking position, Jefferson began by saying he was sure the colonel was up on the latest political developments from reading the newspapers. But he still thought his "general view" might be useful. "At any rate," Jefferson continued, "it will give me an opportunity of recalling my self to your memory, & of evidencing my esteem for you." Burr had responded by assuring Jefferson of "my entire attachment & Esteem."[4]

In seven years, Aaron Burr had gone from esteem to contempt in the Jeffersonian worldview. The president obviously bought the Cheetham-Clinton slanders against Burr down to the last exclamation point. So complete had been their demolition of Burr, or so intense was Jefferson's vindictiveness—perhaps two sides of the same coin—the high-riding president saw no need to take seriously the vice president's threat to cause a rift in the Republican party and buy his silence with an ambassadorship.

As Colonel Burr trudged out of the presidential palace onto dark, cold Pennsylvania Avenue, he could have had no illusions about his relationship with Thomas Jefferson. That left him with only one alternative: a run for the governorship of New York. It was his last chance for political redemption.

III

This stark conclusion did not prompt the vice president to alter his plan to visit Philadelphia, where he planned to confer with leading Republicans—and spend some time with several lady friends. One, Celeste, was the subject of numerous playful references in his letters to Theodosia. Burr claimed he was in love with her and wanted to marry her. But various problems kept cropping up, not the least of which was the lady's disinclination. There was also a lady called "La R," another called "La Planche," and a third, "La Bin." The latter has been identified as Miss Susan Binney, sister of a well-known Philadelphia lawyer.[5] There was also a New Yorker he called "La G," whom Burr claimed to fear, because she might deprive him of his single state.

Two days after his disastrous interview with President Jefferson, Burr left Washington, D.C. Eight inches of snow had fallen that morning. In the cheerfully self-deprecating tone he often adopted in his letters to Theodosia, Burr described his journey: "The vice president, having with great judgment and science, calculated the gradations of cold in different latitudes, discovered that for every degree he should go north he might count on four and a half inches of snow. Thus he was sure of sixteen and a half inches at Philadelphia; twenty-one inches at New-York, and so for all intermediate space. Hence he wisely concluded to take off the wheels from his coachee and to set it on runners."

After a pleasant evening with Madame Bonaparte (nee Betsy Patterson) in Baltimore, Burr sleighed toward Philadelphia. "A hundred times he applauded the wisdom" of abandoning his wheels for runners. Suddenly, as he approached the Susquehanna River, the snow grew thin. In another two miles "the ground was bare." He dragged on to a roadside tavern, where he brooded on a world out of joint. "Having neither wife nor daughter near me on whom to vent my spleen, renders the case more deplorable," he wrote.

After treating himself to a good dinner and a bottle of wine, the vice president felt better about life. The next day, apparently having found wheels for his coachee, he was in Philadelphia, where he reported to Theodosia that everyone was marrying so rapidly, she would not have "a single single acquaintance" left. He went to a wedding supper at the home of a lady whose daughter had married into the wealthy Willing family. He could not resist adding: "Could any one suppose she was *unwilling?* He quickly confessed the pun was "Execrable!"

La R, La Planche, and La Bin seemed to be resisting this romantic epidemic. He reported visiting Miss Binney and her friend Miss Kean, who played the harp for him. He also saw Celeste several times, apparently in the company of her sisters. But there was apparently no progress toward wedding vows or some less licit consummation.

Even less satisfying to the vice president was the way the *Philadelphia Aurora* reported Burr's presence in town with maximum hostility. The paper commented on how little time he had spent in "the chair of the senate," supposedly because he devoted so much attention to his political ambitions. There were even more acid remarks on the Virginia edition of Aristides's pamphlet. The *Aurora*'s editor, William Duane, was a dedicated Jefferson worshipper and he did not take kindly to the lines about Hamilton's support of the president. Duane wondered if Burr was contemplating a "Pennsylvania edition" of Aristides, and added the colonel had "no great hopes" from the state, badly as he could use "fifteen or sixteen votes" in the coming weeks as the Republican party named its candidates for president and vice president.[6]

What Duane omitted from the *Aurora* was the probable reason for Burr's stop in Philadelphia. The Pennsylvania Republican party was being torn apart by savage feuding between radicals and moderates, most of whom disliked Duane's take-no-prisoners style. The Irishman was in the process of anointing himself pope of the state Republican party, sentencing those who disagreed with him to the political equivalent of excommunication. All this was grist for Burr's leadership of a union of honest men.

In Pennsylvania the split was exacerbated by the radicals' attack on the state's judiciary, which earned them execration in Federalist newspapers such as the *New-York Evening Post*. The state's Republican Governor, Thomas McKean, had vetoed the legislature's proposal to set up a system of referees that would have dispensed with much of the court system. On other fronts, the assault on the judicial system was more successful. In

1803 the legislature had impeached and removed a Federalist judge for expressing political opinions from the bench.

That victory led to calls for wholesale removals of any judge whose politics did not conform to the radicals' version of the will of the people. Attention soon focused on three judges of the state's supreme court, whose heads Duane imperiously demanded. Governor McKean let it be known that he sympathized strongly with the judges. Already the moderates were talking about running a separate ticket (for which Burr had a ready name) in the fall elections to blunt the radical rampage.[7]

IV

By February 8th Burr was in New York, where he reported plans to see "La G." He playfully asked Theodosia to pray for him. But her prayers would have been put to better use if they had been directed to the vice president's political problems. Burr found his New York followers in disarray, waiting for word from him on what direction he was going to take. In the Burr paper, the *Morning Chronicle*, Dr. Peter Irving had been running a series of articles, "Who Shall Be Our Next Vice President?" which catalogued Burr's claims to the job. By now Burr knew this was a lost cause.[8]

A great deal depended on whom the Clintonians nominated for the governorship. They were conferring in Albany, and Burr reported to Theodosia that "the Clintons, Livingstons &c [have] not, at last advice, decided on their candidate." The scheme to have the Old Incumbent run for both governor and vice president and then resign in favor of Ambassador Livingston seemed to be faltering. Ominous shifts were occurring beneath the surface of the Clinton-Livingston alliance, as the Clintons concentrated more and more on doing what would please President Jefferson first, last, and always.

Robert R. Livingston was no longer someone Jefferson wanted to see elevated to any office of power. The New Yorker had written unseemly letters to friends, some of which had gotten into the newspapers, claiming he and not the President's favorite, James Monroe, was responsible for the Louisiana Purchase. No small ego in his own right, the Hudson River Valley aristocrat was guilty of the Republican version of *lèse-majesté* in thus failing to give credit where it was politically correct to bestow it—on the wisdom of President Jefferson.[9]

As early as November 1803, Governor Clinton had informed his nephew that he had no desire to run for governor again. Mayor DeWitt had persuaded Uncle George to keep this decision a secret, while he labored mightily to persuade Jefferson to make the Old Incumbent his next vice president. The studied silence from Albany also prevented the Livingstons from trying to beat the political drums for the ambassador or some other member of their ambitious family, such as New York State Supreme Court Chief Justice Morgan Lewis or Associate Justice Brockholst Livingston.[10]

Burr also had his eyes on the Federalist party and there too the news was not encouraging. "Hamilton is intriguing for any candidate who can have a chance of success against A.B.," he told Theodosia. "He would doubtless become the advocate even of Dewitt [*sic*] Clinton if he should be the opponent."[11]

While arguing for Burr's right to another term as vice president, his followers had also been working to position him for a run for the Albany statehouse. In January they issued a call for a drastic widening of the franchise for the election of members of New York City's Common Council, which was still in Federalist hands, thanks to the law limiting voters to "freeholders"—major property owners.

The Burrites' next move must have produced not a little chortling in private: They called for an end to mayors by appointment. They wanted the mayor elected by the vote of the people—and they proposed to make the office a good deal less lucrative by giving the common council the right to license cart men, tavern owners, and other small businessmen who were currently lining DeWitt Clinton's pockets with fees.

The Clintonians responded by flexing the muscles of their political machine. They too recommended widening the city franchise. At a party conclave, they appointed a committee to consider the two sets of proposals. Meeting in private, the committee dropped the mayoralty proposal and sent the franchise recommendation to the state legislature as the supposedly unanimous request of the Republican party.

More important was a move that Colonel Burr made as soon as he arrived in New York. He filed a libel suit against James Cheetham for the many slanderous things he had written about the vice president in his newspaper and his pamphlets. Not a little of the lawsuit was going to be devoted to defending Burr's conduct during the presidential electoral deadlock of 1801. The *Morning Chronicle* excitedly announced that Colonel Burr planned to prosecute the case personally, and predicted it would be a crucial factor in the governorship election if the suit came to trial before the voters went to the polls on April 26.

William Coleman, the editor of the *New-York Evening Post*, watched these maneuvers with a Federalist eye that was by no means anti-Burr. Coleman opined that with the Clintonians in control of the state's courts, there was little chance of an early hearing on Mr. Cheetham's libels. Nevertheless, the lawsuit gave the *Morning Chronicle* an excuse to expatiate on the numerous ways Cheetham had smeared the vice president.

V

Still Burr made no explicit move to announce himself as a candidate. The reason was the continuing silence of George Clinton, whose unpredictability was notorious. There was no guarantee that the Jeffersonians would honor Clinton's request to become vice president. For one thing, Clinton was four years older than Jefferson and his health was poor. If he did not get the vice presidential nomination, there was a very good chance that nephew DeWitt would prevail on him to run for governor again.

On February 14th, the Republican members of the legislature caucused in Albany and named George Clinton as their candidate. The governor promptly declined the honor. Jefferson had confirmed his acceptability as his next vice president weeks ago, but again, the Clintons kept the news to themselves to sabotage a Livingston candidacy. The Albany legislators caucused again the next day to consider an alternative candidate. They settled on John Lansing, the man who had succeeded Robert R. Livingston as chancellor of the state court system.

The choice satisfied two Clinton imperatives: Lansing was not allied with the Livingstons, and he might win Federalist support, putting a large dent in Burr's prospects. The candidate had opposed the Constitution but once it was ratified had followed a moderate course as a judge. In his years on the bench he had stayed out of the political infighting of the era. He was also a scholarly somewhat colorless man who was unlikely to acquire larger political ambitions. What Uncle George and Nephew DeWitt did not factor into their calculations was Lansing's independent mind.

Three days later, on February 18th, fifteen certified Republicans met at Albany's Tontine Coffee House and nominated Aaron Burr for governor. Only two, John Swartout and William P. Van Ness, were from New York City; the rest theoretically demonstrated Burr's appeal upstate. Several of them were prominent citizens, such as Peter Townsend, owner of the Sterling Iron Works in Orange County. Still their numbers were few compared to the mass of party regulars who had nominated Lansing. The *Morning Chronicle* discreetly claimed only that the delegates came from "the different counties of the state." James Cheetham's *American Citizen* sneered at their paltry numbers and printed all but one of the delegates' names, implying that henceforth they were proscribed.

That same night, the Clintonians gathered to plan John Lansing's campaign. Before anyone could say an optimistic word, a letter arrived from the chancellor, announcing that he was withdrawing from the race. Behind the scenes, the candidate had collided with the Clintons' attitude that the state government was their personal fiefdom. Lansing had been summoned to an audience with the Old Incumbent and his nephew, and ordered to issue a statement that he would be a model Republican for his three-year term. Lansing had no difficulty translating this request into a demand for obeisance to DeWitt Clinton. The chancellor demurred at taking orders from Magnus Apollo. To humble him, the Clintons sponsored a story in the *Albany Register*, noting that a veritable laundry list of more prominent and more deserving Republicans had rejected the nomination and the party had turned to Lansing as a last resort. Infuriated, the candidate had resigned.

Frantic behind-the-scenes negotiations ensued. At one point Attorney General Ambrose Spencer reportedly offered to release a letter from a "gentleman at Albany" denouncing DeWitt Clinton as "an assuming young man" who was taking advantage of his uncle in his dotage. But Lansing refused to be placated, and bowed out with a statement that he had discovered too late his candidacy would not promote the political principles in which he long believed.[12] One of Lansing's principles was thinking for himself—something that was going out of fashion in the New York Republican party, with DeWitt Clinton at the helm.[13]

The Republican faithful could only gasp at this revelation of their political machine's malfunctioning. Down in New York City, Colonel Burr's newspaper voice, the *Morning Chronicle* chortled: "The Clintonians might well be compared to a pack of hounds that had lost the scent."[14] On February 20th, an enthusiastic group of New Yorkers met to second the vice president's Albany nomination.[15] Presiding at the Gotham meeting was Colonel Marinus Willett, one of the heroes of the sanguinary upstate Indian warfare of the Revolution.[16]

From Albany Peter Townsend reported that numerous Republicans who resented the "malice and malignance" frequently displayed by the Clintonians and Livingstons had "burst into a flame that will not be easily extinguished." Wealthy Abraham Lansing, the brother of the chancellor, and his friends "begin to be very polite to the friends of Col. Burr." Lansing apologized for not extending the usual civilities to Townsend when he visited Albany during the previous winter. He said that to be seen with a friend of Burr would have been "dangerous."[17] But Burr's candidacy and Chancellor Lansing's embarrassing withdrawal had made the Clintons less menacing.

Meanwhile, the Federalist party was in such disarray, they were not even going to name a candidate. This dolorous decision meant a lot of Federalist moderates might be inclined to vote for the candidate who called for a union of honest men. Suddenly Vice President Aaron Burr's chances of becoming governor of New York did not look so dubious after all.

CHAPTER 8

Resist, Resist, Resist
the Demagogues!

*W*hile Aaron Burr was deciding to run for governor of New York, Alexander Hamilton and Richard Harison completed their preparations for their foray against the Clinton-Jefferson alliance—the appeal of the conviction of the Hudson, New York, newspaper editor, Harry Croswell, for libeling the president. In the second week in February, Hamilton journeyed to Albany. It was a trip he took often to plead cases before the full New York State Supreme Court. In good weather he preferred to rely on his faithful horse, Riddle, but in February he and Harison probably took the mail coach for the three-day journey. The coach was almost certainly on runners. In January the *Evening Post* reported there were six inches of snow on the ground in Albany and the sleighing was "excellent."

On his arrival, Hamilton's first stop was his father-in-law Philip Schuyler's yellow brick mansion, The Pastures, about a half mile outside Albany, overlooking the ice-choked Hudson. General Schuyler had been among the first to urge Hamilton to join Croswell's defense team. A few weeks after the editor's conviction, the old man had written to Elizabeth Hamilton telling her he had been besieged by Federalists asking him to use his influence to draw her husband into the case "against that Jefferson, who disgraces not only the place he fills but produces immorality by his pernicious example." General Schuyler was not a moderate Federalist.[1]

Hamilton was greeted with the usual warmth, but the good cheer that had long prevailed at The Pastures was sadly absent on this visit. The seventy-one-year-old Schuyler was still mourning his wife, Catherine, and daughter Margarita who had died last year. The gout-crippled general was only a ghost of his once commanding presence. Seeing him could only remind Hamilton he would soon lose another aegis, once almost as important to him as George Washington.

II

Another less than cheerful aspect to the Croswell case was news that had arrived from Virginia six months ago: James Thomson Callender, the man on whom Hamilton counted to be an electrifying witness if he won a new trial for Croswell, was dead. His demise was more than a little mysterious. He had apparently fallen into the James River after a night of drinking and drowned—in three feet of water. Another version had him drowning in the same depth while taking a swim—at 3:00 A.M. Jeffersonian supporters were not above reporting that the turncoat Scottish muckraker had drowned in "congenial mud." But more than a few Federalists wondered if some Virginia friend of the president had accelerated Callender's dive into the James River with a blunt instrument.

In fact, George Hay, a member of the Virginia governor's executive council and James Monroe's son-in-law, had viciously battered the newspaperman on the head with a club several months before he died and then persuaded a Virginia court to silence Callender on the extremely dubious argument that English common law entitled the state to require a "common libeller of all the best and greatest men in our country" to post a bond against commiting further offenses. Rather than put up the money, Callender went to jail. Here was more ammunition for a Hamilton assault on the Jeffersonians's two-faced attitude toward freedom of the press.[2]

Moreover, the dead newspaperman had left behind his papers as well as his public statements that Thomas Jefferson had paid him a series of handsome sums—as much as $100 at a time—to support him while he was writing his assault on President John Adams and ex-President George Washington. Jefferson had even read proofs of *The Prospect Before Us* and returned them with a warm letter, declaring: "Such papers cannot fail to produce the best effect. They inform the thinking part of the nation." Practically admitting that he knew Callender was bad news in every sense of the term, Jefferson added: "You will know from whom this comes without a signature." When the newspaperman turned against Jefferson, he had reprinted this damning document in his scandal sheet, the *Richmond Recorder*.[3]

An examination of *The Prospect Before Us* reveals the sort of things that Jefferson apparently wanted people to think about. Callender sneered á la Tom Paine at Washington's contributions to winning the Revolution. He called President John Adams a hoary-headed incendiary and a murderer for fomenting the undeclared war with France. In a somewhat frantic letter to James Monroe, who had delivered some of his contributions to Callender, the president claimed he had only felt sorry for the editor because he was a political refugee from Scotland and was being persecuted by the Federalists under the Sedition Act.

II

Few Federalist editors equaled Harry Croswell's savagery in mocking this presidential evasion.

> It amounts to this then. He (Jefferson) read the book and from that book inferred that Callender was an object of charity. Why! One who presented a face bloated with vices, a heart black as hell—one who could be guilty of such foul falsehoods, such vile aspersions of the best and greatest man the world has yet known–he is an object of charity! No! He is the very man that an aspiring mean and hollow hypocrite would press into the service of crime. He is precisely qualified to become a tool–to spit the venom and scatter the malicious poisonous slanders of his employer. He, in short, is the very man that a dissembling patriot, pretended 'man of the people' would employ to plunge the dagger, or administer the arsenic.[4]

Along with these attacks on the Republicans' hero, Croswell had added nasty satires on New York's attorney general, Ambrose Spencer, and his local Hudson henchman, District Attorney Ebenezer Foote. He called the latter "Spencer's Foot" and published a poem in which he described the attorney general as

> drunk but not with grog
> Power and pride had set his head agog.

The hatchet-faced gimlet-eyed Spencer was a particularly good target because he had been an ardent Federalist until 1798, when he failed to get the job he wanted, comptroller of the state, and suddenly discovered a burning enthusiasm for Thomas Jefferson and George Clinton. Switching parties had paid off handsomely for Spencer. In early February 1804, the Clintons had rewarded him for convicting Croswell by appointing him to the state supreme court.

Croswell's prosecution blended with Spencer's turncoatism to inspire the young editor to one of his wittiest flights of sarcasm. In the January 26, 1803, edition of *The Wasp*, Croswell announced that since publishing "federalism and truth was against the powers that be," he was "resolved to turn his rusty coat" and devote this edition of *The Wasp* to political correctness.

Democracy and Lies

I believe that Thomas Paine and Thomas Jefferson are the two greatest men that ever were or will be upon earth; and that they are both so great that they eclipse each other's greatness. I believe that Jefferson is the greatest friend of religion and Paine the greatest friend of Washington . . . I believe that Paine as he says himself did more good in our Revolution than Washington who (to use the Democrats' ideas) was a mere old woman, led around by the nose by Hamilton.

(Zounds, if I had not turned Democrat, such mis-shapen lies would nearly choak me.)

I believe that Paine never drank a thimble full of brandy in his life; and that Jefferson spends three fourths of his time in prayer . . . I believe that Colonel Burr attempted to obtain the President's chair after having received as many votes as Jefferson and by this act he has forfeited the support and confidence of all good Democrats; and yet I believe that for doing the same thing Jefferson deserves well of his country.

I believe that General Hamilton, for the unpardonable sin of speaking and writing his thoughts freely, ought to be regarded as a dangerous man.

I believe that Ambrose the Turn Coat General, was never a Federalist; that he did not, as some of his enemies contended, become a rampant Jacobin because Governor Jay told him he had not honesty and talents sufficient for a comptroller . . . I do not believe that Spencer's Foot was ever a cobbler; because I do not believe he has ingenuity sufficient for that profession; I do not think that if the said Foot possessed a tail, he would precisely resemble a monkey. I do not believe that Foot has sufficient ingenuity to be a swindler. In short, and to waste no more paper, I do not believe that Foot is a consummate blockhead . . . My dear Ambrose, how do you like this side of my coat? Are you satisfied? —How cursed sheepish this turncoat business makes a man feel![5]

III

Here, surely, was a Federalist that General Hamilton could and would defend with enthusiasm. Richard Harison was an ideal partner in this potentially satisfying task. Not only did Harison have a deep grasp of the history of the law in America and England, as U.S. attorney for the southern district of New York, for eleven years he had been responsible for enforcing federal law in the state. He was an implicit reminder that New York law was not the final arbiter of justice in this case, especially since President Jefferson's guilt or innocence was deeply involved in its outcome.

If Hamilton could drag President Jefferson in front of a jury, either in person or through a deposition, and arraign him for slandering George Washington, he would achieve a huge political victory. In 1804 Washington was still first in war, first in peace, and first in the hearts of his countrymen. Already, his first biographer, Mason Locke Weems, was wandering the countryside, selling wagonloads of his hagiographical book *The Life and Memorable Actions of George Washington.*

At first glance, the composition of the New York Supreme Court did not bode well for Hamilton's cause. Morgan Lewis, the Chief Justice, had presided at Croswell's trial. Lewis was not likely to change his mind about the charge he had given to the Croswell jury: that the libel law of the state of New York made the truth of Croswell's assault on Jefferson irrelevant.

Two other justices, Brockholst Livingston and Smith Thompson, were also Republicans and Clinton appointees. But with either or both, Hamilton had reasonable hopes of persuasion. Livingston had worked with Hamilton on many cases. Their friendship went back to their teenage years, when they attended school together in Elizabethtown. During the Revolution, Livingston had served on General Philip Schuyler's staff and had gone to Spain with John Jay as a diplomat.[6]

Livingston was, however, a dedicated Republican. Smith Thompson was a less political man. There was a good chance that he could be influenced by Hamilton's main hope on the four-judge panel, James Kent, who was by far the ablest legal mind on the bench. In 1804 he was in the early stage of a judicial career that would win him the title of the American Blackstone.[7] Kent was, not entirely coincidentally, a confirmed admirer of General Hamilton. Since 1788, when Kent had watched Hamilton almost single-handedly defeat the Clinton apparatus and persuade New York to ratify the Constitution, he was convinced that the illegitimate refugee from the West Indies was a great man.

Ambrose Spencer, although officially appointed a justice of the court, could not with propriety take his seat. He would have to act as attorney general for a few more days, defending the conviction he had won with Morgan Lewis's help. For his assistant, he chose George Caines, a lawyer who primarily made his living as the court's stenographer. He did not have the best reputation; one justice who watched him at work called him a "profligate"—perhaps best translated as drunkard—and suggested they find someone who could at least keep decent records. [8]

To provide continuity from the trial that resulted in Croswell's conviction, Hamilton retained the services of William W. Van Ness, who had argued ably but in vain against Chief Justice Lewis the previous year. He was a cousin of Aaron Burr's literary lieutenant, William P. Van Ness. The family had long been prominent in the Hudson River valley.

On February 13, 1804, as the judges and the lawyers and defendant Croswell gathered in the supreme court chamber, a ripple of excitement ran through the taverns and boardinghouses of the Empire State's capital, where politics was an obsession on a par with Washington, D.C. Everyone sensed an historic showdown was about to take place.

IV

William W. Van Ness opened for the defense by recapitulating many of the arguments he had made in the earlier trial. He cited a plethora of cases from English common law that suggested the truth was frequently considered an issue in cases of public libel. He took particular pains to cite examples that predated the opinions of Lord Mansfield, the famous eighteenth-century English jurist, whom Lewis and Spencer had cited for their argument that the truth was irrelevant. Mansfield had political appeal to American audiences because at one point in his career he had defended John Wilkes, the English politician who had championed America against George III's policies before and during the Revolution.

George Caines replied for the prosecution. His speech took his listeners through a veritable jungle of English common law all the way back to Anglo-Saxon days, all purporting to maintain the Clintonians' claim that there was a firm tradition as well as a reasonable basis for forbidding the truth to become a bone of contention in seditious libel cases. The reasoning was, in essence, that a seditious libel against a king or other government official tended to "break the peace" and arguing about its truth in court would only tend to further fracture public tranquillity. Ambrose Spencer followed Caines and went even deeper into the underbrush of English common-law cases. Then, turning to American law, he argued that the trial of John Peter Zenger in 1734–35 was the case that created New York's libel law.

Contemporary Americans will no doubt be puzzled by Spencer's reverence for Zenger. The trial has often been cited as a landmark in the evolution of the free press in America. The German-born printer was acquitted of libeling the corrupt colonial governor, William Cosby, thanks to a passionate plea for a free press by Philadelphia lawyer Andrew Hamilton (no relation to Alexander). But in the New York of 1804, the relevant part of the case was the judge's charge to the jury, which the jurors ignored: He told them the truth was irrelevant in a public libel.

The argument was startling evidence of how far the Clintonians were ready to depart from Republican traditions to defuse their political time bomb. They were citing a case from the days of British rule, claiming a continuity that in other contexts they maintained the Revolution had ruptured, thanks to the genius and eloquence of the author of the Declaration of Independence. Spencer curtly dismissed an opinion by the former chief justice of the U.S. Supreme Court, Federalist John Jay, that the jury in a libel trial could consider the motives and facts of the case. Instead, Spencer warbled a rhetorical paean to Lord Mansfield, who he claimed would "flourish in eternal youth" when the actors in this case had vanished into oblivion. Watching this performance, defendant Croswell must have recurred to his line in *The Wasp*: "Zounds, if I were not a Democrat, such mis-shapen lies would nearly choak me."

Richard Harison spoke next, and delivered a sharp rebuttal to the Clintonian claims. He pointed out that the doctrine that the truth was immaterial in libel trials originated in the infamous juryless Star Chamber courts of the British system, used by Charles I and other kings with a tendency to despotism. There were numerous cases that predated the Star Chamber days in which British judges had ruled that the truth was a factor in libel cases. Even some of the Star Chamber judges had said this in minority opinions.[9]

Harison cleared away legal debris and effectively set the stage for Alexander Hamilton. By now the hearing was late in its second day and was absorbing the total attention of both the judicial and legislative wings of the Empire State. Newspapers reported that almost the entire senate and assembly swarmed into the supreme court chamber to hear the climax of the debate. They were there for more than the simple excitement of seeing General Hamilton in action. Already, a legislator had submitted a bill that would permit the truth to be heard in libel cases. The Clintonians were obviously trying to protect their flanks while struggling to contain this explosive threat to their center.

The British parliament had passed a similar bill in 1792. Why Governor George Clinton, the supposed man of the people, had not bothered to follow this lead is one of the many reasons why Federalists considered the Old Incumbent lazy, a faker, or both. In 1788, Hamilton had done him near-mortal damage in the state constitutional convention when Clinton's claque began damning the Constitution because it did not have a bill of rights. Hamilton had pointed out that Clinton had been governor since 1777 and never bothered to add such a document to the New York State Constitution.

V

Such memories must have stirred more than a few tremors in Republican nervous systems as the man whom Thomas Jefferson had called "a colossus" and a "host unto himself" took center stage in the supreme court chamber. Hamilton began by emphasizing the importance of the subject and went on to examine what he called "the two great points": the truth as evidence and the jury's right to examine Croswell's intent. He insisted he was not arguing for "the pestilential doctrine of an unchecked press." In a savage reference to Jefferson's alliance with Callender, he recalled to everyone's mind that the character of "the best man on earth"—George Washington—had been besmirched by such a press.

No, Hamilton declared, he was contending for the right to publish "the truth, with good motives, though the censure light on government or individuals." Above all he wanted to see "the check" on an unfettered press not in a permanent body of judges but in an "occasional and fluctuating body"—a jury. He pointed out that in the American system judges were appointed by politicians, which made them likely to be politicians themselves. The only safe anchor for freedom of the press was the right of trial by jury.

Hamilton now ranged up and down English law and even into Roman law and Biblical texts to prove that the common law had always maintained those rights, until judges became entangled with the English Star Chamber courts, whose corruption only proved his point: "a permanent body of men without the wholesome check of a jury grows absolute." Chief Justice Morgan Lewis must have squirmed at the implications of this remark.

Next, Hamilton startled many listeners by boldly defending the Sedition Act, which specified that the truth could be presented in evidence. He said he had always had "a profound reverence" for the doctrine of focusing on the truth "when public rights and the liberties of the people" were at stake. Giving the back of his hand to Caines and Spencer, he heaped praise on Chief Justice John Jay for having laid down "so correctly and broadly" the power of the jury.

Hamilton wisely made no attempt to defend the way the Sedition Law was administered by angry Federalist judges, especially Judge Samuel Chase. Too often they curtly dismissed attempts by the indicted Republican editors to introduce into the trial evidence that their statements were true. Often, as in Callender's assault on Washington, the lies were so outrageous and patent, one can have a certain sympathy with this judicial impatience. But their political wrath had inflicted near fatal wounds on the Federalist party.

From here, Hamilton soared into a long paean to the juror's rights and duties. What if this was a "capital case" and the jury decided that it did not agree with the court's interpretation of the law? Were they bound to let an honest man like Harry Croswell go to the gibbet without a challenge? Everyone knew that jurors were bound by their oaths to vote according to their consciences. Were he such a juror, Hamilton declared, he would "endure the rack" before he would "immolate his convictions on the altar of power."

Throughout the winter afternoon, Hamilton hypnotized his audience with his swift muscular oratory. James Kent, making notes on the speech, jotted that he was "sublimely eloquent." The next morning, February 15th, Hamilton took up the argument once more. His two-day speech would consume over six hours. Again he worked his way through an impressive number of citations to bolster his argument. But he soon got to the political meat of his morning's work, a philippic on American liberty.

America's most precious heritage was being endangered, Hamilton declared, not from provisional armies (a nice defense of his leadership during the undeclared war with France) but from "dependent judges and selected juries stifling the press and the voices of leaders and patriots." The enthralled Judge Kent jotted "impassioned and most eloquent" as Hamilton soared to his climax.

"We ought to resist, resist, resist until we hurl the demagogues and tyrants from their imagined thrones," Hamilton cried. Never was there a libel case where the question of the truth was more important. "It ought to be distinctly known," he thundered, "whether Mr. Jefferson [be] guilty of so foul an act as the one charged"—paying Callender to slander Washington. This bitter thought catapulted Hamilton into a eulogy of Washington that Kent thought was "never surpassed, never equalled."

Finally, a cooler Hamilton used sarcasm to pay tribute to the "other party's . . . strange and unexpected compliments to the *freedom* of the English nation." Once more, the Republicans squirmed on this self-created petard. For the previous decade, they had never missed a chance to heap abuse on Hamilton for supposedly favoring tyrannical England against revolutionary France. Now here they were, burbling over the magnificence of English law and judges.

Calmly, Hamilton reiterated his fundamental point: A country is free only where the people have a representation in the government and where they have a trial by jury. America had gone further into the "popular principle" than any other nation in history. He joined his prayers with the opposing counsel ("If indeed they do pray," he added—a tart reference to

Jeffersonian Republican hostility to religion). On bended knee he hoped the American experiment would be successful.

Hamilton's doubts on this point were evident when he returned one more time to Washington's administration, which was "unmoved by calumny and faction." It was this tendency to faction that was "the evil genius of republics." If America abandoned the principles of the common law, a faction in power could construe the words "crimes and misde-meanors" in the Constitution to make "any political tenet or indiscretion a crime." This could lead to sacrificing and crushing individuals "by the perverted forms and mask of law"—the most dangerous and destructive tyranny. Here Hamilton was speaking with a national voice, condemning the Jeffersonian attack on an independent judiciary. As the slim figure bowed to the four black-robed justices and retired to his seat, James Kent jotted a final note: *I never heard him so great.* [10]

VI

The senators and assemblymen were equally impressed by General Hamilton's eloquence. They went back to their chambers and completed work on the truth-in-libel bill, incorporating into it many of Hamilton's arguments. But the men whom Hamilton had to convince to get a new trial for Croswell were the four justices. He obviously had Kent, and the future chancellor of New York soon persuaded Smith Thompson to agree with him. That left Chief Justice Morgan Lewis and Brockholst Liv-ingston. Lewis was never going to reverse the opinion that he had handed down in the first Croswell trial. So Kent concentrated all his powers of persuasion on Livingston.

Contemporary opinion described Livingston as a "weathercock" finely attuned to the political winds. But he was also a competent lawyer. His scholarship did not match Kent's but he was open to the power of Hamil-ton's legal arguments. Turning him in the other direction was his memory of Hamilton's ferocious prosecution of the widowed owner of the New

York *Argus* and its hapless printer for accusing him of peculation while he was secretary of the treasury. Livingston had been the defense attorney in that case.

On the other hand, as a Livingston, the judge had no great loyalty to Thomas Jefferson. The president had given his man, James Monroe, far more the credit for the Louisiana Purchase than Ambassador Robert R. Livingston had received. The Jefferson administration's harsh treatment of the ambassador's younger brother, Edward Livingston, in the matter of the misappropriated federal tax money while he was federal attorney and mayor of New York was another counterweight, swinging Livingston back to a pro-Hamilton (or Kent) position. To Kent's delight, at the end of a judicial conference on Croswell's case, Livingston said he agreed with Hamilton and would vote for a new trial. Undoubtedly, Judge Kent soon communicated this good news to Hamilton.[11]

VII

Large political events were taking place outside the chambers of the supreme court. Aaron Burr's candidacy for governor was announced on February 18th, three days after the Croswell hearing ended. In the state capital, where political gossip permeated the atmosphere, everyone knew this nomination was forthcoming. A group of leading Albany Federalists met in the Lewis Tavern on February 16th, the day after Hamilton made his closing remarks on Croswell, to discuss what role, if any, the party might play in the gubernatorial campaign.[12]

General Hamilton attended this meeting with an eight-point speech in his pocket. The points were a blend of new and old charges against Aaron Burr. He began by insisting that Burr had always been a "democratic" politician and was unlikely to change now. It was foolish to think he would suddenly espouse the views of the prostrate Federalist party. Second, Burr was popular with most Clintonians and only detested by a few leaders. If he won the governorship, he would use patronage to create a formidable political juggernaut, including "such Federalists as from personal good will or interested motives" will give him support. The third point reiterated this prediction.

On the fourth point, General Hamilton revealed how much he, the ultimate insider, already knew about the plot to take New England and New York out of the union. He dwelt on Burr's distinguished New England ancestry and warned that this would make him a natural candidate to lead this new confederacy. Points five, six, and seven continued the danger of what Burr could accomplish with this secession scheme, especially if he were elected by a heavy percentage of Federalist votes.

The result would be almost certain disaster. "Every day shows more and more the much to be regretted tendency of governments entirely popular to dissolution and disorder," Hamilton declared—a revealing statement of his pessimism about America's future. Burr would only accelerate this tendency, and, worse, he would "infuse rottenness" into New England, the only part of the country where Federalist principles remained "sound."

Hamilton therefore urged the Federalists to vote for John Lansing, unaware that the chancellor was about to take himself out of the race. He argued that Lansing's personal character was good and his election would, for reasons Hamilton did not explain—and which sound like wishful thinking—divide the Republicans and lead to a revival of the party of "the wise and good."

Unknown to Hamilton and his fellow Federalists, two Burrites were eavesdropping in the next room, taking copious notes on what the General said. Burr's gift for political espionage was one of many things that did not endear him to Hamilton. On February 23rd, the *New-York Evening Post* printed a letter from Albany describing Hamilton's speech as a "harangue" that soured his own party. "The spirit of disappointed rivalship it bespeaks, is censured by all," the writer declared. He added that it was "one of the most fortunate occurrences that could have taken place," because it was bound to elevate Mr. Burr in the eyes of average Republicans. The Clintonians had been spreading the lie that Burr and Hamilton were teaming up to win the election. The writer opined that General Hamilton "rather over rates his controuling influence" on the Federalist party.[13]

To cover himself with Hamilton, *Post* editor William Coleman assured his readers that the paper was not abandoning its neutrality on Burr's candidacy. But anyone with an iota of political sophistication could see he was doing exactly that. Coleman went on to claim that General Hamilton had been reluctant to speak at the Federalist conclave and "did not offer his sentiments until just before [the meeting] broke up." The editor emphatically denied a report that General Hamilton had spoken for two hours. There are good grounds for suspecting that Coleman inserted these comments in an attempt to soften the blow of Hamilton's repudiation by his fellow Federalists.

Another part of this editorial comment bore even stronger marks of Coleman's concern for Hamilton's feelings and his understanding of the General's long-range hopes. It took issue with the "disappointed rivalship" remark. "Rivalship for what?" Coleman asked. "Is General Hamilton, or has he been a competitor with Mr. Burr for office? On the contrary, we now state as a fact, that defies contradiction, that he has more than once openly declared, that, unless called upon in the event of a foreign or civil war, he would never again accept of any office whatever, either under the general or state government."[14]

In the event of a foreign or civil war. Those words underscore how closely General Hamilton was watching developments in Europe as well as in secessionist New England. If Napoléon successfully invaded England, America might soon find herself fighting a French army in Louisiana. If New England's secessionists acted, civil war might well result if the remaining states resisted the Yankees' plan to create a separate country. One thing is clear: The only public future General Hamilton envisioned for himself was that of a man on horseback.

VIII

On February 19th Hamilton was still in Albany, arguing other cases before the supreme court. He found time to write a long letter to Robert Goodloe Harper, who was acting as defense counsel in the upcoming trial of the insane Judge Pickering. The General told Harper he viewed the impeachment of Pickering and the imminent impeachment of Supreme Court Justice Samuel Chase as the "prosecution of a deliberate plan to prostrate the independence of the Judicial Department" and substitute for the present judges "creatures of the reigning party, who will be the supple instruments of oppression and usurpation, under the forms of the Constitution."[15]

Hamilton assured Harper that he would do his best to assist him and other Federalist lawyers in defending judges and editors under Republican attack but he could not "absolutely" promise attendance. "There is hardly a sitting of our Circuit or Supreme Court, at which there are not causes depending, which involve the whole fortunes of Individuals who place a material reliance on my efforts," he wrote. This glimpse of how hard Hamilton was working as a lawyer makes all the more significant the tremendous effort he had made on behalf of Harry Croswell. Those oratorical pyrotechnics did not spring from the mouth of a man who had retired from politics.

Switching to political prediction, Hamilton told Harper that he would not be surprised if the Jeffersonians called off their war on the judiciary for the time being. It was upsetting too many moderates, especially here in New York. There was a "mass of discontent" in the state's Republican party and "Col Burr intends to profit by it, if he can." More or less confirming the letter Coleman published, reporting Hamilton's anti-Burr harangue a failure, the General ruefully admitted to Harper that Burr had "no bad chance of being lifted to the chair of government" by his personal following among the Republicans, plus malcontents disgusted with the Clintons and "federalists too angry to reason."

Again Hamilton predicted the state Republicans were about to "split into fragments, unless hereafter reunited under the more skillful, adroit, and able lead of Col. Burr." These compliments are rather startling, but Hamilton knew Harper was favorably inclined toward Burr. The General could not resist adding that he did not "look forward to his success with pleasure." It was an axiom with him, Hamilton declared, that Burr would be "the most dangerous chief that *Jacobinism* can have." He again predicted Burr's victory would lead to a "dismemberment of the Union." That was why he would rather see Lansing governor, even if it meant the New York Federalist party was "broken to pieces."[16]

The next day, while this letter was still unmailed, Hamilton added what was to him an enormously disturbing postscript. "Since writing the foregoing, Chancellor Lansing has declined and Chief Justice Lewis is the substitute. Burr's prospect has extremely brightened."

Hamilton's words were an understatement. Handsome, egotistical Morgan Lewis was a Republican party man to the core of his being. Married to Gertrude Livingston, Robert R. Livingston's sister, he owed his political existence to his brother-in-law and George Clinton. It was hard to see him attracting a single Federalist vote. Moreover, as a Livingston ally in the shaky coalition, he was liable to stir Clintonian doubts about his fairness when it came to handing out government jobs. That could cost him votes against a deal maker like Aaron Burr.

It must not have been easy for the Old Incumbent and his nephew De-Witt to turn to a man whom DeWitt had denounced in such scathing terms when he elbowed Lewis aside for mayor of New York. Though both Clintons were thorough political actors and would undoubtedly now trumpet Lewis's virtues from Long Island Sound to the St. Lawrence River, some of their followers knew how little real enthusiasm they had for their candidate.

To compound the irony, Hamilton had inadvertently given Colonel Burr powerful electoral assistance by spending two days demolishing Chief Justice Lewis for his truth-is-irrelevant ruling in the Croswell trial—something Lewis's own party was in the progress of repudiating in the legislature.

IX

General Hamilton immediately tried to find a Federalist who was willing to run for governor and siphon off enough votes to defeat Aaron Burr. Hamilton's first thought was the man he had made U.S. senator from New York and then ambassador to England—Rufus King. In the Senate he had ably defended Hamilton's financial policies and had been an equally astute ambassador to London at a time when British belligerence and Jeffersonian hostility kept American relations with England dangerously fragile.

King was a shrewd choice. Considered a moderate Federalist, he inspired nervous tremors among Republicans when he resigned as ambassador and returned to New York in mid-1803. From Paris, Robert R. Livingston had warned DeWitt Clinton that King might establish a moderate party that would seduce voters from their camp—a preview of the movement to the center that Aaron Burr was now attempting.[17]

Hamilton urged King to make the race because even if he lost he would help defeat Burr and prevent "the federalists from becoming a personal faction allied to him." There was also a distinct possibility that a Federalist could come down the middle between the two Republican factions and win. "If an attempt is to be made, You must be the candidate," Hamilton wrote on February 24th. Only someone with King's stature would convince Federalist voters that the party was in earnest, and was not simply trying to defeat Burr.[18]

X

On the same day he wrote this canny letter, General Hamilton became embroiled in a quarrel over a whispered slander against him that was a veritable summary of the kind of politics the Jeffersonian Republicans played—and Hamilton's vulnerability to their tactics. While the General was rhetorically annihilating Chief Justice Morgan Lewis in the supreme court chamber and perhaps again becoming a political force to be reckoned with, Governor Clinton was industriously circulating around Albany an old story that in 1787 Hamilton and John Adams, then ambassador to England, had negotiated with George III about the possibility of cutting a deal with London to make one of George's sons king of America. In return, the British were supposedly ready to cede Canada, Nova Scotia, and all their other American possessions to the new nation. The story purportedly proved the long-standing Republican charge that Hamilton in particular and the Federalists in general were hoping to return America to monarchical government.

The tale had first been aired in the *Pennsylvania Gazette and Journal* in the summer of 1787, while the Constitutional Convention was still in session. It had been repeated and embellished since that time, until it became a project Hamilton supposedly backed by mailing letters from his law office to influential politicians all over the country. There is a strong probability that the originator was one of Jefferson's more devious supporters, John Beckley, the man who had leaked the Maria Reynolds story to James Thomson Callender. Beckley was, not incidentally, a close friend of George Clinton.[19]

Although Hamilton was appearing in court almost every day, arguing complex cases in marine insurance and other commercial matters, he devoted much of his free time to tracking down the source of this slander. With the help of a prominent Albany merchant, James Kane, he traced it to a state senator from Westchester County, Ebenezer Purdy. Hamilton called on Purdy with Kane, who repeated in Purdy's presence the story the merchant had heard from him.

The implication of Hamilton's aggressive confrontation was all too clear. If Purdy did not have a good explanation of where the story originated, he was liable to find himself on the wrong end of General Hamilton's dueling pistol. An agitated Purdy backtracked and evaded to the best of his ability but he finally admitted that he had heard the story from Governor Clinton. The Old Incumbent claimed there was an eyewitness who could confirm the existence of a Hamilton letter discussing the purported negotiation with George III. Crumpling under Hamilton's steely glare, Purdy said that the governor had told him he had a copy of the letter, and had mentioned the name of the man who had originated the story. However, Purdy claimed he could not remember the name; he only recalled the man was from Westchester County.

Two days later, on Saturday, February 25th, Hamilton called on State Senator Purdy again. This time he was accompanied by his friend Nathaniel Pendleton. Choosing this ex-soldier as his partner for the second interview with Mr. Purdy emphasized to the squirming state senator that he was getting closer to smelling gunpowder. Pendleton took extensive notes and drafted a memorandum of the conversation for Hamilton's use. The document described Hamilton grilling Purdy again about the identity of the slanderer, whose name the state senator still declined to reveal. Purdy said he now remembered his name but did not want to mention it without the gentleman's consent.

Is he in Albany? Hamilton bristled.

No, Purdy said. He live[s] in Westchester.

"This is a slander I am determined to trace," Hamilton said. He wanted the man's name from Purdy "as soon as possible." [20]

The following Monday, Pendleton called on Purdy again to obtain the slanderer's name. Purdy would still only confirm that he lived in Westchester County. The previous day, Purdy had informed Governor Clinton that Hamilton was on the rampage. Clinton immediately fired off a letter to the man in Westchester County who Purdy considered the source of the slander. He happened to be the governor's son-in-law, former Republican assemblyman Pierre Van Cortlandt Jr., who had studied law under Hamilton.

In a tone that can only be described as gloating, Clinton wrote: "I presume I shall be honored with a Letter from the General on this subject, and I have thought proper to apprize you of it that you may be on your guard. It will be prudent not to utter a sylable [*sic*] on the subject to any person whatever till you hear further from me."[21] The game was obviously to torment Hamilton as long as possible.

Three days later, Van Cortlandt wrote a nervous letter to an unknown correspondent in which he claimed to have visited Hamilton's law office in mid–1787 and seen the letter in question, signed by John Adams. Hamilton's law clerk at the time, Joseph Strong, tried to conceal it but Van Cortlandt had persuaded him to display the document, which Strong was purportedly copying to send to Hamilton followers in the southern states. Van Cortlandt piously claimed he never planned to say a word about the letter to anyone, "from my personal friendship to Mr. Hamilton at that time." But when he learned that Hamilton had proposed a king for America in the Constitutional Convention, Van Cortlandt decided that patriotism overrode the obligations of friendship and began broadcasting the story of the letter to numerous people, including "the Governor." [22]

This tangle of fact and fiction is a veritable case history of the way a slander grew from a germ of truth—Hamilton's Constitutional Convention proposal of a president for life—to a smear that political enemies manipulated for their pleasure and profit. Van Cortlandt may well have seen a copy of the letter in Hamilton's office. He was probably mailing it to friends, asking them to help him rebut it and/or track down its originator. Hamilton's reemergence as a political force at the Croswell hearing made the governor reach for this old weapon as a tried-and-true retaliation.

As Clinton predicted, Hamilton wrote to him on February 27th, describing the "very odious slander [that had] been in circulation to the prejudice of my character." Now he had tracked it to Clinton's door: "The very mention of your name adds importance to the affair and increases the motives to investigation." He asked Clinton for "a frank and candid explanation of so much of the matter as relates to yourself."

Clinton replied two days later, saying he had told Purdy that he had seen a copy of the letter. It was shown to him in 1787 by a long-dead revolutionary war general, William Malcolm, who by ironic coincidence was Aaron Burr's commander. Malcolm told Clinton he had received the letter from Connecticut. It had no signature and was not addressed to anyone.

This hardly jibed with the story that Pierre Van Cortlandt Jr. was retailing at almost the same time: a letter signed by John Adams and copied in Hamilton's office. Clinton was obviously sidestepping Hamilton's accusation by blaming the whole thing on a dead man and denying that he ever said Hamilton had anything to do with it. In a word, the Old Incumbent was lying. On March 2nd, a dissatisfied Hamilton replied that he wanted to see the letter, if it was in Clinton's papers, and requested permission to make a copy of it.

Clinton replied four days later in a style that emanated menace. He said he could not imagine why Hamilton was still bothering him. Was he questioning the truth of his "explicit declaration" in his previous letter that he never connected Hamilton to the letter? "This I trust will not be attempted," he wrote, implying that if Hamilton called him a liar, he was ready to reach for his dueling pistols.

Clinton then spent several paragraphs claiming he could not remember exactly what he had said to Purdy, nor could he recall whether he had kept a copy of the letter or returned it to General Malcolm. He could not find it in a search of his papers. With supreme nastiness, the Old Incumbent added that he considered the charge of trying to establish a monarchical government in the United States "odious and disreputable" and he was pleased to find Hamilton agreed with him "however much we may differ on other political Subjects."[23] He added that if he found the letter, he would let Hamilton make a copy.

The next day, Clinton wrote again to Pierre Van Cortlandt Jr., enclosing copies of Hamilton's letters. He told his son-in-law that he thought Hamilton wanted to see a copy of the letter because he was afraid it would be in Strong's handwriting, which would prove it had passed through his office. Clinton said he did not tell Hamilton he had seen a copy of "the original Copy only." The governor gleefully added that he "thought it prudent to leave the General in Doubt on this Subject." The use of the term, "original copy" suggests that Clinton was in on the secret of the Beckley fabrication of the slander from the start.[24]

General Hamilton was left swinging in the political wind, mocked and frustrated by the Old Incumbent. To cap the General's woes, he received a letter from Rufus King, turning down Hamilton's plea to run for governor on the Federalist ticket. King thought a man of "virtue & independence" would be very unhappy in the governor's chair, considering the confused state of the political parties.[25] This egotistic rejection by a man who owed his entire political career to Hamilton's backing must have been especially painful. It underscored Hamilton's almost total loss of power and influence among his fellow Federalists. The General was left to brood on the ominous fact that Aaron Burr looked more and more like the only man who was ready, willing, and able to take command of the leaderless party.

XI

By this time the magnificent speech General Hamilton had made on behalf of Harry Croswell, with its smashing attack on Jefferson, had turned to ashes on his lips. The combination of Burr's emergence as a candidate, the General's repudiation by the Federalist caucus, the Clintonians disarray, the Old Incumbent's slander, and Rufus King's rejection left Hamilton feeling helpless and adrift in the midst of events—a demoralizing experience for a man who had once seen himself as the director of the nation's destiny.

Hamilton seized frantically on the only shred of political influence within reach—his opposition to Aaron Burr. He continued to flail accusations at the vice president to anyone who would listen. One evening he went to dinner at the home of Judge John Tayler, an ex–New Yorker who had been an Albany resident for decades. Tayler was a moderate Republican who had served many terms in the legislature as an assemblyman and senator. He had been proposed as a candidate for governor at the Republican caucus but declined the honor in favor of John Lansing.

Judge James Kent was at the dinner, along with Nathaniel Pendleton. Hamilton inveighed against Burr in terms and language that apparently went far beyond what he said in the Federalist caucus at Lewis Tavern. Among the guests was Dr. Charles D. Cooper, who happened to be John Tayler's son-in-law. Judge Kent and Pendleton nodded agreement with Hamilton's characterization of Burr as a "dangerous man . . . who ought not to be trusted." Whereupon Hamilton apparently added a commentary on Burr's character, which no doubt repeated some of his well-worn terms, such as "debauched," "profligate," and "bankrupt beyond redemption." This was, of course, exactly what Tayler and his fellow Clinton allies were eager to hear. Dr. Cooper was one of the most attentive listeners. He forthwith resolved to become a dedicated opponent of Vice President Burr. The earnest young physician could not foresee that his enthusiasm would have fatal consequences for General Hamilton.[26]

With all his insider's astuteness and experience in anticipating the future, General Hamilton was equally unaware that death would be the outcome of his harangue against Aaron Burr at Judge Tayler's dinner table. Like everyone else in the drama, he was groping into the future, living day by day, trying to cope with the unnerving mixture of hatred and admiration, victories and defeats, ambition and regret in which his life had become entangled.

Although the General's political rhetoric retained its youthful depth and brilliance, as his performance on behalf of Harry Croswell demonstrated, no amount of genius could add wisdom to his crowded mind and burdened heart. That required time for rest and reflection, an indulgence his tormented finances did not permit and his soldierly soul would have probably rejected, even if a temporary retreat were possible.

CHAPTER 9

Does Impeachment Justify Secession?

*B*y the time General Hamilton assaulted Aaron Burr's political and personal character at Judge Tayler's table, the vice president was back in Washington, D.C., presiding at the impeachment trial of Judge John Pickering of New Hampshire. Even before Burr returned, he had learned news that considerably dampened the euphoria he and his followers felt, watching the Clinton-Livingston machine flounder in its search for a gubernatorial candidate.

On February 25th, the Republicans in the U.S. Senate and the House of Representatives had caucused to nominate the next president and vice president. Thomas Jefferson had won the top slot unanimously, which surprised no one. For vice president, George Clinton of New York received sixty-seven votes. Senator John Breckinridge of Kentucky was a distant second, with twenty-one votes. A handful of favorite sons received a few votes. Vice President Aaron Burr received none.

This total repudiation by the party that he had lifted to national power only four years ago must have been very hard for a proud man to swallow. It was proof, if any was needed, of the awesome control Thomas Jefferson wielded over his followers—and the grievous mistake Aaron Burr had made in 1801, when he allowed some people to think he was ready to replace Mr. Jefferson as president, even if his intention had been merely to retain the party victory that his energy and leadership had helped to win.

Whatever he felt, Burr maintained his usual aplomb as he took his seat on the Senate's dais for the opening arguments in Judge Pickering's trial.

He was overseeing a drama that had considerable potential for tearing the Republican party apart and splintering Thomas Jefferson's power. That must have stirred dreams of revenge, as John Randolph and the four other House of Representative managers of the impeachment entered the Senate chamber, followed by most of their fellow congressmen.

"Some of our democrats feel uneasy," Senator William Plumer of New Hampshire told a correspondent. "They do not wish to act either as accuser or judges of a madman."

One Republican senator told Plumer that he was "resolved *not* to believe Pickering insane" no matter what he heard. All he wanted to know was whether he had committed the outrageous acts specified in the House indictment. Several other senators were saying the same thing. "But still they feel embarrassed [and] fear to meet the shaft of ridicule . . . should the trial be farcical indeed!" Plumer wrote.[1]

The business began precisely at noon on March 2nd. After assigning special seats to the speaker of the House and to the five prosecutors, Burr left the other congressmen to shift for themselves. They were, Federalist Senator Plumer noted with covert pleasure, "not well accommodated." Why should the vice president be deferential to politicians who had just humiliated him?

Burr ordered the Senate crier to call Judge Pickering. Three times the judge's name rang out—without response. The vice president announced that he had a letter from defense attorney Robert Goodloe Harper, enclosing a petition from Judge Pickering's son, Jacob Pickering, addressed to the court. Burr directed the secretary of the senate to read both documents.

Jacob Pickering reported his father was insane and incapable of defending himself. He asked for a postponement; the old man was in poor health and could not possibly travel to Washington from New Hampshire "at this inclement season of the year." In Harper's letter, the attorney said he wanted to appear as counsel for Judge Pickering's son, not for the judge, who was incapable of authorizing anyone to represent him. Harper said he had evidence to support these facts and asked to be admitted to the trial.

Vice President Burr invited Harper to take a seat on the Senate floor, and the ex-congressman addressed the conclave. He urged a postponement. If a delay was not forthcoming, he asked permission to introduce witnesses who would prove the judge was insane. Vice President Burr said he thought Harper was entitled to be heard.

Immediately, one of the managers, Maryland Congressman Joseph Hopper Nicholson, objected to the vice president's ruling. He argued that the testimony was irrelevant and contrary to the rules the Senate had agreed upon, which limited participants to Pickering, his counsel, or someone delegated to speak for him as his agent. The other managers vociferously concurred. Nicholson demanded to know why the House of Representatives was called to attend the trial when the accused had defaulted. Vice President Burr smoothly replied that until the trial legally began, he could not affirm or deny whether the defendant had failed to appear. As to whether Mr. Harper was entitled to speak for Judge Pickering, he thought this was something the Senate as a whole should decide. They should therefore retire to the nearby committee room and discuss it.[2]

Senator Plumer overheard Jefferson's majority leader, Senator Wilson Cary Nicholas of Virginia, growl to Senator John Breckinridge of Kentucky "shall we obey [that] order to retire?" Breckinridge muttered, "We must." Vice President Burr led the solons into the committee room, leaving the fuming managers and congressmen to stare at each other for the rest of the day. In the committee room, the Jeffersonian leaders argued that Pickering had defaulted and urged that Harper be barred. A ferocious debate erupted, with many senators pointing out that in any court of law in England or America, if a man accused of a crime was said to be insane, the jury was asked to pass judgment on his condition before proceeding to try him. Unable to reach agreement, the senators finally returned to their chamber to announce to the dismayed congressmen that they were adjourning for the day.

The next morning, the Jeffersonians revealed their anxiety to keep Pickering's insanity as little known as possible. They tried to expunge from the previous day's record Jacob Pickering's petition and Harper's letter and appearance. This was "surplusage," Senator Breckinridge blandly declared. All that should be in the record was the judge's default. This motion only brought on another day of violent argument. Breckinridge claimed it was the custom in the courts where he practiced for the presiding judge to correct the record of the previous day's proceedings, limiting it to essential facts. Maybe they did that in Kentucky, he was told, but not in any other court in America. In that retort was an implied dig at the Kentucky Republicans' attempt to undermine their state judiciary.

On Monday, March 5th, Vice President Burr threw more sand into the Jeffersonian machinery. He announced he had "certain affidavits" from Mr. Harper that would prove Judge Pickering insane. Senator Wilson Cary Nicholas immediately objected and more hours of wrangling erupted. The Federalists, led by Senator John Quincy Adams, were determined to include the evidence, because they thought it would bring the whole procedure to a dead stop, and embarrass if not halt President Jefferson's war on the judiciary. Finally, Vice President Burr called for a vote and nine Republicans deserted the president, joining nine Federalists for an 18 to 12 majority in favor of admitting Harper's testimony. The House managers, led by the choleric John Randolph, denounced the decision and withdrew from the proceedings.

They soon realized this behavior got them nowhere and returned to hear Harper's affidavits read. The Maryland attorney closed his appearance with a plea against convicting an insane man of a criminal offense and renewed his request for an indefinite postponement. Once more the Jeffersonians found themselves in a bind. But by this time, urgent pressure was coming from the presidential palace. The Senate's Republicans flexed their majority muscles and voted to continue the trial. Witnesses for the prosecution were called. Senator John Quincy Adams noted in his diary the decision had evidently "been settled by the ruling party out of court."[3]

From that point, Burr's power to influence the outcome largely vanished. So did any resemblance to a fair trial. The hostile witnesses were all Republicans, most of whom President Jefferson had appointed to government jobs. There was no defense attorney to cross-examine them about Pickering's conduct. Robert Goodloe Harper, still insisting he could not represent an insane man, had departed. Ignoring final pleas from New England senators against the cruelty of inflicting disgrace on the family of a man who had long and honorably served his country, on March 12th the Republicans voted to convict Judge Pickering by a vote of 19 to 7. They fudged the issue of his insanity by saying nothing about treason, bribery, or high crimes and misdemeanors in their votes on the articles of impeachment. Nevertheless, eight senators absented themselves rather than vote either way.

On the same day, John Randolph and his fellow House radicals reported articles of impeachment against Supreme Court Justice Samuel Chase for his supposedly criminal treatment of Republican editors who came before him as violators of the Sedition Act, and other political excesses. The Jefferson impeachment machine was not going to slow down because of the bumps in the road encountered in the demolition of Judge Pickering.[4]

II

By that time, Vice President Aaron Burr was on the way to New York. He had left the Senate on March 10th. From Baltimore he wrote to his good friend Congressman Oliver Phelps, whom he had persuaded to run on his ticket for lieutenant governor. Phelps was a Connecticut-born landowner and speculator with large holdings in western New York and elsewhere. He had been wary about joining Burr. As recently as February 1st he had assured Postmaster General Gideon Granger that he was not siding with the vice president.

Phelps's glory days as a speculator were behind him. When the outbreak of the Napoléonic wars dried up immigration and burst the speculative bubble, Phelps had been forced to go into hiding to escape his creditors. He was in no position to offend those in power. But Burr had a long relationship with Phelps, going back to revolutionary war days, when his stepfather, Timothy Edwards, had worked with Phelps as an army contractor. In his early New York land speculations, Phelps had received numerous favors from Burr when the colonel was attorney general of New York.[5]

Phelps may have changed his mind when he learned that Jefferson was throwing Burr out of the party without even a scrap of consolation such as an ambassadorship or judgeship. The president's vindictiveness was bound to stir sympathy for Burr, at least among politicians who did not believe Cheetham's slanders.

Phelps did not attend the congressional caucus that nominated George Clinton and repudiated Burr. His absence immediately triggered letters to New York from watchful Postmaster General Granger. In fact, Granger carried watchfulness beyond the ordinary bounds of political custom. He had a spy in Burr's camp, his brother, Erastus Granger, who worked as an Indian agent in northern New York and pretended to be a close friend of Phelps and other Burrites in that region. He regularly reported what he heard to his brother Gideon, who passed on Burr's plans to President Jefferson and the Clintons.[6]

In his letter, Burr urged Phelps not to leave Washington until he had "the other conversation you proposed." He said it would be worth ten days delay if it could be accomplished. Burr was talking about a visit to President Jefferson, at which Phelps hoped to extract a promise of neutrality in the New York governorship race. Burr had attempted to win such a commitment from Jefferson before he left Washington and failed.[7]

Burr apparently felt a need to block a Clintonian move to claim Jefferson's support for their candidate, Morgan Lewis. Since the president had made it brutally clear that he wanted nothing more to do with Aaron Burr, this attempt to win his silence seems almost superfluous. But in a political contest where every vote counted, Burr probably decided he had nothing to lose by trying to keep Jefferson out of the fight. Also, Phelps thought he could obtain a written declaration of neutrality from Jefferson that might be produced at the right moment with potentially strong impact on the Clintonians.

Phelps saw Jefferson a few days later and soon realized there was no chance of getting a written statement. He had to be satisfied with a verbal declaration of the president's neutrality, plus a warning that any attack on the administration or on Jefferson personally would be resented and would be met with a sharp response. The only thing Congressman Phelps brought with him from Washington was a letter of his own, describing his visit to Jefferson and what he had been told. It was better than nothing, but not a lot better.

Apparently Burr decided Phelps's statement was unsatisfactory. A few days later in March, another upstate pro-Burr congressman, the huge, ebullient Erastus Root, tackled the president on the same mission. He too got the by now standard statement of neutrality—as long as the Burr camp did not attack Jefferson and his policies.

The result of these maneuvers may have been a negative for Burr. In political circles, where every move he made was discussed and analyzed, this attempt to neutralize Jefferson probably made the vice president look weak at the very moment when, running against a dubious candidate, he had a chance to look strong. The president's demand for party loyalty also stifled Burr on subjects where he might have spoken out with considerable effect. Simmering just below the surface of the Republican party in New York was a growing dislike of Virginia's hegemony. The aging George Clinton's pursuit of the vice presidency could have—and probably should have—been ridiculed as an ego trip and little else. The Clintons were playing humble second fiddles to the Virginians in return for control of New York's share of federal jobs. Everyone knew the Old Incumbent would never become president and, in fact, was not qualified to do the job.

New York's Federalists would have been delighted by such a line of attack. But Burr and his advisors thought Jefferson's tacit neutrality was worth more than a confrontational assault on the Clinton-Jefferson alliance. They would soon learn that the president had some maneuvers up his sleeve that would amount to something less than a double cross, but also a good deal less than keeping his word.

Burr may have suspected something along that line. On this trip to New York there were no blithely self-mocking letters to Theodosia or wry references to Celeste, La G, and his other ladies in perpetual waiting. Instead, Burr's mood seems to have grown more and more saturnine as he approached the battlefield. In Philadelphia, he stayed at the home of his friend Charles Biddle. They sat up late, discussing the oncoming contest. Toward the end of the conversation, Burr bitterly described the way he had been slandered by the Clintonians and by Hamilton. He said he was "determined to call out the first man of any respectability concerned in the[se] infamous publications" about him. The words, as Biddle remembered them years later in his autobiography, suggest that Burr's rage was focused at this point on the Clintons. They were responsible for the infamous publications. Hamilton's newspaper, the *New-York Evening Post*, had already declared its neutrality in the race, and would soon reveal editor William Coleman's distinct tilt toward Burr.[8]

III

Colonel Burr was doing something far more explosive than weighing the advantages and disadvantages of attacking Thomas Jefferson. The vice president was continuing to talk to New England Federalists about the plan to create a secessionist northeast confederacy. Although some of these politicians, such as New Hampshire's Senator William Plumer, had been disillusioned with Burr's lack of full commitment to the idea in their talks in Washington, Jefferson's mounting attack on the judiciary inspired new desperation in their hearts and they continued to pursue Burr in spite of their doubts.

Exactly what Burr thought and felt about this idea is hard to pin down. But the colonel was unquestionably sending signals that he was not averse to the proposition. In Connecticut, his brother-in-law, Tapping Reeve, founder of the first law school in America and a judge of the state's superior court, was writing letters in all directions, telling everyone, including his numerous influential graduates, that secession was New England's only hope of escape from the rising tide of Jeffersonian power. Unquestionably, Reeve's secessionist inclinations were spurred by Jefferson's attack on the judiciary and his brother-in-law's opposition to it. "I have seen many of our friends; and all that I have seen and most that I have heard from believe that we must separate, and this is the most favorable moment," Reeve told Connecticut Senator Uriah Tracy.[9]

Senator Timothy Pickering of Massachusetts was more convinced than ever that the secessionist movement had a rendezvous with destiny. He too fastened on the assault on the judiciary as a prime reason, along with the Louisiana Purchase's impact on the national balance of power. "It is the intention to impeach every judge who, in his charges to the grand juries, has given a political opinion," he told one correspondent.

Pickering's hatred of President Jefferson was all consuming. In December 1803, he had written to Rufus Putnam of Massachusetts, a distinguished soldier of the Revolution, whom Jefferson had removed from his job as the federal government's surveyor general: "Alas, mistaken soldier, you find, after the lapse of only twenty years, that liberty is the right of adopting the political opinions of the present chief ruler, & independence the privilege of bowing obsequiously to his will."[10]

Not all Federalists agreed with Pickering's call for early secession. Wealthy former U.S. Senator George Cabot of Massachusetts, one of the leading lights of New England politics, agreed with Pickering's analysis of the Jeffersonian plague, but did not think the people were ready for secession yet. He feared a premature declaration of New England's independence would ruin any politician who made it. But Pickering ignored Cabot's cautious advice and kept widening his net of correspondents.

Other currents flowing from Washington, D.C., also fed the secession movement. President Jefferson's protocol quarrel with Ambassador

Anthony Merry was viewed by the New Englanders as further proof that the Democratic Emperor, as some Federalists called the president, was tilting his foreign policy toward France. This was unacceptable to a region that relied for its wealth on trading with the world's dominant commercial power, England.

Pickering was industriously collecting support from anyone who would listen to him. He persuaded William Rawle of Pennsylvania, a noted Constitutional thinker, to agree that the northern states would "probably separate."[11] The Senator told federal judge Richard Peters of Pennsylvania, who had been linked with Chase as a candidate for early impeachment, that the new confederacy would be "exempt from the corrupt and corrupting influence and oppression of the aristocratic democrats of the South." He predicted that "the British provinces"—Canada and Nova Scotia—would become members of the new Confederacy with the "consent" of the British government.[12] Next would come a treaty of friendship and commerce between Great Britain and this new "Northern League," which the ex-secretary of state undoubtedly envisioned himself negotiating.

IV

There was another reason why the New England men gravitated to Burr, aside from their desperate desire to back a winner. In the years since the American Revolution, the population of New York had grown faster than that of any other state. Almost all the growth had come in northern New York, and almost all the newcomers were New England men, migrating from overcrowded Connecticut and Massachusetts and Rhode Island. The Clintonians had rejoiced in this influx at first. They saw the immigrants as poor, and that made them natural candidates for enlistment in the Republican party. But they soon realized that these people were closer to middle class, and were all thoroughly indoctrinated with Federalist ideas.

It was Aaron Burr who changed this situation. In the two years he spent in the New York State Assembly after he left the U.S. Senate, he concentrated on ingratiating himself with a dozen representatives from the western district, all of them nominal Federalists. He turned them into Republicans and they too had played a part in swinging New York behind the Jefferson-Burr ticket in 1800.[13] It seemed reasonable to assume Colonel Burr could work the same magic on these former Federalists and not only persuade them to elect him governor, but follow him into a New England confederacy.

Moreover, Colonel Burr could call for support not only on a major landowner such as Oliver Phelps. He was also a warm friend of the man who had done more to transform northern New York than anyone else in the state—Charles Williamson. This was the ex-British army officer whom Robert Troup attempted to persuade Alexander Hamilton to join as a secret partner. Williamson had become the agent for a stupendous swath of the Genesee River valley known as the Pulteney Purchase, after the wealthy Englishman who put up most of the money. It totaled 1,264,000 acres and was valued at $2,687,682.25. For a decade, Williamson had toiled along the Genesee to create townships, complete with roads, taverns, even a hotel on Seneca Lake. The energetic Scot had spent a staggering $1,374,470 on this vast scheme. Burr had done him many favors in the legislature. Now Williamson was in New York, renting a house Burr partially owned, transferring his responsibility for super-intending the Pulteney Purchase to Burr's (and Hamilton's) old friend Robert Troup. But as long as Williamson remained in the state, he was a potent spokesman for Burr.

President Jefferson's chief watchdog, Postmaster General Gideon Granger, continued to monitor Burr's campaign. This Connecticut-born, Yale-educated lawyer was an acute student of the political weather. On March 27th, he wrote DeWitt Clinton a very nervous letter about the implications of the numerous Yankees of the ten northern counties of New York and their links to New England. He warned Clinton that the election depended heavily on their vote and he feared they would "go with New England whenever her citizens are agreed among themselves."

Granger was obviously upset by the "violent measures" pursued by the Jeffersonians in Congress, in particular the attack on the judiciary. John Randolph was also still heaping insults on the Yazoo investors, declaring they were a bunch of crooks who deserved to lose their mostly Yankee shirts. The postmaster general, a Yazooist with a 160,000-acre claim, predicted if the administration did not change its policies, in three years the "six eastern states" (New York and the five New England states) will "be united" and "will take with them New Jersey." Even if they did not secede, they would need only four votes in the Senate and fourteen in the House to form a majority and take over the country. Everyone on both sides was acutely aware of what was at stake in Colonel Burr's run for governor.[14]

V

On March 4, 1804, Senator Timothy Pickering wrote to General Hamilton's close friend Rufus King, virtually repeating Granger's prophecy, while coloring it with his hatred of Jefferson: "I am disgusted with the men who now rule, and with their measures." He called the president "a cowardly wretch" who prated like a Parisian revolutionary about humanity while taking "infernal pleasure" in the "utter destruction" of his political opponents. Burr, Pickering told King, was their one hope of breaking the "democratic phalanx." With New York detached from Jefferson's clutches under Burr's administration, "the whole union would be benefited." Jefferson would be forced to temper his policies and if a separation should be deemed proper, "the five New England states, New York and New Jersey would naturally be united."[15]

The secessionists' goal was a gradual conversion of doubters like George Cabot and Rufus King, and the eventual conversion of General Hamilton, with their help. The plan seemed to be working. On March 17th, George Cabot wrote to King, coming very close to endorsing the idea: "An experiment has been suggested by some of our friends, to which I object that it is impracticable." But he added that "the thing proposed is obvious and natural" and "the time may soon come when it will be demanded by the people of the North and East, and then it will unavoidably take place."

Cabot added that he would "rejoice to see Burr win the race" in your state, although he felt "leading" Federalists should not visibly support him. This last cautionary advice may have been an attempt to soothe General Hamilton's vanity by pretending to follow his leadership while most of the party did the precise opposite.

VI

When Congress adjourned on March 27th, some of the foremost secessionists headed for New York. Pickering called on Rufus King to try to persuade him to join them. So far, all Pickering had gotten from the former senator and ambassador was a vague approval of his anti-Jefferson sentiments. King persisted in resisting Pickering's entreaties. On the way out of King's house, the senator encountered John Quincy Adams, who was equally anxious to learn what King was thinking for the opposite reason. Senator Adams strongly opposed the secessionists' scheme, largely because of Pickering's role in it. Pickering hated Senator Adams's father, ex-President John Adams, who fired him as secretary of state, almost as much as he despised Jefferson.

There is no record of a Pickering meeting with Burr, although, considering the senator's all-out endorsement of the vice president, it is hard to believe they did not exchange a few clandestine words. Another conspirator, Congressman Roger Griswold of Connecticut, left a lively account of a conference with the vice president. Griswold wrote to Oliver Wolcott Jr., asking him to arrange the meeting because he had no "intimacy" with Burr. In Washington, the vice president had spoken "in the most bitter terms of the Virginia faction," but Griswold wanted to know more about Burr's "ultimate objects."[16]

On April 4th, Griswold met Burr in New York, probably at his Richmond Hill mansion. The Connecticut congressman undoubtedly asked the pointed questions he had in mind. If Burr won the governorship, would he go along with a New York–New England secession from the union? Was he an authentic opponent of Virginia's hegemony? Was his union of honest men ready to become a reality?

As a spokesman for the North against Virginia and Jefferson, Burr left nothing to be desired. He said the northern states "must be governed by Virginia—or govern Virginia." There was no "middle ground" on this point. He also assured Griswold that a substantial number of Republicans from above the Mason-Dixon line were of this opinion. He mentioned Oliver Phelps, Erastus Root, and two others as cases in point. He also said "some of the leaders" in New Jersey shared the opinion "and likewise in Pennsylvania." Obviously, the vice president had not been wasting his time while traveling between New York and Washington for the past three years.

As for secession, Burr was evasive if not noncommittal. He made it clear that his first task was to win the governorship. If he succeeded, he assured Griswold he would "administer the government in a manner that would be satisfactory" to Federalists—code for a promise to give them a hefty slice of the available jobs. This statement was good enough to draw from Griswold a guarantee of Federalist support, even though he voiced doubts about Burr's character to some of his friends. As a fellow politician Griswold almost certainly realized Burr's pledge was the most he could expect from a candidate in the middle of a do-or-die political struggle. The vice president would have been insane to commit himself openly to a secessionist scheme at this point. But the mere fact that he was talking to Griswold again made it clear that he was still neither shocked nor opposed to the idea. [17]

John Quincy Adams met with Colonel Burr a few days after his meeting with Griswold. Burr knew from their contacts in the Senate that Adams opposed secession, and the vice president avoided the topic. Instead, Burr portrayed himself as a reluctant gubernatorial candidate. He had agreed to run only because he was opposed to "these family combinations" that undercut the whole idea of democracy. In short, he was fighting the Clinton-Livingston alliance. There was a hint in Senator Adams's diary entry that he thought he was hearing less than the whole truth. He wrote "etc etc etc" after Burr's evasive comments. Being a version of a family combination himself, Adams was probably not enthused by the colonel's remarks.

On his visit to New York, Senator Pickering called on General Hamilton. No two men had worked harder to keep the Federalists in power. They were united in their loathing for Thomas Jefferson. But Hamilton refused to countenance the idea of a New England confederacy, because Burr was going to head it. The General restated the opinion he had broadcast in Albany: Putting Burr at the head of any government would open the door to an American version of Jacobinism. In fact, operating within the smaller New England confederacy, Burr's demagoguery might be even more difficult to control. [18]

However, Hamilton agreed to attend a meeting in Boston in the fall, where the wisdom of secession would be thrashed out at length among representatives from all the New England states. Would the General come as an avowed opponent or would he follow his friend George Cabot's course and agree that the thing was "obvious and natural" and the only question to be decided was the right political moment? Pickering obviously hoped for the latter, and probably told himself that if Burr became governor of New York, the right political moment would be at hand, whether General Hamilton liked it or not.

CHAPTER 10

Mudslingers
Front and Center

*M*eanwhile, Aaron Burr was fighting DeWitt Clinton for his political life. From the start of the battle, the vice president sought to exploit Chief Justice Morgan Lewis's embarrassing nomination by running as the advocate of the people against the tyranny and greed of New York's political bosses. In the *Morning Chronicle*, Burr's editor, Dr. Peter Irving, ridiculed the on again off again nominations of the Republican legislative caucus, picturing them as little more than puppets of the Clinton-Livingston machine. Dr. Irving argued that nominating candidates was none of the legislators' business. They had been sent to Albany to make laws for the government of New York.[1]

The *Chronicle* repeatedly described Morgan Lewis as "the aristocratic candidate" or "the candidate of the associated *families*." On the day the news of Lewis's nomination reached New York, the *Chronicle* sneered "the *families* have chosen for the people." Occasionally the *Chronicle* tried to portray Burr as a victim of Clinton-Livingston political greed. The newspaper accused the alliance of trying "to divide the Union and this state between them."[2] Burr, on the other hand, had "no long roll of family connections standing with open mouths and greedy hands to grasp every station of emolument or honor in the gift of government."[3]

To prove their point, the Burr organization put together a smashing handbill, *PLAIN TRUTH*, addressed to "the independent electors of the state." In it were lists of names of Livingstons and Clintons and their relatives and in-laws, with the exact salaries each of them made. The totals came to $53,550 for the Clintons and $33,950 for the Livingstons. In the light of these figures, what would Morgan Lewis's election mean? Voters would be erecting "an order of NOBILITY in the country,"[4] the broadside declared.

In another part of this handbill, which was widely distributed throughout New York's northern counties, the author described Colonel Burr as "at once the soldier, the statesman and the patriot." He was asking the "yeomanry" of New York to support him, in particular the veterans of the Revolution. "Many of you have fought and bled by his side. Old Soldiers, will you forsake your comrade?"[5]

The Federalist organization in Albany may have been one of the converts to this appeal. Not long after it appeared, they passed a resolution to support Burr without reservations. Candidate Morgan Lewis informed DeWitt Clinton of this bad news. Judge John Tayler, at whose table Hamilton had declaimed against Burr, followed up Lewis's cry of alarm with an even more agitated letter, informing the Mayor that Burr's followers were using "every artifice that can be devised" while Lewis's backers seemed to be doing next to nothing.[6]

In fact, the Clinton machine was doing quite a lot. In the *American Citizen*, James Cheetham pounded away at Burr in every issue. He devoted most of January to refuting Aristides's aka William P. Van Ness's *An Examination of the Various Charges Exhibited Against Aaron Burr, Esq, Vice President of the United States*. He noted that Judge Brockholst Livingston, "His Honor the Mayor" DeWitt Clinton, and several others mentioned acerbically in the text were suing the author for libel.[7] Cheetham also censured Aristides for insulting and abusing officers of the government "without a shadow of proof," apparently trusting his readers would forget the smear job the *American Citizen* had done on Vice President Burr the previous year.

On two of Aristides's main points, that Jefferson, not Burr had made backstairs deals with the Federalists to end the deadlock of 1801 and that George Clinton had called President Jefferson "an accommodating trimmer," Cheetham's defense was more than a little labored. Aristides had produced witnesses to both assertions. Cheetham declared that even if it were true that Jefferson cut deals with key congressmen, it was justified, because the Republican cause was at stake. Moreover, the author of the Declaration of Independence never would have been forced to stoop to such a tactic, if Burr had not initiated the crisis by refusing to step out of the contest.

Instead of denying that Governor Clinton had called the president an accommodating trimmer, Cheetham denounced Burr for revealing a remark made in a private conversation. Both arguments drew hoots of derision from William Coleman in the *New-York Evening Post*. This editor's proclaimed neutrality became more and more invisible as the campaign picked up steam. He too published a list of Clinton and Livingston officeholders, complete with salaries, in his February 25th issue. The total amount of money at stake "accounts for the violent persecution of Mr. Burr, who has no family to provide for," Coleman concluded, echoing the Burrite broadside almost word for word.[8]

Cheetham remained unbeaten and unbowed in the face of this ridicule. He wove into his refutation of Aristides every word and phrase and sentence from Van Ness's text that could be construed as an attack on Thomas Jefferson. The Englishman paid particular attention to Aristides's comments on the problems created by a chief magistrate with a "speculative mind" unaware of the "extreme depravity of human nature" and too fond of "visionary schemes of reformation based on human perfectibility." Here, Cheetham raged, was a typical Federalist slander against Jefferson. How could Burr claim to be loyal to the president when he stood behind such a publication?

Cheetham flatly accused Burr of being the real author of the *Examination* even if he did not write it word for word. He had been in New York when the suspected author, William P. Van Ness, brought it to the printer. Burr had obviously read and approved these assaults on the president. By way of further proof, Cheetham noted that Burr had not taken his seat as presiding officer of the Senate until December 7th, although the Senate had convened on October 17, 1803. Where was he during those absent weeks? He was "completing this masterpiece of calumny" and incidentally neglecting the job for which the voters had elected him.[9]

II

Never a man to remain on the defensive for long, Cheetham went over to the attack with a weapon borrowed from Alexander Hamilton. The Englishman printed a detailed description of one of the many anti-Burr letters the General wrote during the electoral deadlock of 1801. Cheetham dwelt with particular pleasure on the way Hamilton called Burr a Catiline who was scheming to seize power. In an open letter to Hamilton, under the pen name Manlius, Cheetham asked if he would admit that he stands the "uncontradicted author" of this charge, which "balances the fate of the second officer in the government."

Cheetham maintained that in the letter Hamilton had accused Burr of an offence "so atrocious, no human language can furnish a term sufficiently descriptive of its baseness." Never before in world history, Cheetham declared, had mankind witnessed such "an enormous complication of fraud, dissimulation, and perfidy . . . assembled in the same individual." Compared with Burr, "even Catiline was innocent." The Roman traitor never abandoned his friends, no matter how industriously he tried to destroy his country's constitution. Burr, by conspiring to replace Jefferson, combined Catiline's "desperate and audacious profligacy" and Benedict Arnold's "consummate treachery."

Cheetham noted that Hamilton had not disavowed the letter. "If I have formed a proper estimate of your character, I am entitled to believe you would never have permitted the public to be deceived by a base and daring imposture or suffered an appeal to your authority for the ruin of an innocent man." As least as important, neither "Mr. Burr nor his advocates" had called upon Hamilton for "the explanation to which the guiltless are entitled, and which an injured individual would not hesitate a moment to demand." There was only one conclusion: either the vice president had "sunk into a condition so abject [and] degraded as to permit General Hamilton to slander him with impunity" or Burr must "stand convicted."[10]

Cheetham was using the customs of the code duello to humiliate Burr and simultaneously taunt Hamilton. He poured on the venom with a totally reckless hand: "Yes Sir, I dare assert that you attributed to Aaron Burr one of the most atrocious and unprincipled of crimes. He has not called upon you—It is enough! How will the most profligate of his followers answer my conclusion? Either he is guilty or he is the most mean and despicable bastard in the universe."[11]

III

The *Morning Chronicle* ignored these attempts to drag Hamilton into the fray. Instead Dr. Peter Irving published an open letter by one Herodnius addressed to President Jefferson, asking him to state his support of Mr. Burr. The writer argued that it would refute rumors that the president had "countenanced" the attacks on Burr and had even extended "pecuniary aid" to some of the perpetrators. This was rather neat; it intimated that Jefferson was secretly backing Cheetham as he had supported the arch calumniator, James Thomson Callender, and simultaneously tried to force Jefferson into a pro-Burr statement in self-defense.

Cheetham reacted to this charge with the predictable fury of a man determined to defend the president, even if the accusation was true: "That a writer like Herodnius should have the vanity to think that he can, by the boldness of his denunciations and the virulence of his falsehoods, entrap the President into a declaration in favor of Mr. Burr is of a piece with the other follies which have marked the conduct of Mr. Burr and his adherents." Cheetham, aka Philo-Manlius, challenged Herodnius to "step forward and prove his allegation." If he remained silent, "he must be classified among the most infamous of liars."[12] All this sound and fury concealed the indubitable fact that the president was one of Cheetham's secret subscribers, and had given him a contract to print the latest federal laws.

IV

Retaliating against this attempt to intimidate Jefferson, Cheetham spilled gallons of acidic ink on Burr's failure to get a single vote for another term as vice president from the Republican nominating caucus in Washington, D.C. The *Morning Chronicle* had tried to mitigate this humiliation by publishing a letter from Washington, D.C., claiming that "the manner in which the business was conducted"—on orders from the presidential palace—"has given great dissatisfaction to considerate men." The *Chronicle*'s correspondent also claimed that DeWitt Clinton had negotiated with three congressmen to put himself forward as a vice presidential candidate and had been forced to settle for his decrepit uncle.

Cheetham declared the mayor's purported candidacy was "palpably a falsehood." DeWitt was too young to become vice president. This sally revealed the Englishman as less than conversant with both Clinton's age and the national charter; it drew hoots from the Burrites. The Constitution clearly stated vice presidents had to be thirty years of age; presidents had to be thirty-five.

Undaunted, as usual, Cheetham assailed the *Chronicle*'s claim that Burr had numerous friends in Congress who were silenced by presidential edict: "But really, had Mr. Burr any friends in Congress, I mean among the *Republican* members? . . . They certainly had a fine opportunity of evincing their *friendship*, for, voting by [secret] ballot, they might have written 'Aaron Burr' upon their tickets without the possibility of discovery."[13] Cheetham printed extracts of several letters from Washington, D.C., supporting his version of the caucus. He also reprinted selections from the *Philadelphia Aurora*, in which editor William Duane concluded that Burr's failure to get a single caucus vote proved that his "wretched efforts" to calumniate Governor Clinton and conceal his own corruption had failed.[14]

This was almost breathtaking in its insouciance, since Van Ness's *Examination* was an attempt to refute two years' worth of smears and diatribes against Burr from Cheetham's pen, financed by the Clintons. But Duane, with an apparently straight face, reproached Burr for attacking the Old Incumbent.

Cheetham tried to make almost as much capital out of the endorsement of Morgan Lewis by the caucus of Republicans in Albany. Brushing aside the *Morning Chronicle's* claim that they had no business nominating candidates, the Englishman solemnly reported the total number of politicians in the state assembly and senate, and subtracted the Federalists, leaving 107 Republicans: "Of the one hundred and seven Republicans, one hundred and four signed the address to the electors of the state in favor of the election of Morgan Lewis." This, declared the *Citizen's* editor, should enable people from other states to "form a pretty correct estimate" of the Burr faction in New York.[15]

Cheetham leveled some of his heaviest verbal artillery at the few elected members of the legislature who were supporting Burr. One was William Taber, an assemblyman from Dutchess County. Cheetham reported Taber had defected because he had asked Jefferson for a federal job and had been turned down: "Mr. Burr prevailed upon William to apply for the office, knowing it would not be given him." Burr had drawn many another poor "gull" into his act in this devious way. Virtually speaking in the official voice of the Clinton-Livingston machine, Cheetham urged the Republicans of Dutchess County to "take care of William" if he did not "immediately turn from the error of his ways."

The Clintons left no one out of their call to arms against Colonel Burr. Their three appointees to the state's supreme court, Brockholst Livingston, Smith Thompson, and the newly elevated Ambrose Spencer all signed the address to the electors of the state, endorsing Morgan Lewis's election. This was a bit too rich for William Coleman's taste. In the *Evening Post* he blasted the idea of judges meddling in politics. He may also have been thinking that Thompson's and Livingston's names on this declaration of naked partisanship dimmed the likelihood of Harry Croswell getting another trial.

Cheetham came back at Coleman in his usual slashing style. He noted that the previous day, the *Post* had printed a story from the nation's capital about a Federalist dinner on Washington's birthday attended by several judges of the U.S. Supreme Court. "Political damnation was dealt out to the Republican Party from the president downwards," Cheetham said, and the "consistent" Mr. Coleman had reported the festivities "in high glee."[16]

V

As the campaign took shape, the Clinton-Livingston strategy became clear. In the pages of the *American Citizen* Burr and his followers were repeatedly characterized as "the little band"—a tiny minority of malcontents in league with the Federalists to undo the great Republican triumph of 1800. Burr was vulnerable to this assault. His organization was relatively small, and they had to travel to various parts of the state to set up local committees and distribute campaign literature. Cheetham began referring to them as "strolling gentry." This soon became "these travellers—these jugglers—these strolling players." Whenever a Burr operative left New York, his itinerary was reported in the *American Citizen* with derisive comments about the little band's "travelling" or "straggling" habits.[17]

Burr was winning support: The *Morning Chronicle* ran names and endorsements from around the state on a daily basis. But the Burrites could not match the numbers that the Clinton machine mustered at their public meetings. On March 19th, the *Citizen* triumphantly printed a "NEW YORK ADDRESS" in support of Morgan Lewis. Most of it was a hymn to the Republican administration's "mild and benevolent ascendancy" and the acquisition of "the fertile and extensive territory of Louisiana." No less than sixty-three delegates from New York's wards signed this chorus of congratulation.

VI

A few days later Cheetham reported that in the town of Kinderhook, headquarters of the Van Ness clan, "Old Peter Van Ness could collect only nine votes for his friend Burr," while ninety-eight Republicans voiced their support of Morgan Lewis at a town meeting.[18]

In Kinderhook lived a twenty-one-year-old attorney named Martin Van Buren, who had studied law in William P. Van Ness's New York office and almost certainly had met Vice President Burr. Some writers have suggested, against all evidence, that Van Buren was Burr's illegitimate son. "Little Van," as he was sometimes called, unquestionably knew Van Ness's total commitment to Burr. Even at this early age, however, he was demonstrating his later reputation for slippery politics.

Van Ness wrote Van Buren an emotional letter, describing Burr as "the intended victim of . . . persecution against which it is the duty of every friend of freedom to sustain him." He urged Van Buren to "reflect maturely" before he chose a side. The colonel's purported offspring replied that he had given the contest "the most mature passionate reflection." Although he abstained from judging whether the charges against Burr were true or false, he had concluded that for a regular Republican to support him "would not under existing circumstances be proper." This was Little Van's way of saying that he wanted to be on the winning side.[19]

VII

To run a campaign of this intensity took money—a lot of it. Printers had to be paid to produce handbills by the thousands and more money had to be spent to distribute them throughout the state. At one point Cheetham remarked that Burr was spending "forty shillings a day" (two dollars) to distribute a handbill. This was twice as much as a laborer was paid, and gives a glimpse (one of the few) into how much money was needed to run a campaign in 1804.

Winning Federalist support meant Burr had access to a lot of cash. These well-heeled gentlemen did not merely resolve to give the vice president their vote. They reached for their checkbooks, in the same realistic way they had put their dollars behind Alexander Hamilton in the past. There were rumors of New Jersey Federalists contributing as much as $10,000–$20,000 to Burr's campaign—and the New England Federalists undoubtedly called on their friends to do likewise.

To bolster his appeal among the merchant class, Burr turned to a device he had used with great success in 1800: backing a new bank. The year before that pivotal election, he had wangled through the legislature something called the Manhattan Company, an organization that promised to supply New York City with decent water to replace the putrid stuff most of the residents were forced to drink from polluted Collect Pond. In the fine print of the charter was the provision that the company could also do a little banking on the side. The Manhattan Company never did get around to solving New York's drinking-water problems but as the Chase Manhattan Bank it flourishes to this day.

A bank was a political weapon wielded by politicians of both sides. Hamilton's Bank of New York and the local branch of the Bank of the United States were controlled by Federalists and they only loaned money to those who were politically reliable. A bank was also a godsend to the debt-encumbered, such as Burr. We have seen how the vice president persuaded the Manhattan Company bank to loan him $112,407 in 1802.

For the gubernatorial election, Burr adopted as his financial wedge the Merchants Bank. It needed a corporate charter from the legislature to stay in business and its backers sent thunderous memorials and petitions to Albany on its behalf. One had 614 signatures. The Burrites backed the bank with resolutions and declarations at public meetings. The legislature stonily ignored them and passed a law toward the end of March banning "unincorporated banking institutions." The Clinton-Livingston machine wanted no competition with the Manhattan Company, which they now controlled. With almost shameless arrogance, the party of the people excepted one unchartered Albany bank, the Mercantile Company, which they also controlled.[20]

The *New-York Evening Post* retaliated with a withering attack on this legal maneuver. They said the legislative committee that recommended the bill received direct orders from His Honor, the Mayor, DeWitt Clinton. They quoted Morgan Lewis as whining to an acquaintance, "You cannot imagine how pressingly DeWitt writes on this subject." The bill was drawn by Maturin Livingston, Lewis's son-in-law, who was quoted as declaring: "My bill will pass. The Merchants Bank will be dam'd." Too late the leaders discovered that Maturin's bill also inadvertently suppressed the Manhattan Company. They had to scramble to tack a rider on another bill to correct matters. The *Post* portrayed Maturin as less intelligent than Tunis Wortman, Mayor Clinton's subhumanoid city clerk. But the bottom line was: good-bye to the Merchants Bank.[21]

Not everyone in Clinton's apparatus thought this was a brilliant move. In line with his union of honest men, Burr had involved a nice mix of Federalists and Republicans in the new bank. One observer wrote to His Honor the Mayor on March 13th: "I am a great friend to the old Clinton Family and I do now believe you are going all wrong." He told DeWitt that the destruction of the Merchants Bank was a "very impolitic measure" and was likely to "cause a ferment that will turn the election." Without some very good management, "Little Aaron will undoubtedly get in."[22]

VIII

Aside from their debatable war on the Merchants Bank, the Clintons displayed shrewd political judgment in their attacks on Burr's candidacy as the campaign unfolded. One of their prime concerns was the vice president's potential appeal to the thousands of New Englanders who had moved into northern New York. The *American Citizen* soon developed a habit of describing Burr as a mocker of all established religions. Editor

Cheetham undoubtedly hoped this would also have some impact on Federalists, who tended to be religious.

A climax of sorts in this branch of the Clinton-Livingston strategy was Cheetham's publication of "The Creed of the Burrites." This was a more direct attempt to discredit Jonathan Edwards's grandson among those who might have some lingering respect for him.

> I believe in one Aaron Burr . . . I believe that Aaron Burr has done more during the late revolution to advance the liberties of America than George Washington himself; I believe that Aaron Burr is so good, pious and devout a man that after he has been governor of the state of New York . . . he will then be made Pope of Rome. . . . I believe Aaron Burr is the perfect model of chastity, piety, virtue and morality. . . . [23]

VIII

To impress voters of a more secular bent, Cheetham produced supposed new evidence of Burr's corruption. One of the most troublesome charges concerned the legacy of Albrecht Behrens, a New York City sugar refiner who had died intestate in 1797. Burr had been named the administrator of his estate, which amounted to some twenty thousand dollars (perhaps a quarter of a million in today's money). The *American Citizen* said the heirs had not seen a cent of it; Burr had stolen it all.

Cheetham launched the attack on March 6th in a series of "interrogatories," as if Burr was a defendant in the dock. The editor cited dates and names. Henry Behrens, the spokesman for the family, had appeared before the legislature in 1798 and asked them to bring in a bill forcing Burr to pay over the money.

> Do you recollect that the assembly went into committee of the whole on said bill, March 24 [1798], Thomas Storm in the chair—and did you, or did you not then and there in solemn assembly declare that the petitioners were the legal heirs of Albrecht Behrens, and that you were perfectly satisfied with the documents that were then produced to that effect? And did you not then and

there, on that occasion, solemnly and sincerely promise that you would pay
over to the heirs of Albrecht Behrens some time in the month of April then
ensuing, the personal property then in your hands belonging to said estate?

Cheetham demanded a "peremptory answer to the aforesaid queries." If
"silence" was Burr's reply, it would be taken "pro confesso" as "evidence of
guilt or defalcation." For the next seven weeks, the Behrens case was constantly in the *Citizen's* pages. When his bill failed to pass in the legislature, Henry Behrens, who claimed to be the dead man's brother, had sued
Burr in the court of chancery in 1799. In later installments, the *Citizen*
published affidavits by Messrs. Isaac Moses and George Schmelzel, now
acting as agents for the heirs, claiming the suit had never been settled and
they were waiting for Burr to make good.[24]

The Burrites could not afford to ignore this smear. The *Morning Chronicle* and the *Evening Post* teamed up to answer it. According to their version
of the story, Henry Behrens had appeared in New York and demanded the
estate for himself and twelve other heirs. Burr had asked two distinguished
lawyers, Alexander Hamilton and Richard Harison, to examine Behrens's
papers. They furnished him with a written statement, concluding that they
were not convinced that Henry was trustworthy. They advised Burr to submit the case to the court of chancery and obtain a decree that would protect
him against possible lawsuits, if other heirs turned up.

The case was still in chancery because that court too was dissatisfied
with Henry Behrens's bona fides. Meanwhile, Mr. Burr, sympathetic to
the distressed as always, had advanced some eight thousand dollars to Mr.
Behrens. The *Post* published affidavits from Messrs. Moses and
Schmelzel, saying they were not in the least dissatisfied with Burr's conduct of the case. These two gentleman had been tricked into accusing the
vice president by that noted subhumanoid City Clerk Tunis Wortman.
"What heightens the baseness of this attack," the *Post* declared, "is that
the true state of the affair must have been well known to the very persons
who are most assiduous in circulating this detestable calumny."[25]

Undeterred, Cheetham went on churning out handbills and stories in the *Citizen* about "Poor Behrens." In his usual pseudodocumentary style, the editor reproduced notarized certificates about Burr's administration of the estate and solemnly announced they had been deposited with the "Chairmen of the Republican Committees in New York and Albany" for honest citizens to examine. Several handbills were published in German as well as English to persuade recent immigrants of Burr's perfidy. The Burrites fought back with a bilingual broadside of their own: "TRUE STATEMENT OF BEHRENS'S CASE," signed by the Rev. John C. Kunze, pastor of New York's German Lutheran Church and five other well-known German-Americans, all exonerating the candidate.[26]

IX

Cheetham was especially irked by the way William Coleman took up Burr's defense in the Behrens case, and in effect used Hamilton's name to trump the *Citizen*'s cards. This put a dent in one of the Clintonians' basic strategies: to try to persuade as many Federalists as possible to vote against Burr by emphasizing Hamilton's opposition to him. Coleman had become "an active electioneer" for Burr, Cheetham raged.[27] It was, in fact, a symptom of what was happening in the Federalist party. The Albany committee was by no means the only group who had decided to ignore General Hamilton's strictures.

Elsewhere along the Hudson, Stephen Van Rensselaer, General Hamilton's brother-in-law, the largest landowner in the state, with property that extended into three counties, had decided to vote for Burr. The word went out to his numerous tenants, who for reasons economic and psychological were inclined to follow "The Patroon" at the polls. This was the man whom General Hamilton had run for governor on the Federalist ticket in 1801. It would be hard to find better evidence that New York's Federalists had discarded the General as their leader.

Even more astonishing was a letter Burr received from Peter Jay Munro, nephew of former Governor John Jay. Munro had studied law under Burr and remained an admirer. The young attorney had a country home in Westchester County. "Gov. Jay will vote for you and Mr. Phelps—he is as decidedly and openly with us as we could wish—" Munro wrote.[28] Here was an endorsement that refuted Cheetham's—and Hamilton's—accusations against Burr. If there was an ultimate pillar of rectitude in American politics, it was Jay, the man George Washington had chosen to be the first chief justice of the U.S. Supreme Court.

If General Hamilton heard about Jay's swing to Burr—and it is hard to believe he did not, for the Burr organization undoubtedly spread the news all over New York State—the General knew why he could no longer claim the allegiance of a man whom he had once considered one of his closest friends. When Hamilton lost the crucial New York City election to Burr in 1800, he had written to Jay, who was still governor, urging him to call the lame-duck legislature into special session and pass a bill enabling presidential electors to be chosen by popular vote, to give the Federalists a second chance. It would have amounted to stealing the election, George Clinton style, using legal technicalities to repudiate the expressed will of the people. The desperate General told Jay it was not a time to be "overscrupulous." Jay had written on the letter: "Proposing a measure for party purposes that it would not become me to adopt" and never answered Hamilton.[29]

Watching Aaron Burr take over the New York Federalist party could only have deepened the dismay General Hamilton experienced in Albany, after his repudiation by the Federalist caucus and his rejection by Rufus King. There is no evidence that he tried to play any further role in the election. It was clear that no one had the slightest interest in his opinion. His dreams of wider fame as Washington's military and political heir were expiring before his eyes. He was experiencing his own political death.

Struggling for consolation, Hamilton veered to his rediscovered religious faith. Writing to a friend who was looking for a job, he advised him:

"Arraign not the dispensations of Providence. They must be founded in wisdom and goodness; and when they do not suit us, it must be because there is some fault in ourselves which deserves chastisement; or because there is a kind intent, to correct in us some vice or failing, [of] which, perhaps, we may not be conscious."[30]

CHAPTER 11

From the Low Road
to the Depths

Other paragraphs in John Jay Munro's letter to Aaron Burr, reporting that ex-Governor John Jay was backing him, were not as encouraging. The young attorney's on-scene Westchester County report was ominous evidence of the thinness of Burr's support among the party regulars, the people who participated in politics and worked to get out the vote: "Your interest in this county, and particularly in the upper towns, has been neglected by your friends, while your opponents have been vigilant [sic] and active. Of course they have made an impression not easily to be removed and which will be felt notwithstanding our present exertions." The most Munro could promise Burr was a 50–50 split in Westchester. That would be "doing as much as we can expect to do."[1]

A particular cause of concern in Westchester was another slander James Cheetham had thrown into the battle, exhumed this time from Burr's revolutionary past. In the April 7th issue of the *American Citizen*, the vice president's editorial nemesis published a letter from James Morgan, a former member of the militia, who claimed Burr had ordered him flogged for no discernible reason.

In 1780 or 1781, Morgan asserted, he had loaned the army a horse to carry a letter to West Point. The next day, when he went to collect his horse, Colonel Burr told him the steed had not yet returned. After staying overnight in a nearby house, Morgan again asked for his horse. Burr supposedly sent him to a nearby farmhouse to collect it, accompanied by a corporal. When they got there, the corporal opened sealed orders he had been given by Burr, telling him to flog Morgan. "I was stripped naked, then tied to a tree, and the corporal who carried the orders was expressly charged to be the executor of his malicious purpose. I then received THIRTY NINE LASHES ON MY NAKED BACK!!" Morgan claimed "acts of a similar nature were frequent with Colonel Burr to gratify his capricious temper."[2]

Cheetham added a totally spurious postscript: "In consequence of the INHUMAN treatment mentioned by Mr. Morgan, Gen. Washington superseded Mr. Burr and appointed Gen. Hull of Massachusetts to the command."[3]

The *Morning Chronicle* swiftly published a refutation, stating that Morgan had been lashed after repeated warnings not to cross the lines. Letters from Westchesterites portrayed Morgan as a suspected spy who was lucky to get off with a flogging. These were capped by a letter from Morgan's brother, who said that the officer who gave the order for the flogging was not Colonel Burr. He had resigned from the army in 1779.[4] Undeterred as usual, Cheetham published a handbill replete with affidavits from Morgan and several Westchester friends confirming his version. The Clinton forces circulated it throughout the state. "Poor Morgan" became a staple beside "Poor Behrens" in Cheetham's arsenal.[5]

II

Burr did not announce Oliver Phelps as his running mate for lieutenant governor until rather late in the campaign, at the end of March. Cheetham immediately made the congressman another target of opportunity, solemnly assuring his readers that "truth shall be our guide."

There were so many things wrong with Phelps, the editor of the *Citizen* did not know where to start. For one thing, he was a *stranger* in New York, settled in Ontario County for no more than four or five years, after birth in Connecticut and a sojourn in Massachusetts. His face, to any student of physiognomy (a popular pseudoscience of the day) bore unmistakable "lineaments of duplicity and distrust." He was a man of "extremely limited understanding," and "illiterate" in the bargain. In Massachusetts, according to a "gentleman of respectability" from that state, he was known as "Lying Phelps" until he was thirty years old. Even worse, he was a land speculator, known for his "low cunning." Worst of all was his attachment to Aaron Burr, "the most immoral, the most perfidious, the most unprincipled of men." Obviously, Phelps deemed the colonel "a man *after his own heart.*"[6]

Having by his lights destroyed Phelps's character, Cheetham now unlimbered his heaviest weaponry to attack the most dangerous thing about Phelps—his role as a bearer of a message from Thomas Jefferson that he was neutral in this struggle between the Republicans contending for control of New York. Hoping to gain as much credibility as possible, the Burr organization had arranged for Phelps's report of his interview with Jefferson to be published in the *New York Commercial Advertiser*, a paper that professed to strike a neutral stance in the contest. The editor, the Reverend Zachariah Lewis, was a Federalist who frequently tilted toward Burr in the style of the *Evening Post.*[7]

Cheetham went after Phelps and Lewis with manic fury: "We deny that Mr. Jefferson made the declaration *in the sense asserted here* . . . IT IS IMPOSSIBLE THAT THE PRESIDENT COULD HAVE MADE SUCH A DECLARATION. His opinion of Mr. Burr is well-known. It does not, I believe, differ essentially from that of General Hamilton." Shifting to his sanctimonious mode, Cheetham added that it was "extremely indelicate and improper to involve Mr. Jefferson in the great question that agitates the state, [and] perhaps the union." That last line suggests the agitated Cheetham momentarily forgot Mr. Jefferson was president of the United States and leader of the Republican party.[8]

The president's nonendorsement of their candidate and seeming toleration of Burr was a major threat to the Clinton-Livingston machine's survival. Behind the scenes there must have been a lot of frantic conferences on how to challenge it. On April 10th, Cheetham found a way. He reported that another New York congressman had visited Jefferson because he doubted the president's supposed statement to Phelps.

According to this congressman (who at first withheld his name and hid behind Cheetham's description of him as "a very respectable citizen of the state") Jefferson had replied that Phelps's statement was true as far as it went. He had told him he would remain neutral in any contest "BETWEEN REAL REPUBLICANS." (The capital letters are Cheetham's.) But Jefferson supposedly continued: "REMEMBER MR. PHELPS THAT I DO NOT CONSIDER THE *LITTLE BAND* AS MAKING ANY PART OF THE REAL REPUBLICAN INTEREST."

The Burr organization struggled to recover from this body blow by publishing a refutation in the *Morning Chronicle* from two other Republican congressmen, Burr's friend Erastus Root and David Thomas of Washington County. They said Jefferson told them he was "very sorry that a division existed." But he considered both candidates Republicans and he would continue to do so, as long as he did not discover that the Burrites were attacking his administration.

The importance of this version to the vice president was evident from the way his organization rushed it into a handbill for statewide distribution. Unfortunately for Burr, this subservience to a Jeffersonian veto—and anxiety to retain a Jeffersonian semiblessing, however lukewarm—was bound to be counterproductive among the Federalists, whose votes Burr needed at least as badly as he needed Republicans. Like all third-party candidates, the vice president was constantly in danger of losing the enthusiasm of both sides.

III

While continuing to belabor Burr for Behrens and Morgan, Cheetham began printing communications from the next world:

My once loved countrymen.

"From the cold mansion of death, from the awful bosom of the grave, permit me to address you. Behold! It is your WASHINGTON who speaks.
Will you refuse to listen to his councils?

Washington the ghost warned New Yorkers to "BEWARE OF AMBI-
TION" and to be even more wary of this awful vice when it was combined with "PROFLIGACY." Character was all important in public
office and every voter should refuse to trust a candidate whose "*moral integrity* is impeachable."

The Father of the Country claimed he was addressing both Federalists
and Republicans. He urged them to disregard a man who had been repudiated by both political parties. It had always been a maxim of his life
"THAT A DESERTER SHOULD NEVER BE TRUSTED." It was
imperative to choose "THE CANDIDATE SELECTED WITH THE
APPROBATION OF YOUR POLITICAL REPRESENTATIVES"
instead of an individual whom "NO HONEST MAN CAN IN CON-
SCIENCE CONSENT TO SUPPORT."[9]

Thus was the man who deplored political parties summoned from the
grave to recommend party regularity above all things, and incidentally
knock in the head Aaron Burr's union of honest men.

In the *Evening Post* William Coleman asked how the Clintonians, of all
people, could claim a fellowship with Washington, who venerated the Constitution. George Clinton had devoted most of his political career to trying
to subvert the great charter. Coleman opined that the Washington speech
had been written by none other than "the master magician" DeWitt Clinton: "The solemn bombast, the profound hypocrisy, the mixture of rage and
terror could come from no one else. Pride, power, revenge and ten thousand
a year [the mayor's take-home pay] all unite to instigate him." Clearly,
Clinton's fervor was bordering on frenzy. "The terrors of political death are
upon him. We read his destiny: thou art found wanting."[10]

Coleman followed this blast with reports of smashing Federalist victories in gubernatorial races in New Hampshire and Massachusetts.

IV

Burr reacted to this relentless drumfire of billingsgate and calumny with his usual composure. He spent most of each day in his headquarters, a rented building on John Street, where he conferred with Van Ness, Davis, the Swartouts, and other key people in his campaign. Aside from writing letters to encourage supporters to speak out on his behalf, there was not much else for a candidate to do in 1804. To stump the state making speeches or otherwise pleading for votes was considered unseemly. The office was supposed to seek the man. A candidate who tried too hard could be accused of unwholesome ambition, which suggested in its train a plethora of dark possibilities.

Burr undoubtedly read all the vicious things said about him by Cheetham in the *American Citizen*. It was a necessity. Rapid replies had to be produced before these charges took root in the minds of the voters. One of the few surviving glimpses of his reaction to them was a letter he wrote to Theodosia.

He began by scolding her for not writing more often: "I had really begun to doubt whether you were not all dead or something worse." He scolded her even more severely for failing to send him a speech her husband, Joseph Alston, had made in the South Carolina legislature: "I shall get the speech, no thanks to you; there is a copy in Philadelphia for which I have written." It would come, he added teasingly, "endorsed by the fair hand of Celeste." He added that her hand—and arm—were "truly handsome." He had not seen her when he passed through Philadelphia. He had taken "great affront" at her coldness and that had led to "explanations &c." There was "nothing like a quarrel to advance love."

Then, almost casually, he added: "They are very busy about an election between Morgan Lewis and A. Burr. The former supported by the Livingstons and the Clintons, the latter *per se*. I would send you some new and amusing libels against the vice-president." But he had the impression that "this sort of intercourse is not desired."

He closed with another scolding, this one about his grandson, Aaron Burr Alston, who would be two years old in May. If Theodosia had "one particle of invention or genius" she would have taught the boy his ABC's before this. As for his tendency to tell lies (a fault that apparently worried Theodosia), he told her not to worry about it. It was "an inheritance, which pride, another inheritance, will cure. His mother went through the process."[11]

An April 3rd letter to Theodosia revealed the pressure Burr was under. He acknowledged receiving her latest letter and added that he was "in the midst of occupations connected with the approaching elections; of course, every moment, interruptions." Four days later, the letter was still unmailed and he added a postscript: "Since the 3rd I have vainly endeavoured to get a minute to write to you. It will not, I fear, be possible before the 30th inst., when, or soon after, I hope to be in Philadelphia, whence you will hear from me."[12]

Even with the election fury swirling around him, Celeste was apparently on Burr's mind. Several days later, he wrote a letter to an unnamed woman correspondent, who may have been this elusive lady. It was the sort of letter a lover might write to a woman with whom he had recently quarreled.

> Your vanity, if in any degree concerned, will be fully satisfied by the assurance that my heart, my wishes and my thoughts will be with you. The mortal part of me is indispensably otherwise engaged. As you cannot fail to have admirers, you cannot fail to be amused. Knowing that you are happy, I shall be so by sympathy, though in a less degree, as reflected light is less potent than direct.[13]

V

In the final days of the campaign, Cheetham devoted much of his newspaper to portraying Burr and his supporters as desperate intriguers, thugs, and bribers. One story concerned "TULLY ROBINSON, a young gentleman of this city," who reportedly delivered a scathing speech against

Burr at the Union Hotel to "upwards of *one thousand citizens* assembled on the occasion." The speech, Cheetham declared "was several times interrupted by the most warm and flattering applause."

The next day a Burr supporter supposedly warned Robinson that Burr intended to sue him for slander. Moreover, if Robinson went anywhere near the polls on election day, he would be mobbed. Robinson declared himself eager to meet the Burrites in court or on the street. It would give him a chance to prove "Mr. Burr is as desperate in private life and as treacherous in public as the ROMAN CATILINE."[14]

Another communication, under the heading "Bribery!! Corruption!! Violence!! and Assaults!!" accused Peter Townsend, Burr's close friend and proprietor of the Sterling Ironworks in Orange County, of trying to buy the vote of one David Westcott, who for reasons obscure reported this to Edward McLaughlin of New York. Townsend supposedly threatened to beat Westcott "most damnably" with a club and actually attempted to do so when he declined to be purchased. In the best Cheetham pseudolegalese, McLaughlin became the "deponent" and swore before Justice of the Peace A. C. Van Slyck that all this was absolutely true.[15]

VI

As William Coleman had predicted, Burr's libel suit against Cheetham had never come to trial. On the day before the election, Cheetham claimed that Burr was responsible for the delay. In defending the *American Citizen*'s claim that Burr's immorality was notorious, Chetham triumphantly informed his readers that he and his agents had obtained the names of "upwards of *twenty women of ill fame* with whom [Burr] has been connected." The names of these prostitutes were "enumerated" in the court papers, along with names of married women who had been "divorced" because they had yielded to Burr's charms, and names of "chaste and respectable ladies whom he has attempted to *seduce*." (Italics are Cheetham's as usual.) When Burr saw this supposedly damning evidence, he responded with a number of "propositions" that made it impossible to begin the trial before the election.[16]

When the polls opened on April 24th, Cheetham stayed on the low road. Polling continued through April 26th, and on each of these days, Cheetham treated his readers to a view of Burr as a moral degenerate and would-be traitor. One correspondent, named Sylphud, claimed that Burr had allowed a prostitute to insult his dying wife. Sylphud added that he knew the Burrites' "rottenness" and could tell tales about them that would "torture the very marrow of their bones."

Another message from "A SERIOUS FRIEND" accused Burr of being a secret agent in the pay of Great Britain. Everyone knew the British were eager to spend huge sums to bribe "desperate and unprincipled politicians." Should the citizens be so insane as to elect Burr governor, he would undoubtedly "sell you, and make stepping stones of you to march into the presidential chair."

Breaking into verse, Cheetham described a Burr play for the Negro vote. The poem, "Aaron's Last Shift," portrayed Burr as desperate until one of his black servants, Alexis (described as his favorite pimp), suggested persuading New York's free blacks to back him by promising them an elegant supper at Richmond Hill. Other advisors protested:

> blacks were faithless, never true,
> fond of deceit, of basest treason.

But a supposedly desperate Burr ignored these warnings and staged a ball at Richmond Hill "for a considerable number of gentleman of color—upwards of twenty" at which they toasted "a union of honest men." [17]

In the same issue, Cheetham reprinted the 1801 handbill *Aaron Burr!* once more describing Burr's seduction of the daughter of a Washington tradesman. He solemnly disclaimed all responsibility for it, pointing out that it was apparently written by a Federalist. In the *Evening Post* William Coleman blasted Cheetham as totally shameless. Never before in New York politics had anyone stooped so low as to publish such charges in a newspaper, Coleman wrote.

From Albany came reports that Chief Justice Morgan Lewis was appalled at the depths to which DeWitt Clinton had sunk to stop Burr. The *Commercial Advertiser* quoted Lewis as saying "he would rather have seen the government in ___ than he would have been a candidate, had he known how the election would have been conducted."[18]

VII

In the last week of the campaign, the vice president remained at his John Street headquarters almost twenty-four hours a day. Only a letter from Theodosia could distract him from the all-consuming task. When one arrived on April 25th, the middle of the three polling days, he somehow found time to answer it. Theodosia had apparently described a violent thunderstorm that was raging as she wrote to him.

"I too write in a storm; an election storm," Burr replied. "The thing began yesterday and will terminate tomorrow . . . I have, since beginning this letter, been already three times interrupted."

He then segued into an attempt to persuade Theodosia and her husband and their son to come north to spend the summer at Richmond Hill. He assured her that there were ample servants on hand and the cellars and garrets were well stocked with food and wine. He himself would rent a house in town and live with them only as much as they wanted him.

Almost casually, Burr returned to the subject that had absorbed him for the previous two months: "I forgot to speak of the election. Both parties claim majorities, and there never was, in my opinion, an election of the result of which so little judgment could be formed. A.B. will have a small majority in this city *if tomorrow should be a fair day*, and not else."[19]

VIII

On that same day, April 25th, the *Evening Post* published a fateful letter under the heading "Electioneering Arts." The letter was from Dr. Charles D. Cooper, Judge Tayler's son-in-law, who had been so impressed with General Hamilton's harangue against Burr at the judge's dinner table back in February. The *Post* described it as an extract from a handbill from Albany.

GENUINE REPUBLICANS

The following is a copy of a letter written by Dr. Charles D. Cooper of the City of Albany to Andrew Brown, Esq of the City of Bern in the same county.

THE LETTER VERBATIM
Albany 12th April 1804

Dear Sir:

You will receive some election papers and some of them also in the German language. I presume you will make use of them to the best advantage. Have them dispersed and scattered as much as possible—the friends of Col. Burr are extremely active and will require all our exertion to put them down—it is believed that most of the reflecting Federalists will vote [for] Lewis. Genl. Hamilton, the Patroon's brother-in-law it is said has come out decidedly against Burr, indeed when he was here he spoke of him as a dangerous man and ought not to be trusted. Judge Kent also expressed the same sentiment—the Patroon was quite indifferent about it when he went to New York—it is thought that when he sees Genl. Hamilton and his brother-in-law Mr. Church (who Burr some time ago fought a duel with, and who, of course, must bear Burr much hatred)—I say many feel persuaded that Mr. Rensselaer will be decidedly opposed to Mr. Burr—if you think any of us can aid you in the election in your town, let us know and we will give you what assistance in our power—can you send me word what you think will be the result of the election in your town?

Yours Sincerely,
Charles D. Cooper
Addressed to A. Brown, Esq.

Postscript:
Perhaps it [would] be of use to shew part of this letter that relates to the Patroon, Hamilton and Church to some of the patroon's tenants—I leave it to your discretion.

Post editor Coleman added some scathing comments to this reprint. He declared that Dr. Cooper was trying to impose on Andrew Brown Esq. "by the most palpable falsehood and misrepresentation." Cooper knew that "few or none of the 'reflecting Federalists' would give their votes to Judge Lewis."

Coleman went on to claim that General Hamilton had "repeatedly declared" he would not oppose the election of Colonel Burr in favor of Morgan Lewis "or any other candidate nominated by the prevailing tyrannical faction, after they drove the Honorable Chancellor Lansing to decline." Coleman asserted that Dr. Cooper had been "personally told so in plain and pointed terms by a highly respected Federal character and near connection of General Hamilton." Coleman was referring to General Philip Schuyler.

Editor Coleman maintained that Dr. Cooper also knew that Judge Kent was determined to give his vote for Colonel Burr and that he had "candidly informed Judge Lewis so." Cooper also knew that the Patroon (Stephen Van Rensselaer) had "determined on giving a firm and decided support to the election of Colonel Burr. Judge Tayler himself had reported hearing the Patroon say this a few days before he departed for New York."

Determined to annihilate Dr. Cooper, Editor Coleman continued: "The falsehood and malice of the above letter will be seen by all who shall read the following."

Below these lines was a letter from General Schuyler, Hamilton's father-in-law, stating that Hamilton had favored Lansing but after Lewis's nomination had said he would not interfere in the election. Schuyler also confirmed the Patroon's support for Burr, and declared Judge Kent had told him personally that Burr was getting his vote.[20]

The exchange reiterated the desperate attempts by leading Republicans to persuade Federalists that their leaders were anti-Burr, and the equally determined efforts on the part of these leaders to give the vice president their support. Both the handbill and the Schuyler letter had already appeared in the *Albany Register*. Neither Coleman nor General Schuyler could foresee that young Dr. Cooper, outraged by being publicly denounced as a liar, would reply in heated terms.

In an April 23rd letter to Schuyler, which was published in the *Register* on April 24th, Dr. Cooper protested the "malignant attack" on his character. He claimed somewhat lamely that he never intended his letter to be made public—it had been broken open and used without his consent—a statement that his postscript seemed to refute. Then, recalling the dinner at Judge Tayler's house, several days after Morgan Lewis's nomination, Dr. Cooper angrily declared that Nathaniel Pendleton and Judge James Kent had both said they would not vote for Burr, and General Hamilton had not hesitated to hold forth on his detestation of the vice president. In quoting these gentlemen, Cooper maintained he had been unusually cautious: "For really sir, I could detail to you a still more despicable opinion which Gen. Hamilton has expressed of Mr. Burr."[21]

Those words were scarcely noticed in the salvos of vituperation and slander being flung at the vice president by James Cheetham and the other members of the Clinton-Livingston machine. But they would lie beneath the tumultuous surface, acquiring deadly force, as the election churned to a climax.

IX

The next day, April 26th, the *Evening Post* left no doubt whatsoever about who it wanted to win the election. A lead story recounted statements by various Republican leaders, including Chief Justice Morgan Lewis, about their post election plans to humiliate the Federalists in every possible way. Ambrose Spencer purportedly declared that after the election a Federalist "would know what it was to be scourged in reality." DeWitt Clinton exulted that he had his foot on the Federalists' necks and would never let them up.

Coleman followed this with a sworn statement by a Federalist who said he heard James Cheetham say the Federalists were voting for Aaron Burr

because he was "a damned contemptible rascal." Along with ruthless electioneering, this story suggests that Coleman was hoping to draw some
Burr gunfire in Cheetham's direction. "Is there a Federalist in this city
having the spirit of a man in him whose indignation does not instantly
kindle at the sight of this?" Coleman cried. "To the polls then—to the
polls!! And down with this insolent, malevolent, villainous faction."[22]

X

In an era when information traveled by horse or boat, and frontier counties such as Ontario were five hundred miles from New York, it would
take at least five days to count the ballots. The only total reported on the
day after the polls closed was the New York City vote. Almost exactly as
Aaron Burr predicted, he had carried Gotham by 100 votes—roughly the
same narrow margin that had lifted him to victory in 1800. Was that an
augury of another triumph?

Cheetham attempted to dismiss Burr's Manhattan victory as meaningless. He sought solace in reporting that "Gen. Hamilton, Colonel Troup,
John B. Church" and several other prominent Federalists had not voted
for either Burr or Lewis. "Their conduct has been honorable and manly,"
Cheetham declared.[23] This was a long way from previous Republican
boasts that most reflecting Federalists were voting for Lewis.

It would take another four days to learn what voters had decided elsewhere in the Empire State's polling places. The suspense was exquisite.
General Hamilton waited to find out if he was permanently discarded as
the leader of the Federalist party. A Burr victory would make his rival the
leader not only in the state but in the nation. Colonel Burr undoubtedly
contemplated the possibility of using a victory to run against Jefferson in
the fall as the Federalist candidate for president.

With New York under Burr's control, President Jefferson stuck with a
repudiated George Clinton as his running mate, Burr's son-in-law's family, the Alstons, eager to spend their money to give him South Carolina's

electoral votes, and New England behind Jonathan Edward's grandson in a fervent phalanx, there was more than a little chance that Virginia's hegemony could be broken by a union of honest men. If that electoral effort failed, there was still the secession option. In Massachusetts and Connecticut and New Hampshire, followers of Senators Pickering and Tracy and Plumer and Congressman Griswold were offering fervent toasts: "To Aaron's rod! May it bloom in New York!"[24]

Judge James Kent, on circuit in New York City from his Supreme Court chambers in Albany, thought Burr was all but in the governor's chair. "The Burrites appear flushed with the laurels of victory," he told his wife. The judge gave the Federalists credit for the triumph. They had been "generally brought out," he said, although the "cold reserve and indignant reproaches of Hamilton may have controlled a few." As we have seen, Hamilton-devotee Kent, was not one of these few, even though he admitted to admiring Morgan Lewis's character.[25] He too was unable to swallow George Clinton's perpetual greed for public office and his nephew DeWitt's amoral arrogance.

Both Clintons must have slept poorly, dreading a Burr victory. The governor would end his political career as a laughingstock and DeWitt would be faced with no career worth mentioning—and the imminent loss of that juicy $10,000–$15,000 he pocketed as mayor of New York. As for James Cheetham, the *Evening Post*'s editor, William Coleman, had offered a bet that the editor of the *American Citizen* would be nowhere to be seen in New York within three months. There were no takers.

CHAPTER 12

A Distracted Dictator and
an Etiquette-Mad President

*I*n the world beyond Manhattan Island, events were unfolding that could alter the future at least as drastically as New York's gubernatorial election. By far the most important was the situation in France. There Napoléon Bonaparte prepared to launch his 200,000-man Army of England across the channel.[1]

Immense efforts and a huge amount of money had been poured into building a "national flotilla" of some two thousand landing craft. When his frantic subordinates complained of a shortage of workers, Napoléon snapped: "Conscript them." Soon thousands of men in Belgium and along the Rhine were hammering and sawing in the service of France.

Even more awesome were the engineering projects launched by Bonaparte's imperious will. Over three thousand men labored to enlarge the harbor of the fishing port of Ambleteuse, near Boulogne, so part of the invasion armada could be sheltered there and launched on the same tide as the hundreds of boats scheduled to sail from the bigger port. Boulogne too was being enlarged by additional swarms of workmen and engineers. Napoléon's readiness to alter the very geography of the French coast only added to his legend.[2]

The Man of Destiny remained furiously determined to cross the Channel even though most of his naval officers had told him his flat-bottomed landing craft would be badly battered if the British navy caught them in open water. With typical ruthlessness, Napoléon replied that even if he lost twenty thousand men, what did that matter if he got one hundred thousand ashore and France became master of the world? "One loses that number in battle every day, and what battle promised such results as a landing in England?"[3]

No detail was too trifling to escape the first consul's attention. On February 13, 1804, he wrote to Marshal Soult, the commander of the camp near Saint Omer, ordering him to seize the crew and gear of a French fishing boat that had been caught communicating with a patrolling English frigate. "Make the skipper speak, and I even give you the authority to promise him his pardon if he gives information. If he should seem to hesitate . . . squeeze his thumbs in the hammer of a musket."[4]

From the cliffs of Ambleteuse, Napoléon wrote to a friend in Paris: "I [can] clearly see the English coast . . . It [the Channel] is a ditch which one can jump whenever one is bold enough to try it." To a French admiral, he wrote: "Eight hours of darkness with suitable weather [will] decide the fate of the universe."[5]

The admiral told Bonaparte his invasion plan was "extremely chancy . . . but not altogether impractical." After a major storm the English Channel often experienced a period of "utter calm" that would give Napoléon the eight hours he needed. The storm would scatter the patrolling English fleet and the utter calm would leave them with their sails flapping haplessly while Napoléon's veterans bent to their oars and rowed toward victory.[6]

The British were stunned by the furious energy Napoléon evoked from the French people. George III's ambassador to Paris, Lord Whitworth, had been confident that a war-weary France would overthrow the first consul if he plunged them into another conflict so soon. Instead, shipyards and factories were churning out weapons and men-of-war from Calais to Marseilles. The French truly believed there was no difficulty Napoléon Bonaparte could not overcome. "Let the English see with terror the hero of France advancing to proclaim on the ruins of Albion the commercial independence of Europe!" cried the Prefect of the Somme.[7] French generals talked confidently of reviewing the Army of England in St. James's Park.

Adding to the suspense was the English people's almost total lack of confidence in their government. William Pitt, the charismatic prime minister who had rallied England to resist the lure of the French Revolution and led the nation through a harrowing decade of war had been replaced by the uninspiring Henry Addington. He assembled a cabinet of mediocrities that was, in the words of one English wit, deficient in only three things: "brains, blood and gold." Assuring everyone that the "experimental peace" of Amiens would last, Addington had junked the income tax, which had funded the previous war, beached a good part of the Royal Navy, and reduced the regular army to a mere forty thousand men.[8]

The declaration of war had sent shock waves of panic through Addington's government. Their reaction to the invasion threat was the military amateur's instinctive resort: sheer numbers. They called on every able-bodied British male between sixteen and sixty to offer himself for some form of military duty. Hundreds of thousands rushed to join "volunteer" regiments, drying up the regular army's ability to recruit men they needed to expand their shrunken battalions.[9]

The defense of the realm became an even more colossal muddle when the government confessed to the 300,000 volunteers that it did not have enough muskets to arm more than a third of them. The only weapons available for most of the impromptu army were pikes. Addington found himself with a huge amorphous force of untrained, unarmed, quarrelsome novices, all determined to make their own rules and defiant of regular army attempts to discipline them. It was exactly the sort of patriotic horde that a well-trained army such as Bonaparte's could shatter in a day.

Add to this disarray the magic of Napoléon's reputation and it is easy to see why panic was coursing through England. George III wrote a letter to the bishop of Worcester, entrusting him with the preservation of the crown jewels.[10] Solemn plans were made for the evacuation of the royal family to refuges in the interior of the island. Redoubts were built along the roads to London and a huge armed camp constructed at nearby Chelmsford.

The French navy captured a British East Indiaman with a packet of confidential letters written by Englishmen to friends and relatives abroad. All expressed a dismaying defeatism. "I fear lest the people in their discontent,

[will] join the French if they should attempt to land," one writer confessed. Another admitted if the French landed, they "would carry the whole country." Others reported banks and businesses failing and the prices of everything skyrocketing.[11] Pundits bemoaned the "pitiful squirting politicians" around Addington. The *New-York Evening Post* reported from a reading of the latest London newspapers that "the public mind continues to be distracted."[12] Apparently, all Napoléon needed was the mighty storm, followed by the pregnant hours of dead calm, to achieve his ultimate victory. But on February 14, 1804, an upheaval that had nothing to do with the weather abruptly shelved the great invasion. As the first consul was shaving himself before a mirror held by his devoted valet, Constant, into the bedroom rushed the Paris chief of police to announce the discovery of a conspiracy to assassinate Napoléon and restore royal rule.

Unable to organize his country for defense, Prime Minister Addington had fallen back on a weapon that had long served England well: subversion. The government shipped to the continent a red-haired bull-necked Breton peasant and dedicated Napoléon hater named Georges Cadoudal, with orders to eliminate the first consul. On his heels came somewhere between forty and sixty fellow conspirators, under the command of General Jean-Charles Pichegru, a talented soldier who had switched to the royalist side.[13]

It was not the first attempt on Napoléon's life. Little more than three years earlier, he had narrowly escaped a Christmas Eve bomb that had killed and wounded almost a hundred Parisians. Vigilant police had intercepted another team of killers who planned to stab him to death while at the opera.

Postponing the invasion, the first consul launched a massive manhunt for his would-be slayers. On March 9th Cadoudal was captured after a gun battle with gendarmes. Asked why he had waited so long to strike, the Breton told his interrogators that he had orders to synchronize his attack with the arrival of a royal prince in Paris. From another Breton source came a report that the prince was Louis-Antoine, duc d'Enghien.

This thirty-one-year-old member of the House of Bourbon was living just across the border from France in the neutral principality of Baden.

Fig. 1   Grief, even depression, are visible in this portrait of General Alexander Hamilton, painted by Ezra Ames after his fall from political power in 1800 and his son Philip's death in a duel in 1801. In spite of his losses, the general remained the de facto leader of the fractured Federalist Party. The last letter he wrote was a plea to abandon the New England Federalists' plan to secede from the Union.

Fig. 2a Elizabeth Schuyler brought to illegitimate Alexander Hamilton a connection with one of the most powerful families in New York. Hamilton regretted that she excelled most of her sex in "amiable qualities" but not in "the more splendid ones." She remained devoted to her husband even after he made a public confession of his adultery with a voluptuous woman-about-Philadelphia, Maria Reynolds.

Fig. 2b Hamilton's country house, The Grange, was named after his family's ancestral estate in Scotland. It comprised 32 acres on Harlem Heights. The house cost Hamilton the equivalent of $300,000 in modern money and put him deeply in debt. A splendid house was almost a social necessity for a powerful politician to entertain important visitors.

Fig. 3a In this painting by John Trumbull, Angelica Schuyler Church, Elizabeth Hamilton's sister, poses with her son, Philip, and a servant. Beautiful, witty, intensely interested in politics, Angelica was married to dull, gouty, extremely wealthy John Barker Church. Friends cautioned Alexander Hamilton that his fondness for Angelica was in danger of becoming a scandal.

Fig. 3b Philip Schuyler, Hamilton's father-in-law, owned thousands of acres in the Hudson River Valley. A major general in the army of the Revolution, Schuyler enjoyed political combat as much as Hamilton, especially against "that Jefferson, who disgraces not only the place he fills but produces immorality by his pernicious example."

Fig. 4a Hudson River manor lord Robert R. Livingston was American ambassador to France when the Louisiana Purchase was consummated. He headed a clan of voracious office seekers who maintained an uneasy reliance with President Jefferson and his party in New York. Livingston resented Jefferson's attempt to downgrade his role in the historic purchase.

Fig. 4b Napoléon Bonaparte's power and fame cast a shadow on American politics in 1804. Bonaparte had a 200,000 man "Army of England" massed on the English Channel coast. If his invasion suceeded, many thought he would turn his imperial eyes toward America and demand the return of Louisiana.

Fig. 5   Vice President Aaron Burr's ruling passion, according to one of his closest friends, was "an ardent love of military glory." He was the theoretical heir apparent to the presidency. But Thomas Jefferson had grown hostile to his 1800 running mate. He suspected Burr of considering a switch to the Federalist Party, a prospect that also deeply disturbed Alexander Hamilton.

Fig. 6a Theodosia Burr Alston read Greek and Latin, spoke and read Fench fluently, and was well-versed in English Literature. Her father had supervised her education personally. Many thought the motive for her marriage to wealthy South Carolina planter Joseph Alston was political rather than romantic—to give her father a power base in the South.

RICHMOND HILL.

Fig. 6b Aaron Burr's country estate, Richmond Hill, occupied 26 acres at the intersection of what is now Charlton and Varick Streets in New York's Greenwich Village. The mansion's furnishings included inlaid card tables, mahogany chairs, a library lined with hundreds of books, and a well-stocked wine cellar. It was the chief reason why Burr was deeply in debt.

Fig. 7 In 1802, President Thomas Jefferson seemed in serious trouble when a journalist accused him of fathering several children by his mulato slave, Sally Hemings. But his political fortunes rebounded when Napoleon Bonaparte offered to sell the territory of Louisiana to the United States. Alexander Hamilton considered Jefferson a "contemptible hypocrite." Aaron Burr's opinion was equally scathing.

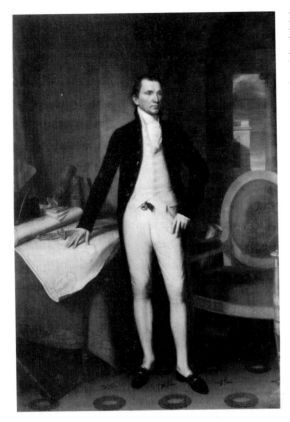

Fig. 8a   Future President James Monroe almost fought a duel with Alexander Hamilton for the Virginian's role in leaking the story of Hamilton's affair with Maria Reynolds. Monroe's second, Aaron Burr, helped resolve the quarrel short of gunfire. Later, Burr characterized Monroe as "naturally dull and stupid . . . indecisive to a degree that would be incredible to one who did not know him."

Fig. 8b   Ex-President John Adams blamed Alexander Hamilton for his 1800 loss to Thomas Jefferson. He filled the mails with vituperative, often scatological comments on Hamilton's morals and hunger for power. His wife, Abigail, agreed that General Hamilton hoped to become America's Napoléon Bonaparte.

Fig. 9a George Clinton was known in New York as "the old incumbent" because he had held the governorship for all but two terms since 1777. He hated Alexander Hamilton and never missed a chance to smear his reputation. President Jefferson chose the ailing sixty-four year old Clinton over Aaron Burr for his vice president in 1804, even though Clinton had called Jefferson "an accommadating trimmer."

Fig. 9b Thirty-four year old DeWitt Clinton began his political career as the secretary of his aging uncle, Governor George Clinton. DeWitt was called "Magnus Apollo" for his good looks and arrogant manner. When Governor Clinton won reelection in 1801, DeWitt launched a campaign to destroy Vice President Aaron Burr. With President Jefferson's covert cooperation, Clinton succeeded, thereby becoming New York's political boss.

Fig. 10a Privately, DeWitt Clinton said Morgan Lewis's two ruling passions were avarice and vanity. But Clinton chose him as his candidate for governor of New York because his distinguished record as a colonel in the Revolution gave him a chance of beating Aaron Burr. In this late portrait by Charles Curran, Lewis wears the uniform of a major general in the War of 1812. He carried the sword at Washington's inauguration in 1789, at which he was master of ceremonies.

Fig. 10b General James Wilkinson, commader in chief of the American Army, was known as Agent 13 on the Spanish secret service payroll. Wilkinson concealed his hatred of President Thomas Jefferson and paid a late night visit to a defeated, depressed Aaron Burr, proposing a plan to detach the western states from the Union and conquer Texas and Mexico.

P. Hamilton, Alexander DEATH OF ALEX. HAMILTON.

Fig. 11a Burr and Hamilton met in Weehawken because dueling was illegal in New York. Contrary to myth, a duel was not necessarily fatal. The death rate was about twenty percent. Most duelists missed. George Washington was on record as saying duels were decided by luck. If so, Hamilton's luck was bad. Burr cut him down with his first shot.

Fig. 11b Dr. David Hosack was the personal physician of many prominent New Yorkers, including Alexander Hamilton and DeWitt Clinton. In 1804 he was treating Hamilton for stomach and bowel complaints. Hosack also lectured at the Columbia College medical school. On July 11, 1804, he accompanied Hamilton and his second to Weehawken for the duel with Aaron Burr and was at Hamilton's bedside until he died the following day.

Fig. 12   This memorial page was typical of the many expressions of grief for Hamilton's death. Eventually, the *New-York Evening Post* published a book of the sorrowful sermons and poems. A few years ago a prominent rare book dealer advertised a copy of it with the owner's name inscribed on the first page: Aaron Burr.

One version of the story had him pining for the love of a nearby German princess. Another had him plotting a rebellion in the French province of Alsace-Lorraine through agents in Strasbourg.

An infuriated Napoléon sent three hundred dragoons and a small army of gendarmes across the Rhine to seize Enghien. Dragged before a military court, the yo ung nobleman admitted he had been receiving 4,200 guineas a year from the English, who ordered him to wait on the Rhine, where he would soon find a part to play in the great drama of Napoléon's downfall. The court sentenced the prince to death and Napoléon grimly approved the sentence. Enghien died before a firing squad on the morning of March 21, 1804. [14]

The Enghien-Cadoudal-Pichegru plot soon developed a momentum of its own in another direction—one that would have large meaning for politicians in the United States.

Virtually echoing General Hamilton's remarks about the fragility of postrevolutionary France, Napoléon began searching for a better answer to Bourbon plots than midnight kidnappings of witless young princes. After an earlier plot, he had told his followers: "These fanatics will end by killing me and putting angry Jacobins in power. It is I who embody the French Revolution." [15] The answer to the problem, in the opinion of many of the first consul's advisors, was to make Napoléon "immortal."

How was that to be done? By electing the Man of Destiny emperor of France. That would create a legal process for passing power to his family and his descendants, nullifying the danger of his death leaving France leaderless. For the moment, persuading the erstwhile Republicans of France to accept this idea became more important than the great invasion.

II

In Washington, D.C., early in March, the Spanish ambassador to the United States, the marqués de Casa Yrujo, burst into the office of Secretary of State James Madison and screamed curses and insults in his face for the better part of twenty minutes. Yrujo threatened war and thus the destabi-lization of Louisiana. Everyone immediately wondered if this was part of some subtle Napoléonic plan to give him an excuse to take back Louisiana soon after he hoisted the tricolor over the ruins of Parliament in London.

The root of the trouble was the vague boundaries of Louisiana. The primitive sixteenth- and seventeenth-century maps of the original terri-tory allowed for wildly different interpretations. One version suggested the Americans had bought everything down to the Rio Grande. Another more plausible argument seemed to include the east bank of the Missis-sippi and the port of Mobile.

This chunk of the continent was the old British colony of West Florida, which the Spanish had captured, along with the peninsula known as East Florida, in the closing years of the American Revolution. Anxious to bar the Americans from spreading their unsettling ideas about liberty to the citizens of Mexico and South America, the Spanish angrily contested the American claim. Yrujo was infuriated when Jefferson per-mitted (or more probably, sponsored in deep background) a bill to create a customs district of Mobile. When Jefferson signed the bill into law, the Spanish ambassador lost his self-control and paid his highly undiplomatic visit to Madison's office, shouting that his country had been libeled and his king insulted.

Jefferson and Madison retreated somewhat, designating nearby Fort Stoddert as the headquarters of the customs district. Meanwhile they drafted elaborate instructions to James Monroe, who was in England, try-ing to persuade the British to stop impressing seamen from American ships on the high seas. They ordered Monroe to Madrid to try to buy both Floridas from Spain. Simultaneously they urged Robert R. Liv-ingston, the outgoing American ambassador in Paris, to persuade Napoléon to pressure the Spanish into selling.

Alas, Jefferson and Madison soon learned that Napoléon's attitude to-ward the United States was continuing the downturn Livingston had noted not long after the first consul sold Louisiana. Napoléon blamed the Americans for supplying black rebels on the island of Saint Domingue with guns and ammunition that helped them drive the French army off the island and declare independence under the old Carib Indian name Haiti.

More evidence of France's negative attitude soon reached Washington from American ship owners and captains. French officials who had fled Saint Domingue to Cuba and nearby islands issued privateering commissions (called letters of marque) to every ship that asked for one of these licenses to piracy. The French and Spanish captains began seizing American ships by the dozen, accusing them of supporting the Haitian rebels. The captured ships were sailed into Cuban ports, their cargoes plundered, and the ships sunk. Their unfortunate crews were left stranded and in danger of starvation.

Madison angrily told Yrujo that the United States would hold Spain responsible for this assault on her ships. The ambassador replied that if the Americans were going to supply "poignards and torches" to assassins in the colony of a friendly country, they had no one to blame but themselves. American sailors, not inclined to take such treatment meekly, began going to sea with as many as twenty cannon on the decks of their merchantmen. A first-class naval war, only slightly less sanguinary than the one that ignited hostilities between France and America in 1798, seemed to be brewing, and Jefferson, with most of the tiny U.S. Navy fighting pirates in distant Tripoli, could do little to stop it.[16]

III

From Louisiana came rumbles and portents of even more serious trouble. The Spanish and French officials and their soldiers seemed in no hurry to leave New Orleans. Their presence nonplussed Jefferson's inexperienced choice for governor of the territory, William C. C. Claiborne. The president had originally hoped to lure the Marquis de Lafayette to America for this vital job. But the pressure to ratify and occupy before Napoléon changed his mind ruined that idea.

Public balls were among New Orleans's favorite pastimes. They swiftly became an arena where the Americans and their new subjects clashed. French officers drew their swords when they were told that only sissies danced quadrilles and from now on they were going to do jigs and reels. When one of the French musicians failed to cooperate, he was threatened with a caning by an obstreperous American. At one dance, General James Wilkinson had to restore order with fixed bayonets.

At another ball, the general and the governor got into an idiotic singing contest with the inhabitants. Wilkinson had arrested a Frenchman for refusing to follow the order of the dances. Excitement mounted and the two top American officials decided the best answer was a chorus of "Hail Columbia." The French responded by singing the Marseillaise, ending with a shout: *"Vive la république!"* The next day the governor and the general invited French leaders to a "banquet of reconciliation"—a gesture that only seemed to emphasize American weakness.[17]

The pleasures of New Orleans also made inroads on Wilkinson's handful of soldiers. No mean consumer of John Barleycorn himself, the general visited nearby Fort St. Louis, the bastion that was supposed to guard the city, and found the entire garrison passed out or too drunk to walk. This state of rampant indiscipline did not exactly inspire awe of American military might among the restless and resentful creoles.[18]

General Wilkinson himself did not inspire much confidence. Along with a fondness for the bottle and the pleasures of the knife and fork, the portly commander adored military magnificence—an odd contrast to the Republican simplicity favored by his commander in chief. The general's self-designed uniform glittered and dripped with gold braid. His horse wore a saddle cloth of leopard's hide with dangling claws, and stirrups and spurs of gleaming gold.

Worse, the province was filling up with refugees from Saint Domingue, some of whom had brought slaves with them. Other slaves, shipped from the island by the French before they fled, turned up on the auction block at New Orleans. The news of Saint Domingue's black triumphs soon traveled through the slave quarters of Louisiana, stirring thoughts of local revolt and inspiring French planters to loathe Americans for contributing to this sable revolution.

Another aspect of slavery's complexities had the planters in a fury at the American government. Congress, responding to Federalist diatribes against the trade, had voted to ban the importation of foreign slaves and also blacks from the other slave states. The only slaves who could be brought into Louisiana had to be demonstrably owned by immigrants from other slave states. The French planters regarded this legislation as a body blow at their rights and their future prosperity.[19]

The frantic Claiborne, whom Congressman John Randolph considered "a pompous nothing," bombarded President Jefferson with anxious letters.[20] The uncertain young governor reported widespread dissatisfaction because he had decreed that English would be the only language in the courts. He had no choice; Jefferson's lone judicial appointment understood nothing else. (Claiborne might have added he did not understand a word of French himself.) The governor was even more anxious about the lingering Spanish and French officials and their circle who were ready to "resort to every expedient short of assassination" to hamper his government. Their chief motive was greed. When the Spanish intendant heard that his country had given Louisiana back to France, he immediately issued a series of huge land grants to his friends.

Also among the troublemakers was Daniel Clark Jr., the former American consul in New Orleans, who thought Jefferson should have made him governor, and Edward Livingston, DeWitt Clinton's scandal-tarred predecessor as mayor of New York. Livingston still nursed his grudge against Jefferson's administration for failing to rescue him from the shame of embezzlement. Both Americans were stirring up the locals by criticizing Jefferson's appointive government as a betrayal of their rights under the treaty. The mayor of New Orleans had resigned in protest. The former French prefect and commissioner, Pierre Clement Laussat, was also in this worrisome picture, constantly second-guessing and interfering with Claiborne's attempts to keep order. Writing to his superiors in Paris, the Frenchman described Governor Claiborne as incompetent and General Wilkinson as a drunk.[21]

As a climax to this portrait of impending disaster, General Wilkinson decided the timing was perfect to renew his lapsed relationship as Spanish Agent 13. Behind the general's assiduous courtship of Thomas Jefferson still lurked a carefully concealed rage at the president and his administration.[22] In February 1804, Vicente Folch, the governor of West Florida, visited New Orleans. A charming man who spoke fluent English, he was soon deep in midnight conferences with General Wilkinson. The commander in chief of the American army told him that if the Spanish increased his stipend to $4,000 a year and paid the $20,000 that they owed him, the king of Spain would never have to worry about anyone encroaching on his American dominions.

Folch told the general he did not have that kind of money in his treasury but the marqués de Casa Calvo, designated by Spain as a commissioner to determine the proper boundaries for Louisiana, had $100,000 for "expenses"—a word that frequently included bribes in 1804. Wilkinson transferred his offer to the marqués, after swearing him to secrecy. The Spaniard offered $12,000. Wilkinson demanded the privilege of selling sixteen thousand barrels of flour in Havana, which would make him twice that sum. The marqués promised to pass on the request to the governor general of Cuba, and meanwhile handed over the $12,000.

General Wilkinson rewarded Calvo with twenty-two pages of "reflections,"—a farrago of advice and observations on how to keep the Americans at bay. Among his bits of wisdom: Hold onto both Floridas, no matter how much the Jeffersonians blustered and passed bills in Congress claiming all or part of them; if the pressure grew too strong, offer to trade them for everything west of the Mississippi in the Louisiana Purchase. To back this offer, Wilkinson urged Spain to bring Napoléon's France into the game. As for the expedition led by Meriwether Lewis and William Clark that President Jefferson was about to launch from St. Louis to explore America beyond the Mississippi—arrest them. [23]

Wilkinson's dalliance with the Spaniards was soon the gossip of New Orleans. He brushed aside the stories as attacks from envious enemies. He knew he had nothing to worry about in Washington. He was Thomas Jefferson's favorite soldier, even though in 1802 Secretary of War Henry Dearborn expressed his strong suspicion that Wilkinson was a Spanish agent.[24] The general wrote letters to Jefferson crammed with descriptions of the flora, fauna, and Indians of the region and filled the mails to Washington with petrified bones, Indian knives, and meteorological observations, all of which charmed the president. [25]

Given the rampant hostility to the Americans among the French population, one may assume that Napoléon soon learned that the commanding general of the American army was for sale. With this kind of information in his files, Bonaparte could only conclude that Louisiana was his for the retaking as soon as he crossed the English Channel and finished off perfidious Albion.

IV

In Washington, D.C., President Jefferson's feud with British ambassador Anthony Merry about American dining-room etiquette was producing its own brand of evil fruit. The British government of Prime Minister Henry Addington had tried hard to mend relations with the United States. They were as friendly as any English politicians could be, with George III glowering over their shoulders, still brooding about his lost colonies. Merry's reports to London soon became a jarring dissonance in this attempted harmony.

Rather than try to soothe the outraged Briton and his wife, President Jefferson and Secretary of State Madison stiffly defended their right to entertain as they pleased. They claimed they were merely introducing the Merrys to Republican etiquette, where everyone was equal and the discomfited pair objected because they were (by implication) a couple of royalist snobs.

The president compounded this misunderstanding by continuing to call Ambassador Merry's large outspoken wife a "virago." He used this term in a letter to Special Envoy James Monroe in London and apparently repeated it to visitors to the presidential palace.

Stubbornly refusing to admit they had done anything wrong, and ignoring the political "buzz," as former ambassador to London Rufus King called it, the president and his secretary of state spent hours drawing up a promulgation called "Canons of Etiquette" that established Republican standards of *pêle-mêle* for all official gatherings in Washington, D.C. It had begun to dawn on Jefferson that he was verging on the ridiculous, but he did not know how to back out of this social cul-de-sac. "I blush to have put so much trash on paper," he confessed to Special Envoy Monroe.

Waxing toward the extreme, as he was inclined to do when he had pen in hand, the president told another former diplomat, Virginian William Short, that he was trying to establish "the true principal of equality" at his dinner table. He fumed that American ministers had to submit to the practices of foreign courts and that justified forcing diplomats to accept the absence of manners among Americans. Completely carried away, Jefferson revealed his underlying isolationist streak. "I have ever considered diplomacy as the pest of the peace of the world," he told Short. The president boasted that he had gotten rid of half the American diplomatic corps and wished he could jettison the rest.[26]

Next, Jefferson took the time to write an anonymous article for the *Philadelphia Aurora*, defending *pêle-mêle* as quintessential Americanism. He lashed out at "unfounded stuff" in Federalist papers and accused them of trying to foment "misunderstandings with other nations"—an attempt to put the shoe on the other foot. He ranted on about how the Jefferson administration had abolished the "court of the United States"—a nasty reference to the mild formalities observed at receptions given by Presidents Washington and Adams. *Pêle-mêle* and "next [nearest] the door" were the social rules that Americans followed, roundly declared the president.

Undeterred, the Federalists spread the story of Jefferson's rudeness far and wide. Congressman Manasseh Cutler of Massachusetts, who often referred to Jefferson as "His Democratic Majesty," strenuously disagreed with the president's characterization of Mrs. Merry. At a formal visit to their home with Senator John Quincy Adams, Cutler found her "just as easy and social as if we had been long acquainted" and praised her "agreeable conversation."[27]

Merry in turn took seriously the New England Federalist plan to secede from the union and urged the same attitude on his government. He gave splendid dinners for as many as thirteen Federalist congressmen at a time, and undoubtedly filled their ears with his contempt for President Thomas Jefferson. Refusing to submit to *pêle-mêle*, he had declined all invitations from the president or his secretary of state.

From London came a low cry of distress from the president's special envoy, James Monroe. Although he repeatedly told Jefferson that no one in the British government or out of it took Merry's complaints seriously, the Virginian could not help noticing numerous slights. At a royal reception, Queen Charlotte had looked through him as if he were invisible. Whenever he attended a diplomatic dinner, he was seated last, after diplomats from piffling German states such as Liechtenstein and Anhalt Lippe.

Although there were undoubted elements of comedy in this situation, Federalists could also find in it proof that in a world at war, Jefferson the political theorist was in charge and common sense was as scarce as traditional diplomacy in Washington, D.C.

V

In the midst of this hugger-mugger, fate dealt Jefferson a cruel blow. Only two of his seven children had reached maturity. The older, thirty-two-year-old Martha, nicknamed Patsy, was a tall, ungainly female version of her father. She lived near Monticello with her moody, unstable husband, Thomas Mann Randolph, and their seven children.[28] The second daughter,

Maria, called Polly, was Martha's opposite in almost every way—auburn-haired, clinging, beautiful. She was reputedly the image of her mother, Martha Wayles Jefferson, who had died in 1782—a loss that drove Jefferson to the brink of suicide.

Maria had married her cousin John Wayles Eppes in 1799 and had already given him a son. Like her mother, she seemed to decline when her husband was away, and Eppes was away a good deal since he had been elected to Congress. Both he and his brother-in-law, Thomas Mann Randolph, won seats in the 1802 congressional elections. Pregnant with her second child, Maria went into an even steeper decline. Martha was soon reporting to her father that Maria's spirits were "bad."

In letters to her husband, "the best beloved of my soul," Maria reported her health was so poor, she could take almost no solid food. Her symptoms suggest she had inherited the illness that had killed her mother, the kidney disorder known as Bright's disease. Pregnancy was especially dangerous for any woman with this malady, but no one in the early nineteenth century was aware of this grim fact. Jefferson wrote warm letters, urging Maria to rely on her courage. She gave birth to a healthy child early in March and the president congratulated her, presuming the worst was over.

Alas, exactly like her mother after her last pregnancy, Maria failed to recover. By the time Jefferson returned to Virginia in April, he found her too weak to walk. Her husband had her carried in a litter to Monticello, and Jefferson tried to revive her with a regimen of sweet wines and simple foods. But nothing could stop Maria's sad, slow decline. On April 23, 1804, as the election in New York swirled to a climax, he reported Maria's death to James Madison. The family's hopes and fears had, he wrote, taken their "ultimate form."[29]

To a friend of his youth, John Page, the president was far less stoic. "Others may lose of their abundance, but I, of my want, have lost the half of all I had," he cried. He added a long lament about growing old, wondering if the loss of so many loved ones and friends through death or political alienation was tolerable. [30]

Maria's death had a political postlude. Abigail Adams, reading the story in the newspapers, wrote Jefferson a tender letter, recalling how fond she had been of Maria when she had stayed with the Adamses in London, enroute to join her father and sister in Paris, seventeen years before. But the former first lady could not resist adding a political sting to her final lines. She closed by describing herself as someone who had once been Jefferson's friend.

The president replied with rare emotion, declaring that in spite of their political differences, he still had a warm place in his heart for Abigail and her husband. In fact, he careened unwisely on, there was only one political act of John Adams that he considered unfriendly: his passage of the judiciary act and his appointment of the corps of Federalist federal judges—his "ardent political enemies," Jefferson called them—as Adams was leaving office. Abigail sent him a scorching reply, asking him how the moment he became president he could have pardoned James Thomson Callender, "a wretch" who had published "the basest libel, the lowest and vilest slander that malice could invent" against her husband.[31]

Revealing how acutely the Callender story disturbed him, Jefferson completely lost his judgment and wrote a wrathful answer, damning the Sedition Act under which Callender had been imprisoned as a "nullity" as palpable as if Congress had ordered Americans to worship a golden calf. Abigail furiously defended the act in her reply, demanding to know where and how Jefferson and his fellow Virginians thought they had the right to annul any law passed by Congress. She wondered if he really believed there was any difference between a republican and a "despotic government." In a vitriolic close, she told him she had once felt "respect and esteem" for him, believing him to be "an affectionate parent, a kind master, a candid and benevolent friend." But experience had forced her to change these opinions. Never again would she "esteem" him.[32]

This was ugly stuff. Abigail was telling Jefferson she believed Callender's story about his seduction of Sally Hemings—and she was stating even more firmly that she was convinced he had hired Callender to slander Presidents Washington and Adams.

VI

In Albany, another side of Jefferson's unsavory connection with James Thomson Callender was being played out in the legislature and in the chambers of the state supreme court. The lawmakers were hard at work, trying to mitigate Chief Justice Morgan Lewis's truth-is-irrelevant ruling in the Croswell trial and the additional damage Alexander Hamilton had wreaked on the candidate in the hearing before the supreme court. On the last day of the legislative session, "An Act Relative to Libels" was delivered to the Council of Revision, a body composed of the supreme court's judges and the state's chancellor, who had the responsibility to examine all laws passed by the legislature. The act stated that the truth would henceforth be relevant in libel cases in New York, and juries would have the right to judge an accused libeler's intentions.

James Cheetham's *American Citizen* and other Republican papers had publicized the bill as it went through the legislature. The Clinton-Livingston machine could now claim they had corrected a slight glitch in their commitment to free and untrammeled speech, as good Republicans must. Unfortunately, this still left Harry Croswell, the convicted editor of the Hudson *Wasp*, facing a jail term. Judge James Kent, keenly aware that the legislature had tacitly repudiated Chief Justice Lewis's ruling, wondered if this meant Croswell would get a new trial. Recalling Judge Brockholst Livingston's statement to him in favor of such a decision, Kent could only conclude—or at least hope—that his fellow jurist would be even more inclined in this direction now. During next fall's presidential elections, General Hamilton might yet have a chance to accuse Thomas Jefferson of hiring a literary assassin to besmirch the good name of the father of the country.[33]

CHAPTER 13

A Ruined Politician
Has a Midnight Visitor

On April 30th, James Cheetham began printing in the *American Citizen* voting returns from districts within easy reach of New York City. It soon became apparent that Vice President Burr's Manhattan majority of 100 was not an omen of victory. Orange County, where Burr had hoped his friend Peter Townsend's influence as an ironworks tycoon would give him an advantage, reported a majority of 650 for Morgan Lewis. A letter from Westchester reported an expected majority of 400 for Lewis. Another letter from a single town, Southhampton, on Long Island, gave Lewis a 300-vote majority. A writer from Albany reported Burr had a majority of only 92 in that crucial town, less than Stephen Van Rensselaer had received when he ran in 1801 with Alexander Hamilton's backing.[1]

Cheetham continued to reprint returns for the rest of the week, most of them reporting majorities for Lewis. The editor interspersed the reports with gloating remarks from his correspondents. From Albany, one writer crowed: "THANK GOD THE TRAITORS ARE UNMASKED in all quarters and consigned to political oblivion."[2]

On Saturday, May 5th, Cheetham added a very large chortle of his own: "All parties now admit that Chief Justice Lewis . . . will be elected by a majority of from 7000 to 8000 . . . At our last governor election in 1801, Governor Clinton, the most popular man in the state, had a majority of 3965 only. So much for Burrism and Federalism in 1804!" He added a special barb for William Coleman, who had declared that in every county in the state "thousands were crying out for Aaron Burr as our next governor."[3]

Two days later, Cheetham proclaimed conclusive proof that President Jefferson had never been neutral in the election. Congressman Beriah Palmer, now sure he was on the winning side, came out of hiding and allowed the Englishman to use his name on a letter, affirming that the president had told him he never considered the "little band" real Republicans. Thus, crowed Cheetham, the character of their beloved chief executive was now freed from "the vile aspersions of Oliver Phelps." Congressman Palmer was rewarded by being hailed as "a gentleman of correct understanding, and of unsullied reputation."[4]

II

By this time Burr knew the worst. He reported it in a letter to Theodosia on May 1st. He told her he was writing in the dining room of Richmond Hill beside a good fire on a chilly spring evening. He began by answering her queries about his various lady friends. He had planned to visit Celeste but now it looked as if other matters had intervened. As for his New York inamorata, La G, she was about forty-one, "talks much . . . is certainly good tempered and cheerful; rather comely, abating a flat chest; about two inches taller than Theodosia." He assured her things had not yet "gone to extremities," meaning he was not close to proposing. But he conceded: "There is danger—"

In his inimitably cool way, he added: "The election is lost by a great majority: tant mieux." (It's just as well.) Burr made a point of seeming imperturbable to Theodosia, who worried incessantly about him.[5]

III

On May 3rd, William Coleman devoted a column in the *Evening Post* to a rueful analysis of why Burr lost. He insisted that the vice president had been ahead until "just previous to the opening of the polls." The chief reason for his sudden downturn was "the very extraordinary attacks on his private character, which were circulated with an industry and an expence [*sic*] hitherto unexampled." Coleman also concluded that the Clintonian-Livingston assault on the Burrites as "feeble folk" had been very effective. Many New Yorkers who resented the Clinton-Livingston monopoly of jobs and power concluded it would be a waste of time to publicly support Burr, and even politically dangerous, given the vindictive tendencies of the Old Incumbent and his nephew. Finally Coleman blamed the upstate weather for preventing many Federalists from getting to the polls. Drenching rain had fallen on all three polling days, turning the roads to quagmires. "Generally speaking the Federalists are very much your fair weather sort of people," Coleman concluded.[6]

Before William Coleman published this tombstone on the election, the *Evening Post*'s editor devoted the previous day's front page to a reprint of a long essay from the *Boston Repertory*. The writer deplored the way Americans had been so distracted by "dissensions between the Federalists and the Democrats" that they have overlooked "the aggrandizement of the Southern States and their accumulating power." That, the writer maintained, was Jefferson's main object in acquiring Louisiana. His outrageous flattery of Bonaparte proved he was not a "sincere democrat." The real question before the country was whether "the states from the Chesapeake to the River St. Croix" were to be "satellites of Virginia."

There was only one way to prevent this: The "aristocratical" power of the southern states had to be reduced by amending the Constitution to bar their millions of Negro slaves from being represented in Congress. Under the compromise adopted by the Constitutional Convention, the South was granted representation in Congress for three-fifths of its black population. But the representatives were all "white aristocrats." If the slaves were going to be represented, this contentious Yankee proposed, "let us have at least their members in black—real negroes."

When the French troops withdrew from Haiti, the new black rulers had massacred every white person left on the island. Drawing on the shock waves of fear that this carnage had sent through America, the New England essayist went on to argue that the southern states were defenseless because of their restless negroes. If an enemy attacked the United States, "the yeomanry of the North will have to rescue Virginia just as they did during the Revolution." The one hope of national salvation was a union of the states north of the Chesapeake. Only then would the nation cease to resemble a serpent "whose head is directed by its tail."[7]

With the election lost, William Coleman was no longer campaigning for Aaron Burr. But he was well aware of the New England plan to propose secession at a meeting of political leaders in the fall. He seemed to be suggesting with this story that the idea was still alive and meaningful, even if Governor Burr could no longer include New York in the movement.

IV

Cheetham and the Clinton-Livingston organization had carefully avoided the secession plot throughout the campaign. It was too loaded with potential damage among the heavily New England–populated upstate counties. But they reacted to Coleman's story with violent rhetoric in the *American Citizen* on May 7th. Cheetham called the editor of the Boston *Repertory* "an impertinent meddling ignoramus" and he condemned the "anti-union doctrine he so sedulously and zealously inculcates."

The *Repertory* had backed Burr throughout the governorship race. Why? "It is not generally known that the *eastern federal prints* abound with speculations on the DISSOLUTION OF THE UNION!" (The capitals are Cheetham's, as usual.) Worse, the "conductors and patrons" of the scheme "view Aaron Burr as the man best fitted to effect this most disastrous of national calamities." That explained why in the recent election, most of the New England Federalists residing in New York backed Burr. Warming to his conspiracy theory, Cheetham asserted that Aaron Burr and Oliver Phelps were New England men and so were William Coleman of the *Evening Post* and Zachariah Lewis, editor of the *Commercial Advertiser.* These "desperate adventurers" schemed to destroy the union by seizing power in Albany.

V

In succeeding days, Cheetham returned to gloating. He reported that New York had sent fifteen Republicans and only two Federalists to Congress. The previous ratio had been twelve to five. The two assemblymen who had dared to endorse Burr had lost their seats. He quoted approvingly from the *National Intelligencer*, the president's semiofficial paper, which congratulated New York's voters for standing "firm to their principles" and rejecting "acts subversive of the public good." From the Republican *Register* of Salem, Massachusetts, came a mocking comment that "the little Bonaparte"—Aaron Burr—could now only exclaim "Farewell, a long farewell to all my greatness."[8]

On May 10th, Cheetham congratulated himself for being the man who had first exposed Burr's perfidy. The rehash of his accusations went on for dozens of smug paragraphs. He recalled that he had challenged the vice president to hold a judicial inquiry on his charges and he had responded only with "monkish legerdemain," persuading friends to write deceptive letters in his defense. Burr's performance was typical of "men abandoned to vice," and he had proved his depravity by forming an alliance with the despicable Federalists.

Switching to his pious mode, Cheetham exempted from his remarks General Hamilton, Colonel Troup, Rufus King, and Richard Harison. These Federalists refused to stoop to using "the worst means"—Aaron Burr—to overthrow the Republican party. Cheetham doubted that any of them had performed an "essential disservice" to Burr's cause, but their "honorable" neutrality had won the editor's respect.[9]

VI

On May 18th, Cheetham opened an assault on The Merchants Bank, "the crafty work of Aaron Burr and his minions." He declared it was Burr's one hope of escaping the financial "embarrassments" that would soon overwhelm him. The vice president had hoped it could buy the election for him. It was to be the focus of "eastern federalism" (New England) and of "New York opposition to the state and federal governments." According to Cheetham, Burr was hoping to pocket gains of as much as 20 percent on the original stock.[10] But the citizens of the state of New York had announced in the election that The Merchants Bank was a "dangerous political institution."[11]

What was going on here? It was a continuation of the take-no-prisoners war that Cheetham and DeWitt Clinton, two natural-born extremists, were waging against Burr. They were making it clear that they intended to destroy him not only politically but financially and in every other conceivable way.

Cheetham also went to work on demolishing any hope of Burr becoming the head of the Federalist party in New York State, even though he had run a losing race. On May 29th the Englishman devoted numerous paragraphs to showing that the Federalists had actually lost support by backing Burr. The vice president had polled 103 less votes than Stephen van Rensselaer in 1801, while Morgan Lewis ran ahead of the previous Republican total by almost 6,000 votes. (The final count would give him a majority of over 8,000.)[12] The Republicans, in short, had gained by discarding Burr and the Federalists had suffered. "So much for the union of all honest men," Cheetham sniggered.

VII

What was Aaron Burr doing while this abuse continued to rain on him? The most revealing document that has survived is a letter to Theodosia. He began it on May 8th, responding to a letter she had mailed to him on April 26th. He told her that the "affair of La G." was becoming serious. She had the feminine qualities he wanted and needed: prudence, cheerfulness, and good temper. He had decided to "offer homage" (propose marriage) and wanted to know if Theodosia approved. "Answer quickly," he added.

The next paragraph reported that "Madame Bonaparte and husband" were in New York. But he had only "just seen them and no more."

For reasons unknown, "we are become strangers." Burr suggested it was doubtless "some state policy." Behind this offhand remark lurked a major snub by the Bonapartes. After all, the vice president had entertained the couple royally in Washington, D.C. To ignore him in New York was a rather brutal commentary on how low Burr's political stock had dropped.

Abruptly Burr switched the subject to his grandson. "Of all earthly things I most want to see your boy," he wrote. "Does he yet know his letters? If not, you surely must want skill, for, most certain, he can't want genius. You must tell me of all his acquirements."

Then the letter switched back to La G. Burr admitted that he had not seen "my inamorata" since the last time he mentioned a meeting, "which you may think passing strange."

Next came a space, and another date: May 26th. Almost three weeks had passed since Burr wrote the first five rambling paragraphs of this letter. "I think I will never again be so long without writing to you," he began this new section. "It has been a daily and nightly reproach to me . . . The matter there spoken of seemed to be in so precarious a state, that I did not like to send you that page alone, and in fact I did not know what to add to it." He was referring to La G, of course. From the day he began the letter on May 8th until he resumed it on May 26th, he had not seen her "owing partly to accident and partly to apathy."

Apathy. For three weeks, Burr had apparently hidden himself at Richmond Hill. He did not answer an importunate letter that his boyhood friend, Senator Jonathan Dayton of New Jersey, wrote to him on May 12th. On May 18th, Dayton wrote again, pressing him urgently about money due him from one of Burr's supporters. Dayton had not dunned the man for it during the campaign, because he knew that the family's backing (political and probably financial) was important to Burr. Now he hoped Burr would help him collect the debt.

Dayton added a paragraph about $2,500 he had loaned Burr in 1800. "I cannot possibly do without it," he wrote. In fact, he needed it so badly, he did not even ask Burr whether he would pay it. "It seems not to admit of a question."

Dayton was a friend of Daniel Clark, the former New Orleans consul whom Jefferson had disappointed by not naming him governor of Louisiana. In another part of the letter he enclosed a letter from Clark, reporting serious dissatisfaction in New Orleans over Congress's decision not to permit the importation of slaves into the territory.[13]

Burr's silence was evidence not only of a deep depression. It intimated that he had no hope of repaying the money he owed Dayton or of helping him collect the other debt. The Merchants Bank was not likely to loan him any money now. Instead, with the growing evidence that he was a political pariah, the bankers were more likely to ask him to distance himself from their operations.

Not everyone in New York had abandoned Burr. In the third week in May he received a letter from his friend Charles Williamson, the land speculator who had bought millions of upstate acres for English investors. Writing from Bath, in Albany County, Williamson was seeking Burr's advice on how to get a divorce from his angry American-born wife, Abigail. The Scot had not been the most faithful husband and Abigail had developed "the temper of a devil." The process of transferring supervision of his million-plus acres to Robert Troup was almost completed, and the ex-soldier planned to return to England later in the year. As to politics, he would say nothing until they met. Writing on May 16th, Williamson planned to visit Burr in "one month's time." Meanwhile, he wanted the vice president to know that "no circumstance can lessen the most respectful and sincere regard and esteem of your affectionate friend."[14]

VIII

On May 23rd, the apathetic vice president received a clandestine visit from a friend who was on his way to Washington, D.C.—Brigadier General James Wilkinson. The general's letter could not have been more covert: "To save time of which I need much and have little, I propose to take a bed with you this night, if it may be done without observation or intrusion—Answer me and if in the affirmative I will be with [you] at 30 after the 8th hour."

Here was an interesting scene. The commander in chief of the American army—the flatterer who had worked overtime to win President Jefferson's favor in spite of the rumors about his Spanish treason, and who secretly hated Jefferson almost as much as Burr now did—sneaking under cover of darkness to see the president's greatest enemy little more than three weeks after Burr's political power had apparently been shattered at the polls. What was going on? No one knows what this double-talking general discussed with Burr on that dark May night. But in the light of what soon transpired, there are some plausible conjectures.

Almost certainly, Wilkinson brought confirmation of the growing unrest in New Orleans and what it might—or might not—portend for both him and Aaron Burr. Without quite admitting he was on the Spanish payroll, the general probably bragged that he had the Spaniards totally gulled. They were ready to believe anything he told them. The opportunity was wide open for an enterprising man to lead a foray into Spanish territory and carve off a chunk of their tottering empire.

Wilkinson was in touch with numerous adventurous types in Kentucky and Tennessee who had discussed with him conquering some part of Spain's dominions. This army of western warriors could easily be evoked by Colonel Aaron Burr, who was already known as their friend and supporter in Washington, D.C. The most tempting and eminently grabable prize was Texas, an immense territory peopled by a few wandering Indians and a handful of Mexicans.

If all went well in Texas—a certain amount of shooting would be required to convince the Spanish they meant business—who knows what could happen next? A man who had been vice president of the United States and a colonel in the American Revolution, and who had just routed a Spanish army in Texas, might appeal to a lot of Mexicans as the Bonaparte they needed to lead them from the medieval darkness of Spanish tyranny into the bright sunlight of a modern republic. With General Burr would come the men of Kentucky and Tennessee, whom Wilkinson frequently said were "as greedy after plunder as ever the old Romans were."

Mexico! The very word meant gold and silver beyond calculation—and equally vast amounts of political power. By Burr's side would ride magnificently uniformed General Wilkinson on his gleaming steed, with his leopard-skin saddlecloth and stirrups and spurs of polished gold.

The conquest of Mexico, or even of Texas, would inspire the citizens of Louisiana, already angry at their Jeffersonian masters, to throw in their lot with the new country, and it was more than likely that the states along the Mississippi and Ohio would make a similar decision. What could be more delicious than to whisk President Jefferson's Louisiana Purchase out from under his nose and convert it into a vehicle for the fame of Aaron Burr? [15]

The next day, Wilkinson sent Burr another brief letter as he resumed his journey to Washington, D.C.: "You are deceived, my friend, with respect to the size of the rum barrel of Louisiana the answer being 450 lbs," the brigadier wrote. This was probably a veiled reference to the number of American troops in Louisiana. Henceforth, the two men frquently communicated in masked phrases and ciphers. Wilkinson added that he was on his way "with prayers and wishes for your prosperity and happiness" and "with warm prospect." He closed, describing himself as "your affetiate [affectionate] and faithful friend."

Within a few hours came another note, indicative of still rising enthusiasm, urging Burr to visit the general before he left New York "to see my maps." Wilkinson had brought with him from Louisiana a collection of manuscript maps of Texas and the rest of the Spanish Southwest—extremely useful tools for planners of an invasion. [16]

Here was the answer to Vice President Burr's apathy. Within three days he was assuring Theodosia that he would "never again be so long without writing to you." The implication that he was on his way to becoming his old sanguine self was unmistakable. He ordered Theodosia to resume her education. He wanted her to read philosophy and Latin and Shakespeare. He proposed they jointly read the Bard's collected works and mark the passages they consider "beautiful, absurd or obscure," and then compare notes. "Gods!—how much you might accomplish this year."[17]

Suddenly James Cheetham's gloats and chortles, DeWitt Clinton's vindictive determination to annihilate Aaron Burr, no longer seemed important. The future was alive with possibility for the vice president, his daughter, and the heir apparent.[18]

CHAPTER 14

Light
in the Labyrinth

*W*hile Vice President Aaron Burr's political hopes soared and then plunged to a humiliating crash at the hands of the Empire State's voters, General Alexander Hamilton spent most of his time in his law office toiling on briefs and in the courtroom arguing cases. But he could not ignore the election, which had much more profound meaning for him as an insider than it had for the ordinary voter. Judge James Kent visited Hamilton at The Grange during the last weekend of the campaign and found he was almost constantly melancholy. The General saw nothing but evil emerging from a Burr victory. He was sure it would lead to the secession of New York and the New England states, with Burr as their leader. He was equally pessimistic about the reckless assault on the judiciary in Washington, D.C., and in Pennsylvania. He lamented to Kent the "sway of artful and ambitious demagogues."[1]

On the Saturday of Kent's visit, a terrific northeast storm erupted, which lasted most of the night. It hit The Grange particularly hard. Kent told his wife in a letter a few days later that "the second story, where I slept . . . rocked like a cradle." Hamilton visited the judge in his bedroom to make sure he was not getting blown away.[2]

His host's solicitude reminded Kent of the time he and Hamilton were riding circuit in wintry upstate New York. Kent had a very bad cold. After he went to bed, he was awakened by a shadowy figure tucking an extra blanket around him. It was Hamilton. "Sleep well, little Judge," he said. "If anything happened to you, what would we do?"

In the same letter to his wife, Kent remarked that Hamilton's deranged daughter Angelica, now nineteen, "has a very uncommon simplicity and modesty of deportment." It is hard to tell whether the judge was trying to say something nice about this pathetic young woman or had somehow convinced himself there was nothing wrong with her.

Gouverneur Morris was supposed to join Hamilton and Kent for dinner, but he sent a message from Morrisania that the "Jacobinical winds" made travel impossible. In several hours of talk, Hamilton confided to Kent that he was planning to write "an investigation" of the history and science of government and the impact of the various forms on the freedom and happiness of mankind. He hoped to enlist six or eight fellow lawyers, including John Jay, Rufus King, and Gouverneur Morris, in the project. He wanted Kent to join in the venture and the judge readily agreed. The goal was to be a demonstration that any scheme of government based on a transformation of human nature was doomed to fail. In short, the treatise would be a projectile aimed at Jeffersonian and Jacobinical ideas about changing mankind through politics. It was also a mournful admission on Hamilton's part that his political career was probably over.

Undoubtedly, Kent and Hamilton discussed the Croswell case. The supreme court was going to hand down its decision during the May term. Kent almost certainly reported that he had half persuaded Judge Brockholst Livingston to side with him. But Kent said nothing about this news igniting a flash of the General's old pugnacity. Instead, Hamilton probably expressed considerable scepticism about hoping too much from this very political judge.

Kent came away from the weekend, he told his wife, resolved to pursue his ruling passion: "literary and elegant retirement and a glowing and vehement attachment to my wife and children." He was "assuredly" not interested in "ambition or glory." Forty-eight hours with the Hamiltons had given him a sobering look at the wages of fame.[3]

II

A few weeks later, in early May, Hamilton displayed the sort of hospitality he had in mind when he built The Grange. Jerome and Betsy Patterson Bonaparte were guests of honor at a glittering dinner party for sixteen people. The General rushed a special invitation to Gouverneur Morris. The master of Morrisania did not let the weather or anything else interfere with a chance to meet a young man who might say something indiscreet—and revealing—about Napoléon and his plans for the future of Europe and America.

Unfortunately, no one left a record of what was discussed at the dinner. But the spectacle of two leaders of the New York Federalist party exchanging toasts with an unofficial spokesman for the latest stage of the French Revolution was a commentary in itself. General Hamilton was publicly expressing a certain acceptance—even a degree of admiration—for the man who had restored order to France.

III

Another Grange party of even larger dimensions was an all-day fête that Elizabeth Hamilton gave for her sister Angelica. No less than seventy people were invited to a 9:00 A.M. breakfast, followed by a ball and climaxed by a dinner. Angelica, used to late hours like most women of fashion, confided to her son, Philip, that people would "have to wear their nightcaps" to arrive on time for breakfast. She also remarked that her countryfied sister had made the possibly fatal mistake of failing to hire New York's best caterer, a Frenchman named Contois.[4]

Gossip continued to swirl around General Hamilton and his flirtatious sister-in-law. Her dour gouty husband left her alone in their lavish town house on Robinson Street (now Park Place), staying out until dawn four or five nights a week, playing cards for heavy money. Five nights a week, Hamilton was a few blocks away in his house on Cedar Street. Only on weekends did he seek the company of his wife and family at the Grange. Incontrovertible evidence of a continuing affair remains elusive. But at the very least Angelica was a tantalizing figure on Hamilton's emotional horizon. She was the sort of woman a soldier who acquired power—perhaps, in American terms, became president for life—would take for a mistress.

IV

At one point, General Hamilton was asked to involve himself as a lawyer in one of Aaron Burr's primary concerns. The backers of the Merchants Bank approached the General to represent them before the governor's council when the Clinton-Livingston–controlled legislature refused to give them a charter. Hamilton's response underscored his awareness that his political career was over. He did not respond with his patented diatribe against Aaron Burr, or haughtily declare he would have nothing to do with an organization backed by such a nefarious character. He seemed more than willing to take the case. In the end he was asked only to comment on an early draft of the bill banning the bank, because it seemed to bar individuals or partnerships from receiving deposits of goods or money. Hamilton agreed the wording was ambiguous and "dangerous to the Mercantile interest."[5]

One Hamilton law case exhibited an oblique interest in politics—and in making some badly needed money. Having lost political control of New York City, he and a group of fellow Federalists decided to build an even greater city on the other side of the Hudson. They formed the Associates of the Jersey Company and bought up much of what is now downtown Jersey City, which in 1804 was called Powles Hook. They planned to level the hilly peninsula, divide it into a thousand lots, and launch a Federal metropolis on the somewhat debatable maxim that most great cities arise on the west banks of major rivers.

The city of New York did not look kindly on this venture. No sooner were the lots advertised for sale than Mayor DeWitt Clinton and his cohorts launched a lawsuit claiming that New York owned all the land on the Jersey shore below the low-water mark. The agitated associates asked General Hamilton if this meant their wharves and docks would be under the jurisdiction of the state of New York. If so, it aborted any prospect of the future city becoming a major port.

Hamilton replied on May 3rd that in his opinion, the corporation of the city of New York had no right to the land under water adjoining Powles Hook. He therefore concluded that there would be "adequate security" to the purchasers of the future city's lots. Neither side was aware that they were firing the first shots in a legal struggle that would last for another forty years. Eventually the U.S. Supreme Court would declare Hamilton was right. But by that time Mayor DeWitt Clinton and his successors had achieved their goal: They had effectively destroyed the possibility of a major city arising in New Jersey to compete with New York.[6]

V

Around this time, General Hamilton received a letter from James Wilkinson. The U.S. Army's commander in chief had fond feelings for Hamilton. He had treated Wilkinson well when Hamilton commanded the army during the undeclared war with France. The brigadier told his former chief that New Orleans was attracting "men of all nations, ages, professions, Characters & Complexions, and *women* too." Underlining that last word suggested Wilkinson thought Hamilton would enjoy sampling the charms of these newly arrived and presumably adventurous ladies.

The current commanding general added that he would give "a *Spanish* province for an interview with you." The underlining of the word Spanish was also not accidental. Wilkinson apparently had not forgotten General Hamilton's inclination to take a large slice of Spanish America by force. He added that the "infernal design of France" was "obvious to me," suggesting he was one of those insiders who thought Napoléon planned to take back Louisiana as soon as possible. As for the "destinies of Spain," they were in "the hands of the U.S." That meant the Floridas, Texas, and perhaps Mexico were plums waiting to be picked by a government with a little energy. Wilkinson closed by asking General Hamilton to remember him fondly to Gouverneur Morris—another man who thought the United States should have long since taken Louisiana and the Floridas by force.[7]

The letter was written several weeks before General Wilkinson's visit to Vice President Burr. It is a revealing look at what was on the brigadier's mind.

VI

The month of May in New York was enlivened not only by James Cheetham's sustained gloating over Aaron Burr's political corpse in the *American Citizen* but also by the appearance of another literary effort by Thomas Paine. The aging revolutionist had been pondering Napoléon's projected invasion of England. Bonaparte was not—and in fact should not have been—one of this radical democrat's favorite people. In 1797, when Napoléon returned from his victories over Austrian armies in Italy, he had met Paine and embraced him, declaring that the author of *The Rights of Man* should have a statue of gold. Dazzled by this flattery, Paine had become an instant convert. When Napoléon announced a plan to invade England in 1798, Paine had donated a hundred livres (about $25.00) to the effort and sent with it "all the wishes of my heart."[8]

A few months later Paine wrote Jefferson that Bonaparte's invasion had been "only a feint." Paine soon discovered that Napoléon's fondness for the rights of man was another feint. Not long before Paine returned to the United States, he confided to an English journalist that he could not abide Bonaparte because he had promised Paine he would make France a "pure republic" and had gone back on his word. Paine considered him "a perjurer."

In America, Paine discovered his friend Thomas Jefferson still retained his enthusiasm for Napoléon as the personification of his beloved French Revolution. Jefferson even managed to swallow the first consulship for life, pointing to Napoléon's contributions to peace and order in France: his civil code, his creation of schools dedicated to modern education and science. When England declared war on France in May of 1803—an act which almost everyone agreed was rooted in fear of France's growing strength—Paine felt a rush of revolutionary fervor.

Reading about Napoléon's stupendous preparations to invade England, Paine decided this time the Man of Destiny was not feinting. This conclusion inspired Paine to write an open letter to the British people, urging them to welcome Napoléon as the champion of liberty. Paine's praise of the Frenchman was, to put it mildly, extravagant. He called him "the most enterprising and fortunate man, either for deep projects or daring execution, the world has known for many ages." Paine sniffed that "not a man in the British government" could match Bonaparte. They should never have pushed him into another war. Napoléon's ambition was satisfied. All he had wanted to do was improve France. He had said as much to the British ambassador. Yet the oligarchs in the British establishment remained determined to destroy him. That was why they had renewed the war. Average Englishmen, groaning under aristocratic tyranny and unbearable taxes, should welcome Napoléon's army as saviors.[9]

At almost the same time that Paine was publishing this effusion, John Mercer, one of the lesser diplomats attached to the American embassy in France, was writing to James Monroe, who was still in England vainly trying to alter the Royal Navy's arrogant habit of boarding American ships. Mercer told Monroe that the "public prints" would probably give him information on events in Paris. "I mean [the] new form to the government of France." The form was to be "hereditary in the family of the present chief magistrate, who is to be vested with the title of Emperor."[10] On May 18, 1804, Napoléon announced he was accepting this title in accordance with the will of the French people, as expressed in resolutions and petitions from his followers across France.

This stunning news would take another six weeks to reach America. It would make Thomas Paine look like the biggest fool in the country. By implication it should have made his friend and patron, Thomas Jefferson, look almost as foolish. But for the time being, the Louisiana Purchase had made the president impervious to even the most shocking shifts in the political weather.

VII

Underscoring this indubitable fact was a magnificent celebration Mayor DeWitt Clinton staged on Saturday, May 12th, to celebrate Jefferson's continental-sized real estate coup.[11] At sunrise cannon on the Battery at the foot of Manhattan thundered a "Grand National Salute" and guns in the federal fort on nearby Governor's Island boomed a response. The American flag was hoisted over all the principal buildings of the city: the "Great Wigwam" of the Tammany Society, the City Hotel, the Union Hotel, and, of course, City Hall. All the ships in the harbor also raised the national colors. While all the church bells in the city pealed triumphantly, a procession gathered in the City Hall park.

Cavalry, infantry, and artillery formed resplendent ranks and Mayor Clinton, the sheriff, and other city officials strode to the head of the column. In the lead, on a richly decorated white horse, rode the commander of the city's militia, carrying a white silk banner on which was inscribed: "Extension of the Empire of Freedom in the Peaceful, Honorable and Glorious Acquisition of the Immense and Fertile Region of Louisiana, December 20th, 1803, 28th Year of American Independence, and in the Presidency of Thomas Jefferson."

In the center of the Tammany Society, marching behind the soldiers, members carried a fifteen-foot-long white muslin map of the Mississippi River and the surrounding 828,000 square miles of Louisiana. The procession marched down Chatham, Wall, Broad, and Beaver Streets to the Battery, where a huge crowd gathered. The Battery's cannon boomed another salute and the Governor's Island fort answered them. Bands played appropriate songs, including "Hail, Columbia," the closest thing the

United States had to a national anthem, and "Bonaparte's March." Reforming, the parade returned up Broadway to City Hall Park, where the soldiers fired a salute and spectators gave three tremendous cheers for Louisiana and Thomas Jefferson.[12]

For both General Hamilton and Colonel Burr, the celebration was a kind of public message from the triumphant Clinton-Livingston-Jefferson alliance: Your political careers are *over.*

VIII

From Albany at the end of May came news of the final disposition of the hearing for a new trial for Harry Croswell. Early in the May term, Judge James Kent, Judge Smith Thompson, and Judge Brockholst Livingston were in court without the commanding presence of Chief Justice Morgan Lewis. Editor Croswell had been sitting in the courtroom for several days waiting for a verdict. Judge Livingston startled the other two justices by asking them if they were in favor of a new trial. They replied emphatically in the affirmative. Judge Livingston again said he was too, based on his opinion that the rights of the jury had been violated in the previous trial, when the chief justice, now the governor-elect, declared the truth was irrelevant.

Judge Kent could scarcely believe his ears but he and Judge Thompson promptly agreed to discharge defendant Croswell on the posting of a $500 bond and his promise to appear in Columbia County's court the next time the circuit judge sat there. It was almost unbelievable, Judge Livingston seemed indifferent to what might be said about Thomas Jefferson in this second trial. Was it an indication of a secret split between the Livingstons and the Clintons? Ambassador Robert R. Livingston had been shamefully neglected in the latest disposition of political spoils. He had been passed over for governor and vice president, and the Jeffersonians had sponsored a whispering campaign to give James Monroe most of the credit for the Louisiana Purchase. Perhaps Aaron Burr's assaults on Virginia's hegemony had borne fruit here.

Editor Croswell was accordingly discharged and went back to Hudson, New York, a relatively happy man. But the supreme court had yet to issue a formal verdict on his case. As days passed and Chief Justice Lewis said nothing about it, Kent and his convert to Hamiltonism, Judge Smith Thompson, grew uneasy. One day in the final week of the term, Brockholst Livingston suddenly remarked that he was satisfied with the opinion the chief justice had written, which meant that Croswell would not get a new trial after all. Obviously, Chief Justice Lewis and Judge Livingston had had a private conference.

On the last day of the term, Judge Kent announced he wanted to read his opinion on the case, which at least might have gotten some attention in the newspapers. Chief Justice Lewis said he did not think it was necessary, and his fellow Republican, Smith Thompson, lamely agreed with him. Kent's only consolation was Brockholst Livingston's evident embarrassment. On the last day of the term, rather than face him, the judge sent a letter, claiming to be ill. In his notes, Kent ruefully recorded that Livingston never wrote an opinion on the case, nor did he ever read Kent's opinion, although he offered it to him several times.[13]

Underscoring how acutely the case embarrassed the Republicans, the state government, under Governor Morgan Lewis never made any attempt to punish Harry Croswell for the guilty verdict that the supreme court let stand. The matter was simply and silently dropped. Two years later, Judge Brockholst Livingston, who had rescued the Clintons as well as Thomas Jefferson from an extremely tight spot, received his reward. The president nominated him to the U.S. Supreme Court.

For Alexander Hamilton, the Croswell decision was only one more example of the politicization of the court system. With impeached Supreme Court Justice Samuel Chase scheduled for trial in the next session of Congress, who knew where President Jefferson and his cohorts would stop in their reckless determination to embody the will of the people in their political party? All in all, the disposition of the Croswell case could only have added to General Hamilton's pessimism about the future of the

American Republic and its Constitution, which he considered a "frail and worthless fabric" in the first place.

VIII

In the *American Citizen*, James Cheetham continued to gloat over Aaron Burr's defeat. He broadened his retrospections to include a report on a similar attempt to create a coalition between disaffected (Cheetham called them apostate) Republicans and Federalists in Pennsylvania. There too the alliance had gone down to calamitous defeat. It was one more proof that Thomas Jefferson was golden for the time being. The Louisiana Purchase had added immense numbers of cubits to his and the Republican party's political stature.

Cheetham chose to see it as a victory of truth over falsehood, virtue over depravity. He repeatedly referred to the Pennsylvania coalition as a union of "so called honest men." Never one to hesitate to underscore the obvious, the Englishman pointed out that New Yorkers had just escaped similar peril. Who or what was responsible for thus rescuing the Republic? "A free unbiased unshackled press," crowed Mayor DeWitt Clinton's favorite character assassin.[14]

In the same June 4th edition, Cheetham published a long exchange between the Federalist editor of the *Albany Gazette*, which had backed Burr, and a farmer named Scott, who described himself as illiterate, but nonetheless managed to fill up several columns expressing his indignation because the editor had told him a committee of Albany Republicans had endorsed Burr. Scott rehashed the Behrens case to prove Burr was a crook and then added: "Gen. *Hamilton* has declared in substance that he looked upon Mr. *Burr* as a dangerous man and one that ought not to be trusted." There was more than a little irony in the way Cheetham seemed to be the only journalist who thought General Hamilton was still worth quoting.[15]

IX

Although General Wilkinson's visit may have jarred the vice president out of his apathy, this continuing drumfire of abuse from Cheetham soon diminished that brief euphoria. Again, we have to rely largely on Burr's letters to Theodosia to find evidence of what he was thinking and feeling. On June 11th, he sent her a cheerful commentary on a letter that included a scrawled postscript from his grandson. Burr had studied "every pothook and trammel" of this "first literary performance" looking for signs of genius. He invoked some experts on handwriting to support his hopes.

But the second paragraph of the letter collapsed into the defeated politician again. Burr described himself as "unlocomotive." He had done nothing about Madame La G and reported that she had expressed "a sort of surprise, approaching to vexation" at his continued "apathy." He had promised to meet her the following day, and meanwhile was impatiently awaiting Theodosia's "permission or dissent."[16]

On June 13th, Burr reported his interview with La G, and predicted "one more will be fatal and final." He promised to answer letters he had received from Theodosia and her French stepsister, Nathalie Delage, "tomorrow." On a visit to Paris, beautiful Nathalie had met and married South Carolinian Charles Sumter, Ambassador Robert R. Livingston's secretary, and was living happily in South Carolina's high hills of the Santee.

Almost two weeks later, Burr's next letter revealed that on the following day he had been laid low by "an ague in the face." The indisposition, probably maxillary sinusitis, was a disease that frequently had a strong stress component, like the migraine attack Burr had suffered in January, shortly before he went to see President Jefferson, He told Theodosia on June 24th that he had been "nursing [it] from that day to this, in great ill humor."[17]

X

In January Burr's migraine had occurred in the midst of a struggle to decide which political course to follow. Now another anguished bout of indecision had produced (or coincided with) this excruciating pain in his face, accompanied by chills, fever, and prolonged "ill humor." What were Burr's options, at this point? He still had nine months left in his vice presidential term. His serious creditors were not likely to pursue him in the courts while he was the second officer of the government. In nine months a great deal could happen—nationally and internationally.

Although he had been trounced in New York, by no means everyone considered Aaron Burr a political pariah. The fact that he had won the support of four-fifths of the Federalists in the Empire State was not to be dismissed with a sneer, as Cheetham was trying to do. Men such as Stephen Van Rensselaer and the incorruptible John Jay had voted for him. Compared to the Clinton-Livingston-Jefferson combination, Burr had fought an honorable campaign. He had slandered no one; he had not stooped to comment on anyone's private life. He might reasonably assume he was still on the short list of possible leaders, if the New England states decided to secede. The mere fact that he had an intimate knowledge of this potential political earthquake would, one might think, persuade him to sit tight and await events for a while.

Burr had retained Daniel D. Tompkins, a young but able lawyer (and future governor of New York) as his attorney in the libel suit against James Cheetham. The *American Citizen*'s editor had successfully stalled—and even more successfully lied about his stalling—until election day. But Tompkins continued to press the case. On May 19th, Cheetham's lawyers asked the court to appoint "commissions" to examine Edward Livingston, Robert Goodloe Harper, David A. Ogden, and others whom Cheetham claimed Burr had tried to corrupt during the frantic weeks of the presidential deadlock in 1801. For these three-man teams, each side would chose a representative, with the third choice decided by a coin toss.[18]

On May 29th, Burr had written to Robert Goodloe Harper, telling him about the lawsuit and asking him to suggest commissioners in Baltimore who might interview Harper as well as Congressman James A. Bayard of Delaware and other politicians who would be reachable while they were in nearby Washington, D.C., during the next session of Congress.[19] Doggedly pursuing this suit seemed to be the act of a man who was determined to retrieve his political reputation by honorable means. If Burr won the lawsuit—and he seemed to have no doubt that all these men would testify that he had done nothing to try to steal the presidency from Jefferson—he had William P. Van Ness standing by to spread the news around the United States in the same blazing prose that had made the *Examination* a best-seller.

In short, Burr was not out of the political game. Given his insider's knowledge of the instability of the world at home and abroad, he could have reasonably concluded that a period of watchful waiting and circumspect behavior was in order. Not only might the global war or upheaval at home turn things in Burr's favor, but a dignified low-keyed course would help disprove the slanders that had been piled on him.

Burr was convinced that some sort of violent transformation was in the works. In his letter to Robert Goodloe Harper, the vice president referred to a letter that Harper had written to him in March, in which the ex-congressman had remarked that their world was pregnant with change, and wondered what Burr's predictions were. Burr replied that the world was indeed pregnant but "the Gestation will be longer & the parturition more remote, [and] probably, more critical, than you seem aware." This comment suggests two things: that Burr thought Jefferson was going to fall on his face eventually or New England would secede, or both, and the country might well collapse into disunion and chaos. But as a realistic politician, Burr had no doubt that in the short run the Louisiana Purchase guaranteed Jefferson a second term as president.[20]

Burr's comment to Harper also suggests that time was a crucial factor in the colonel's decision making. His burden of debt did not give him the luxury of sitting around practicing law for the next several years, waiting for the Jefferson administration or the Union to unravel. Out of power, he had no hope of persuading a bank to help him with a hefty loan or of recruiting a group of wealthy friends to rescue him if his creditors closed in.

Colonel Burr might wind up in debtor's prison, or at the very least be forced to sell Richmond Hill and live in straitened circumstances. This was not an acceptable option. Not only did it threaten a proud man with humiliation, it would cast grave doubt on his political future. It was far too late to change his image and embrace Republican simplicity. Burr had projected himself as a leader with an aristocratic aura, ready and eager to be generous to his friends and followers with jobs, favors, money. To be reduced to living in a few rented rooms on a New York side street would be an admission of the totality of his defeat. Even Matthew Davis and the other loyalists of the Tenth Legion would abandon him and make the best political deal they could get with the triumphant Clinton-Livingston-Jefferson apparatus.

XI

While Burr sat there brooding on his situation and nursing his facial ague with mounting ill humor, into Richmond Hill came a copy of the April 24th *Albany Register* with Dr. Charles D. Cooper's letter in it. Who sent it? Or brought it? James Cheetham and Mayor DeWitt Clinton himself are not beyond suspicion. Cheetham was still devoting an occasional chortle in the *American Citizen* about General Hamilton's refusal to support Burr during the governorship race. At the outset of the campaign, we saw Cheetham try to taunt the vice president into a challenge with Hamilton's 1801 comparison of Burr to the Roman degenerate Catiline. Sending Burr this additional Hamilton insult would be of a piece with the vindictive malice Cheetham and his backer, Mayor Clinton, had displayed in their assault on Burr.

There is another, more probable bearer of this explosive piece of newsprint: Charles Williamson. On May 16th, the land speculator had written from Bath in Albany County, well within the *Albany Register*'s circulation range, telling Burr he intended to see him in "one month's time." The tone of his letter was heavy with sympathy, even pity, for his defeated, slandered friend. He may have brought the April 24th *Register* and other editions of the newspaper along to show Burr how viciously his enemies had smeared him upstate as well as in New York.

When Williamson met Burr at Richmond Hill, the Scot's sympathy for his fallen friend could only have redoubled. The vice president's face was still covered with woolen "wrappings" to assuage his ague. The future of both men almost certainly was the main topic of discussion, although Burr no doubt also advised the Englishman about the best American state in which to get a divorce. He had handled the divorce of Maria Reynolds, Hamilton's femme fatale, from her husband, James.

Another topic they may well have discussed was Robert Troup, to whom Williamson was handing over the supervision of the million acres in the Genesee Valley that he had bought for his English clients. Troup's health continued to be alarming. His ulcerated tongue and mouth still made eating and drinking agony. His reputation as a man among men was not in much better condition, since he evaded William Stephens Smith's challenge to a duel. But it was too late for Williamson to start hunting for a replacement. He was anxious to unload the weight of those Genesee acres from his shoulders and settle his accounts with his employers. According to his bookkeeping, they owed him $175,000 (over $2 million in modern money) for his ten years of labor.[21]

Williamson probably was more forthcoming with his plan for the future. He called it "The Levy." With the backing of the English secret service, to which he had ready access thanks to his friendship with Henry Dundas, Lord Melville, the political boss of Scotland and a powerful presence in the English government, the Scot planned to recruit an army of recent English immigrants to America and use them to attack Spanish possessions in the New World.[22]

The coincidence of this plan with General Wilkinson's dreams of military glory in Texas and Mexico may have been too breathtaking for Colonel Burr to believe, at first. When the vice president told Williamson about Wilkinson's visit, the two men felt fame was stalking through the shadowed rooms at Richmond Hill to embrace them. Williamson assured Burr that the colonel could rely on The Levy to bolster his army of conquest. Moreover, when Williamson returned to England he would persuade the government to back Burr with a naval squadron.

The ebullient Englishman departed, leaving behind the *Albany Register* with Dr. Cooper's letter. Alone, a restless agitated Burr read and perhaps reread it. There was the earnest young physician telling Philip Schuyler that he could supply him with a "still more despicable opinion" that General Hamilton had expressed of Aaron Burr.

In the context of what James Cheetham and other Republican editors had called Burr in the past two years, and especially during the past two months, *despicable* seems a mild term, hardly worth a flicker of emotion. But the word fused in Aaron Burr's mind with a host of bitter memories of the times General Hamilton had reportedly attacked him in private letters, especially in 1801. The word also coalesced with General Wilkinson's vision of Bonapartean fame in the Spanish southwest and Charles Williamson's confident assurance of English support for the venture. In a scarifying flash, Aaron Burr saw a way to exit from New York and head for that future, not as a beaten politician, or a patient litigant, humbly interviewing fellow politicians for the next year to prove he was not a traitor to his party, but as a soldier, with a reputation restored on a soldier's terms.

CHAPTER 15

Honor's Deadly Ritual

*A*lthough Burr's face was still swathed in "mufflings" to heal his ague,[1] the vice president summoned William P. Van Ness, the faithful, even worshipful, Aristides, to Richmond Hill on the morning of Monday, June 18th, and showed him Dr. Cooper's letter in the *Albany Register*. Van Ness's feelings must have been strongly affected by the sight of Burr with his face wrapped in cloth, his voice ragged with what he called "ill humor" and we would call depression. The younger man listened while Burr raged that many people had told him "General Hamilton had at different times and upon various occasions used language and expressed opinions highly injurious to [my] reputation."[2]

Until now, Burr continued, General Hamilton's statements had not appeared "sufficiently authentic" to justify action. This was hardly the case, as Van Ness himself must have—or should have—known. If authenticity was what the colonel needed, Cheetham's report in the *American Citizen* that Hamilton had called Burr a degenerate like Catiline would surely have done as well or better than this single word in Dr. Cooper's letter, six weeks after the governorship election was over. Moreover, as an insider Burr knew that Hamilton had played little more than a spectator's part in the election, once he was repudiated by the Albany Federalists in February. William Coleman's statements in the *Evening Post*, as well as Cheetham's remarks in the *American Citizen*, confirm this fact. If Burr's purpose was to exact revenge for losing the election, his only logical target was Mayor DeWitt Clinton. Hamilton was chosen for an entirely different

reason: He was a soldier, competing for the same role Burr was now seeking—the Bonaparte of America.

II

William P. Van Ness was the perfect choice to play the unwitting accom-
plice in this drama that Burr was constructing. A gentleman in Van Ness's
situation was supposed to try to avoid a duel by offering to act as an intermediary to resolve the quarrel short of gunfire. Burr had played this role
when Hamilton challenged James Monroe in 1797. But Van Ness made
no attempt to calm the vice president or point out the illogic of choosing
Hamilton as a target for his wrath. Committed heart and soul to Aaron
Burr, Van Ness was probably as depressed as his hero and ready to see
some sort of revenge enacted for the vice president's persecution. The
young lawyer apparently did not say a word in disagreement when Burr
declared this newspaper copy of Dr. Cooper's letter entitled him to demand an explanation from General Hamilton under the mores of the duelist's code.

At 11:00 A.M. on June 18th, Van Ness appeared at General Hamilton's
law office with the following letter.

> N York 18 June 1804
>
> Sir,
>
> I send for your perusal a letter signed Ch. D. Cooper which, though appar-
> ently published some time ago, has but very recently come to my knowledge.
> Mr. Van Ness who does me the favor to deliver this, will point out to you
> that Clause of the letter to which I particularly request your attention.
>
> You might perceive, Sir, the necessity of a prompt and unqualified ac-
> knowledgment or denial of the use of any expressions which could warrant
> the assertions of Dr Cooper.
>
> I have the honor to be
> Your Obdt s^t
>
> A. Burr[3]

III

In his busy office, with clerks toiling over briefs a few feet away, General Hamilton read Burr's curt letter in a glance. He took more time to absorb Cooper's longer epistle. Outside, the curses of Irish cart men mingled with the cries of the street vendors in the humid June air.[4] Glancing up at Van Ness, Hamilton said that he doubted if Colonel Burr had any right to "call upon him" this way, on the basis of Dr. Cooper's language. The word *despicable* was too "general and undefined" to warrant a "specific answer." Hamilton told Van Ness to go back to Burr and ask him to identify "particular expressions" and he would be glad to "recognize or disavow them."

Van Ness replied with considerable asperity that he did not think Colonel Burr was inclined to do this. Dr. Cooper obviously referred to remarks by Hamilton that were "derogatory" to Mr. Burr's reputation, and the "laws of honor" entitled the colonel to ask a fellow gentleman whether he had been guilty of saying anything that "imparted dishonor." Hamilton replied somewhat testily that he did not think Van Ness was correct. But he would examine Dr. Cooper's letter in more detail and answer Colonel Burr later in the day.[5]

At one thirty on the same day, Hamilton visited Van Ness at his house and said "a variety of engagements" would prevent him from giving the matter his full attention until Wednesday. At that time the General hoped he could give Van Ness an answer that was both "suitable" and "compatible with his feelings." Hamilton added that he was sorry that Mr. Burr had adopted this course. It required Hamilton to give the subject "some deliberation."

Van Ness said he would be perfectly willing to wait until Wednesday for Hamilton's answer. The General spent Tuesday at his wife's party for Angelica Church, no doubt playing the gallant witty courtier whom this exquisite woman of fashion loved. On Wednesday, Hamilton spent the morning in court. He saw his fellow lawyer Van Ness there and told him he would have the answer to Colonel Burr ready that afternoon. Van Ness waited at his home for it until 8:00 P.M. and finally went out, probably for supper. When he returned, the answer was there.

Hamilton's letter opened by confirming what he had told Van Ness on Monday: He could not "without manifest impropriety" avow or disavow anything about the phrase "still more despicable." Hamilton then looked back at earlier paragraphs in Dr. Cooper's letter and found the lines in which he was quoted as saying that Burr was a dangerous man and should not be trusted with the reins of government. Apparently, Dr. Cooper thought this was a despicable remark, and a second one, unspecified, was still more despicable. This was simply too indefinite to discuss, Hamilton maintained. Between gentleman, despicable and more despicable were not worth the "pains of a distinction."

Hamilton was trying to turn Burr's argument back on him. If the vice president was willing to accept one despicable opinion, what was wrong with another one, slightly or even extremely more despicable? If he accepted the first one without comment, he ought to accept the unstated second one as within the limits to which political opponents might extend their attacks on each other. He was also reminding Burr that Dr. Cooper, not he, had used the word under contention.

The tone thus far was wry, almost mocking, as if all this was a mere bagatelle that could and should be dismissed. Hamilton dropped this pursuit of the meaning of "more despicable," lest it lead to "embarrassment"—presumably, Burr's, for bringing forward such an unanswerable complaint. Hamilton repeated his refusal to acknowledge or deny this vagary, and abruptly shifted his tone: "I will add, that I deem it inadmissible, on principle, to consent to be interrogated as to the justice of the *inferences*, which may be drawn by *others*, from whatever I may have said of a political opponent in the course a fifteen years competition." To accept such an interrogation would expose him to "injurious imputations" from every person to whom he may have talked or written during this decade and a half.

Hamilton, having been involved in at least eleven exchanges that might have led to duels, plus a half dozen others in which he served as an intermediary or second, was speaking from experience here. The language of insult between gentlemen usually required a specific term, unmistakably from the lips of the insulter, such as *rascal, coward, liar, scoundrel,* to bring things to the brink of gunfire. What was wrong with the reply was its tone of mockery, even condescension, and the sudden shift to almost outright hostility.

Even more mistaken was the offhand reference to fifteen years of competition. This slip of the pen would soon haunt General Hamilton. In the closing paragraph, instead of suggesting even a hint of conciliation, the General reiterated his determination to demand a "precise or definite" accusation. He hoped "on reflection," Burr would agree with him. If not, "I can only regret the circumstances, and must abide the consequences."

This sentence was an explicit declaration that the General was not backing away from the possibility of a duel. It left Burr with the unpleasant choice of either retreating or insisting on some sort of answer.

The letter might well have ended there. For all effects it did end there. But Hamilton added one more line that seemed closer to an afterthought than part of his reply. "The publication by Dr. Cooper was never seen by me till after the receipt of your letter."[6]

Here was more than a hint that Hamilton did not want to fight a duel if he could avoid it. He was telling Burr that this whole matter was not of his doing. That was true, up to a point. He had never intended his remarks at Judge Tayler's dinner table to get into the public prints, any more than he would have wanted his vicious letters during the 1801 presidential deadlock to appear in a newspaper. But the General was also obliquely confessing he had said things that would have been infuriating to Burr if the vice president had heard them.

All in all, Hamilton's reply revealed a man riven by conflicting emotions and necessities. As General Hamilton—the one public role he still reserved for himself—he could not let Colonel Burr humiliate him. He had no doubt if he wrote a humble apology to Burr, it would appear in the

Morning Chronicle the next day. That would almost certainly destroy whatever influence General Hamilton might still have in the New York Federalist party. It might also eliminate him as the potential leader of a New England army, if the Federalists of Yankeedom decided to secede. It would certainly disqualify him as the leader of a national army if Napoléon succeeded in conquering England and headed across the Atlantic to regain France's colonial empire. Although dueling was already in some disfavor in New England and New York, it was still the quintessential test of a man in the South and West.

The letter, with its shifts in tone, its final note of defiance, followed by an oblique admission of guilt, shows evidence of hasty composition. Hamilton had written it in a single afternoon and had talked to no one about it—another grievous mistake. The reply was composed by an overworked lawyer too busy to concentrate on this sudden threat, even though he spoke of giving it serious deliberation. Hamilton was trying to confine this matter to an argument over the meaning of *despicable* and simultaneously play the soldier, ready to reach for his pistols. The General should have known this was impossible.

IV

On Thursday morning, June 21st, William P. Van Ness delivered General Hamilton's reply to Colonel Burr at Richmond Hill. Van Ness stayed with him for the rest of the day, helping him work on an answer. Van Ness would seem to have written a wordy first draft. The vice president trimmed Aristides's verbiage to the precision of a sword blade in his version, which was only half the length of Van Ness's effort. In fact, Burr's letter was so superior, it makes one suspect that the colonel had more than a little to do with the writing of Aristides's pamphlet, as James Cheetham claimed.

> Sir
>
> Your letter of the 20th inst. has been this day received. Having Considered it attentively I regret to find in it nothing of that sincerity and delicacy which you profess to Value.

Political opposition can never absolve Gentlemen from the necessity of a rigid adherence to the laws of honor and the rules of decorum: I neither claim such priviledge nor indulge it in others.

The Common sense of Mankind affixes to the epithet adopted by Dr. Cooper the idea of dishonor: it has been publicly applied to me under the Sanction of your name. The question is not whether he has understood the meaning of the word or has used it according to Syntax and with grammatical accuracy, but whether you have authorised this application either directly or by uttering expressions or opinions derogatory to my honor. . . . Your letter has furnished me with new reasons for requiring a definite reply.[7]

Burr added that he was indifferent to when Hamilton made the statement. The "calumny has now first been disclosed" and that entitled him to seek an explanation. The reference to "now" strengthens the probability that Charles Williamson brought the letter to Burr's attention. At the very least it confirms that the discovery of the letter triggered the decision to challenge General Hamilton, even though he had little or nothing to do with Burr losing the election.

The reiterated demand for a definite reply suggests at this point that Burr would still be satisfied with some kind of disavowal from Hamilton. With Robert Troup's recent humiliation by Colonel William Stephens Smith vivid in his mind, the vice president was not necessarily thirsting for General Hamilton's blood. A retraction would remove Hamilton from the public stage as America's military hero and open Bonapartean possibilities for Burr.

On Friday morning, June 22rd, Van Ness delivered this letter to General Hamilton in his law office. The General grew visibly upset as he read it. He said it was a letter he had been hoping he would not receive. Several of the expressions were "offensive" and it seemed to close the door to any possibility of an accommodation. Hamilton, as Van Ness later recalled, said he had hoped his letter would give a "different direction" to the controversy. Why couldn't Mr. Burr see it was impossible for him to make a "specific reply?" to a general term such as *despicable*?

Then, in a strange about-face, similar to the abrupt shifts of tone in his reply to Burr's first letter, Hamilton said if the vice president had asked him to state "what had fallen from him that might have given rise to the inference of Doctor Cooper," he would have done this "frankly." He believed his remarks "would not have been found to exceed the limits justifiable among political opponents."

It is hard to fathom the difference between this offer and the reply Burr demanded. Hamilton seemed to be saying that Colonel Burr's offensive second letter was now the problem. He proposed that they consider the second letter "not delivered." But if Burr refused to withdraw it, the General said he could "make no reply" and Mr. Burr must pursue "such course as he should deem most proper."

Once more, in virtually the same breath, Hamilton went from expressing an eagerness, almost an anxiety, for an accommodation to a bristling readiness to reach for his pistols. Van Ness, by now remembering that his primary duty as a second was to prevent bloodshed, responded with a peace offer. He told Hamilton that if he had said in his first letter that he could "recollect the use of no terms" that would justify Dr. Cooper's choice of the word *despicable*, Van Ness thought an immediate accommodation would have been more than possible.

General Hamilton absolutely and totally refused to consider this alternative. Van Ness said he "stated the same objections" he had made in his reply to Colonel Burr.[8] The reason for Hamilton's rejection is fairly clear. He had undoubtedly used terms that warranted Dr. Cooper's use of the deadly word *despicable*, and he saw no point in calling the young physician a liar. Cooper was already outraged by General Schuyler's assault on his character. Hamilton was now acutely aware that he was performing in the public spotlight, and he would get nowhere if Burr published his letter and Dr. Cooper came railing back with vivid recollections of some of the offensive things General Hamilton had said about Colonel Burr. The General would be forced to disavow them and wind up eating the same diet of crow that he was determined to avoid, even if he had to fight a duel to do it.

As Van Ness left, Hamilton called after him that he was ready to put in writing his refusal to answer on Burr's terms. Van Ness said that was not necessary. He would report what Hamilton had said verbally. Hamilton nodded and repeated his determination to remain silent, and again added that Burr would have to decide to do whatever he thought was "proper."

Van Ness, probably growing appalled at the slide toward gunfire, again tried to play the role of a peacemaker. He urged Hamilton not to force him to deliver that obviously defiant final remark. Why not "take time to deliberate?" Perhaps tomorrow he would find himself with a calmer or at least different opinion. Van Ness said he would be happy to return to hear it. Hamilton growled that unless Burr took back his second letter and sent him one that would give him a chance to make a "different reply," it would be a waste of time for Van Ness to call again.[9]

V

Later on Friday morning, June 22nd, General Hamilton realized that unless someone intervened on his behalf, he was on his way to a New Jersey dueling ground, For a spokesman he chose his fellow ex-soldier, Nathaniel Pendleton—the same man who had escorted him four months ago in Albany in his vain attempt to track down the old smear of conspiring to create an American king. It is worth noting that the bristling language Hamilton had used with Burr was similar to the exchanges between the General and Governor Clinton. Yet Hamilton would soon profess an abhorrence of dueling. It was another indication of the General's inability to integrate the ideas that were roiling his mind and heart.

Pendleton saw the dispute with Burr had already reached a crisis point. He listened with dismay as Hamilton told him that he had rejected Burr's second letter as "rude and offensive" and described his rebuff of Van Ness's attempt to suggest a less truculent answer. Hamilton gave Pendleton a letter addressed to Burr and asked him to give it to Van Ness. Whereupon the General departed for The Grange to spend the weekend of June 23–24 with his family.

Hamilton's letter only increased Pendleton's dismay. It seemed designed to demolish any possibility of further negotiation.

> Sir
>
> Your first letter, in a style too peremptory, made a demand, in my opinion, unprecedented and unwarrantable. My answer, pointing out the embarrassment, gave you an opportunity to take a less exceptionable course. You have not chosen to do it, but by your last [i.e. second] letter, received this day, containing expressions indecorous and improper, you have increased the difficulties to explanation, intrinsically incident to the nature of your application.
>
> If by a "definite reply" you mean the direct avowal or disavowal required in your first letter, I have no other answer to give than that which has already been given. If you mean any thing different admitting of greater latitude, it is requisite you should explain.

Van Ness, meanwhile, reported to Colonel Burr Hamilton's verbal answer, including his truculent final statement and overall tone of defiance. Burr said he wanted a few hours to consider the situation. Van Ness promised to return to Richmond Hill that evening, but he was detained in town and did not get back until Saturday morning, June 23rd. He found Burr with another letter for General Hamilton.

In this phase of the deadly dance, the vice president altered his tone. After dismissing Hamilton's verbal remarks as mostly unworthy of a gentleman's notice, Burr adopted the voice of an injured party. He declared he had tried to make the matter as simple as possible, relying "with unsuspecting faith that from the frankness of a Soldier and the Candor of a gentleman I might expect an ingenuous declaration." The reference to Hamilton as a soldier is significant. It was a triumph over a soldier that Burr wanted and needed, in particular a soldier of General Hamilton's reputation—the man who was considered Washington's heir.

The colonel's letter went on in this injured tone, declaring he thought if General Hamilton had dishonored him, he would have "the Spirit to Maintain or the Magnanimity to retract" his remarks. Instead, Burr had received a letter that he considered both evasive and "not altogether decorous." But he was not deceived about one point: Hamilton's unvarnished statement that he was ready to "meet the consequences."

Those words alone would have justified him in sending an "immediate message," Burr wrote. But he had decided perhaps Hamilton's defiance was the result of "false pride" rather than "reflection," so he wrote his second letter, refuting Hamilton's complaints about indefiniteness. He had done this because he "felt the utmost reluctance to proceed to extremities while any other hope remained." But General Hamilton had simply reiterated his refusal to reply, leaving him no alternative "to the course I am about [to] pursue."[10]

As he handed this letter to Van Ness, Burr added some remarks that revealed personal animosity boiling to the surface. The vice president claimed he had never felt political rivalries entitled a man to say dishonorable things about an opponent. He had strictly observed that rule with John Jay, John Adams, and General Hamilton—the three men he considered rivals on his political level. This grouping reveals the contempt Burr felt for George Clinton and his nephew. He would not even consider them worthy of the term *rival*.

In Hamilton's case, Burr continued, there had never been any "reciprocity" of restraint. For several years he had loaned his name to "base slanders" that he had never had "the generosity, the magnanimity, or the candor to contradict or disavow." Burr claimed that all his forbearance toward these slanders had produced was "repetition of injury." He could only conclude that Hamilton had a "settled & implacable malevolence" toward him. "These things must have an end!" Burr snarled.

Even allowing for some restraint in Van Ness's account of this conversation, the portrait of a profoundly depressed and angry man is more than visible. The whole monologue mounts from the opening stanzas of dignified reproach to a swirling tirade of self-justification and sweeping accusation. Hamilton was transformed in a few sentences from a gentleman to a monster. Vehemently though he denied it, revenge had begun to play a part in the vice president's psyche.[11]

Van Ness decided not to deliver Burr's letter to Hamilton at The Grange. He would also be forced to deliver Burr's wrathful verbal message, which he feared would lead to an angry response from Hamilton. The young lawyer was also loath to upset the General's wife and children. Instead he sent Hamilton a note by messenger, asking when and where it would be "convenient" for him to receive a "communication."

Hamilton sent the messenger back with a note thanking Van Ness for his "delicacy." He said he would be in his town house at 52 Cedar Street on Monday morning and would be glad to see him there.

VI

While Hamilton relaxed with his family, Burr was doing something similar at Richmond Hill. His facial ague had subsided, enabling him to dispense with his "wrappings." He invited a few friends to join him to celebrate Theodosia's birthday. He reported the party to Theodosia in a cheerful letter on June 24th. For a while they set her portrait on a chair at the table. But because it was in profile and "would not look at us," they replaced it with her stepsister Nathalie's, "which laughs and talks to us." He exchanged barbs with her about La G. She had apparently told him she did not care what he did with this elusive lady. Her permission, he wrote, "seems to be that I may hang or drown or make any other apotheosis that I may please. Dear indulgent creature, I thank thee."[12]

VII

Meanwhile, Nathaniel Pendleton sought out Van Ness to explore the possibility of an accommodation. They met several times over the weekend. The Virginian did not hand over the letter Hamilton had written on June 22nd. He obviously felt it should be withdrawn or at least concealed for the time being. As a first step Pendleton tried to persuade Burr to retract his second letter. Instead, in a substitute letter, the vice president should ask if General Hamilton had alluded to any "particular instance" of dishonorable conduct in his conversation with Dr. Cooper. In response, General Hamilton would write a letter denying he had cited any particular incident, and stating to the best of his recollection what he had said. Van Ness said he and Burr and would take this proposal under advisement.

On Monday, June 25th, Van Ness found Hamilton at his Cedar Street house and gave him Colonel Burr's third letter and added the raging verbal communication "as much softened as my instructions would permit." Both seconds were now trying hard to prevent bloodshed.

In response to this softened message, Hamilton disclaimed "every idea of personal enmity." He admitted he had been a "uniform public opponent of Colonel Burr" but his opposition had been rooted in "public principles." Then, veering back to hostility, Hamilton told Van Ness he had written a reply to Burr's second letter. Later that morning, Pendleton reluctantly handed the letter over to Van Ness.

Burr's second swiftly delivered this letter to his principal, who had left Richmond Hill for his city house to bring the negotiations to a climax. As Pendleton feared, the letter triggered an outburst of fury. The vice president raged that it was nothing more than a snide elaboration of the hostile verbal reply Van Ness had already delivered. Why should he explain anything to Hamilton when he was the injured party?

One can easily see the infuriated Burr pacing up and down, playing the inflexible leader to the awed young Van Ness. He had begun this business requesting a very simple statement, Burr said. Hamilton's intransigence had convinced him of what he had often suspected: there was a long history of traducing him that the General was trying to conceal.

Whereupon Vice President Burr escalated the confrontation to the ultimate level. He would not be satisfied with anything less than a "general disavowal" by Hamilton (the pun, surely unintended, is nonetheless suggestive) that he had *ever* intended to impugn Burr's honor in any letter or conversation over the last fifteen years.

At about 2:30 on this same Monday, June 25th, the anxious Pendleton called on Van Ness again. Burr's second reported the colonel's response to the letter the Virginian had tried to conceal. Toward the end of the conversation, Van Ness revealed Burr's new position: a demand for a general disavowal. No doubt to Van Ness's amazement, Pendleton replied he believed General Hamilton would have "no objection" to making such a statement.[13]

For the first time, Pendleton revealed his weakness in dealing with this crisis. Although he had become close to Hamilton in recent years, he was not a long-standing confidant on the level of Gouverneur Morris or Rufus King. Pendleton was not aware of how often and how ruthlessly Hamilton had slandered Burr.

Now came a scene not reported in Pendleton's narrative of his brief career as Hamilton's second. He returned to Hamilton and told the General that he had agreed to a general disavowal. What transpired is beyond the documents of the historians. But it is easy to imagine Pendleton encountering an explosive mixture of anger and embarrassment. Never would or could General Hamilton agree to such a proposition. It would have made total the partial humiliation that Burr had been seeking in his original letter about Dr. Cooper's smear. For Hamilton an exoneration of Aaron Burr was unacceptable—and, even worse, impossible—without becoming a coward and a liar in the eyes of the very men on whose opinion he was relying to elevate him to fame.

Fame. That word lurks and looms in every corner and crevice of this confrontation. It was fame that controlled almost every word that Hamilton spoke or wrote during this deadly week. Burr, the man whom Hamilton had accused of not being interested in this lofty ideal as one more proof of his unfitness for high office, was proving he too was ready to risk his life for a chance at this elusive prize.

VIII

At six o'clock on the same June 25th, as the twilight gathered in the crooked streets of New York, Van Ness called on Pendleton to learn if General Hamilton would agree to a general disavowal. A sobered Pendleton informed Burr's second that Hamilton refused to do so. Lamely, and perhaps sadly, Pendleton added that he "did not then perceive the whole force and extent" of such a statement. Clearly, General Hamilton had explained to his friend why the statement was out of the question. Both words, *force* and *extent*, are significant: One refers to the impact it would have on Hamilton's reputation (fame), the other how wide and deep the General's attacks on Burr had been.

In a gesture that was almost forlornly foredoomed to failure, Pendleton again tried to persuade Burr to take back his cutting second letter. The Virginian gave Van Ness a statement he and Hamilton had prepared as a possible solution. It called for Burr to write a "properly adapted" letter that asked Hamilton to apologize for any specific imputation of dishonorable conduct.

As Pendleton probably feared, this proposal ignited a new explosion of Burr fury. The vice president told Van Ness it was "a worse libel than even the letter of Dr. C." It manifested in every word a continuing attempt to "evade." Burr took particular umbrage at the suggestion that the letter should be "properly adapted" to enable Hamilton to make a satisfactory reply. The vice president growled that his first two letters were "very properly adapted." He found even more fault with Hamilton's continued insistence that Burr specify "any particular instance of dishonorable Conduct" to which the General might have referred. Burr thought it left too much room for the suggestion that there were "general opinions and general charges."

Burr said he was sending this commentary to Van Ness as additional material to "interweave" into the formal challenge that he would now deliver to Nathaniel Pendleton. Before the end of the day, this longish letter was in Pendleton's hands. It recapitulated the twists and turns of the argument and reiterated the new demand that "No denial or declaration will be satisfactory unless it be general." The only other solution was a request for a "personal interview"—the sanitized term gentlemen used for a duel. Van Ness asked Pendleton to tell him at what hour he could call on him to deliver the formal challenge.

On the evening of June 26th Hamilton's harried second wrote and delivered to Van Ness a letter pointing out that Burr had "greatly changed and extended" his expectations since his opening letter and that this had led General Hamilton and, by implication, Pendleton—to presume that Burr was motivated by "predetermined hostility." This charge was a last desperate attempt to keep Burr at bay. A gentleman was not supposed to fight a duel with such a motive. It could be construed as a misuse of the duello code to commit murder.

At noon on Wednesday, June 27th, Van Ness arrived at Pendleton's house with another long letter that he had written as Burr's spokesman. The young lawyer reiterated the justice of demanding a general disavowal and tautly defended his principal against the charge of predetermined hostility. Van Ness closed on a somber note: "The length to which this correspondence has extended" only proved to Colonel Burr that "satisfactory redress, earnestly desired, cannot be obtained." The vice president deemed it "useless to offer any proposition except the simple Message which I . . . now have the honor to deliver."[14]

Speaking in General Hamilton's name, Pendleton glumly accepted Van Ness's delivery of Burr's challenge. His only response was a request for a postponement. The General was extremely busy before the circuit court and he would like some time to complete several cases on the docket and arrange his affairs. Van Ness said that was perfectly agreeable and he would call on Pendleton tomorrow to learn what time and place General Hamilton preferred for the "interview."

XI

Pendleton reported this conversation to Hamilton late on Wednesday, June 27th, and gave him Van Ness's letter. The General seemed stunned by the challenge. He told Pendleton he had the impression that there would be at least one more meeting with Van Ness. Anxiously scanning the letter, he said he felt called upon to answer some of the points Van

Ness made. While Pendleton waited, the General wrote a reply, which only testified to his desperate desire to somehow avoid a duel. It reiterated Hamilton's readiness to explain to Burr "any and every" objection of "a specific nature" but not to answer "a general and abstract inquiry." This was "inadmissible in principle" and "humiliating in practice." Those words cut close to the bone of the General's dilemma.

The next day, Thursday, June 28th, Van Ness called on Pendleton at 10:00 A.M. and was surprised to find him with Hamilton's letter in his hand. The Virginian said it contained "some remarks" on Van Ness's final letter. Van Ness said if it offered a "definite and specific proposition" he would receive it "with pleasure" and show it to Colonel Burr immediately. But if the letter was only additional observations on their quarrel, he would have to decline it, because Colonel Burr considered the correspondence "terminated."

With a sigh, Nathaniel Pendleton agreed. By now he realized, without quite percieving the motivational depths the historian can explore, that there was never any real hope of preventing General Hamilton from meeting Aaron Burr on the field of honor.

CHAPTER 16

Why Soldiers Why?

O n Wednesday, June 27th, not long after Nathaniel Pendleton left Alexander Hamilton's town house, the General began writing an essay, which he described as "some remarks explanatory of my conduct, motives and views" in regard to his expected duel with Colonel Burr. Clearly, he had no hope of achieving anything with his hurried reply to William P. Van Ness's challenge letter. The General worked on this statement intermittently from that night until the following Wednesday, July 4th. It might best be described as a letter to the American public.

Hamilton began by stating what was evident in the letters he exchanged with Burr: He was "certainly desirous of avoiding this interview." He listed four "cogent" reasons for this desire.

1. His "religious and moral principles" were strongly opposed to dueling. It would "give [him] pain" to shed the blood of a "fellow creature" in a "private combat" that was "forbidden by the laws."

2. His wife and children were "extremely dear" to him, and his life was of "the utmost importance" to them.

3. He felt a sense of obligation to his creditors. If he was killed there would be a forced sale of his property. As a "man of probity" he did not think he was at liberty to expose them to financial loss.

4. He was conscious of no ill-will to Colonel Burr "distinct from political opposition." But this opposition was based on "pure and upright motives."

After this collection of seemingly overwhelming imperatives to shun the duel, Hamilton nevertheless maintained it was impossible to avoid it. He gave two explanations for this conclusion. One was the *"intrinsick"* [*sic*] difficulties of the situation. The second was the "*artificial* embarrassments" created by Burr's "manner of proceeding."

The intrinsic difficulty was the "not to be denied" fact that he had made "extremely severe" attacks on Colonel Burr's political principles, character, and overall view of life. Although General Hamilton considered his motives "commendable," it would be very hard to explain or apologize for these statements, unless Burr or someone else convinced him that they were "erroneous." He cited the advice of a "very moderate and judicious friend" against making a general disavowal of his long career of assaulting Burr's reputation. Then there was the problem of Colonel Burr's assumption of an "unnecessarily peremptory and menacing" tone at the outset, which in his subsequent letters became "positively offensive."

In spite of these obstacles, Hamilton felt he had tried "to leave a door to accommodation." He thought his letters and his conversations with William P. Van Ness would bear this out. In fact, Hamilton feared he may have gone too far in this direction, possibly impugning the courage that a "punctilious delicacy" required a man to display. His motive for this error would, he hoped, be visible from the four reasons he cited for avoiding the encounter.

At the same time, Hamilton protested that he was not trying to "affix any odium" on Colonel Burr's conduct. Hamilton realized that some of the "animadversions" Burr may have heard no doubt "bore very hard upon him." Moreover, there was a strong probability that they had been exaggerated by others. Hamilton again insisted he had never attacked Burr on light grounds or from unworthy motives. He had strong reasons for saying the things he said. But he admitted that sometimes he may have been wrong. He hoped Burr's conscience was satisfied with the way he had acted in the negotiations. In fact, it was Hamilton's ardent wish that Burr's future conduct would show he was worthy of esteem. He even hoped he would become an "ornament" to his country.

Because he may have injured Colonel Burr (although Hamilton again protested that his opinions were well founded and his motives pure) the General declared that he had decided "to *reserve* and *throw away* my first fire." He even had thoughts of reserving his "second fire." This would give Colonel Burr two chances to "pause and to reflect." But the General said he did not intend to give Burr any inkling of this decision. "Apology," he wrote, "from principle, I hope, rather than pride, is out of the question."

Finally, Hamilton returned in a last tortured paragraph to why he was going ahead with the duel. He realized he was violating his own "principled opposition" to the practice of dueling and giving a bad example to other Americans. Yet Hamilton felt his *relative* situation" created a "peculiar necessity" to respond to Burr's challenge. Public prejudice required a man who wanted to remain in politics to conform to the code of honor. At stake was the General's "ability to be in future useful, whether in resisting mischief or effecting good, in these crises of our public affairs, which seem likely to happen."[1]

II

When General Hamilton acquired his principled opposition to dueling, he did not say. Four months earlier, he seemed to show no hesitation to use the threat of a duel to track down the old slander about conspiring to give America a king. He never made a public statement condemning dueling, even after his son Philip's death. He did not make the slightest effort to rescue his friend Robert Troup from humiliation in his clash with Colonel William Stephens Smith. On the contrary, Hamilton's comments seemed to approve Smith's menacing style.

Writing twenty-five years later, John Quincy Adams offered a succinct explanation of why General Hamilton, in spite of the almost insuperable objections he had stated at the opening of his extraordinary remarks, still went ahead with the duel. Adams, no friend of the man who had wrecked his father's chances for reelection in 1800, coldly reduced the General's tormented words about hoping to remain useful to a single, damning noun: "AMBITION."[2] There is some truth in this reduction, but it is inadequate as an explanation of why General Hamilton chose to risk his life.

To fully appreciate the situation, it is necessary to see General Hamilton's ambition in more concrete terms. Hamilton had declared his only future public role would be as a soldier. He had taken himself out of electoral politics, for reasons that are also apparent. But in a world shadowed by Napoléon Bonaparte, Hamilton was intensely aware that election was not the only way a man could achieve power. Far more congenial to General Hamilton was the soldier's role. Having reserved for himself the part that Bonaparte had played in restoring order to revolutionary France, he could not let Aaron Burr, of all people, usurp this last hope of ultimate fame.

John Quincy Adams was aware that Hamilton's status as a soldier was the heart of his ambition. "Should he decline to meet Colonel Burr," Adams wrote, "some doubt at least of his personal intrepidity would be entertained by the men of military mind. He could no longer expect to be the favorite candidate for the chief military command."[3] Adams did not go the next step, and suggest that Colonel Burr was likely to be a foremost contender for that military command. That likelihood is essential to understanding why a man deeply in debt, with seven children to support, including an insane daughter, could make such an unreasonable decision. General Hamilton's antagonism to Colonel Burr was too deep for reason or prudence to control.

John Quincy Adams thought Hamilton was obsessed with the threat of secession that was fermenting in New England. He argued that Hamilton's references to "resisting mischief and effecting good" and "crises in our public affairs" were directly connected to what he had heard and read from New England visitors and letter writers. These were terms that someone would use about a civil rather than a foreign war. At the same time Adams believed—and Hamilton biographers point out—that the General opposed Senator Pickering's scheme. But Adams felt Hamilton's objections were primarily tactical: He did not think the Louisiana Purchase was a good reason to launch a civil war.

General Hamilton hoped to go to the Boston meeting and talk the New Englanders out of doing anything for the moment. But Adams thought Hamilton was convinced that other crises would bring these same feelings of virulent hostility to Virginian and southern hegemony to the fore in "more felicitous auspices." With heavy irony Adams added that he preferred to "disbelieve" that Hamilton would ever destroy the Union to which he often stated his deep devotion. But Adams could not resist noting that Hamilton was a man whose "sense of rectitude" was often swayed by "the impulses of the heart." The purity of his virtue was tempered by "the baser metal of the ruling passion."[4]

III

However astutely John Quincy Adams grasped the persistence of Hamilton's ambition, the New Englander's deep dislike made him incapable of seeing that the General's strange essay bore witness to the journey of a soul. Part of General Hamilton had become the Christian that his twentieth-century admirers yearned to see. But he had not integrated this new faith into his personality. There was a psychological split between the Christian Hamilton and the man who was still involved in the struggle for power and fame.

This split in Hamilton's psyche explains the essay's painful dissonances. Mingled with Hamilton's protestation that he bore Burr no enmity is an attempt to take the high moral ground away from his antagonist. Hamilton's repeated emphasis on admittedly "severe" onslaughts being well founded undercuts the apology and transforms it into a covert attack. The pious hope that the man whom he had repeatedly slandered (supposedly with good reason) would nevertheless become an "ornament" to his country is too cloying for moral digestion. These are not the sentiments of a fully committed Christian. They are not even halfway to the Christian state of true contrition and forgiveness.

More complex is Hamilton's solemn declaration that he intended to throw away his first and possibly his second rounds rather than wound or kill Burr. Other sources confirm that Hamilton told Pendleton and Rufus

King of this intention. Both men were appalled and tried to talk him out of it. King told his friend that if he was going to make an appearance on the field, he "owed it to his family and the rights of self defence" to shoot back. But neither man could change Hamilton's mind. King later wrote that the General's thinking on duels was a "fallacy [that] could not fail to be seen by any man of ordinary understanding."[5]

More than Christianity was involved in this decision, although Hamilton used his new faith to justify it. Grief and regret for his slain son were also tormenting this divided man. A genuine Christian would not have told anyone, not even Pendleton, about the decision. The divided Hamilton, still hungry for fame, not only announced his noble intention in his remarks, which he left with his will and other letters, but told his second and his close friend, Rufus King. This public display of his sensitive conscience—even if it was sincere—converts it into a political statement that degrades the purity of the spiritual gesture. Again, Hamilton seems to be telling the world: See what a noble man I am. He was trying to outwit possible defeat and death by mounting fame's pedestal in advance.

This is not the Christian way. Jesus made that clear in his parable of the man who stood in the front of the synagogue, announcing to God and the world what a virtuous, charitable worshipper he was. The man Jesus preferred stood in the back of the church, head bowed, murmuring, "Oh Lord I am not worthy," making no claims for his goodness.

Anyone who has given some thought to the journey of the human soul can summon compassion for this divided, tormented man. Hamilton was, like most of us, absorbed, even obsessed with the things of this world. Faith had invaded his soul without warning. Riven with regret for his adultery with Maria Reynolds and perhaps with Angelica Church, for his son Philip's death, and his daughter Angelica's insanity, he had veered toward the God-man who had died on the cross saying "Thy will be done." But Hamilton had not yet grasped the deeper dimensions of his new faith when Aaron Burr flung his challenge.

IV

Seeing the General as a divided man is the best solution to the argument advanced by some recent writers: that for Hamilton the duel was a disguised suicide. Those final lines in his remarks about being useful in a coming crisis make it clear that Hamilton hoped to survive, even though he was daring fate or, more precisely, the Christian God's mysterious providence.

Such dares were the essence of a soldier's code. At Yorktown, twenty-three years earlier, in the closing days of the famous siege, Lieutenant Colonel Hamilton had commanded a frontal assault on a British redoubt. He had browbeaten Washington into giving him the assignment. Hamilton had led from the front, taking his chances against whistling enemy bullets and lunging bayonets, and considerably enlarged his stature as a soldier. He was going to meet Burr with the same reckless fatalism that had sustained him there.

At the same time, one suspects another darker motive in the divided Hamilton's moral posture. If he was killed, he wanted his death to destroy Burr as a political and military leader. It would have taken a year of prayer and fasting to scour hatred of Aaron Burr from General Hamilton's soul. The ongoing animosity is all too visible in his repeated insistence on good reasons for his attacks on the vice president, in his declaration that his conscience was clear, and in his pious hope that Burr's was in the same pristine condition. No matter how often Hamilton declared he had no personal enmity toward Aaron Burr, the General's loathing for the man only becomes more apparent.

V

On July 1st, Colonel Burr wrote Theodosia Burr Alston a letter in which he told her he had been "shivering with cold all day" and was sitting before a fire in the library of Richmond Hill. He was enjoying the fire "if that word can be applied to anything done in solitude." Later in the letter he added that there were "three shiploads of South Carolinians" in New York, all complaining mightily of the heat. Burr's shivers and constant sensation of feeling cold—he told Theodosia he had slept under a blanket throughout the month of June—suggest his ague was still troubling him, even though the pain in his face had subsided. His decision to challenge General Hamilton and use his apology—or his corpse—as a stepping stone to fame only compounded the underlying stress that had triggered the illness.

The portrait Burr draws of himself, alone in his mansion on a Sunday evening in midsummer, only underscores his sense of isolation and loss. In the letter he struggled to find some consolation in urging Theodosia to continue her self-education. He recommended she start keeping a list of books she would like to buy for a personal collection. He urged her to subscribe to a new magazine, the *Edinburgh Review*, which would soon become de rigueur for novelists, poets, and cultivated readers in England and America.

Burr told Theodosia that Jerome Bonaparte, trapped in New York by a swarm of patrolling British frigates, had rented an elegant country house on Manhattan Island for a summer retreat. The comment only underscored Burr's isolation. The vice president had not heard a word from the young Frenchman. The letter trailed off with a wistful reference to Montalto, the house Theodosia and her husband were building in northern Manhattan. Even in its unfinished state it was "one of the curiosities or beauties" of the island.[6]

At one point in the letter, Burr felt impelled to explain his solitude. Instead he decided to "drop the subject," because it might lead to "another on which I have imposed silence on myself." He knew Theodosia would be enormously upset if he mentioned the duel.

The vice president was growing more and more impatient to settle the matter with Hamilton one way or another. But the seconds proceeded at a more deliberate pace. Nathaniel Pendleton called on William P. Van Ness on July 3rd and informed him that the Manhattan session of the supreme court's circuit would conclude its business on Saturday, July 7th, and General Hamilton would be ready to "meet" Colonel Burr on the following Monday or Tuesday. The two seconds agreed to ride out into the country as soon as possible and settle on the day and place.

VI

On Wednesday, July 4th, the day that General Hamilton completed his remarks on the coming duel, he and Colonel Burr attended the annual dinner of the New York chapter of the Society of the Cincinnati. This organization, composed of the officers of the revolutionary army and their male descendants, had been created in the 1780s and aroused a storm of criticism because of its decision to make membership hereditary. To the more politically sensitive members of the revolutionary generation, including Thomas Jefferson and Benjamin Franklin, it smacked of an attempt to create an American aristocracy.

The ex-soldiers had gone ahead with their plans, although some, including George Washington, had misgivings. Washington overcame his uneasiness and served as the society's first president. Hamilton succeeded him. A majority of the members were Federalists whose army experience had given them a keen appreciation of the need for a strong central government. A minority of officers, especially those of a Republican persuasion, had declined to join. One of these was Aaron Burr. He had only added his name to the rolls in 1803, around the time that he had begun to see his political future linked to acceptance by the Federalists.

The society, which drew its name from the Roman general Cincinnatus, who retired to his farm after his military triumphs, met at Fraunces Tavern, the red brick building still standing on the corner of Broad and Pearl Streets. Here Washington had said farewell to his officers nine days after the British army evacuated New York in late 1783. Hamilton was among those who attended that tearful scene. Although Burr was living in New York, he was not invited—evidence of his lifelong antagonism toward Washington.

The dinner carried the adversaries back to their military youth, to the Revolution that had transformed the rest of their lives. The great upheaval had made possible the nation building, the savage struggle for political power, the pursuit of fame. The occasion could only have reinforced the sense of history encircling them, with fate, destiny, in control.

The two men sat next to each other at the long banquet table. Burr was brooding and silent. His ill humor apparently still gripped him. He barely participated in the ritual toasts to General Washington and Louis XVI of France (for signing the 1778 treaty of alliance that rescued the Revolution). Hamilton was strangely ebullient. He laughed and joked with his numerous friends in the group. Toward the end of the evening, he leaped up on the table and sang his favorite song, an enormously revealing lyric. It was supposedly written by General James Wolfe the night before he died assaulting Quebec in 1759—the victory that drove the French off the North American continent and set the stage for the American Revolution.

Wolfe was the only British general to achieve fame in Hamilton's lifetime. He was almost certainly one of Hamilton's boyhood heroes. If Wolfe had survived, he would have been rewarded with riches and power by the British establishment. He might have become a kind of viceroy of North America, an arbiter of the destiny of the continent. Not only did the verses sum up Hamilton's passion for fame, they also spoke to the threat he would soon confront at the end of Colonel Burr's pistol. Here was the soldier's creed, defiantly sung in death's saturnine face.

> Why, soldiers, why
> Should we be melancholy, boys?
> Why, soldiers, why
> Whose business 'tis to die!
> What! sighing? fie!
> Damn fear, drink on, be jolly boys!
> 'Tis he, you, or I
> Cold, hot, wet, or dry,
> We're always bound to follow, boys,
> And scorn to fly.

'Tis but in vain
(I mean not to upbraid you, boys),
'Tis but in vain
For soldiers to complain:
Should next campaign
Send us to Him who made us, boys,
We're free from pain;
But should we remain,
A bottle and a kind landlady
Cures all again.[7]

VII

After the party, General Hamilton returned to his Cedar Street house. Burr's grim expression and icy eyes had communicated an ominous chill. The General sat down at his desk and wrote a letter to his wife.

New York, July 4, 1804

This letter, my dear Eliza, will not be delivered to you, unless I shall first have terminated my earthly career; to begin, as I humbly hope from redeeming grace and divine mercy, a happy immortality.

If it had been possible for me to have avoided the interview, my love for you and my precious children would have been alone a decisive motive. But it was not possible, without sacrifices which would have rendered me unworthy of your esteem. I need not tell you of the pangs I feel, from the idea of quitting you and exposing you to the anguish which I know you would feel. Nor could I dwell on the topic lest it should unman me.

The consolations of Religion, my beloved, can alone support you; and these you have a right to enjoy. Fly to the bosom of your God and be comforted. With my last idea; I shall cherish the sweet hope of meeting you in a better world.

Adieu best of wives and best of Women. Embrace all my darling Children for me.

Ever yours
AH[8]

General Hamilton added this sad epistle to the possibly posthumous remarks he had already completed. Did he also think that it would be one more nail in Aaron Burr's political coffin? One hopes not.

VIII

The circuit court closed roughly as Pendleton had predicted, on Friday, July 6th. Pendleton told Van Ness that Hamilton wanted to spend the weekend with his family but he would be ready any time after Sunday.

On Saturday, the Hamiltons gave a dinner party for William Short, Thomas Jefferson's former secretary when he was ambassador to France. Later Short had been American minister to the Netherlands, where he had helped Hamilton negotiate some vital loans when he was secretary of the treasury. Among the other guests were Colonel William Stephens Smith, John Adams's son-in-law, the humiliator of Hamilton's friend Robert Troup in their aborted 1803 duel. Smith was with his wife, Abigail, evidence that not all the Adams clan considered Hamilton a monster.

For Hamilton, Smith represented a lost dream of a British-American rapprochement. In 1790–91, Smith had circulated around London, promoting the news of Hamilton's financial system and the opportunities it offered for British investment. He returned to America with heady orders to purchase stock in the Bank of the United States. But Jeffersonian hostility—and anti-Americans in the British government who seized on it—had stifled this hopeful vision.[9]

Like Hamilton, Smith was an ex-Washington aide. But he had never adjusted to civilian life. He was constantly afloat on schemes of financial glory, all of which turned out to be chimeras that left him deeper in debt. At one point his father-in-law had to rescue him from debtor's prison. As John Adams was leaving the presidency, he had reluctantly named Smith surveyor of customs for the port of New York. "All the actions of my life and all the conduct of my children have not disgraced me so much as this man," he wrote as he made the appointment. "His pay will not feed his dogs, and his dogs must be fed if his children starve." In spite of her father's scorn, Abigail Adams Smith remained devoted to her erratic husband.[10]

Also in the party was the painter John Trumbull, who was about to depart for Boston. As the son of Connecticut's revolutionary war governor, he moved in the highest circles. According to one of Hamilton's sons, John Church Hamilton, who was thirteen at the time, the General took the artist aside after dinner and said: "You are going to Boston. You will see the principal men there. Tell them from me . . . for God's sake, to cease these conversations and threatenings about a separation of the Union. It must hang together as long as it can be made to."[11]

On Sunday, July 8th, John Church Hamilton recalled his father spent the early morning strolling with his wife around their thirty-two acres. Back in the house he gathered the family for the Episcopal service. At the end of the long, hot day, he called his children around him and they trooped out to a large tree on the lawn. Sprawling on the grass, he urged them to imitate him. They lay there, John Church Hamilton said, "until the stars shone down from the heavens."[12]

Later that night, John Church Hamilton was sitting in one of the Grange's downstairs rooms when his father appeared in the doorway. "John," Hamilton said, "won't you come and sleep with me tonight?" John Church recalled that Hamilton's expression was tender, "without any of the preoccupation of business" that he often saw on his father's face. The next morning, Hamilton arose early to leave for New York City. He awoke his son and together they recited the Lord's Prayer.[13]

IX

On Monday, July 9th, a rampantly impatient Colonel Burr wrote to William P. Van Ness, telling him he did not want to "pass over" another day. He had no "predilection" for the time, although he considered the morning, from seven to twelve, the "least pleasant." He was ready to agree to anything "so *but* we get on."

That afternoon, Pendleton and Van Ness agreed on Wednesday, July 11th, as the day. The place would be the dueling ground in Weehawken where Hamilton's son, Philip, and many others had fought. That same day, alone in his house at Cedar Street, Hamilton wrote his will. He appointed his brother-in-law, John Barker Church, Nathaniel Pendleton, and lawyer Nicholas Fish the executors. He left everything to his "excellent and dear Wife" and enjoined his children "if they . . . shall ever be able" to make up the losses that a forced sale of his property would inflict on his creditors. He trusted his wife's "patrimonial resources"—General Schuyler's fortune—would save her from "indigence."

He signed this document in the presence of John Barker Church and three neighbors. He left to Church the collection of some $2,510 in legal fees and a statement of his assets and debts. In spite of his resolutions to economize, Hamilton's expenses since January 1, 1804, had amounted to $11,840.27—well beyond his income of $8,000.[14] His assets were mostly speculations in land in upstate New York and Ohio, the value of which he vastly overestimated. His debts, to which he could not apply this sort of delusional accounting, totaled $54,722 (well over a half million in today's dollars). By kiting the value of his real estate, Hamilton managed to convince himself that he was leaving a balance in his favor of $25,778.

As a hard-nosed businessman who was well aware that the General tended to keep inaccurate accounts, John Barker Church probably did not believe a scrap of Hamilton's financial balancing act. But it was hardly the time to be critical. The Englishman somberly handed his brother-in-law the same pair of dueling pistols that Philip Hamilton had used in his fatal encounter with George L. Eacker in 1801. Made by Wogdon, a well-known London gunsmith, the pistols were beautiful weapons, with dark walnut stocks and gleaming solid brass barrels. They had a hair-trigger adjustment as well as standard trigger pull—not unusual among dueling pistols of the era. In fact a gun shop in New York advertised in the New York *Evening Post* that it specialized in guns with this device.[15]

When the hair trigger was set (by pushing the trigger forward) a duelist could get off a shot with only a half pound of pressure. The ordinary pull required considerably more pressure—about ten to twelve pounds—and more time. The two trigger choices gave a man the option of betting on a quick but possibly inaccurate shot or relying on a more deliberate aim. Unusual for dueling pistols was the guns' large calibre: .544. Most dueling pistols of the period fired a .50-calibre bullet. The Wogdon bullet weighed a full ounce. As one twentieth-century expert has put it, these guns "were heavy enough to shoot horses."[16]

Later that afternoon Hamilton went to dinner at the home of Oliver Wolcott Jr., his successor as secretary of the treasury and one of his warmest admirers and friends. Two days later a stunned Wolcott would tell his wife that the General was "uncommonly cheerful and gay." The same ebullience that had animated him at the Society of the Cincinnati dinner was still present.

On the way home from this party, or possibly the following day—the sequence from the surviving records is unclear—Hamilton paid a call on his oldest friend in New York, ailing Robert Troup. The overworked fat man, still suffering from his multiple illnesses, seemed too sick to deal with a serious discussion of the looming confrontation with Burr. In the context of Troup's failure to fight William Stephens Smith, it would have been too painful, in the first place. Troup later recalled that the General's "composure and cheerfulness of mind" made it impossible for him even to suspect that there was a rendezvous with death just over the horizon.[17]

Later, on the tenth of July, Hamilton wrote another letter to his wife. He urged her to be generous to his mother's cousin, Ann Mitchell, who had emigrated from the West Indies to Burlington, New Jersey, and was growing old in straitened circumstances. She had tried to help young Alexander and his brother after their mother died on St. Croix. Hamilton told Betsy that he had failed to do his duty to Mitchell. He had hoped to be able to make the "Evening of her days" comfortable. Now all he could do was draw a bill of exchange for $100 and leave it with his papers.

His final words were exclusively for his wife.

> The Scruples of a Christian have determined me to expose my own life to
> any extent rather than subject myself to the guilt of taking the life of another.
> This must increase my hazards & redoubles my pangs for you. But you had
> rather I should die innocent than live guilty. Heaven can preserve me and I
> humbly hope will, but in the contrary event, I charge you to remember that
> you are a Christian. God's Will be done! The will of a merciful God must be
> good.
>
> Once more Adieu My Darling
> darling Wife
> AH[18]

Heartbreaking though this letter seems at first reading, it makes no
sense. Hamilton once more reveals a totally confused idea of what he was
required to do as a Christian. The fifth commandment, Thou Shalt Not
Kill, does not prohibit a Christian from self-defense. This sudden dread
of taking the life of another was also totally at variance with the General's stated readiness to take command of the American army in the
event of a war, in which, presumably, he would kill a great many people.
Nor is there any evidence that Elizabeth Hamilton would have preferred
to see her husband die innocent rather than shoot Aaron Burr. On the
contrary, she seems to have nursed an extremely unchristian hatred for
Burr and Hamilton's other adversaries for the rest of her long life.
Decades later, when James Monroe called on her, she refused to see him
because she believed he had leaked the Reynolds scandal to James
Thomson Callender.

The scruple that was tormenting General Hamilton's conscience was
the death of his beloved son. Hamilton seems to be saying to God, if not
to his wife: I am going to throw away my fire to expiate the bad advice I
gave Philip. The tormented General was transferring his reluctance to see
Philip kill a man whom he had insulted but did not hate to Aaron Burr—
a man Hamilton thoroughly hated. He could not explain this to Elizabeth Hamilton—or to himself.

X

That same night, Hamilton revealed how much his passion for fame still pervaded his divided soul. He wrote a letter to Theodore Sedgwick, one of the leaders of Massachusetts's Federalists. As a congressman Sedgwick had received Hamilton's omnibus denunciation of Burr during the presidential deadlock of 1801. The New Englander, who was also an old friend of Aaron Burr, had rejected Hamilton's advice. This recollection, and the imminence of tomorrow's meeting, added a tinge of desperation to Hamilton's prose.

The General said he had been working on a long letter in response to two letters Sedgwick had written to him about the New England threat to secede from the Union. He had intended to explain at length "my view of the course and tendency of our Politics" and how he planned to conduct himself. But he had been delayed by several things, including "a growing distaste for politics," and the treatise lay unfinished. He was writing now to let Sedgwick know his silence was not caused by any lack of regard for him.

Hamilton said he only wanted to express one sentiment: "Dismemberment of our Empire will be a clear sacrifice of great positive advantages, without any counterballancing good." The choice of the word *empire* is significant. Creators and rulers of empires were those who won fame. His hostility to "dismemberment" (secession) was rooted in his vision of the future might of a united, continental America. World power was the great positive advantage for which Hamilton believed America must contend.

Then General Hamilton added one of the saddest and most revealing lines he ever wrote. Secession would administer "no relief to our real disease; which is DEMOCRACY."[19] Here, stated in the starkest terms, was the reason for Alexander Hamilton's failure as an American politician. Entwined with his immense gifts was a fundamental lack of faith in the ability of the average citizen to participate in government. Temperament and experience had rooted this pessimism deep in his soul.

XI

Alone in his Richmond Hill mansion, except for his three black slave servants, on that same Tuesday night Aaron Burr was also writing farewell letters. He had no reason to assume he was going to survive the duel. He too wrote his will and a covering letter to his son-in-law, Joseph Alston, who would be his executor, along with John Swartout and William P. Van Ness.

The vice president told Alston, "It would have been a great satisfaction to me to have had your assurance that you would assume my debts." This was an oblique way of saying he hoped Alston would undertake this favor. He added that the sale of his "property"—Richmond Hill and his land speculations and some lots in New York City—would "undoubtedly" produce more than his debts. This fond hope was based on the same sort of creative accounting that General Hamilton was doing on Cedar Street.

Burr asked Alston to extend his friendship to Charles Biddle and his numerous sons. The vice president also mentioned five young lawyers who had supported him in the recent governorship campaign, and asked Alston to give them some "token of remembrance." He urged his son-in-law to make an effort to "attach them all to you." Obviously, he was hoping that Alston would somehow acquire the talent and personality to became his political successor.

"If it shall be my lot to fall," Burr wrote, "yet I shall live in you and your son. I commit to you all that is most dear to me—my reputation and my daughter. Your talents and your attachment will be the guardian of the one—your kindness and generosity of the other."

Taking up a theme that he never tired of pursuing, Burr urged Alston to "stimulate and aid Theodosia in the cultivation of her mind." He wanted her to acquire a "critical knowledge of Latin, English, and all branches of natural philosophy." In the future, he was certain "all this would be poured into your son." Perhaps sensing that this educational passion was beyond Alston's grasp, he begged him to do it as "a last favor." He guaranteed that Theodosia "will richly compensate your trouble."[20]

Finally, Burr turned to a farewell letter to his daughter. He began by making her the custodian of all his letters and papers. If her husband ever undertook a sketch of his life, he might find some of these useful, Burr wrote. He added that no one could do it as well—a compliment to Alston's considerable literary gifts, which he never displayed in public. For the rest, Burr ordered Theodosia to burn anything that would "injure any person," if by some accident it became public. This of course especially applied to his female correspondents. One bundle of letters, to a woman named Clara, he thought Theodosia and eventually, Aaron Burr Alston, might find amusing in the future.

He wanted "my dear Natalie [*sic*]"—his adopted daughter Nathalie Delage Sumter—to have one of his portraits, and any other token she might want. Other tokens should go to his stepsons, Bartow and Frederick Prevost. He directed that a lot in the city worth about $250 should be sold for his slave, Peggy, who ran Richmond Hill, and urged Theodosia to persuade her to move to South Carolina and work for the Alstons. His valet, Peter, "the most intelligent and best-disposed black" he had ever known, would make a superb valet for Aaron Burr Alston.

Burr urged Theodosia to be especially kind to her half brother, Frederick Prevost, still a rustic farmer in Westchester County. "He loves *me* almost as much as Theodosia does; he does love *you* to adoration." He ordered her to give Frederick all his clothing, and any other token that occurred to her. Frederick had supported Burr valiantly in the governorship election, while his brother Bartow had stayed cautiously neutral. Finally, Burr found special words for the only person in the world he truly loved.

> "I am indebted to you, my dearest Theodosia, for a very great portion of the happiness I have enjoyed in this life. You have completely satisfied all that my heart and affections had hoped or even wished. With a little more perseverance, determination, and industry, you will obtain all that my ambition or vanity fondly imagined. Let your son have occasion to be proud that he had a mother. Adieu. Adieu.[21]

CHAPTER 17

This Is a Mortal Wound, Doctor

That same night, July 10th, in his New York City house, Nathaniel Pendleton was writing the regulations for tomorrow's duel. He dated the paper July 11th—perhaps a sign of his inner agitation or of the way that date loomed in his mind. The parties were to leave New York for the dueling ground at 5:00 A.M. The distance was to be ten paces—about thirty feet. The pistols were not to exceed eleven inches in the barrel. The choice of positions would be determined by a coin toss.

The previous day, William P. Van Ness had written his own set of regulations, which agreed with Pendleton's almost verbatim. Oarsmen had been hired by the seconds to row the three miles across the Hudson to Weehawken. For a doctor, both sides had agreed to call on Hamilton's family physician, David Hosack.[1] There was nothing more for anyone to do but try to get some sleep.

The night was hot and muggy—typical New York weather for July. How or if Hamilton slept in his Cedar Street house has gone unrecorded. We know Burr threw himself down on a couch in the Richmond Hill library. William P. Van Ness, John Swartout, and Matthew Davis found him there in the predawn darkness, sleeping soundly. He dressed quickly in black pantaloons, half boots, and a coat of dark bombazine. They hurried down to the shore of the Hudson, where a boat was waiting for the colonel and Van Ness. Duelists generally did not breakfast. It was widely believed that food in the stomach would lead to rapid infection if a bullet penetrated that organ.

Van Ness and Burr reached the dueling ground first, and began clearing away tree limbs and underbrush. No one had exchanged shots on this grassy ledge below the cliffs known as the Palisades for some time. The outcropping was about six feet wide and eleven yards long. At one corner was a granite boulder. Nearby stood a large cedar tree. The site had become a dueling ground because of its inaccessibility. There was no path leading down the cliff face from the village of Weehawken. Walkers along the Hudson shore could only reach it at low tide. The future town of Hoboken, two and a half miles to the south, was unborn. The isolation was a virtual guarantee against an interruption of the deadly business transacted there.

Hamilton set out from another dock in what is now Greenwich Village, not far from the country house of New York merchant William Bayard, a client and friend. The General and Nathaniel Pendleton may have been delayed by the necessity to collect Dr. Hosack. They seem to have arrived on the Weehawken shore considerably after Burr and Van Ness. The physician stayed down on the water's edge with the boatmen while the General and his second clambered up a narrow path to find Burr and Van Ness in their shirt sleeves, clearing away nature's debris. The two parties greeted each other in gentlemanly fashion. The seconds conferred on the regulations and found they were in agreement. They had already decided to use the Church pistols.

Burr put on his coat and waited at a distance. Hamilton stayed at a roughly equal distance on the other side of the seconds while they tossed a coin to see who would have the choice of positions and who would give the order to fire. Pendleton won both tosses. By now it was approaching seven o'clock. The July sun had begun beating down on the river, creating an intense glare. The sun itself was still low enough in the sky to strike the dueling ground at an angle. Pendleton chose to position Hamilton with his back to the cliff, facing the light. Some people have criticized him for this move, but Pendleton probably thought Burr was a better target, outlined against the glistening river. Hamilton had said he was going to throw away his first fire, but he had not decided on his second round, if Burr insisted on one.

II

The two seconds now loaded the pistols with powder and a "smooth ball," as the regulations required. The inside of the guns' barrels was also smooth. This made a handgun, with its short barrel, though precision made, even more inaccurate than a musket. Inside and outside the barrel, the spinning bullet was subject to forces over which the gun wielder had no control. A rifled barrel, prohibited by the dueling code, would give a marksman far more accuracy. Beyond thirty yards, a smoothbore pistol was almost a useless weapon, and even at that range it was extremely un-predictable. These ballistics were part of the reason why the duel was not always a fatal encounter.

With the pistols loaded, the duelists took their positions, and their sec-onds walked over to hand each his weapon. As Pendleton gave General Hamilton his gun, he asked: "Do you want the hair spring set?"

"Not this time," Hamilton replied.

Pendleton stepped back and walked out of the line of fire. He briefly explained the rules they were following. First he would ask them if they were ready. If they answered in the affirmative, he would say "Present!" Thereafter, each could fire whenever he pleased.

Both men nodded. At this point, according to Burr and William P. Van Ness, General Hamilton raised his pistol "as if to try the light," and asked them to pardon him. He said the "direction of the light" made it hard for him to adjust his eyes. With his left hand, he drew spectacles from his pocket and put them on.

Pendleton asked if they were ready. "Yes," both said.

"Present!" Pendleton said.

By this time, both men had assumed the duelist's stance, the right foot about twenty-six inches in front of the left foot, the face positioned over the right shoulder, the stomach sucked in, the right thigh and leg covering the left leg. The goal was to present as little body surface as possible. Even the pistol was wielded with protection in mind; it was held somewhat to the left, where it could deflect a bullet.[2]

Both men leveled their pistols and the guns boomed within seconds of each other. Van Ness thought Hamilton fired first. He spun his head to see if Burr was hit. At that instant the colonel fired and almost simultaneously his body seemed to jerk as if Hamilton's bullet had struck him. Later, Van Ness would discover Burr had stepped on a stone as he assumed the oblique position and as he fired he must have pressed his foot on it.

Pendleton thought Burr fired first. His eyes remained on Hamilton and the Virginian saw his arm jerk upward as he pulled the trigger. To his horror he realized the General was hit. A swirl of gunsmoke enveloped both duelists. For a moment, time, perception, understanding froze. Still clutching his pistol, Hamilton pitched forward on his face, The oversize lead ball had penetrated his right side a little above the hip, torn through his liver and diaphragm, and lodged in his vertebrae.

The vice president uttered a small sound of dismay and started toward him. Pendleton shouted: "Dr. Hosack!" Van Ness rushed forward and led Burr down the path toward the water. One account has him shielding Burr with an umbrella so that the boatmen and Dr. Hosack, who were rushing up the same path, could not testify that they had seen him there. When Burr and Van Ness reached their boat, the vice president hesitated. "I must go and speak to him," he reportedly said. Van Ness persuaded him this was out of the question and the boatmen soon had them out on the river.[3]

Dr. Hosack found Hamilton half sitting on the ground in Nathaniel Pendleton's arms. "This is a mortal wound, Doctor," he gasped. A second later he lost consciousness and Hosack thought he was going to die on the spot. The doctor pulled up his bloody shirt and saw at a glance that Hamilton was probably right. Hosack could find no pulse, nor was Hamilton breathing. He put his hand on the General's heart and found "no motion there." Hosack thought Hamilton was "irretrievably gone."

Against the cliff the air was dense with heat and humidity. Hosack decided the only hope was to get the General on the water as soon as possible. Together he and Pendleton carried him down the path to the point where the land fell steeply to the water's edge. As they labored, an anguished Pendleton told Hosack about Hamilton's refusal to fire at Burr. With the help of the oarsmen they got the wounded man into the boat and pulled off. Hosack began rubbing Hamilton's face with spirits of hartshorne. He applied this invigorating potion to his neck and chest and wrists and palms, and even tried to get some into his mouth.

About fifty yards from shore, Hamilton gave a great sigh and began breathing again. The hartshorne, along with the cooler air on the river, had restored him to life. His eyes wandered across the water and around the boat and he muttered: "my vision is indistinct." Gradually, his pulse returned to near normal, his breathing became regular. Hosack tried to examine the wound but even a slight touch caused Hamilton such pain, he "desisted."

III

As Hamilton's sight returned, he saw John Barker Church's pistol case open in the bottom of the boat, with the gun he had used lying outside it. "Take care of that pistol," he said. "It is undischarged and still cocked—it may go off and do harm." Attempting to turn his head to Pendleton, who was sitting behind him in the stern, Hamilton added: "Pendleton knows I did not intend to fire at him."

"Yes," Pendleton said. "I have already told Dr. Hosack that."

Hamilton fell silent. After a few minutes with the only sound the grunts of the sweating oarsmen, Dr. Hosack began asking the wounded man how he felt—nauseous, dizzy? He was trying to get some idea what organs the bullet had struck. Hamilton told him he had lost all feeling in his body from the waist down. He could not move his legs. Hosack tried to rearrange his legs hoping circulation would be restored, but Hamilton reported no improvement. Once or twice he asked Hosack to take his pulse, which the doctor reported was still fairly normal.

As they approached the shore, Hamilton told Pendleton and Hosack to send for his wife. He asked them to break the news to her gradually. "Give her hopes," he said.

A moment later they were alongside the dock from which they had set out. Looking up, Hamilton found his friend William Bayard gazing down at him. A servant had seen Hamilton and Pendleton and Hosack setting out in the dawn and told Bayard, who immediately knew where they were going. Bayard already feared the worst. As the boat approached he saw only Hosack and Pendleton sitting up. When the merchant saw Hamilton lying in the bottom of the boat he burst into tears.

Hosack told Bayard to prepare a bed for his wounded friend. Bayard was so overwhelmed by grief, he was almost useless. His whole family was soon weeping and wailing. Pendleton and Dr. Hosack almost joined them. In his account of this part of the return from Weehawken, the doctor noted that only Hamilton kept his composure.

IV

When they finally got the General to a bed on the second floor of Bayard's lamentation-filled house, Hamilton seemed almost comatose. But Dr. Hosack revived him with some wine and water. With help from others, the doctor undressed him and administered a strong "anodyne"—a painkiller. He rubbed it on the parts of Hamilton's body where he complained of pain, particularly his back. The drug did little to assuage the wounded man's agony.

Dr. Hosack sent for Dr. Wright Post, professor of anatomy at Columbia College and one of the New York's leading physicians. Dr. Post soon arrived but he only confirmed Dr. Hosack's opinion that the wound was mortal.

Several hours later, the French consul sent surgeons from two men of war in New York harbor in the hope that their experience with gunshot wounds might help. But they too concluded that General Hamilton was a dying man.

The General had no doubts about this diagnosis. His thoughts were already focused on the next world. He asked the Bayards to send a servant to Benjamin Moore, Episcopal bishop of New York and president of Columbia College. The bishop came as requested, but was unhappy to learn that Hamilton had been wounded in a duel, an activity Moore considered sinful. Worse, the dying man had never joined the Episcopal church. When Moore learned that Hamilton wanted to receive holy communion, the Bishop demurred. This reception of the body and blood of Jesus, in a consecrated wafer of bread, was for Christians a central act of faith, and could not be administered casually. The bishop departed, declaring he wanted to give the dying man "time for reflection."

Hamilton asked Bayard to summon another clergyman, the Reverend John M. Mason, pastor of the Scotch Presbyterian Church. This was the faith that had stirred Hamilton in his youth, when a Presbyterian minister had befriended the orphaned boy on St. Croix. Mason hurried to Bayard's house. But the minister sadly informed Hamilton that his church forbade him to give communion privately. It could only be done at the altar, in the course of a Sunday ceremony. He tried to assure Hamilton that communion was only a "pledge" of the forgiveness of sin that Jesus had purchased by his death on the cross. The same forgiveness was available to Hamilton by faith.

The dying man did not find this idea satisfactory and pleaded for someone to persuade Bishop Moore to return as soon as possible. Meanwhile, around noon, Elizabeth Hamilton arrived. In obedience to the General's wishes, no one had told her the truth about his condition. She believed Hamilton was suffering from stomach spasms. But a few minutes with her husband must have revealed everything. When Betsy grew frantic with grief, Hamilton reminded her in a strong firm voice: "Remember, Eliza, you are a Christian."[4]

V

The news that General Hamilton was dying of a mortal wound inflicted by Vice President Burr spread swiftly through New York. Oliver Wolcott Jr., who was preparing to leave the city to join his wife in Connecticut, rushed to Bayard's house but was advised that a visit to the General's bedside was out of the question. Returning home, Wolcott scribbled a distressed letter to his wife, telling her that he would be delayed. One line exposed the central truth of the tragedy. Wolcott wrote that Hamilton had convinced himself that while dueling was criminal, "peculiar reasons . . . rendered it proper for him to expose himself to Col. Burr in particular" (underlining is Wolcott's).[5]

About 1:00 P.M. Bishop Moore returned to the Bayard House and spoke with Hamilton. As the bishop recalled it later that day, Hamilton said: "My dear sir you perceive my unfortunate situation, and no doubt have been made acquainted with the circumstances which led to it. It is my desire to receive the communion at your hands. I hope you will not conceive there is any impropriety in my request." Hamilton added that for some time it had been "the wish of my heart" to join the church. He did not explain why he had never gotten around to it.

The Bishop lectured him. Hamilton was putting him in a "delicate" situation. He wanted to relieve "a fellow mortal in distress." But he had to uphold the law of God, which required him to "unequivocally condemn" dueling. Hamilton humbly assured the bishop that he agreed with him and he viewed his trip to Weehawken "with sorrow and contrition." The Bishop sternly asked him, if he regained his health, to promise never to fight another duel. Hamilton said that was his "deliberate intention."

Mollified, the bishop asked the General if he repented of his past sins and had a "lively faith" in God's mercy through Jesus Christ. Was he disposed "to live in love and charity with all men?" Hamilton lifted his hands and vowed he could answer yes to all these questions. He said he had "no ill will" toward Colonel Burr. He had met him with a "fixed resolution" not to do him any harm. He forgave him for "all that happened"—the challenge and the duel.

The bishop gave Hamilton holy communion. He said the dying man received it "with great devotion" and "his heart afterwards appeared perfectly at rest."[6] Dr. Hosack gave a somewhat amended version of his patient's condition. He said Hamilton, as he writhed in agony, repeatedly muttered: "My beloved wife and children."[7] The General spent the rest of the day in terrific pain. That night he had what Dr. Hosack called "some imperfect sleep," no doubt helped by the ounce of laudanum that the physician gave him.

VI

In Richmond Hill, a half mile away from the Bayard house, Vice President Burr was hearing things, perhaps from his servants, perhaps from friends who had contacts with visitors to the Bayards. He scribbled a letter to William Van Ness: "There is in circulation a report which is ascribed to Mr. Pendleton & which he must forthwith contradict." Almost certainly Burr was referring to Hamilton's determination to throw away his first fire. Pendleton had already told this to Dr. Hosack and probably to Bayard and some of the visitors.

If Van Ness could not come to Richmond Hill, Burr was ready to visit him in the city, even though the latter "would you know, not be very pleasant."[8] Already the vice president was discovering that the reaction to Hamilton's death was drastically altering his assumption of what he could achieve in the duel.

VII

In the morning Hamilton's pain was less but his other symptoms—the inability to move his legs or feel his body from the waist down—were "aggravated." Hosack hesitated to give him a purgative because of the stomach and bowel problems from which Hamilton had been suffering. No doubt the doctor was disinclined to try any of the other so-called heroic methods common in the medicine of his time such as bloodletting and blistering because he knew the case was hopeless.

Sometime during the previous day or night, Elizabeth Hamilton had brought the seven Hamilton children down from The Grange. They accompanied her to their father's bedside. Hamilton gazed for a moment at their weeping faces and closed his eyes until they were led from the room. What could he say to them? The distraction on his daughter Angelica's face must have been especially painful. His passion for fame had inflicted a second even more terrible wound on her psyche.[9]

Bishop Moore visited Hamilton later in the morning. With a faltering voice, the dying man again expressed his confidence in God's mercy through Jesus. The bishop stayed by the bedside for the next hours, as Hamilton's life signs ebbed. He was joined by a grief-stricken Angelica Schuyler Church. The man she loved more than her husband or any other person on earth did not try to say anything intimate. Her presence was enough, for both of them.

From Aaron Burr, in nearby Richmond Hill came a letter to Dr. Hosack.

> Mr. Burr's respectful Compliments. He requests Dr. Hosack to inform him of the present state of Genl. H. and of the hopes which are entertained of his recovery.
>
> Mr. Burr begs to know at what hours of the [day] the Dr. may most probably be found at home, that he may repeat his inquiries. He would take it very kind if the Dr. would take the trouble of calling on him as he returns from Mr. Bayard's.[10]

At around the same time, a grief-stricken Nathaniel Pendleton was writing a letter to Rufus King, who had left New York for Massachusetts a few days before the duel took place. "Before you read this, our dear and excellent friend Hamilton will be no more." Aware that Hamilton had consulted King about the clash, Pendleton omitted most of the details, simply saying: "Burr's first shot was fatal." He described the probable course of the bullet through Hamilton's body and mournfully reported: "I have just left him and the doctors say he cannot outlive the day." Pendleton added that he did not have time to discuss the reflections that were crowding upon his mind "on this . . . public and private calamity." He would only add that the news had already "occasioned a strong public sensation which will be much increased when he is dead."[11]

VIII

Late on the previous day, a friend had told Gouverneur Morris that Hamilton was dead, killed by Aaron Burr. The statesman rushed from Morrisania to New York on the morning of July 12th, to be told that Hamilton was still alive in Bayard's house. Hurrying there, he found Hamilton "speechless"—comatose and obviously dying. "The scene is too powerful for me," Morris later told his diary. "I am obliged to walk in the garden to take breath."[12]

Regaining his self-control, Morris returned to the bedside, where he was joined by several other Hamilton friends. At two o'clock in the afternoon, the General died. Bishop Moore reported that he expired "without a struggle, and almost without a groan." Tears streaming down his face, one friend turned to Morris and said: "If we were truly brave we would not accept a challenge. But we are all cowards."[13] Morris morosely observed that the friend was one of the bravest men alive, but he doubted if he would "so far brave public opinion as to refuse a challenge." Dr. Hosack found words from the Roman poet Horace (mourning the death of another general) swirling through his head.

> Incorrupta fides, nudaque veritas,
> Quando ullum invenient parem?
> Multis ille bonis flebilis occidit.
>
> *When will incorruptible Faith and naked Truth*
> *Find another his equal?*
> *He has died wept by many.*[14]

CHAPTER 18

Muffled Drums
and Beckoning Destiny

The next melancholy step was the preparations for General Hamilton's funeral. On Thursday evening of July 12th, the day the General died, Colonel William Stephens Smith, no doubt speaking for a committee, asked Gouverneur Morris to give an oration. Morris promised to do it, "if I can possibly command myself." For the moment he confided to his diary that he thought it was "utterly impossible." He was "wholly unmanned" by what he had seen and heard at the Bayard house: Hamilton's wife "almost frantic with grief, his children in tears, every person deeply afflicted."

The next day, still agitated, Morris dined with Richard Harison, the attorney who had joined Hamilton in the appeal for another trial for the Hudson, New York, editor Harry Croswell. Morris wanted to discuss the points he could safely "touch" in the speech. It was going to be a difficult task for a man who could not command "all his [oratorical] powers."

Somehow, Morris told his diary after the dinner, he would have to pass over Hamilton's illegitimate birth, but do it "handsomely." The dead man was also "indiscreet, vain and opinionated." Somehow Morris would have to mention these faults without destroying the "interest" of the audience. Even more difficult were Hamilton's politics: "He was in principle opposed to republican and attached to monarchical government" and these opinions were "generally known and long and loudly proclaimed."

Other problems troubled Morris beyond this brutally candid—and somewhat distorted—summary of Hamilton's politics. The General had opposed dueling in principle, yet he had been killed fighting one. "I cannot thoroughly excuse him without [in]criminating Colonel Burr, which would be wrong." That morning, Colonel William Stephens Smith had visited Morris and they discussed this dilemma. Smith hoped that "in doing justice to the dead," Morris would not "injure the living."

Morris told Smith that Colonel Burr should be considered in the same light as any other man who had killed someone in a duel. He may have been thinking of Brockholst Livingston, who was a judge of the highest court in the state, six years after he had sent Federalist James Jones to the grave. Morris assured Smith that he would "excite no outrage" at Colonel Burr. But Morris thought it would be a good idea if Burr stayed far away from the funeral. Among Federalists, indignation against him was intense. There was a good chance that "legal steps" would be taken against him.[1]

William P. Van Ness and Aaron Burr were already keenly aware of this possibility. On July 11th, the fatal day itself, Van Ness had written to Nathaniel Pendleton, inquiring about Hamilton's condition. Burr's second said he had heard that Dr. Hosack had pronounced the wound mortal but he hoped this was not the case. Getting to the real point of his letter, Van Ness said he hoped Pendleton would not publish anything in the newspapers until they conferred on a statement that was acceptable to both sides.

On July 12th, William Coleman published a long letter from Bishop Moore in the *New-York Evening Post*. It recounted the story of his summons to Hamilton's bedside, the dying man's plea for communion, his contrition, his claim that he had no ill will against Burr. The bishop's chief purpose was visible in the last paragraph, which was an exhortation to "the Infidel" to abandon his opposition to the gospel, which "the strong, inquisitive and comprehensive mind of a HAMILTON" had accepted on his deathbed. The bishop followed his call to unbelievers with a denunciation of dueling, which had left Hamilton's family "afflicted," deprived his friends "of a beloved companion," and his country of "a great statesman and real patriot."[2]

While the bishop's chief purpose seems to have been an advertisement for the Episcopal church, there were elements in his letter that tended to exonerate Hamilton and by implication indict Burr. Certainly no one, not even an unbeliever, could read it without deep sympathy for the fallen General. Meanwhile New York's Common Council was meeting to discuss the funeral. They decided to shut down all the businesses in the city for the day. The funeral would be at public expense. They also suspended the ordinance banning the tolling of church bells at funerals and directed those in charge to muffle the bells and toll them at suitable intervals throughout the services.

Merchants and stockbrokers met at the Tontine Coffee House and seconded the council's decision to close all businesses. They asked captains of vessels in the harbor to lower their flags to half-mast and requested everyone in New York to wear black crepe on his left arm for thirty days as a gesture of respect for "the Integrity, Virtues, Talents and Patriotism of General Alexander Hamilton."

The bar association met at Lovett's Hotel, and Richard Harison made a brief memorial address in a tremulous tear-choked voice. The lawyers passed a resolution declaring their "universal confidence and veneration" for Alexander Hamilton, calling him "the brightest ornament of their profession." Other organizations issued similar statements, including the Tammany Society, whose Republican members until recently regarded General Hamilton as the incarnation of evil.

On that same July 13th, William P. Van Ness and Nathaniel Pendleton conferred at Dr. Hosack's house on a joint statement for the press. They discovered they did not agree on significant details such as why Van Ness had refused to accept Hamilton's final letter. Far more important, Pendleton insisted Burr had fired first. Extremely agitated, Van Ness argued that he and Burr had a right to prevent the publication of anything that made them look guilty. The seconds parted, agreeing to consult their notes and reach an agreement at their next meeting.

Sometime on July 13th, the vice president wrote a troubled letter to Van Ness: "The most abominable falsehoods are current and have issued from the house where H. now lies." Shortly after Burr wrote this note, a letter (since lost) from Van Ness arrived, containing a draft of the proposed joint statement. In a postscript, Burr took strong exception to several points. He was particularly exercised about "the falsehood that H fired only when falling & without aim." That "has given rise to very improper suggestions—the fact does appear to me to be important."

Another concern in this letter was money. Burr was anxious to obtain at least $1,000 in cash as soon as possible. He begged Van Ness to help him make up a "deficiency" of $780. The vice president was apparently preparing to take a trip.[3]

On this same Friday the 13th, the following paragraph appeared in James Cheetham's *American Citizen*: "Death has sealed the eloquent lips of GENERAL HAMILTON! . . . As soon as our feelings will permit, we shall notice this deplorable event, this national loss."[4]

II

Preparations for the funeral on Saturday morning gathered momentum. By now it had acquired the characteristics of a state occasion. The arrangements also became distinctly military. Hamilton's body was moved to John Barker Church's residence at 25 Robinson Street and on Saturday morning the Sixth Regiment of New York's militia assembled in front of the house, with their guns reversed, muzzles down, as a sign of mourning.

At noon the Churches' door swung open and eight pallbearers, including William Bayard, Richard Harison, and Oliver Wolcott Jr., carried Hamilton's body in a mahogany coffin into the street. The soldiers formed into a line of march, led by six artillery pieces. A military band, beating on muffled drums, struck up the dead march. Behind the Sixth Regiment marched members of the Society of the Cincinnati, followed by numerous clergymen. Behind them came the coffin escorted by the pallbearers, followed by Hamilton's gray horse, carrying his boots and spurs reversed. Two black servants dressed in white, wearing turbans trimmed with black, led the horse.

The Hamilton family, Gouverneur Morris in his carriage (his wooden leg prevented him from marching), the members of the bar, and numerous other dignitaries lengthened the procession. The students and professors of Columbia College marched in mourning gowns. Behind them came the Tammany Society, the Mechanic Society, and "citizens in General." Ex-Governor Clinton had the good taste not to appear in mourning for the man he had been slandering only four months ago. Nor did Burr's chief slanderer, Mayor DeWitt Clinton, march as a member of the corporation of the city of New York. He was out of town, probably at his country estate on Long Island.

The procession wound along Beekman, Pearl, and Whitehall Streets and then up Broadway to Trinity Church. In the *Evening Post*, William Coleman reported "the streets were lined with people; doors and windows were filled, principally with weeping females, and even the house tops were covered with spectators." On the Battery and on Governor's Island and aboard men-of-war in the harbor, cannon fired a steady salute.[5]

In his carriage, Gouverneur Morris was still having troubled thoughts, many of them about Aaron Burr. "I can find no Way to get over the Difficulty which would attend [describing] the Details of [Hamilton's] Death," he told himself. "It will be impossible to command [control] either myself or my Audience; their Indignation amounts almost to a frenzy already."

Morris was also worried about any reference to Hamilton's "domestic life." Too many people still remembered the way he had "foolishly" published his confession of infidelity with Maria Reynolds. But the master of Morrisania felt he had to say something to excite "public pity" for his family, whom Hamilton had left "indigent." Morris had probably talked to John Barker Church, who had given him a ruthless analysis of Hamilton's chaotic finances.[6]

At Trinity Church, a stage had been built in the portico. Morris debarked from his carriage and asked Hamilton's four sons to join him on this structure. Around them spread an immense crowd, jamming every square inch of Broadway and nearby streets. It was the first time Morris had ever spoken in the open air and in his diary he reported that he was dismayed to discover "my voice is lost before it reaches one tenth of the Audience." Yet he felt he got through the oration "tolerably well" in spite of feeling "the Impropriety of acting a dumb Shew [show]" for those who could see him but could not hear him.[7]

Morris began by declaring he was going to express only his personal feelings. Instead of the language of a public speaker, they would hear the "lamentations" of a friend. He would try "with bursting heart" to portray Hamilton's "heroic spirit." He quickly narrated Hamilton's early career, decorating it with apostrophes. He was so brilliant, many had heard his name before they knew him. "It seemed as if God had called him suddenly into existence, that he might assist to save a world!" Soon he attracted the "penetrating eye" of Washington and he became a "principle actor" in the Revolution.

Recounting the General's role in the creation of the Constitution, Morris admitted that Hamilton did not think the document was strong enough to prevent America from collapsing into anarchy and ending in despotism. He never concealed this opinion and this "generous indiscretion" led to criticism from those who did not understand "the purity of his heart." They accused him of "deliberate designs" to overthrow the Constitution when in fact he constantly struggled to preserve and strengthen it. Surely the people would pardon "that single error" in a life devoted to their service.

Morris dwelt at more length on Hamilton's creation of the nation's financial system and his role in Washington's cabinet. His "rising family" forced him to resign but he never abandoned public service. When Washington chose him as his second in command in the undeclared war with France, Hamilton once more sacrificed his income as a lawyer to serve the nation. Morris combined this praise with an attempt to prove that Hamilton had risen above political ambition. He had vowed he would never hold public office again unless a "foreign war" forced him to unsheathe his sword.

Finally, Morris urged the people to protect Hamilton's fame. It was all he had left to his "poor orphan children." This fame was also a treasure that the American people shared. Henceforth, he urged them to test the decisions of their politicians by asking: *Would Hamilton have done this thing?*

Morris said he could not and would not dwell on how Hamilton died. He did not want to excite emotions "too strong for your better judgment." In Hamilton's name, he urged the people to avoid any act that might "again offend the insulted majesty of the law." As if he feared these words would not be sufficient, he cried: "Let me entreat you to respect yourself!"

Hamilton's coffin was now carried into Trinity churchyard, where Bishop Moore read the service for the dead. A detachment of soldiers fired three volleys over the grave. On the ships in the harbor and in the forts, the cannon continued to boom. In the *Evening Post*'s next edition, William Coleman wrote that the scene "was enough to melt a monument of marble."

III

Morris soon found that his oration did not "answer the general expectation." He knew this would be the case, because he had spoken with the conscious intention to "allay the sentiment" that he was expected to arouse. What Morris meant by this becomes clear in the next sentence in his diary: "How easy it would have been to make them for a Moment absolutely mad!" Clearly, the mood of New York City was not friendly to Vice President Aaron Burr.[8]

That evening, William Coleman visited Morris in a state of great agitation. He had taken notes on the statesman's speech but he found, on examining them, that they were useless. He had been too overwhelmed by grief to write coherently. For the vice president, the editor's distress was another ominous sign. Coleman was no longer an admirer of Aaron Burr. Morris agreed to expand the editor's fragmentary notes into a coherent speech.

Elsewhere, William P. Van Ness and Nathaniel Pendleton were still negotiating a joint public statement. It finally appeared in the *Morning Chronicle* and in the *New-York Evening Post* on Tuesday, July 17th. It contained thirteen documents, beginning with Burr's first letter and continuing through the exchanges between Hamilton and the vice president as well as the seconds, to a summary description of the duel. On the crucial point of who fired first, they compromised: "The pistols were discharged within a few seconds of each other." After describing Hamilton's fall, the narrators continued: "Col: Burr then advanced toward Genl H—n with a manner and gesture that appeared to Genl Hamilton's friend to be expressive of regret." Then followed the account of Van Ness hurrying Burr from the field. The concluding sentence was: "We conceive it proper to add that the conduct of the parties in that interview was perfectly proper as suited to the occasion."[9]

Meanwhile, a coroner's jury began hearing evidence concerning Hamilton's death. They interrogated Pendleton, who pleaded the Fifth Amendment and was permitted to depart. Rather than appear, Van Ness went into hiding. When Matthew Davis was called before the jury and he refused to answer certain questions, he was committed to the city's prison, the Bridewell. The jury arrested another Burr backer, Colonel Marinus Willett, and issued a warrant for the arrest of a third friend, William Irvine. The manhunt was based on a report that the Burrites had met in secret caucus and decided Colonel Burr should fight one of a list of four or five people, presumably including both Mayor DeWitt Clinton and Governor George Clinton, and Burr had chosen Hamilton as his preferred target.[10]

This bizarre tale was only a sample of the rumors that were sweeping New York. There was talk of burning Burr's town house and dispatching a mob to do a similar job on Richmond Hill. From elsewhere in the nation, as the news spread, the reaction was similar: grief and rage at Vice President Burr. Philadelphia declared a day of mourning. Federalist newspapers denounced Burr and envisioned the American eagle in deep mourning while Hamilton and Washington met around the celestial throne.[11]

More immediately painful to Burr were the assaults of the New York newspapers. The Federalist editor of the *Commercial Advertiser*, Zachariah Lewis, a paper that had more or less backed Burr in the gubernatorial campaign, now wrote: "Who would believe that the son of venerable President Burr [of Princeton] . . . the second officer in the United States . . . should take cool and deadly aim against the first citizen of our country—the father of a numerous family—the husband of a most affectionate wife—an ornament to his country and to human nature? Could nothing . . . allay the cool persevering resentment of his antagonist but the heart's blood of such a man?"[12]

James Cheetham, who had spent a good part of his newspaper career denouncing Alexander Hamilton, the Federalist party, and all its works, suddenly discovered an adoration for the fallen general that was little short of miraculous. He opened with the only point he really wanted to make: this *"national loss [was] the inevitable and deplorable effect of a long premeditated and predetermined system of hostility on the part of Mr. Burr and his confidential advisors."* [Italics are Cheetham's.] William Coleman reprinted this charge in the *Evening Post*, along with Cheetham's eulogy of Hamilton, another ominous sign of a radical change in Coleman's opinion of Burr.[13]

IV

Cheetham was soon reporting evidence of Burr's malevolence. Three of the vice president's followers had supposedly spent weeks combing newspapers for something that would entitle Burr to issue a challenge. Cheetham seemed oblivious to the fact that his own newspaper was the best possible source for such material. Like many a newsman since his time, Cheetham relied on the public's short memory.

Cheetham cited a paragraph in the *Morning Chronicle* about an Englishwoman who had escaped serious injury when a silk handkerchief deflected a bullet aimed at her breast. From this he concocted a story that

Burr had immediately ordered a suit of silk for the duel. The *Morning Chronicle* replied that Burr's coat had been bombazine and his pantaloons cotton. This only gave Cheetham a chance to publish a veritable treatise on bombazine as a variety of silk.

As Hamilton lay dying at the Bayard house, Cheetham claimed that Burr and his chief lieutenants celebrated with heavy drinking and toasts to the colonel's accuracy at Richmond Hill. Even better (or worse) was the Englishman's story that Burr had spent three months practicing every day with a pistol, and had even spent the morning of the Fourth of July in target practice at Richmond Hill.[14] For Cheetham and his mentor, Mayor DeWitt Clinton, Hamilton's death was a priceless opportunity to destroy Burr politically forever, and they made the most of it.

V

William Coleman's new aversion to Burr was almost as obvious. He began by publishing in the July 19th *Evening Post* "an amended version" of the Pendleton–Van Ness statement on the conduct of the duel. In this document Pendleton said he had a "sacred duty" to "this exalted man" to report that General Hamilton did not fire first and that "he did not fire at all at Col. Burr." Pendleton went on to describe Hamilton's statement about his intention to throw away his fire, made to him and to Bishop Moore (and to Rufus King, who was not mentioned). He described Hamilton's comments on the pistol that he thought was still loaded, in the boat returning to New York.

Pendleton said he was sure William P. Van Ness was sincere in his insistence that General Hamilton had fired first. To clear up his own doubts, on July 13th, the day after the general died, Pendleton and a friend had returned to Weehawken and tracked the bullet from Hamilton's pistol. It had passed through the limb of the cedar tree that grew on or near the ledge; the limb was twelve and a half feet from the ground and four feet wide of the mark on which Colonel Burr had been standing.

Pendleton theorized that the shock of Burr's bullet had caused Hamilton to squeeze his trigger and inadvertently fire this wild shot.[15]

On that same July 13th, the day after Hamilton's death, Burr had written to his son-in-law, Joseph Alston, that the Federalists and the Clintonians were uniting to destroy him: "Thousands of absurd falsehoods are circulated with industry." Five days later, as public indignation, fanned by Cheetham and others, continued to rise, Burr told Alston that he was about to be driven into a "sort of exile," and the uproar might end in "an actual and permanent ostracism." With rhetoric worthy of a Federalist, he wrote that "our most unprincipled Jacobins [read Clintonians] are loudest in their lamentations for General Hamilton after describing him for years as "the most detestable . . . of men."

The coroner's jury continued to sit, with the obvious intention of indicting Burr for murder. If and when this happened, he would be arrested and no bail would be allowed. Murder was not a bailable offense in the New York criminal code of 1804. Burr did not like the thought of being in Bridewell, at the disposal of Mayor DeWitt Clinton's followers.[16]

VI

From Charles Biddle came an anxious letter asking for some details that he might use to answer the uproar against Burr in Philadelphia. Before the vice president received this letter, he wrote to Biddle on July 18th, warning him that he might be heading his way soon. "You can judge what chance I should have in our Courts on a trial for my life," he wrote. Yet he obviously hated to run, and stood his ground in Richmond Hill, hoping for a change in the public mood—something that was unlikely to occur, with every newspaper except the *Morning Chronicle* against him. Even that journal seemed cowed into silence. It took Dr. Peter Irving almost two weeks to begin publishing a cautious defense of Burr's actions.[17]

Later on the same day, July 18th, Burr wrote another letter to Biddle, replying to his plea for information. He told him to read the seconds' account in the *Morning Chronicle,* particularly the letters that led to the duel. Burr added details that "shew [*sic*] what reliance may be placed on those declarations of H which assert that he did not mean to injure me." If true, Burr added, these statements were "contemptible." The vice president described the way General Hamilton had halted the proceedings to test the light and put on his glasses. When the word *present* was given, "he took aim at his adversary & fired very promptly." Burr said he fired two or three seconds later and Hamilton fell exclaiming "I am a dead Man."

Of all the narrators of the fatal day, Burr was the only one who put this quotation in Hamilton's mouth. Continuing his defensive-offensive mode, the vice president said both Hamilton and Pendleton were "a good deal agitated" when they arrived—not a state of mind conducive to accurate observation. In fact, Burr thought Hamilton looked "oppressed with the horrors of conscious guilt." Most "considerate men" in New York thought Burr's only fault was "bearing so much & so long."

Some of this smacks of laying it on rather thick, and the line about considerate men was close to an outright lie. Still unsatisfied, the besieged vice president added: "The last hours of Genl H (I might include the day preceding the interview) appear to have been devoted to Malevolence and hypocricy." He was referring, of course, to Hamilton's various statements about refusing to shoot at him and his pious claim to a clear conscience. After a denunciation of unprincipled Jacobins similar to the one he had sent Joseph Alston, Burr closed with a cry of anguished rage: "The friends of Genl. H. and even his enemies who are still more my enemies, are but too faithful executors of his malice."[18]

Perhaps two days later, Burr asked Van Ness to write to Biddle, urging the second to corroborate his description of how Hamilton had put on his eyeglasses and gave every evidence of intending to shoot it out. Burr even told his second the exact language he had used in his letter to Biddle. Van Ness promptly obliged, sending the Philadelphian a letter twice as long as Burr's, full of details about Hamilton's actions. Sometimes Van Ness's language is virtually identical to Burr's: *He then levelled his pistol in several di-*

rections as if to try the light.[19] Elsewhere he echoed Burr's letter almost as closely. Were these two gentlemen trying too hard to establish a fact that made Hamilton a liar and a hypocrite about his intention to throw away his fire? If Pendleton were the only witness to this statement, there might be more reason to doubt him and believe Burr. But Dr. Hosack and Bishop Moore and Rufus King, as well as Hamilton's "remarks" and letter to his wife, all confirm this "fixed resolution."

On the other hand, Hamilton's actions before firing as described by Burr and Van Ness (and never denied by Pendleton) are not incompatible with his determination to go through with the duel and take his chances on Burr's aim. The only point on which Pendleton and Van Ness publicly disagreed was who fired first. If Burr had missed, Pendleton would have had an opportunity to write a glowing report about General Hamilton's savoir faire in the face of death and his religious refusal to return Burr's fire, proved by his subtly contemptuous discharge of his pistol into the air. Since Hamilton had accepted the challenge to preserve his role as America's Bonaparte, a certain amount of playacting is neither unlikely nor strange.

As for who fired first, the two guns went off almost simultaneously and it was not hard for Burr and Van Ness to convince themselves that Hamilton's was first. Hamilton had told Pendleton he planned to let Burr fire first and "fire in the air."[20] The trajectory of his bullet, high over Burr's head, seems to fit the image of him raising his arm to do this. When Burr's bullet struck him, the General's finger involuntarily jerked the trigger before his pistol was vertical.

VII

On July 21st, William Van Ness published his own amended version of the joint statement in the *Morning Chronicle*. In his letter to Biddle, which is undated but probably written on July 20th, Van Ness claimed that Burr had fired "a few seconds" after Hamilton. In the amended version he improved on this claim, writing that it took Burr "five or six seconds" to return Hamilton's fire. There is not much difference between "a few" and "five or six"—certainly not enough to accuse Van Ness of lying. The young second further diminished the difference between the two statements by writing elsewhere that Burr fired "immediately after" Hamilton. It seems more likely that this devoted Burrite was simply straining to improve every tiny detail in favor of his hero.

Burr's observation that Pendleton and Hamilton were too agitated to be accurate observers applies equally well to him and Van Ness. After two hundred years of controversy, including some absurd magazine articles portraying Hamilton as a dishonorable sneak who had secretly set his hair trigger when Pendleton was not looking, it seems simplest to assume everyone was telling the truth as he saw it, with a minor amount of embellishment inevitable on both sides.

VIII

Far more revealing about the underlying pattern of the duel, if not about the minutiae, was a letter that Nathaniel Pendleton wrote to his nephew-in-law and friend, William Bard, two weeks later. He thanked Bard for a sympathetic letter that had helped him deal with "the loss of our excellent, our noble friend." Aside from his admiration for Hamilton's "sublime talents," Pendleton told Bard that he could not have refused the General's request for help because he was under "particular obligations" to him for "acts of kindness"—a reference to Hamilton's aid in helping Pendleton establish himself in New York's legal world after he retreated from Georgia in the wake of the Yazoo scandal. Pendleton added that "of late" he had also been "much more in the habits of confidence with [Hamilton] than any other man in New York." Still it was good to know that friends such as Bard supported him. Then came words that confirm the contradictory mixture of hostility and attempts at avoidance that were sadly visible in the spiritually divided Hamilton's letters.

The truth is that General Hamilton had made up his mind to meet Mr. Burr before he called upon me, provided he should be required to do what his first letter declined; and it was owing to my solicitude and my efforts to prevent extremities that the correspondence was kept open from 23 June to the 27th. I have, therefore, the satisfaction of knowing I did all I could to prevent it . . . [21]

The words also refute the accusation by Cheetham and others, eventually including William Coleman, that the duel was the result of Colonel Burr's predetermined hostility. Pendleton never joined this vindictive chorus. But the Virginian's testimony does not alter Burr's hidden motive—the Bonapartean dream of fame in the West and Mexico. The deliberate nature of the vice president's challenge, invisible to everyone at the time, left a more elusive but nonetheless serious stain on his honor.

IX

On the night of Saturday, July 21st, perhaps after reading Van Ness's amended statement in the *Morning Chronicle,* Vice President Burr decided that reason and evidence were not enough to save him from indictment for murder. Through the Swartouts, he apparently had friends on the coroner's jury (three of the fifteen members resisted indicting him to the end) and he knew the odds against him were heavy. He had already asked Van Ness to bring him $780 in cash. "I rely on seeing you this evening," he wrote earlier in the day, renewing his request for the money.

Around 10:00 P.M., accompanied by John Swartout and his black valet, Peter, Burr boarded a boat on the Hudson shore near Richmond Hill and headed down the river. They spent the night on the water, rowing through New York harbor and around Staten Island to Perth Amboy, New Jersey. There the vice president sent Peter ashore to ask Commodore Thomas Truxtun for shelter. It was a glimpse of how badly Burr's psyche had been battered by the public reaction to the duel. He was not sure how Truxtun would receive him.

The commodore was amazed to discover that Burr was still in the boat offshore. He rushed to the landing and beckoned him to the dock. As they walked to the house, Burr introduced John Swartout, told Truxtun how many hours they had been on the water, and said they would appreciate "a dish of coffee." The Commodore assured Burr coffee and more would be supplied promptly. After breakfast, John Swartout returned to New York and Burr asked Truxtun where he could find horses to continue his journey to Philadelphia. Truxtun told him he would have to wait until Monday.

The commodore and Burr spent an uncomfortable twenty-four hours together. "Little was said of the duel," Truxtun later recalled. It was a delicate subject. But the commodore observed that Burr "appeared to feel much more sorrow and regret" than he had seen in other men on similar occasions. At one point, Truxtun remarked on how much he admired General Hamilton; Burr became quite agitated. The commodore hastily added that he had a similar esteem for Burr, and would have greeted Hamilton as cordially as he was now greeting Burr, if the situation were reversed.

On Monday, Truxtun drove Burr to Cranbury, New Jersey, in his carriage, where Burr hired horses for the trip to Philadelphia. The commodore soon learned that he was persona non grata with a great many people for offering the vice president this modest hospitality. Truxtun felt compelled to publish a long letter in the *New-York Evening Post*, defending himself and blaming Dr. Charles Cooper for instigating the duel by revealing things a gentleman may have said but never intended to be made public.[22]

X

In the *American Citizen*, James Cheetham gloated that Burr had "abdicated" the state of New York. "He made his escape last Saturday night," the editor reported.[23] The vice president's conduct did, in fact, bear some resemblance to that of a fugitive from justice. He approached Philadelphia cautiously, turning into byroads when an innkeeper recognized him. He sent an anxious note to his friend Charles Biddle, who was in his summerhouse outside the city. Burr told Biddle he would be staying with another friend, Captain William Jones, a veteran of the revolutionary navy, now a prominent Philadelphia merchant and Republican politician.[24] By July 24th, Burr was at Jones's house, writing a reassuring letter to Theodosia.

> I absent myself from home merely to give a little time for passion to subside, not from any apprehension of the final effects of proceedings in courts of law. They can, by no possibility, eventually affect my person. You may find the papers filled with all manner of nonsense and lies. Among other things, accounts of attempts to assassinate me. These, I assure you, are mere fables. Those who wish me dead keep a respectful distance. No such attempt has been or will be made. I walk and ride about as usual.[25]

The *Trenton Federalist* confirmed the latter part of this message. The newspaper marvelled that the vice president had "the hardihood" to show himself in Philadelphia's streets.[26] The city's newspapers, led by William Duane's *Aurora*, were equally harsh. The *United States Gazette* huffed: "Colonel Burr, the man who has covered our country with mourning, was seen walking with a friend in the streets of this city in open day."[27] The friend may have been Alexander J. Dallas, the federal attorney for Pennsylvania, who was criticized severely for appearing in public with Burr.[28]

Although the vice president retained his composure in public, an August 2nd letter to Theodosia revealed that the ordeal was causing not a little inner stress. Joseph Alston had probably told Burr that Theodosia was extremely upset about the duel and its aftermath, and not a little critical of her father. Burr asked her not to force him to think "you are dissatisfied with me a moment. I can't just now endure it. At another time you may play Juno if you please."[29] Juno, the mother of the Gods, frequently censured Zeus for his peccadillos.

XI

Back in New York, General Hamilton's friends met in mournful conclaves to discuss how to rescue his family from destitution. At first they debated asking Congress to pass a bill, absorbing his debts. This was the English style. George III, the elder William Pitt, and other public servants had benefited from such parliamentary generosity. Jefferson had recently persuaded Congress to vote a generous land grant to the cash-short Marquis de Lafayette.[30] But the chances of persuading the penny-pinching Jeffersonian Republicans to be equally generous to the fallen leader of the Federalist party were slim. If they did so, the gift would come drenched in sarcasm. A public subscription was also ruled out, for a similar reason: It was too humiliating to admit that the former secretary of the treasury had been so inept in handling his own finances.

Oliver Wolcott Jr. decided to form a committee to appeal to "gentlemen of easy fortunes." The goal was to raise $100,000 quickly. Wolcott told the hoped-for contributors that without Hamilton's financial system, they might not be rich men today. [31]

The project ran into difficulty almost immediately. Many on Wolcott's list wondered why they were being asked when Hamilton's father-in-law, General Philip Schuyler, was one of the wealthiest men in the country. An embarrassed Wolcott had to confess that Schuyler was up to his eyes in debt from his canal building and other failed business ventures. Still, the charity came in a discouraging trickle. Only a few close friends, such as Gouverneur Morris, wrote substantial checks. Boston Federalists were especially chilly, remembering Hamilton's sabotage of John Adams's re-election race in 1800.[32]

XII

Elsewhere in New York, at 2:00 A.M. on August 2nd, the coroner's jury finally stopped wrangling and reported that Aaron Burr had made an assault with a pistol "loaded with Gun powder and a leaden bullet," which he had held in his right hand ... "against the right-Side of the Belly of ... Alexander Hamilton" and shot "the said Alexander Hamilton a little above the Hip," inflicting "one mortal Wound." William P. Van Ness and

Nathaniel Pendleton were also accused of having willfully and with malice aforethought murdered Hamilton "against the peace of the People of the State of New York and their Dignity."[33]

By this time, it was widely known that the jury had displayed considerable reluctance to accuse Burr and the seconds of a crime that was not committed in the state of New York. The indictment tried to get around this embarrassment by describing Hamilton as "languishing" at Bayard's house until he died from the mortal wound inflicted by Burr in New Jersey.

John Swartout rushed a messenger to Philadelphia with the news of the long-delayed verdict. He also reported that the hysteria against Burr was subsiding. Governor Morgan Lewis, pressed by the Clintons to extradite Burr, revealed his underlying antagonism to his sponsors by calling the proceedings "disgraceful, illiberal and ungentlemanly." But the courts in New York City were controlled by Mayor DeWitt Clinton and they issued warrants to arrest Burr, Van Ness, and Pendleton.[34]

Around this time, Philadelphia was swept by a rumor that a band of Clintonites and Federalists was coming from New York to seize Burr. Charles Biddle hurried from his country house and spent several nights in the city with Burr, by way of reinforcement. "He would not have been taken easily," Biddle later wrote.[35]

Biddle was unaware that in the midst of all this excitement, the vice president was conferring with Charles Williamson, the former agent for the vast Pulteney lands in upstate New York—the same man who had visited Burr at Richmond Hill shortly before he had challenged General Hamilton and assured the colonel of British support for his plan to invade Texas and Mexico and create a new empire.

Williamson was the person Burr had journeyed to Philadelphia to meet—a trip that we have seen him planning as early as July 13th, two days after the duel. Williamson intended to sail for England from the Quaker city toward the end of August. The reason for Burr's anxiety to reach Philadelphia as soon as possible was the presence of another man in the city—British ambassador Anthony Merry. He had come to Philadelphia for the treatment of a painful medical condition—hemorrhoids.

Ambassador Merry had sailed to America on the same ship with Williamson in 1803 and the two had become good friends. Soon Williamson was conferring with the ambassador, by now one of President Thomas Jefferson's most confirmed enemies, about an extraordinary proposal he had received from Vice President Burr. On August 6, 1804, Merry wrote a revelatory letter to the British foreign secretary, Dudley Ryder, Lord Harrowby.

Most Secret

My Lord,

I have just received an offer from Mr. Burr the actual vice president of the United States (which Situation he is about to resign) to lend his assistance to His Majesty's Government in any Manner in which they may think fit to employ him, particularly in endeavouring to effect a Separation of the Western Part of the United States from that which lies between the Atlantick [*sic*] and the Mountains, in it's whole Extent.—His Proposition on this and other Subjects will be fully detailed to your Lordship by Col. Williamson who has been the Bearer of them to me, and who will embark for England in a few Days.—It is therefore only necessary for me to add that if, after what is generally known of the Profligacy of Mr. Burr's Character, His Majesty's Ministers should think proper to listen to his offer, his present Situation in this Country where he is now cast off as much by the democratic as by the Federal Party, and where he still preserves Connections with some People of Influence, added to his great Ambition and Spirit of Revenge against the present Administration, may possibly induce him to exert the Talents and Activity which he possesses with Fidelity to his Employers—[36]

There it was in smooth diplomatic prose: Colonel Aaron Burr's dream of a Bonapartean empire based on the guns of the swaggering men of the West. Here was the reason why he had challenged General Alexander Hamilton to pistols at ten paces. It was a fevered dream, an unstable compound of fame, politics, and revenge against both General Hamilton and President Jefferson.

Already Burr had discovered that in public affairs, between the dream and reality frequently falls the shadow of the unexpected. In challenging General Hamilton, the vice president had encountered the unpredictable reactions of the human heart. How could he have known that the General was tormented by regret for his slain son and by spiritual longings that transcended politics? Even more unexpected was the eruption of public grief for a man who seemed to have disgraced and humiliated himself morally and politically. Soon Colonel Burr would confront even more unforeseeable developments in national and international politics and in the treacherous mind and heart of his fellow conspirator, Brigadier General James Wilkinson. But the vice president pressed on, clinging to faith in his special destiny.

Afterward

*I*n New York, the findings of the coroner's jury, accusing Vice President Aaron Burr of murder, were presented to a grand jury, which quickly threw out the charge of murder, since the fatal shot had been fired in another state. However, the grand jury, obedient to Mayor Clinton's wishes and still simmering public indignation, indicted Burr and William P. Van Ness and Nathaniel Pendleton for participating in a duel. This might be a crime under New York law. The matter was uncertain because no public official had ever tried to arrest anyone for dueling in or near New York. When Brockholst Livingston killed James Jones in 1799, outraged Federalists demanded that he be prosecuted. The sheriff had protested that he would also have to arrest the seconds, the doctor, the boatmen; it was just too much trouble.[1]

Word soon reached the vice president in Philadelphia that Governor Morgan Lewis was under severe political pressure from the Clintons to extradite Burr for a show trial. The colonel may have foreseen such a development. On August 3rd, he had written to his friend Dr. Benjamin Rush, Philadelphia's leading physician, asking him for medicines that might be suitable to take with him into the unhealthy southland. He told the doctor he was planning to visit his daughter in South Carolina and perhaps "more southern latitudes."[2]

On August 11th, the vice president told Theodosia he was embarking for a voyage to Saint Simon's Island, the home of his friend South Carolina Republican politician Pierce Butler, with whom he had served in the Senate. Burr did not choose this refuge by accident. Not only was it well beyond the reach of New York subpoenas, it also gave him an opportunity to explore Spanish Florida, one of the plums that General Wilkinson felt was ripe for plucking. With him went his black valet, Peter, and twenty-one-year-old Samuel Swartout, youngest of that faithful clan.

On September 1st, Burr wrote Charles Biddle that he was safe and comfortable on Saint Simon's. He was also pleased to report that there was little or no public censure of him for killing General Hamilton in a duel. On the contrary, he was "overwhelmed with all sorts of attention and Kindness—Presents are daily sent . . . I live most luxuriously."[3] This local reaction was typical of the way most southerners felt about Burr's deed.

In a letter to Congressman Joseph Hopper Nicholson of Maryland, John Randolph of Virginia, Jefferson's floor leader in the House of Representatives, expressed his contempt for the Clintonians who had been shedding crocodile tears over Hamilton. Randolph dismissed them as "the vile mire of seaport politics."[4] After reading the exchange of letters preceding the duel, Randolph concluded that Hamilton's guilt was obvious and Burr had every right to call him out: "How visible is his [Burr's] ascendancy over him [Hamilton] and how sensible does the latter appear of it!"[5]

For ten days in September, Swartout and Burr explored Florida by canoe and horseback, Burr pretending to be a British businessman named King. On October 1st they landed in Savannah, Georgia, where a swarm of leading citizens greeted the vice president as if he were a conquering hero. From Georgia he progressed to South Carolina for a happy reunion with Theodosia and his grandson. There he found letters from New York telling him that the Clintonians and the Federalists were still determined to prosecute him and the duel's seconds. Even more worrisome was the news of a grand jury being convened in New Jersey. But Burr doubted they could do anything to him because dueling was legal in the Garden State. He would have been less sanguine if he had read an editorial in the *Trenton Federalist*, which fulminated that "the honor of New Jersey demands that its shores should no longer be made places of butchery for the inhabitants of New York and Pennsylvania."[6]

Heading north on October 19th, Burr reached Petersburg, Virginia, in ten days and found himself the guest of honor at a public dinner staged by local Republicans as well as at an "elegant supper" given by an old friend. In the midst of these celebrations, Burr discovered the New Jersey grand jury, under the guidance of an angry Federalist judge, had indicted him for murder. This was upsetting. He had toyed with returning to New York and daring the Clintonians to arrest him. He decided instead to stay in Washington, D.C., where he would be immune from subpoenas.

Even more unsettling was the news that his creditors had moved on his New York assets. Richmond Hill had gone under the hammer for $25,000—less than one-fifth of what it was valued at when he considered selling it in 1802.[7] An ex-fur trader named John Jacob Astor had bought the land at a bargain price. In the near future, he would divide it into four hundred small house lots and make a fortune. The mansion's elegant furniture had also been sold by the public auctioneers. Burr's friends were able to save only the library and the wine. Burr wrote to Joseph Alston, offering both to him as a gift.[8]

In Philadelphia, the Federalist *Gazette of the United States* was outraged by Burr's appearance in Washington, D.C. The paper correctly saw that Burr planned to resume his vice presidential seat at the next session of Congress and preside over the impeachment trial of Justice Samuel Chase. Their indignation against this Jeffersonian assault on the judiciary merged with their more recent hatred of Burr as the killer of Hamilton. The editor said it was proof of the "deep degradation" of American politics under Thomas Jefferson. "Hands stained with the best blood of our nation" were about to be "sacrilegiously laid upon the judges of the land."[9]

In the Senate, where Burr took his dais seat on November 5, 1804, sharp-eyed Senator William Plumer noticed the vice president had changed. "He appears to have lost those easy graceful manners that beguiled the hours away the last session," Plumer told his journal. "He is now uneasy, discontented, and hurried." This observation did not stop

Plumer from concluding that Burr's arrival boded ill for Justice Chase and the country. "We are, indeed, fallen on evil times."[10]

II

While Burr was traveling around the South and then trekking back to Washington, D.C., Americans were voting in the seventeen states for the next president and vice president. The Twelfth Amendment, putting the two offices on a single ticket, had been approved before the voting began, so there was no danger of a repetition of the 1800 deadlock. Hamilton, Burr, and the Clintons, among many other politicians, had already perceived that Jefferson was unbeatable, and the results more than proved their judgment. The only thing surprising about the president's reelection was the stunning breadth of the victory for the Jefferson-Clinton ticket. They swamped the hapless Federalist candidates, Charles Cotesworth Pinckney and Rufus King, by a mortifying 162 to 14 vote in the electoral college. Even Federalist Massachusetts and New Hampshire went Republican. The only two holdout states were Connecticut and Delaware.[11]

Jefferson's triumph demolished the secessionist dreams of Senator Pickering and his New England circle. They did not even bother to hold their scheduled meeting, to which General Hamilton had addressed his last passionate denunciation of democracy. The anticipated civil war that had played a large part in persuading the General to accept Burr's challenge was postponed, so it seemed, indefinitely.

III

Behind his imperturbable mask, Vice President Burr was laughing at both political parties. He had plans that transcended their ideological wars. For the time being he concentrated on quashing his indictment for murder in New Jersey. He thanked Charles Biddle for writing to the Garden State's governor, Joseph Bloomfield, an old Burr friend. Bloomfield in turn had written to Burr, confessing he wanted to help but he was in a political bind. He could not pardon Burr until he was convicted and that, Burr told Biddle, "can never be submitted to." Only the New Jersey legislature could solve the problem with a joint resolution, and Burr urged Biddle to round up Philadelphians who had friends in that body and start a letter campaign on his behalf.

The vice president was pleasantly surprised to discover that many congressional Republicans wanted to help him dispose of this indictment. Senator William Branch Giles of Virginia drafted a letter to Governor Bloomfield that would eventually be signed by ten Republican colleagues, asking the New Jersey governor and his council to quash the murder indictment without referring it to the legislature. [12] Senator Plumer was appalled. He told his journal he had no doubts about the Jeffersonians' secret joy at Hamilton's death. But he never thought they would show it by "carressing his murderer."[13]

Senator Giles was not the only Jeffersonian Republican who was eager to befriend the vice president. Secretary of State James Madison and Secretary of the Treasury Albert Gallatin made a point of greeting Burr on his return to Washington. The president himself climaxed this strange rapprochement by inviting Burr to dinner at the palace not once but several times.

Even more remarkable was a sudden rush to give Burr followers jobs in Louisiana. The vast purchase was divided into two districts: the lower half, called the Orleans Territory, and the upper half, the Louisiana Territory. The vice president's stepson, Bartow Prevost, was made judge of the superior court of the Orleans Territory and his late wife's brother-in-law, Dr. Joseph Browne, was made secretary of the Louisiana Territory. Most significant was the appointment of Brigadier General James Wilkinson as governor of the Louisiana Territory—while continuing to keep his rank and salary as commander in chief of the U.S. Army.

Vice President Burr did not have the slightest illusion about the motive of the president and his followers. It was almost blatantly obvious. They wanted and needed his help to impeach Supreme Court Justice Samuel

Chase. Smiling inwardly at the Jeffersonians' naïveté, Colonel Burr put friends in high places where he hoped they would help him create a new empire. "Wilkinson and Brown will serve most admirably as eaters and laughers," he casually remarked in a letter to Theodosia. "And. I believe, in other particulars."[14]

IV

In New York, donations for the fund to keep General Hamilton's family out of the poorhouse were painfully slow. By October 1st, they totaled only $19,000. Some Federalists were reacting against the extravagant praise that had been heaped on Hamilton, particularly by clergymen. The men of the cloth were giving the departed general credit for every note-worthy American achievement since 1776, including the idea for the Constitutional Convention and the Constitution itself. Somewhat grumpily, Noah Webster wrote to James Madison, whose claim to being the "father of the Constitution" was widely acknowledged, asking him if he remembered getting a letter from Webster urging a convention months before Hamilton issued his call in 1786.

Some Jeffersonian Republicans outside New York were also ready to be less than kind to Hamilton's memory. John Beckley, the man who had leaked the Maria Reynolds story to James Thomson Callender and earlier concocted the 1787 smear about Hamilton wanting a king for America, wrote to Burr's friend Senator John Brown of Kentucky: "Federalism has monumented and sainted *their* leader up to the highest heavens, whilst the presses are made to groan under the weight of orations, eulogies and mournings . . . The clergy, too, are sedulously endeavoring to canonize the double adulterer, as a *moralist*, a *Christian* and a *saint* . . . " The reference to "double adulterer" suggests Beckley knew—or at least believed—that Angelica Church had been the General's mistress.

Thomas Paine hated Gouverneur Morris even more than he despised Alexander Hamilton, because Morris had purportedly let Paine rot in his

Paris jail cell while the New York aristocrat was ambassador to France. So Paine combined a nasty satire on Morris's funeral eulogy with sneers at Christian believers, asking them why their God had arranged to have Hamilton killed in the duel.[15] John Adams was equally disinclined to say a good word over Hamilton's corpse. "A caitiff had come to a bad end," old John Yankee wrote. He blamed Hamilton's "fifteen years of slander" against Burr and would only concede a hope that the General was "pardoned . . . in his last moments."[16]

Jefferson was more restrained about Hamilton's demise. In a letter to his friend Philip Mazzei, he simply included the General's name in a list of "remarkable deaths lately." Writing to his daughter, Martha, the president devoted one brief sentence to his rival's fall, referring her to the newspapers for details.[17]

On November 18, 1804, a heartbroken Philip Schuyler died. He had spent the last four months of his life in an agony of regret for inadvertently triggering Dr. Charles Cooper's second letter, about Hamilton's "more despicable opinion" of Burr. The old man left Elizabeth Hamilton some land in various parts of New York but little or no cash. Oliver Wolcott Jr. was in despair. "The property [Hamilton's] will all be sold & the Estate after all be insolvent," he wrote.[18]

Wolcott, Gouverneur Morris and a few friends formed the Alexander Hamilton Association in late November of 1804 and began selling shares in it, paying the subscribers in upstate New York lands Hamilton had bought on speculation. Nine months after Hamilton's death, the memorial fund had risen to $39,700—still far short of the projected goal of $100,000.

However, a cadre of wealthy supporters made sure Elizabeth Hamilton and her children were not left homeless. When The Grange went under the auctioneer's hammer to pay the General's debts, they bought the estate for $30,000 and sold it back to the widow for $15,000. The devoted Wolcott kept soliciting potential donors for another four years, eventually raising $80,000, enabling Mrs. Hamilton to live in dignified if not lavish comfort for the rest of her long life. She died in 1854 at ninety-seven, surviving her husband by a full fifty years.[19]

V

One of the few innocent beneficiaries of General Hamilton's death was Robert Troup. Within a month of the duel, the overweight attorney's ulcerated tongue and mouth vanished, and his health took a startling turn for the better. For those who believe in psychosomatic illnesses, or at the very least how the mind can influence the body, there would seem to be a connection with the tragic result of Hamilton's decision to accept Burr's challenge.

Troup had refused a similar challenge from William Stephens Smith and suffered acute humiliation as a result. He must have identified closely with Hamilton's dilemma. Troup too had a large family and heavy debts. Hamilton's lost gamble with Burr may well have struck Troup as a vindication of his decision. The universal execration of dueling that followed the meeting in Weehawken added still more balm to the fat man's troubled soul. He soon quit the law and moved to upstate New York, where he became a very successful manager of the Pulteney properties, returning over $1 million in rents to the English investors before his death in 1832.[20]

VI

In Washington, D.C., the U.S. Senate convened on February 4, 1805, for the impeachment trial of Justice Samuel Chase, with Aaron Burr presiding. The vice president made sure it was a solemn occasion. He draped the two story high walls of the Senate chamber in brilliant crimson and green, in the style adopted by the British House of Lords when Parliament impeached the viceroy of India, Warren Hastings, in 1788. To deal with the expected crush of spectators, Burr had carpenters erect a new semicircular gallery in front of the permanent one. The senators' tables were moved out and their crimson leather chairs arranged in tiers. The members of the House sat in tiers of green-covered seats facing the senators. Between them was the vice president's chair, flanked by two boxes for the prosecutors and the defendant's attorneys.[21]

What was Burr doing, with this virtual redesign of the Senate? He was subtly sabotaging the Jeffersonian impeachment program. Throughout the month of January, he had watched William Branch Giles working on fellow senators to convince them that impeachment was not a particularly significant process. It was no more serious than passing a law or an appropriation. John Quincy Adams overheard Giles express his contempt for the idea of an independent judiciary. The Virginian told Senator Israel Smith, a Republican from Vermont, that every justice on the Supreme Court except one "must be impeached and removed" because they were Federalists. The exception was a Republican appointed by Jefferson in 1804. [22]

Giles argued that impeachment had nothing to do with criminal acts. He dismissed as verbiage the constitutional stricture that only a conviction for treason, bribery, or high crimes and misdemeanors could remove a judge. "A removal by impeachment," Giles said, "was nothing more than a declaration by Congress to this effect—you hold dangerous opinions, and if you are suffered to carry them into effect you will work the destruction of the nation." Growing more candid with every word, Giles said the process merely amounted to saying: "We want your offices" so we can give them to "men who will fill them better."[23] There was no need for any arguments. All Justice Chase had to do was show up, and the Senate would take a vote and they could all go back to their boarding houses.

This was American Jacobinism, pure and simple, with the emphasis on the latter. The will of the people, expressed by their representatives in Congress, was the only law of the land. That Giles's party line was also the opinion of the president of the United States made it even more alarming. The Jeffersonians' ideological hubris was bolstered by their enormous presidential victory. Giles acted as if the Chase verdict were a foregone conclusion, hardly worth holding a trial to decide.

Evidence of how intimidated other members of the Supreme Court were by the Jeffersonian juggernaut came from no less a personage than Chief Justice John Marshall. In the previous year, ruling on the case of *Marbury* v. *Madison,* a relatively trivial dispute over whether a minor official appointed by John Adams had the right to force the Jefferson administration to confirm his appointment, the chief justice had declared that the high court had the power to rule an act of Congress unconstitutional, infuriating Jefferson and his followers. Now a jittery Marshall, trying to save his job, suggested perhaps Congress had the right to review Supreme Court rulings and override them by a majority vote.[24]

Burr, already loathing Jefferson, was determined not to let the president prevail. His redesign and redecoration of the Senate chamber was his way of saying that Giles and Jefferson were wrong; impeachment was very serious business. One Federalist Senator, Uriah Tracy of Connecticut, said the vice president had converted the trial into "a great, interesting and super spectacle."[25]

For the senators, the arrangements were a striking contrast to the trial of the insane Judge Pickering in 1804. There, Vice President Burr, still with some hopes of Republican support for his union of honest men, had made no attempt to impose a special solemnity on the proceedings, and the senators had avoided deciding whether Pickering was guilty of high crimes and misdemeanors. They had simply voted to impeach the demented judge without referring to the requirements in the Constitution.[26]

Throughout the Chase trial, Burr presided with almost ferocious intensity. When one senator strolled around munching an apple, Burr rebuked him in uncompromising terms. Another solon was censured for wearing a loose, ill-fitting coat, a third for leaving before a session ended. Senator Plumer grew so vexed at being treated like a schoolboy, he confided to his journal: "Really *Master Burr*, you need a ferule or birch to enforce your lectures on polite behavior."

Burr was again making the point that impeachment was serious business, not a lot of folderol that could be ignored until the time came to vote. He forced the senators to listen closely to the arguments, and they slowly realized that the Jeffersonians did not have a case. Their accusations against Judge Chase ranged from the trivial to the political. There was nothing criminal about them. Moreover, John Randolph and the other so-called managers of the impeachment were no match for the legal knowledge and skills of Chase's defenders: Joseph Hopkinson of Philadelphia, Charles Lee of Virginia (a former U.S. attorney general); and Robert Goodloe Harper, Philip Barton Key, and Luther Martin, all from Maryland.

With Alexander Hamilton dead, the unkempt, alcoholic Martin was the greatest trial lawyer in America. He and Burr were linked by their joint friendship with Associate Supreme Court Justice William Paterson of New Jersey, with whom Burr had studied law. Few lawyers in America could match Martin for learning, eloquence—and hatred of President Jefferson. When Martin wanted to insult a man, he said he was "as great a scoundrel as Thomas Jefferson."[27]

In the middle of the 1804 governorship race, Martin had written Burr a warm letter, wishing him "a compleat triumph" over his enemies. "I have never feared to trust you," Martin told Burr. "But was I to perish [at Burr's hands], I would prefer perishing by a Generous Animal—to be torn to pieces at once by a *Lion*, than to be *nibbled* to Death by Rats and Mice" [Clintonians and Jeffersonians].[28]

Martin and Justice Chase's other defenders keyed much of their oratory to the vice president's cue, reminding the senators again and again that history, not the voters, would be the final judge of what they decided. They insisted that the portly short-tempered Chase, a signer of the Declaration of Independence, may have been guilty of some indiscreet partisan comments from the bench, but nothing he had said or done could be called a high crime or a misdemeanor.

At first, the Federalist senators were sure Burr would favor the Jeffersonians. He treated Justice Chase rather coldly when he first appeared before the tribunal, wondering whether he was entitled to a chair, then denying him a table on which to take notes. John Quincy Adams morosely noted the vice president allowed William Branch Giles to speak longer than anyone else.[29] But as time passed, Federalist hopes rose. An amazed Timothy Pickering began predicting that Chase would survive. Not only were Chase's lawyers mauling Randolph and his fellow prosecutors, but the Jeffersonian case was "paltry."[30]

Not even the testimony of a humble fearful Chief Justice John Marshall, who allowed Congressman Randolph to lead him into several damaging statements against Chase, altered the overall momentum of the trial. In his summing up, Luther Martin flatly accused the Jeffersonians of trying to destroy the Supreme Court. He said he was not only defending Justice Chase, a friend of thirty years, but he was also defending his fellow citizens against a pernicious scheme to demolish a bulwark of their liberty.[31]

A crucial point in the proceedings came on the last day, when Senator (formerly Congressman) James Bayard of Delaware, the man who had desperately wanted Aaron Burr as president in 1801, proposed that each senator should vote on whether Judge Chase was guilty of high crimes and misdemeanors. The resolution passed by one vote, 17 to 16, with Senator Giles feebly protesting that it should not become a precedent.[32] This move, which a partisan Burr could have ruled out of order, based on the way the Senate had voted for the impeachment of Judge Pickering, focused everyone's attention on the facts rather than the politics of the case.

At noon the next day, March 1, 1805, the vice president announced to the senators: "You have heard the evidence and arguments adduced on the trial of Samuel Chase, impeached for high crimes and misdemeanors: You will now proceed to pronounce distinctly your judgment on each article." Burr ordered the secretary of the senate to poll the senators on the eight charges, asking each man whether he considered the particular charge a high crime or misdemeanor. The chamber was jammed, with both galleries filled and perhaps four hundred standees in the rear, as each senator said: "guilty" or "not guilty" eight times and the count was recorded. Finally the secretary handed the results to the vice president.

Burr pondered the tallies for a long moment. With grave solemnity he declared: "Samuel Chase Esquire, stands acquitted of all the articles exhibited by the House of Representatives against him." The Jeffersonians had failed to win a two-thirds majority on any charge; on most articles they did not come close.[33]

The stunned Federalists struggled to readjust their opinion of the vice president. General Hamilton's killer had, Senator Plumer conceded to his journal, "done himself, the Senate and the nation honor." One newspaper declared Burr had presided "with the dignity and impartiality of an angel, but with the rigour of a devil."[34]

The infuriated Jeffersonians retreated to the House of Representatives, where they called for a constitutional amendment to allow any federal judge to be removed by a simple majority vote of the House and Senate. For good measure, they proposed another amendment, permitting a state legislature to recall a sitting senator by majority vote, anytime it so pleased.[35] Neither of these ideas went anywhere. But they were stark evidence of how far the radical wing of the Jeffersonian Republican party wanted to go. They underscored the accuracy of General Hamilton's fears for the Constitution. What irony that the man who stopped this national left turn was Hamilton's killer, Aaron Burr.[36]

VII

Near the midpoint in this historic clash, Vice President Burr was forced to interrupt the proceedings to perform another duty. He broke the seals on the ballots of the electoral college and handed them to tellers, who quickly tabulated them and gave him the results. Burr proclaimed to the chamber and the world that Thomas Jefferson had been reelected president for another term and George Clinton had been chosen as his vice president. More than one senator and congressman, not to mention the mob of spectators, studied the vice president intently to detect some cracks in his magisterial calm.

No matter what he may have felt inwardly, Burr retained his composure. Dr. Samuel Latham Mitchill, New York's latest senator, marveled at the vice president's self-control. There was not "the least deviation from his manner," Dr. Mitchill told his wife. It was all the more remarkable when one considered "that the most outrageous wrongs had been done him."[37]

Dr. Mitchill was a moderate Republican. Two weeks later, he voted down the line to acquit Samuel Chase. In fact, both New York senators voted for acquittal. It was a sign of the Empire State's growing uneasiness at Virginia's hegemony. Mitchill's comments also reveal that Governor Morgan Lewis was not the only New York Republican who recognized that the Clintons and Thomas Jefferson were guilty of an unparalleled political vendetta against Aaron Burr.

VIII

On Saturday, March 2nd, the day after the Chase impeachment trial ended, Vice President Burr returned to his usual chair on the dais overlooking a restored senate. The crimson and green hangings and the scaffolding had been removed. The senators' tables had been returned. Two days remained in the vice president's term. But there would be no business on Sunday, and March 4th would be President Jefferson's second inauguration day. About 1:00 P.M. Burr surprised the senators by announcing that a "slight indisposition"—a sore throat—had made him decide this might be the best time for him to withdraw.

In a calm, almost conversational tone, he began a farewell address. He told them that he was aware that he may have hurt the feelings of a few members with his orders. His only defense was his concern for the dignity of the Senate. He may have made an error in his rulings now and then but decision was preferable to indecision. For his part, he had no injuries to complain of—and he had no memory for injuries in the first place. He had tried to rise above party and friends in his official conduct and hoped he had succeeded.

He also hoped they would continue to insist on the rules of decorum he had tried to establish. Nothing was more important to the future of the country than the dignity of the Senate. He had come to revere this place, in which he had spent ten years of his life as a senator and vice president. It was a "sanctuary and a citadel of law, of order, of liberty." Whenever Americans struggled to resist "the storms of popular phrenzy and the silent arts of corruption" the final battle would take place here. If a demagogue or a usurper ever succeeded in destroying the Constitution, a calamity he hoped God would avert, the "expiring agonies will be witnessed on this floor."

Wherever he went, Burr said he would remain interested in the proceedings of the U.S. Senate. For each individual in the chamber, he felt a personal friendship. He hoped the regret he felt on parting with them was mutual. "I have now, Gentleman, only to tender you my best wishes for your personal welfare and happiness."[38]

With those words, the compact elegantly dressed man who had seemed on his way to the presidency four years ago rose from his chair and walked out of the Senate chamber, leaving behind him emotional chaos. Senators Samuel Latham Mitchill and John Smith of New York were weeping profusely. Tears trickled down the cheeks of several other solons. "There was a solemn and silent weeping for perhaps five minutes," Senator Mitchill told his wife in a letter written at his table. It took Senator Smith fifteen minutes to regain his self-control. Three hours after Burr's departure, Mitchill wrote that he had "scarcely recovered my habitual calmness."[39]

Eleven days later, the Washington *Federalist* published a summary of Burr's speech, with a note praising its "elevation and dignity." The editor also liked it because it displayed "a consciousness of superiority." It had nothing of "whining adulation . . . canting hypocritical complaints of want of talents, assurances of his endeavors to please them, hopes of their favor etc etc." This may well be the best explanation of why the senators were so deeply moved. Senator Mitchill summed up this sentiment in his letter to his wife: "He is a most uncommon man, and I regret more deeply

than ever the sad series of events which removed him from public useful-
ness and confidence . . . Where he is going or how he is to get through
with his difficulties I know not."[40]

IX

The ex-vice president seemed poised to make a political comeback. But
there were other less promising reactions to Burr's speech. In New York,
when the *Morning Chronicle* reprinted the *Washington Federalist*'s praise,
James Cheetham sneered at the speech as "melodio, harmonico pathos"
and asked if the voters were to be "wept out of our knowledge of [Burr's]
poltical degeneracy?" William Coleman intimated the *Federalist* story was
really a hoax. He assailed the *Chronicle*'s editor, Dr. Peter Irving, for having "dealt it out as if it were a real panegyric." Coleman added with an almost audible snarl: "I trust in God there is not to be another attempt to
build up Burr and a Burr party here."[41]

Personally, Burr was far more troubled by what had already happened
to William P. Van Ness and Nathaniel Pendleton at the hands of
the Clinton-controlled courts. In January, they had been tried and found
guilty of participating in a duel, and disenfranchised for twenty years.
"I sincerely wish that all the personal inconveniences which flow from
this transaction could fall on me alone," Burr told Van Ness in early
February of 1805. "Those which are suffered by my friends are a source of
most mortifying regret." Even James Cheetham thought this prosecution
was outrageous and called New York's antidueling law unconstitutional.
But he would have sung a very different song if Burr had been in the
dock.[42]

In New Jersey, the indictment for murder had resisted all Burr's attempts to quash it, mostly because of Governor Joseph Bloomfield's lack
of political courage. In December the colonel had hired attorney Aaron
Ogden to represent him in the tedious process of appealing it to higher
courts. Ignoring the Ogden family's long and close relationship with Burr,

James Cheetham promptly denounced the lawyer for betraying his friendship with Alexander Hamilton.[43]

To his son-in-law, Burr wrote a wry letter that graphically revealed his thinking at this time: "In New York I am to be disfranchised, in New Jersey hanged. Having substantial objections to both, I shall not, for the present, hazard either, but shall seek another country." He assured Alston that he had not "become passive, or disposed to submit tamely to the machinations of a banditti." He added a remark about President Jefferson that disclosed his loathing—and his expectation of triumphing over him: "———— and his clan affect to deplore, but secretly rejoice at and stimulate the villainies of all sorts which are practiced against me. Their alarm and anxiety, however, are palpable to a degree perfectly ridiculous. Their awkward attempts to propitiate me reminds one of the Indian worship of the evil spirit."[44]

In the ex-vice president's mind as he wrote these words, his offer to Anthony Merry and the ambassador's positive response were traveling to England with Charles Williamson. Trapped in the present, and goaded inwardly by bitter resentment, Burr ignored the first portents that Jefferson's phenomenal streak of political luck was running out. The newspapers devoted far more space to the president's failed attempt to Justice Samuel Chase than they gave to the second inaugural address. Chase told Senator Plumer that if he were twenty years younger, Jefferson's blunderous attempt to destroy the supreme court would have made the justice a presidential candidate. Burr, who could claim credit for rescuing Chase, would have been a far more viable man.

In Pennsylvania, a month before Chase was acquitted, the radical Republicans in the legislature had tried to impeach three Federalist judges of the state's supreme court on grounds similar to the assault on Chase. The lone Republican judge was so outraged, he insisted they impeach him too. Burr's friend Alexander J. Dallas, the Republican federal attorney for the state, had defended the judges in a tumultuous trial. All were acquitted and the state Republican party had collapsed into rancorous factions.

William Duane, editor of the *Aurora,* spilled venom on anyone opposed to the radical side. He called his antagonists *tertium quids* (third things)—a term that would cause him and Jefferson much grief when the breakaway Republicans adopted it as a badge of honor.

In New York, the Clinton-Livingston alliance began coming apart, thanks largely to DeWitt Clinton's overbearing style, Governor Morgan Lewis's unenthusiasm for taking orders from the mayor, and the general perception that the Empire State had sold too much of its political power to Virginia.[45] In Congress, John Randolph, infuriated by the Republican moderates' refusal to back him in the Chase impeachment and disgusted by Jefferson's support of the Yazoo claimants, edged toward a break with the administration.

No one could have fished more expertly in these troubled waters than Aaron Burr. Moreover, a friend in Congress offered him advice and support on how to organize a new political base in the west, from which he might regain his leadership role. Congressman Matthew Lyon visited Burr one day, shortly before his vice presidential term expired. This radical Republican had moved from Vermont to Kentucky, where he found a more receptive audience for his ideas. Lyon told Burr he came at the suggestion of General Wilkinson, who was spending the winter of 1804–5 in Washington. The general was anxious to help Colonel Burr make the transition from vice president to some office worthy of his talents.

Lyon urged Burr "to mount his horse the fourth of March, and ride through Virginia to Tennessee," telling everyone along the way that he was going to settle in Nashville and practice law. By next July he would have numerous friends, attracted by his celebrity and suavity, who would be eager to send him to Congress. There, Lyon was certain he would soon become speaker of the house—the third-ranking officer in the government.

Burr's reaction to this proposal was cool. He told Lyon that he had ordered a houseboat to be built for him in Pittsburgh, and he planned to take a journey of exploration down the western rivers, perhaps to New

Orleans. Lyon warned him that this would ruin any chance of getting elected to Congress in Tennessee. Burr shrugged and said so be it.

Apparently, Burr was more influenced by three other visitors General Wilkinson sent to his door. Spokesmen for the disenfranchised citizens of Louisiana, they arrived from New Orleans, armed with a "remonstrance" written by Burr's friend and fellow Jefferson-hater Edward Livingston. The phrasing of this document was designed to embarrass the author of the Declaration of Independence for the government he had created in Louisiana. "Do political axioms on the Atlantic become problems when translated to the shores of the Mississippi?" the remonstrance asked, referring to the lack of voting rights and other democratic niceties. Distributing their document all around Washington, the deputies demanded self-government and virtual statehood. They also wanted the right to import as many slaves as they needed, and threatened to head for France and air their complaints to Napoléon. General Wilkinson made sure these protestors met Vice President Burr, who assured them of his sympathy and support.[46]

At the same time there is evidence that Burr continued to balance alternatives. During another conversation with Matthew Lyon, the ex-vice president revealed he was still interested in the appointment he had tried to get from Jefferson in January of 1804—an ambassadorship to Paris or London. He asked Lyon if he would be willing to go to Jefferson and intercede for him. Hothead though he was, Lyon was still a politician, and he was keenly aware of the president's intense dislike of Burr. "I told him very bluntly, I would not," Lyon later recalled.[47]

That refusal and Burr's rejection of Lyon's advice to head for Tennessee left the ex-vice president with only one destination in Washington, D.C.— the British embassy and a meeting with Anthony Merry. Again, the proof is in black and white—the long letter that the Jefferson-hating ambassador sent to his London superior, Foreign Secretary Lord Harrowby, on March 29, 1805. The letter described Merry's conversation with Colonel Burr and outlined his plan to detach Louisiana and the western states from the

Union. Merry added a report of his personal contacts with the complaining deputies from Louisiana, mentioning that Burr had become "very intimate" with them during their sojourn in Washington. Both Burr and the deputies had convinced Merry that Louisiana was eager to declare its independence from the United States.

To support this declaration of sovereignty, the westerners would need some naval support from England—a squadron of perhaps two or three frigates and some smaller vessels to scatter any attempt by the Jefferson administration to blockade New Orleans. Merry did not add—but Burr probably told him—that almost the entire U.S. Navy was now in the Mediterranean trying to redeem Jefferson's floundering naval war with Tripoli.

Merry pointed out at length "the great commercial advantage" the British would derive from making this new western nation an ally. Through New Orleans and Canada, their rapidly growing population would "almost exclusively" become customers for English products, and they would never compete with England on the high seas, as the other Americans were doing all too successfully, because they had only "one bad port," New Orleans, from which to ship their goods, making it unlikely they would acquire a merchant marine. All in all, Merry thought backing Burr looked like a brilliant move, and the price was a bargain too. Burr thought he could manage the whole enterprise for a hundred thousand pounds.[48]

Buoyed by Merry's encouragement, Burr set out for the West in high spirits. On April 10, 1805, he wrote to Theodosia: "As the objects of this journey, not mere curiosity, or *pour passer le tems* [sic], may lead me to Orleans, and perhaps farther, I contemplate the tour with gayety and cheerfulness."

X

The Burr Conspiracy, as it came to be called, took almost two years to unfold and in its course developed so many variants, no one has ever successfully untangled its web of lies, half-truths, and aspirations. In broad outline it remained the vision unfolded by General Wilkinson on his clandestine visit to Burr in New York. At its heart lay the long-standing dream, shared by Burr and Hamilton and many others, of revolutionizing Spain's South American colonies, in particular Mexico, with its supposedly fabulous gold and silver deposits.

The separation of the western states remained linked to this goal in Burr's mind, as a sort of adjunct. The army he needed to win the prize would come from the fighting men of Tennessee, Kentucky, and Ohio. It seemed more than probable, after they got to Mexico City and proclaimed their empire, that those who had stayed behind would rush to join the standard of the American Bonaparte. Burr was convinced that this act of secession would trigger New England's withdrawal from the Union, leaving Jefferson incapable of stopping the formation of the new empire.

Like Hamilton in his heady days as President George Washington's chief advisor, Burr was ready to negotiate with the British for help but he had no intention of letting his new nation become an English client state. With Mexican gold and ports, he would be able to build a navy that would dominate the Gulf of Mexico and the Caribbean and defy any attempt to intimidate him. The vision was unquestionably grand, but the gritty realities of raising a western army and obtaining British aid were soon dogged by the long shadow of the unexpected.

XI

On May 18, 1804, the day that Napoléon declared himself emperor, the English government of Prime Minister Henry Addington collapsed and William Pitt again became the leader of the nation. Almost immediately, London's policy shifted to an offensive posture, but the focus was on Europe not America. Pitt had been prime minister throughout the first Napoléonic War and had sent expeditionary forces in all directions, with only moderate success.

Far more pressing was the specter of Napoléon's 200,000-man Army of England, still waiting for the word from the new emperor to lunge across the English Channel. Pitt decided the only way to eliminate that threat was to build some backfires in Napoléon's rear. English diplomats were soon shuttling through Europe, dangling million-pound subsidies before the governments of Austria, Prussia, and Russia. Burr's plan to attack Mexico was small potatoes compared to these large political-military calculations.

Pitt's new strategy succeeded and failed simultaneously. Angered by the rise of anti-French parties in Vienna and St. Petersburg, Napoléon marched his huge invasion army eastward with a swiftness that confounded his opponents. At Ulm and Austerlitz, he smashed Austrian and Russian armies and became the unassailable master of Europe. Only the English Channel barred Bonaparte from world domination. But the invasion's repeated delays had led him to lose faith in waiting for the perfect storm that would paralyze the British fleet.

Napoléon decided to achieve naval supremacy by uniting the French and Spanish fleets. As the combined armada headed for the English Channel, Admiral Horatio Nelson intercepted it off Cape Trafalgar, on the southwest coast of Spain, and on October 21, 1805, demolished it in a battle that cost Nelson his life. Napoléon's dream of dictating peace in London sank with his fleet. He abandoned the invasion and turned to creating a continental empire that would force the English to surrender or starve. England began a lonely struggle against seemingly awesome odds that would last for the next ten years. They could spare neither time, money, or attention for overseas adventures in Mexico.

Burr could foresee none of this in the fall of 1805, when he returned from his first trip to the West, ablaze with enthusiasm. From Pittsburgh to New Orleans, he had been received with acclaim and admiration. Not only was he known as the politician who had fought for Tennessee's statehood and western rights in the Senate. He was also the man who had killed General Hamilton, creator of such evils as banks and land speculators. Beyond the Allegheny Mountains, this feat established Burr as a soldier, a gentleman, and a leader of men. Westerners such as Andrew Jackson, no mean duelist himself, assured him that they were ready to raise troups by the thousands to take Florida, Texas, and Mexico from the hated and despised "Dons."

XII

Others were not so enthusiastic, particularly in the East, where rumors of Burr's activities soon got into the newspapers. Philadelphia's Federalist organ, the *Gazette of the United States*, published a particularly hostile story on August 2, 1805. Hamilton had once controlled this newspaper, and those inclined to believe in such things might well have imagined from the pointed nature of a set of questions the irate editor printed that the spirit of the slain Federalist leader was pursuing Burr. The more probable sponsor was the Spanish ambassador, the marqués de Casa Yrujo, who was always alert to threats to his nation's American territories.

> Is it a fact that Colonel Burr has formed a plan to engage the adventurous and enterprising young men from the Atlantic states to come into Louisiana?
>
> Is it one of the inducements that an immediate convention will be called from the states bordering on the Ohio and Mississippi to form a separate government?
>
> Is it another, that all the public lands are to be seized and partitioned among those states, except what is reserved for the warlike friends and followers of Burr in the revolution?
>
> How soon will all the forts and magazines in all the military ports at New Orleans and on the Mississippi be in the hands of Col. Burr's revolution party?
>
> How soon will Col. Burr engage in the reduction of Mexico, by granting liberty to its inhabitants, and seizing on its treasures, aided by British ships and forces?

This revelation of his overall plan before Burr had done more than confer with a few willing western conspirators would have intimidated a less driven man. But Burr's enmity for Jefferson—and his contempt for newspaper attacks—made him immune to such storm signals. Even more ominous—and equally ignored—was a distinct coolness manifested by

General Wilkinson. Burr's fellow conspirator had originally planned to travel with the Colonel on his western tour but had managed to delay his trip out of a desire—it soon became clear—to distance himself from Aaron Burr. With his appointment as territorial governor almost doubling his army salary, the brigadier was not inclined to risk Jefferson's wrath unless Burr presented him with a sure thing.

By the time the two men finally met in September 1805 at St. Louis, the capital of the Louisiana Territory, the *Gazette of the United States*'s queries had been reprinted in newspapers all over the country, including several in the West, which caused Wilkinson to grow even more wary. He was also keenly disappointed that Burr had no news of British assistance.[49] But the colonel was so enthralled by the warm reception he had received from Andrew Jackson and others that he was more amused than threatened by the brigadier's coolness and occasionally even treated Wilkinson with a condescension bordering on contempt.[50]

XIII

Back in Washington, D.C., Burr's euphoria suffered a sharp decline. The colonel was "greatly disappointed and mortified" to learn that the long enthusiastic letter Ambassador Merry had sent to Foreign Secretary Lord Harrowby on March 29, 1805, had been put aboard a mail packet that was captured by the French. It had taken Merry more than six months to learn this dismaying fact. All the ambassador could do was lamely send copies with a covering letter, telling his superiors that Burr's plot was still very much alive.

The agitated Burr told Merry he had made a firm commitment to his friends in the West to "commence operations" in March of 1806. The colonel urged the ambassador to tell his government to send a fast frigate to the southern port nearest Washington with the badly needed 100,000 pounds and word that the British would commit a naval squadron to the mouth of the Mississippi.[51]

The British ambassador was more than willing to send this message, but Merry gave Burr news that made them both wonder if anyone in London would listen. In May of 1805, Charles Williamson had lost his chief patron in the government, Prime Minister Pitt's good friend Henry Dundas, Lord Melville, the first lord of the admiralty. Accused of massive corruption, Melville was forced to resign and was facing impeachment.

Burr learned other news in Washington that further diminished his optimism. The Jefferson administration had continued to quarrel with the Spanish about the boundaries of Louisiana and threatened to use force to seize both Floridas if Spain refused to sell them. A war or at least the threat of imminent war had become vital to the Burr and Wilkinson plan. Hostilities would assemble an army of western adventurers which they would take over and deploy for their own purposes.

Burr soon discovered the Jeffersonians were distracted by a crisis on the high seas. The Pitt government had announced a new policy that enabled the British navy to seize American ships wholesale to prevent trade with Napoléon's continental empire. All thoughts of a war with Spain went glimmering. "We are to have no Spanish war except in ink and words," Burr glumly wrote to Wilkinson on January 6, 1806: "Great Britain is just now making alarming and systematic encroachments on our commerce."[52] Even worse news arrived from London several weeks later. Prime Minister William Pitt was dead, extinguishing all hope of British support.

XIV

Not even these major discouragements deterred Burr from a scheme that was becoming less and less viable. Twice he revealed a desire to find another path but both instances only underscored a growing inner instability. Late in 1805, after he returned from the West, Burr asked Charles Biddle to intercede for him to persuade the Pennsylvania Republican Quids to appoint him chief justice of the state. The idea bordered on the fantastic, since he was not a citizen of Pennsylvania.[53]

Another attempt at a respectable political alternative fluttered aloft in New York. Burr's followers, encouraged by the growing split between the Livingstons and the Clintons, opened negotiations with DeWitt Clinton. (James Cheetham, proving the elasticity of his principles or his doglike devotion to DeWitt Clinton or both, made the first gesture of reconciliation.) The Burrites agreed to back Clinton, if the mayor quashed Burr's dueling indictment and agreed to his return to New York in some political form. At a dinner supposedly consummating peace between the two factions, Dr. Peter Irving, editor of the *Morning Chronicle*, offered a toast to "Aaron Burr, late vice president of the United States, dignified in the chair, prompt in the cabinet; gallant in the field—may his country duly appreciate his talents and his services."

In the *Evening Post*, William Coleman commented that "anything so unparalleled in profligacy, so abhorrent to principle, so totally destitute of sentiment, so outrageous upon decency, never before was obtruded upon the public eye."[54] Even more negative was a letter from Vice President George Clinton, telling his nephew that restoring Burr to good standing in the party "would not add to my pleasure." Implied was the even stronger unlikelihood that it would increase President Jefferson's pleasure. Mayor Clinton obediently reneged on the deal and organized a fifteen-hundred-man mass meeting that unanimously resolved: "Aaron Burr does not & ought not to possess the confidence of the Republican party."[55]

XV

In spite of these omens, in March of 1806, Burr sought and obtained another meeting with President Jefferson. Once more, Jefferson's account is the only evidence we have for what was said. If it was accurate—Jefferson waited a full month to write it down—Burr acted more like a man on the verge of a nervous breakdown than the cool consummate conspirator that James Wilkinson envisioned when he unfolded his dreams of Mexican plunder to the vice president during his midnight visit to Richmond Hill.

Burr's opening remarks were a replay of his disastrous January 1804 meeting with Jefferson. In surly tones he complained that Jefferson had once said he wanted him in his administration but he had never offered him an appointment. The president had always "used him with politeness but nothing more." Burr reminded Jefferson that he had helped bring on "the present order of things" and had supported the administration but he was now in a mood to do Jefferson "much harm." Jefferson replied that Burr had lost the confidence of the public, pointing out by way of proof that "not a single voice" had been raised to renominate him for vice president. As for doing him harm, the president told the colonel he had no worries on that score.[56]

There did not seem to be any visible purpose for this conversation. It did nothing but further antagonize Jefferson. From a psychological point of view, Burr seemed to be asking the president to stop him from going ahead with his western plan by offering him a job. The ex-vice president seemed oblivious to the strong probability that Jefferson, with his conviction that the Federalists were evil, was unlikely to have a sunny smile for a man who had just run for office with their massive support and undermined the president's plan to impeach Justice Chase and the other members of the hated party on the Supreme Court.

A month later Burr wrote Wilkinson that "the execution of our project is postponed till December." In this letter he began referring to himself in the third person, something he occasionally did in his playful letters to Theodosia. Here it seemed like the onset of megalomania. "Burr will be throughout the United States this summer," he wrote, adding portentously, "Administration is damned."[57]

Burr was referring to an open break between President Jefferson and John Randolph, which threatened the president's control of Congress. Jefferson was already in political trouble for his failure to do anything about British depredations on the high seas. His attempts to buy the Floridas remained stalled by Spanish intransigence and Napoleonic hostility, adding to the growing public perception that he was not a strong president in the George Washington tradition.

In fact, Colonel Burr's private perception of the government's weakness grew so acute, he contemplated invading Washington, D.C., with five hundred men and chasing Jefferson back to Monticello. He told several people that "men of property energy and talents" would welcome such a revolution—and he had no doubt that Congress would accept him. If nothing else, this feverishly imagined replay of the way Napoléon had taken over France proves that Bonaparte was becoming an ever larger part in the colonel's growing megalomania.[58]

Burr revolved between Washington and Philadelphia for the next several months. He raised money from other sources—his son-in-law Joseph Alston and a gullible Anglo-Irishman, Harman Blennerhasset, who had settled on an island in the Ohio River. The colonel borrowed $25,000 from an Indiana canal company, which he helped turn into a bank, not unlike his legerdemain with the Manhattan Company in 1800. But he made no attempt to inveigle New York's Burrites into the western plot. John Swartout told William P. Van Ness: "Poor Burr is still wandering. What his ultimate destination will be is uncertain."[59]

XVI

In Philadelphia Burr tried to persuade his closest friend, Charles Biddle, to join the enterprise but he would have nothing to do with it. The colonel journeyed to New Jersey to try to talk Commodore Truxtun into becoming commander of the navy he planned to build when he conquered Mexico. Truxtun too declined and tried to talk Burr out of the scheme. Only ex-Senator Jonathan Dayton of New Jersey remained a true believer, spurred by his youthful memory of the Aaron Burr who had assaulted Quebec in 1776, and by hopes of regaining political power in the new western confederacy. Dayton had recently purchased 25,000 acres of land in Ohio and had already committed himself to the region.

By this time, several people had warned Jefferson of what Burr had in mind. The president, distracted by his other large political problems, did nothing. So the conspiracy swirled to its denouement in December of 1806.

Recruiting in northern New York, western Pennsylvania, and Ohio, Burr gathered a force of about a thousand men on Blennerhasset's Island and headed down the Ohio and Mississippi Rivers to New Orleans. Ahead of him he sent two messengers to General Wilkinson with a cipher letter announcing the great adventure was about to begin.

The immediate situation seemed propitious. The Spaniards had continued quarreling with Jefferson about his claim to West Florida, and also about the boundary between Louisiana and Texas. They had sent thirteen hundred men across the Sabine River to sieze a slice of land east of this stream, which supposedly marked the Texas border. The president ordered General Wilkinson to confront them with his army and force them to retire. The war with Spain, so essential to Wilkinson's and Burr's plan, seemed theirs for the starting.

But General Wilkinson was still Agent 13, on the Spanish payroll, and the British alliance, so essential to controlling the mouth of the Mississippi, had never materialized. The general decided there was more in it for him, from the Spaniards and from Jefferson, if he double-crossed Burr. He arrested Burr's messengers and seized their cipher letters, which had been written by Jonathan Dayton. Claiming the letter was from Burr (which for all effects it was) Wilkinson sent a message to President Jefferson, announcing he had just uncovered a nefarious plot to revolutionize the West and start a war with Spain. The general also rushed letters to the Spanish governor of Florida and the imperial viceroy in Mexico City, telling them of his good deed on Spain's behalf and demanding an appropriate reward.[60]

Jefferson's reaction had none of the philosophical detachment he had displayed about the eventual separation of the western states at the time of the Louisiana Purchase. The president knew Burr was trying to deprive him his ultimate claim to fame. Jefferson issued a proclamation denouncing Burr's treasonous conspiracy and ordered the U.S. Army and federal officials in the

West to treat Burr and his volunteers as traitors. By the time Burr reached Natchez, the president's proclamation and Wilkinson's translation of the cipher letter were in the newspapers. Burr's flotilla surrendered to militiamen and the soldiers and their leader tried to flee to Spanish territory.

Arrested, Burr was hustled to Richmond, Virginia, for trial on a charge of treason. President Jefferson, totally enraged at his former vice president, announced his guilt was "beyond question." Other people had different ideas about the captive's fate, most notably Chief Justice John Marshall. He was not going to let the president hang the man who had rescued the Supreme Court from Jeffersonian Republican devastation.

XVII

Putting himself in charge of the case, the chief justice held a hearing in the main hall of the Virginia capital's House of Delegates, the only room large enough to accommodate the crowd that swarmed to see the show.[61] The arguments for and against jailing Burr were relatively brief but they drew the battle lines for the trial to come. Burr's attorneys and Burr himself savagely attacked the government's two charges, that he had tried to start a war with Spain and planned to revolutionize the western states.

Even if Burr had been planning to assault the Spanish empire, the deed was "meritorious," argued John Wickham, Burr's chief attorney and the leader of the Virginia bar. President Jefferson himself, at the opening session of Congress, had denounced Spanish "provocations" along the vaguely defined border and said war between the two nations was imminent. Burr's other lawyer, former Attorney General Edmund Randolph, attacked the treason charge, ridiculing the idea that someone could commit this crime by "supposed intention" when the Constitution clearly stated an overt act was required. [62]

The reply that Jefferson's attorney general, Caesar A. Rodney, made to these arguments was feeble. He expressed regret that he was prosecuting a man whom he had once considered a friend. But he insisted that Burr's activities in the West formed a "chain of circumstances" that showed beyond doubt the former vice president was guilty of a "most heinous crime." Rodney also insisted the government was not persecuting Mr. Burr; he would receive a fair trial. Whereupon the attorney general vanished from the scene, leaving the conduct of the trial to the federal attorney for Virginia, George Hay.

Not every Republican was as eager as Thomas Jefferson to hang Aaron Burr. But for the moment, the president was more than satisfied to have Hay in charge of the prosecution. He was the same man who had battered newspaperman James Thomson Callender's head with a club for revealing Jefferson's supposed liaison with his slave Sally Hemings. In spite of—or perhaps because of—this unorthodox demonstration of loyalty, Jefferson had appointed Hay federal attorney for Virginia. He was as totally devoted to Jefferson as his father-in-law, James Monroe.

The following day, John Marshall ruled on the government's motion. The chief justice stunned Prosecutor Hay by announcing that he could only find probable cause for trial on the misdemeanor of waging war against Spain. On the charge of treason, he found the government's evidence of probable cause—the cipher letter purportedly written by Burr to General Wilkinson, detailing the revolutionary plans of the conspirators—too weak to commit Burr to prison. Quoting from the famed British jurist William Blackstone, Marshall declared he could not allow "the hand of malignity" to seize an individual and deprive him of his liberty.

A murmur of amazement swept the audience. They knew exactly whose hand was being accused of malignity. The angular, dark-eyed chief justice added in his deliberate drawl that he was not suggesting any specific malignity in the case before him. Setting bail at $10,000, which Burr's friends readily met, Marshall adjourned the court until May 22nd, the opening of the summer term.[63]

How did Marshall, a man enormously proud of his integrity, justify his determination to protect Burr? How did Burr attract such outstanding lawyers as John Wickham and Edmund Randolph? As Federalists, hostile to Jefferson's purchase of Louisiana and even more disapproving of the government he had established there, they were more than ready to accept Burr's claim that he never intended to revolutionize the West by force. He had gone there intending to take charge of a popular movement that was clamoring for his leadership.

In Washington, D.C., where news of the chief justice's ruling reached Thomas Jefferson on the fastest horse George Hay could find, a presidential tantrum ensued.[64] In angry letters to fellow Republicans, the chief executive predicted that Marshall's tactics would spur the constitutional amendment Jefferson's followers had recommended after the Chase trial, permitting Congress to remove any judge who failed their standard of good behavior.[65] The president's threat was obvious: If Burr was acquitted, John Marshall would find himself on trial.

The chief justice, buoyed by the Chase acquittal, refused to blink. In his ruling on refusing to commit Burr to jail for treason, he emphasized the importance of adhering strictly to the Constitution. Treason, Marshall said, was a charge that was "most capable of being employed as the instrument of those malignant and vindictive passions which may rage in the bosoms of contending parties struggling for power."[66]

President Jefferson vowed to answer the chief justice's challenge on the treason charge. Money was drawn from the government's contingency fund and federal marshals streamed over the Alleghenys to find proof of Burr's plan to create a new empire from the western states, Texas, and Mexico by force of arms. Over the next seven weeks, they ordered to Richmond 140 potential witnesses.[67]

Burr and his attorneys did not waste the seven weeks in idleness, though the ex-vice president sometimes gave that impression. He invited friends and sympathizers to a number of splendid dinners and attended many others in sociable Richmond and the nearby countryside. Along with working on the strategy and tactics of his defense, Burr added four more lawyers to his list of defenders. Overshadowing three talented younger men was the bibulous, disheveled figure of Luther Martin.

XVIII

By the time the trial resumed on May 22nd, the population of Richmond had leaped from five thousand to ten thousand. Frontiersmen in muddy boots and pantaloons mingled with elegant New Yorkers in brilliant English waistcoats and breeches. Among the westerners was Andrew Jackson, who mounted tree stumps and the steps of the capitol to tell crowds Burr was innocent, Jefferson was a tyrant, and General Wilkinson was an abominable liar in the pay of the Spanish.[68]

On May 22nd, Burr and his attorneys returned to another crowded Hall of Delegates to confront the grand jury which the government had assembled. The composition of this body was stark, even shocking evidence of President Jefferson's determination to get a conviction. It was, Burr told his daughter Theodosia, "twenty democrats and four federalists." Prominent among them was glowering William Branch Giles, the senator from the Old Dominion that Burr had outgeneraled in the impeachment trial of Justice Chase. On the floor of the Senate, Giles had already declared Burr guilty.[69]

Once more John Marshall rattled U.S. Attorney Hay by letting Burr challenge the grand jurors—something usually permitted only for trial jurors. The ex-vice president questioned the impartiality of Senator Giles and ex-Senator Wilson Cary Nicholas of Virginia, another close friend of the president. They hastily withdrew. When Burr interrogated the rest, it became evident most believed he was guilty. Congressman John Randolph, now a Jefferson enemy, was one of the few who admitted his mind might be changed by fresh facts and arguments. Marshall appointed him foreman. [70]

The embarrassed federal prosecutor, George Hay, now confessed that General Wilkinson, the one man who could verify the authenticity of the cipher letter, had not yet arrived from New Orleans. Aaron Burr responded with another offensive thrust. He asked Chief Justice Marshall to issue a subpoena *duces tecum* ("bring with you") to President Jefferson, ordering him to hasten to Richmond with the full text of the letter as well as copies of his response to Wilkinson and of the orders for Burr's arrest.[71]

Would Burr turn the tables and put the president in the dock? The crowd breathlessly followed the tremendous argument that erupted over the constitutionality of the motion. Federal Attorney Hay declared it out of the question. The defense, especially Luther Martin, seized the opportunity to assail Jefferson's role in this "peculiar case." Marshall carefully stated his disapproval of what was said "in the heat of debate"—though he made no attempt to stop the raging rhetoric—and again stunned the prosecution by issuing the subpoena.[72]

In his ruling, Marshall maintained that the president, unlike a king, was no more immune to a subpoena than any other citizen. His only exemption would be if his duties as chief magistrate demanded his "whole time." However, it was "apparent" that this demand was not "unremitting." That may have been a purely general observation or a dig at how much time Jefferson spent at Monticello. The chief justice added another comment that was even more explosive. He said it was also apparent the government "wished" to convict Burr and it was the duty of the court to give him every means to exonerate himself.

Marshall here had the delightful opportunity to enunciate one of the greatest principles of American jurisprudence—that no citizen is above the law—while simultaneously galling a politician he detested. When the prosecution rose to protest the use of the word *wished*, the chief justice artfully withdrew it, substituting *expected*, which he let stand in spite of additional protests.[73]

Jefferson responded to the subpoena by declaring he was perfectly willing to surrender the Wilkinson letter but only he, as president, could decide what other papers might properly be sent. Further affirming his coequal powers, Jefferson stated in a letter to Hay, which the federal attorney read in open court, that the "paramount duties" of the nation made his personal attendance in Richmond impossible.

Jefferson's letter defused the confrontation and the defense accepted the promised delivery of the documents as a fulfillment of the subpoena. The prosecution's vacuum was solved by the arrival of General Wilkinson, resplendent in his gold-braided uniform. The fleshy brigadier exuded self-confidence and righteous wrath against Burr. After a lengthy conference, Hay told Jefferson he was utterly convinced of the general's "unsullied integrity" and would defend him against all comers. Jefferson chimed in with an effusive letter of welcome that assured Spanish Agent 13 of wholehearted presidential support.

The grand jury, under the baleful leadership of John Randolph, took a somewhat different view of the army's commander in chief. Before he reached the witness chair, Randolph described Wilkinson as "the most finished scoundrel that ever lived."[74] The general's performance before the grand jury must have given Hay and Jefferson some sleepless nights. He was forced to admit he had erased portions of the cipher letter which revealed a previous correspondence with Burr. On another question, whether he had prior knowledge of the plot, Wilkinson declined to answer on the grounds of possible self-incrimination.

Chief Justice Marshall solemnly defended the general's right to hide behind the Fifth Amendment but the grand jurors entertained a motion to indict the government's star witness for "misprision of treason"—the crime of knowing treason was being committed and doing nothing about it. The motion lost by a vote of 9 to 7—a commentary in itself from a jury weighted with Republicans. John Randolph wrote a friend the next day lamenting that "the mammoth of iniquity" had escaped.[75]

The prosecution scored a point with the public, if not with the law, when John Randolph asked Burr to produce the prior letter to Wilkinson mentioned in the cipher. Wrapping himself in the mantle of offended honor, Burr said he could never reveal a confidential letter unless he was forced to it by "the extremity of circumstances."[76] This evasion seemed to prove John Randolph's suspicion that both men were guilty, which was nothing less than the truth.

The government produced some fifty witnesses who testified that in the fall of 1806, Aaron Burr had organized an armed force on Blennerhasset Island in the Ohio River near Marietta, Ohio, for the purpose of seizing New Orleans, revolutionizing the West, and attacking Mexico. On June 24th, The jurors indicted Burr for treason and misdemeanor. Charged with the same crime was the owner of the island, hapless Harman Blennerhasset, who had given Burr almost every dollar he possessed, and five other conspirators, notably ex-Senator Jonathan Dayton.[77]

Burr was remanded to the county jail, a verminous place where, his lawyers complained, it was impossible to confer with him. Never before in human history, Luther Martin wrote Burr's son-in-law, Joseph Alston, "did any government thirst more for the blood of a victim."[78] Burr urged both Theodosia and her husband to attend the trial, arguing that it would be less agonizing than learning about it by letter and newspaper. Also, he added darkly, he wanted "discerning" witnesses to his conduct, which would demonstrate that even if he was "murdered in legal form" he would not be "humiliated or disgraced."[79]

XIX

On August 10, 1807, the trial began in a sweltering Richmond with beautiful Theodosia Alston Burr and her son and husband among the spectators in the packed Hall of Delegates. The selection of a jury consumed days of wrangling. Many prospects referred to Burr as "the traitor" and one man accused the defense of being afraid of him because his first name was Hamilton. After examining almost ninety prospects, Burr offered to let the final choices be made at random. It was clear that if he was to escape the rope, it would depend on John Marshall, not the conclusions of twelve good men and true.[80]

From the start, the legal contest centered around whether treason had been committed on Blennerhasset Island, where Burr assembled his armed force, and what connection the colonel had with the events that took place there while he was a day's journey away in Frankfort, Kentucky.

Among the first prosecution witnesses was Commodore Thomas Truxtun. He told of conversations with Burr in the East, during which he outlined his plans. The defense objected mightily, claiming that the testimony had no connection whatsoever to Blennerhasset Island. Marshall permitted the commodore and several similar witnesses to report revealing conversations with Burr on the presumption that the government would eventually connect the plot to the overt act.

The prosecution now tried to prove treason had been committed on Blennerhasset Island. Their star witness was Jacob Allbright, a Blennerhasset-hired laborer, who described the events of December 10, 1806. The local Ohio militia under the leadership of General Edward Tupper had raided the island and tried to seize Harman Blennerhasset. Allbright said several muskets had been leveled by Burr's band of adventurers and General Tupper had hastily departed.

Aaron Burr took personal charge of cross-examining Allbright. He asked him if he knew General Tupper. Allbright said he did and identified him sitting in the audience. Burr had no more questions but everyone in the Hall of Delegates suddenly had a very large one. Why did not the prosecution immediately call General Tupper to the stand? The answer, never supplied at the trial, was a deposition Tupper had made, in which he said he never had a warrant to arrest anyone, and no guns had been leveled at him on the night of December 10th. He had spent a pleasant half hour chatting with Blennerhasset and withdrew.

The prosecution hastily called several more witnesses who embroidered the activities of the armed men on the island, noting that they were making bullets and talked largely about conquests. But no one corroborated Allbright's tale of threatened violence. Burr's attorneys swarmed to the bench and plunged into a vehement conference with the Chief Justice. Was Marshall planning to let Prosecutor Hay parade his entire 140 witnesses to the stand when all he could offer as proof of the overt act was the dubious Allbright and the silent Tupper?[81]

Once more, a thunderstruck George Hay heard the chief justice agree with the defense and rule that it was time to hear arguments on whether further collateral evidence was admissible. The lawyers knew they had reached the climax of the trial and nerved themselves for maximum efforts. The prosecution faltered, confounded by their inability to produce an overt act.

Luther Martin summed up for the defense. He spoke for three full days, adding 118 pages to the trial record. In his closing, the Marylander tried to add a moral dimension to Marshall's decision. He discussed the public clamor against Burr and wondered if American justice had already become "mere idle form and ceremony to transfer innocence from the gaol to the gibbet." He ended by hoping that God would illuminate the court's "understandings." [82]

The chief justice spent the weekend writing his decision. It was one of the longest opinions in his career, citing reams of authorities—a rarity in Marshall's legal canon. He argued that a man who conspired to assemble an army to commit treason can only be convicted if the government proves both the conspiracy *and* an overt act. In Burr's case, the government had proved neither. Therefore all the collateral evidence in the mouths of the government's witnesses was inadmissible.[83]

The chief justice closed his decision by noting that the government's attorneys had hinted several times he was risking impeachment if he ruled for Burr. "That this court dares not usurp power is most true," he declared. "That this court dares not shrink from its duty is no less true."[84] Here, with Burr's help, the chief justice threw down the gauntlet to President Jefferson.

The next day, September 1st, Hay informed the jury he had nothing to offer in response to the ruling. Attorney William Wirt, who had assisted Hay on the prosecution side, had no illusions about the verdict. "Marshall has stepped in between Burr and death," Wirt told a friend.[85] The jury retired for less than an hour while the Hall of Delegates seethed with animosity against Marshall and Burr. Returning, the foreman reported sourly: "We of the jury say that Aaron Burr is not proved to be guilty under this indictment by any evidence submitted to us."

Burr and his lawyers protested the wording of the verdict. But Marshall, perhaps feeling he had done more than enough for them, let it stand, although he directed the court record to read "not guilty." Burr still had to survive a trial for the misdemeanor of waging war against Spain, and an attempt by Hay to transport him to Ohio for another treason trial. But with some help from Marshall, who repeatedly barred testimony he deemed irrelevant, the ex-vice president and his attorneys weathered these perils with little or no difficulty. Ex-Senator Dayton, Blennerhasset, and the other indicted co-conspirators were released without any effort to bring them to trial.[86]

General Wilkinson did not fare as well as he had hoped when he portrayed himself to Jefferson as the savior of the country. The brigadier was caught in numerous lies and contradictions by Burr's defense lawyers, until a disgusted George Hay confessed to Jefferson he had lost all confidence in him. Wilkinson's sorry performance, which Jefferson stubbornly refused to admit, probably explains why Congress ignored the president's thinly veiled call for Marshall's impeachment when he sent the record of the trial to the legislature.

With the help of some clever lies by his Spanish paymasters, Wilkinson survived a military court of inquiry, which almost everyone but Jefferson considered a whitewash. Three congressional investigations also failed to penetrate his evasions.[87] The only person who achieved a modicum of justice in regard to the president's favorite soldier was Congressman John Randolph. Wilkinson challenged him to a duel for calling him a finished scoundrel, among other things. Randolph replied: "I refuse to sink to your level." The enraged general "posted" Randolph in various parts of Washington, D.C., calling him "a prevaricating, base, calumniating scoundrel, poltroon and coward." Randolph ignored him—and lost no respect from anyone in Congress or out of it.[88]

The Constitution of the United States fared better than the principals in this bizarre clash. In spite of the personal animosity in which it was born, John Marshall's ruling in Burr's favor banned the evil genie of "constructive treason"—the conspiracy without the overt act—from American jurisprudence forever, affirming, most scholars agree, the intent of the founding fathers. It was a verdict that Alexander Hamilton, always eager to strengthen the judiciary as the first line of defense against runaway legislatures and corrupt presidents, would have warmly approved. As in the impeachment of Judge Chase, Aaron Burr, driven by his hatred of Thomas Jefferson, ironically acted as a kind of inadvertent surrogate for General Hamilton in a judicial-political triumph that profoundly strengthened the conservative side of the American experiment.

XX

Colonel Burr may have defeated Thomas Jefferson in court but the former vice president lost the contest in the newspapers. With the help of damning quotes from the collateral testimony Chief Justice Marshall had ruled irrelevant, Burr was vilified as a traitor by almost every editor in the country. All the vicious slanders James Cheetham and DeWitt Clinton had flung at him during the 1804 gubernatorial campaign seemed confirmed.

In mostly rural America, Burr's attempt to seduce the western states into secession was seen, one suspects, in very personal terms. The bonanza of open land that Jefferson had obtained from Napoléon was a sort of national surplus which almost every American considered on deposit for himself or his children or grandchildren. Anyone who tried to transmogrify it into another country was stealing John Q. Citizen's inheritance—an angle of vision that gave the word *treason* an especially dastardly ring.

Not even Burr's most devoted supporters could find it in their hearts to say a good word for him. Matthew Davis called the colonel's western adventure "a damn foolish undertaking."[89] William P. Van Ness made it clear that he was no longer a Burrite. Only the Swartouts remained loyal, though they made no attempt to defend him.

In Baltimore, enroute to Philadelphia, a mob of about fifteen hundred enraged citizens threatened to hang the colonel, Samuel Swartout, and Harman Blennerhasset. The next day Burr and Swartout accepted an armed escort to the Philadelphia stagecoach. That night the mob attacked Luther Martin's house, smashed the windows, and paraded effigies of Martin, Marshall, Burr, and Blennerhasset through the streets, screaming insults at them.

In Philadelphia Burr went into virtual hiding with his friend Charles Biddle. For a while he was a spent man, depressed, morose, embittered. Biddle feared Burr might commit suicide at any moment. His condition was so pitiable, there were times when Biddle thought death might be the best solution.[90]

Burr slowly recovered his emotional balance. His ever optimistic friend Charles Williamson wrote to him from London, reviving hopes that the British might yet finance an assault on Mexico. With no future in America, Burr decided to pursue this chimera and, disguised as "Mr. Edwards," departed for England in June of 1808. For the next two years, Burr tried to convince the English that his vision of a Mexican empire founded on American guns was plausible. Although there were flickers of interest, Britain's struggle against Napoléon remained focused on the continent of Europe. Charles Williamson, sent to Jamaica on another secret service venture, died of yellow fever on the return voyage. The American government's representatives in England pursued Burr relentlessly, eventually persuading the British to expel him in 1810.

By that time the twists and turns of war had made Spain an enemy of France. In Paris, Burr tried to interest Napoléon in backing a foray to Mexico. When that idea faltered, he proposed expeditions to Jamaica, Louisiana, and Canada. He struggled to make all these dreams of glory plausible in lengthy proposals submitted to the emperor through intermediaries. Harassed by larger worries, such as a civil war in Spain, Bonaparte kept Burr at arm's length.

XXI

For a while, the continuing decline of the Jefferson administration sustained Burr's hopes. Still without a navy worth mentioning, except for his gunboats, the president could do nothing to stop the British from continuing to seize American ships or to board them and impress American sailors into their ranks. Some historians estimate the number of these hapless victims reached ten thousand.

Napoléon decided to get into the game, and seized $13 million worth of U.S. shipping in European ports on the pretext that they were violating his blockade of England. Jefferson's answer was the Embargo Act, which proved all the things that Hamilton and the Federalists had said about him as a theorist in the disguise of a politician. The president declared that henceforth Americans would trade with nobody.

The law expressed Jefferson's vision of an isolated agrarian America. But it was horrendously out of touch with American economic realities. It brought most of American business to a dead stop and caused enormous unrest in the middle states and New England. Shipowners and merchants compared the embargo to cutting a man's throat to cure a nosebleed. Farmers were equally dismayed as prices for their surplus grain and corn collapsed.

William Coleman, still editing the *New-York Evening Post*, made the embargo his prime target of opportunity. He pointed out that the law was costing the United States $50 million a year, more than enough money to build a navy that could protect every American merchant ship on all the oceans of the earth. He mocked Jefferson's theory that the embargo would force the British to negotiate. Instead, the law handed over to the British merchant marine a monopoly in world commerce.[91]

Smuggling became widespread along the Canadian border, and the dismayed president had to order the U.S. Army into action to enforce his unpopular law. When a fanatic Jeffersonian supporter, Nathaniel Macon of North Carolina, backed the use of troops, William Coleman accused him and Jefferson of being indifferent to the starving laborers and bankrupt merchants of the North. Why should they worry? They each had a hundred slaves working for them. They would have food on their tables.

In the closing weeks of Jefferson's term Congress repealed the embargo—a virtual confession of its failure. Jefferson's prestige collapsed and so did the idea of presidential leadership for the next twenty years. "I am now . . . chiefly an unmeddling listener to what others say," Jefferson confessed in December 1808.

XXII

Without Hamilton or Burr to rally them, the Federalists were so supine, they could not prevent the Republicans from electing Jefferson's hand-picked successor, James Madison, even though roughly 30 percent of the congressmen boycotted the caucus that nominated him "unanimously." President Madison could think of no solution but a modified embargo, so called "non-intercourse" with the two belligerents England and France.

The impact of these policies was visible in a memorandum Burr submitted to the French Ministry of Foreign Affairs in March of 1810: "There are at this moment forty thousand American sailors unemployed by reason of the Embargo Act and the suspension of trade. The majority of these sailors are ready to engage in any undertaking whatsoever . . . provided that it offers a remote prospect of honor and rewards."

Elsewhere in this document, Burr commented on the continuing decline of the Jeffersonian Republican party: "All classes of people are today discontented with the actions of the government. Even the friends of the administration share this dissatisfaction, but they uphold and justify, as best they can, the timid policy that is being followed."[92] While these words may have stirred hope in Burr the conspirator, they must also have caused acute anguish in Burr the politician.

If the colonel had bided his time and dismissed Brigadier Wilkinson and his braggadocio visions of Mexican gold, Aaron Burr might not have shot General Hamilton. Even if he had yielded to that deadly temptation, if he had aborted his floundering western adventure before Jefferson could call him a traitor, Burr might still have been the politician to whom Americans turned as Republicanism tottered into political futility in the hands of Jefferson's inept successor.

XXIII

In 1811, as England and America drifted toward war, a discouraged Burr decided to go home. After some difficulty securing a passport, he sailed for New York under the pseudonym, "Mr. A. Arnot."[93] The colonel returned to heartbreak far deeper than the extinction of his political hopes. As he began to reestablish himself as a lawyer in New York, he learned of the death of his ten-year-old grandson, Aaron Burr Alston.

Theodosia Burr Alston was distraught. Her health deteriorated, along with her marriage to Joseph Alston, who found it hard to forgive Burr for luring him into the western adventure. The South Carolinian had to pay Harman Blennerhassett $10,000 in blackmail when the bankrupt Irishman threatened to reveal Alston's part in the conspiracy.

Suffering from symptoms that suggested cancer, Theodosia decided to return to New York to see her father and seek medical treatment. On December 30, 1812, she boarded the schooner *Patriot* in Charleston. The ship never arrived in New York. Rumors that it had been captured by pirates and the passengers and crew murdered did nothing to assuage Alston's and Burr's anguish. "Oh my friend," wrote Alston, "If there be such a thing as the sublime of misery, it is for us that it has been reserved." Burr said he felt "severed from the human race."[94]

XXIV

The ex-vice president was a mute spectator while Madison's administration, cheered on by the British-hating Jefferson, declared war on England in 1812. Jefferson predicted Canada would fall within six months, with a minimum of bloodshed. Sounding more like General Hamilton or Colonel Burr, the Sage of Monticello urged Madison to use "hemp and confiscation" to deal with antiwar protestors in New England.[95]

The bloodshed turned out to be anything but minimal and the Canadian invasion became a series of military disasters for the Americans.

They were fighting a Jefferson-style war, with a tiny regular army bolstered by hordes of untrained militia. Among the generals who proved their incapacity was James Wilkinson, who was forced to resign in disgrace after one humiliating campaign.

One of the great what-ifs of American history is the part General Alexander Hamilton might have played in this war, which began only eight years after his death. Not only would he have had incontrovertible evidence of Jeffersonian inability to fight a war, he would have been able to point to an equally egregious blunder on the financial front. In 1811, the charter of the Bank of the United States came up for renewal in Congress. In the Senate the vote was a tie, and Vice President George Clinton, whose still insatiable appetite for public office had allowed Jefferson to drag him into another term under Madison, cast the deciding vote—no.

This denouement of the Old Incumbent's long enmity for Hamilton left the United States with no reliable means for financing the war against England, adding to the political and military chaos. By 1814, the American government was literally bankrupt, without enough money to pay the salaries of clerks in Washington, D.C. When a desperate President Madison tried to borrow from New York bankers, William Coleman, as if the avenging spirit of Hamilton possessed his pen, denounced the government's offer of 6 percent interest as much too low and Gotham's bankers invested in British treasury notes instead.[96]

For Burr the spectacle was leavened with irony when his old enemy DeWitt Clinton co-opted the colonel's game plan and ran for president with Federalist support in 1812. He was backed by mass meetings in New York at which Gouverneur Morris, Rufus King, John Jay, and other former disciples of Hamilton denounced the war with England.[97] It was an attempt to break Virginia's hegemony by a politician who had done too much to create it—and Clinton lost, 128–89 in the electoral college. But he carried all of New England except Vermont, plus New York and New Jersey. It was a grim index of how unpopular the war was in the Northeast.

The climax of this sorry tale was the British attack on Washington, D.C., in 1814. Landing 4,100 men from their fleet, George III's men scattered President Madison's pickup militia army with a bayonet charge and marched to the nation's capital, while the president and his first lady fled to Virginia. The British burned the White House and other public buildings and spent the better part of a week ashore without a shot being fired at them. It was the worst humiliation ever inflicted on an American president by a foreign enemy. Jefferson assured his protégé that had "General Washington himself been at the head of our affairs, the same event would probably have happened."[98] This may rank as the most dubious sentence the man from Monticello ever wrote.

There is little doubt that if General Hamilton had been alive, the demand for him to rescue the nation as a man on horseback would have been irresistible. Even a Colonel Burr with Hamilton's blood on his hands might have been a candidate for power in the nightmarish closing months of 1814, if he had not been stained by his western adventure. As it was, national pride was restored and even worse humiliation, including possible dismemberment of the Union, was prevented by another military leader.

In the closing weeks of 1814, the British landed seventy-five hundred veterans near New Orleans, apparently following the broad outline of Burr's prophecy that a takeover of the city would give them control of the economy of the western states and might even persuade the westerners to secede in disgust from the effete East. But Major General Andrew Jackson's army of frontiersmen turned out to be much tougher opponents than President Madison's eastern militia. On January 8, 1815, Jackson's sharpshooters routed the British in a decisive battle that put the Tennessean on the road to the presidency.

While Jackson defended the West's jugular, New Englanders were meeting at Hartford to discuss the long-simmering scheme of regional secession. If Jackson had lost at New Orleans, the two prongs of Colonel Burr's plan—western and northeastern declarations of independence from Jeffersonian-Madisonian military incompetence and economic blundering—might well have come true. Instead, the news of Jackson's victory rescued Madison's administration from panic and threw the New England secession movement into history's dustbin once and for all. The English accepted a status quo peace and the Americans were able to convince themselves—or at least future generations—that the War of 1812 had ended victoriously.

XXV

Federalist disarray over the Hartford Convention enabled the Virginians to retain control of the fractured Republican party. President Madison was even able to eat his own and Jefferson's denunciations and recharter the Bank of the United States in 1816 without being laughed out of the country. With warm approval emanating from Monticello, Madison designated his fellow Virginian, Secretary of State James Monroe, as his heir apparent.

Aaron Burr, watching from New York, could no longer remain silent. On November 15, 1815, he wrote Joseph Alston a letter that summed up all his frustration and bitterness. Alston had served as governor of South Carolina from 1812 to 1814, performing creditably. Theoretically he was still a politician who could speak for his wealthy and populous state.

Burr began by telling (or reminding) Alston that a congressional caucus would soon nominate Monroe and call on "all good Republicans to support the measure." The colonel laid into Monroe and the whole idea of nomination by caucus. The memory of his own humiliation at the hands of this body was obviously still raw. "Whether we consider the measure itself—the character and talents of the man or the state whence he comes, this nomination is equally exceptionable and odious."

Burr denounced "congressional nominations" as "hostile to all freedom and independence of suffrage." More galling was the way "a certain junto of actual and factitious Virginians" had run the federal government for twenty-four years and now thought of it as "their property." The

Jeffersonians had stayed in power, Burr maintained, by "promoting state dissentions" (sic) which made it impossible for a strong leader to emerge elsewhere. Again, the Colonel was probably thinking of the way Jefferson had secretly cheered on the Clintons to demolish him.

As for Candidate Monroe, Burr characterized him as "naturally dull and stupid—extremely illiterate—indecisive to a degree that would be incredible to one who did not know him—pusillanimous and of course hypocritical—has no opinion on any subject and will always be under the gov[ernmen]t of the worst men." This, Burr declared, "is a character exactly suited to the views of the Virginia junto."

Burr urged Alston to rouse himself and South Carolina to action. The time was "extremely auspicious for breaking down this degrading system." There was a man on the political horizon—born in South Carolina—who could do it. He was a leader of firmness and decision and real standing with the public. His name was Andrew Jackson. Burr urged Alston to organize "a respectable nomination" before the congressional caucus named Monroe. The Tennessee general's success would be "inevitable."[99]

Here is enough irony to start an industrial revolution. Colonel Burr was nominating a man who had, thanks to history's perpetual unpredictability, achieved the military fame that he and General Hamilton had assigned to themselves as their exclusive property—the Bonapartean reputation over which they had exchanged bullets on the Weehawken shore eleven years ago. Through his son-in-law, Burr was trying to ignite a movement that would revenge the colonel—and General Hamilton—on Jefferson and his followers. Piling irony on irony, this American Bonaparte came with a democratic label, a hero who preached a western-style equality that left many of the Jeffersonians of the East as dismayed and hostile as the Federalists were to that explosive idea.

In 1815, Colonel Burr was expending his rhetorical fire on a spent man. Alston was devastated by the deaths of his son and his wife. He told Burr that he agreed with him but "the spirit, the energy, the health necessary to give practical effect to sentiment, are all gone." This husk of a man, who must have occasionally wondered what evil spirit had involved him with the Burrs, added that he felt "too entirely unconnected with the world, to take much interest in any thing." A few months later, the ex-governor joined Theodosia in the shadows.[100]

XXVI

This outburst was virtually Aaron Burr's last recorded attempt to influence American politics. He recognized that he had become a pariah whom no politician could touch without contagion. He made no attempt to retrieve his reputation by writing books or persuading others to defend him in print.

Most of Burr's political lieutenants fared poorly. Matthew L. Davis made the mistake of trying to oppose Martin Van Buren in New York and was soon driven from the field by that devious politician. "Little Mercury" no more, Davis retired to newspapering. William P. Van Ness played the fractured politics that followed the breakup of the Clinton-Livingston alliance well enough to procure a federal judgeship—another form of political retirement.

Samuel Swartout was one of the last Burrites to hold office, thanks to his and Tammany Hall's flamboyant support of Andrew Jackson's victorious run for the White House in 1828. Old Hickory appointed Sam collector of the port of New York. Eight years later, Swartout's accounts were found to be a million dollars short and he fled to Europe. It seems that Sam, like his mentor, had dreams of Southwest glory. He apparently invested most of the mulcted money in Texas land, betting on the early admission of the Lone Star State to the Union and a rush of settlers, neither of which materialized.[101]

Meanwhile, Burr quietly continued the practice of law in New York, gradually building up a comfortable income. He was generous to old friends. When Luther Martin's alcoholism reduced him to a bankrupt derelict, Burr took the attorney into his house and cared for him until his death. Still intensely paternal, Burr adopted several children he may or may not have fathered and raised them with generosity and affection. He probably found some silent satisfaction in reading about Thomas Jefferson's frantic attempts to escape bankruptcy in the last year of his life and the sale of Monticello, its slaves, and its furniture shortly after the third president's death in 1826.

XXVII

Occasionally, the colonel encountered fragments of the event that had altered his life. One day in downtown New York City Judge James Kent saw Burr on the other side of the street. By this time Kent was chancellor of the state and one of the most esteemed jurists in the country. Kent lost his customary self-control and rushed through the traffic to shout in Burr's face: "You are a scoundrel sir! A scoundrel!"

Once, that epithet would have led to pistols at ten paces, but Burr was a wiser, if sadder man now. He simply raised his hat, bowed, and said: "The opinions of the learned chancellor are always entitled to the highest consideration."[102]

Did Burr show any sign of regret? Two contradictory stories are worth telling. One has him reading *Tristam Shandy* in his old age. This comic English novel by Laurence Sterne, with its sentimental live-and-let live philosophy of life, was a great favorite of the revolutionary generation. Burr must have read it in his youth. Rereading it in his last years, he supposedly pointed to the passage where the main character, Uncle Toby, puts a fly out the window rather than kill it. Burr reportedly said: "Had I read Sterne more and Voltaire less, I should have known the world was wide enough for Hamilton and me."[103]

More convincing is a tale told by a young friend who persuaded the colonel to revisit the Weehawken dueling ground with him. Burr was silent as the friend rowed them across the Hudson. Together they clambered up the rocky path to where Colonel Burr and General Hamilton had stood decades ago. (The outcropping has long since been demolished by developers.) As Burr began describing what happened on July 11, 1804, his friend said, "his eyes blazed, his voice rose." He recited a veritable catalogue of smears and slanders he had suffered from Hamilton. The cool ironic old man vanished. "His very form seemed to rise and expand," the friend said. With ferocious intensity, Burr described Hamilton as malevolent and cowardly. It was not true, Burr raged, that Hamilton did not fire at him. He had heard the bullet whistle in the branches above his head. As for Hamilton's remarks on the forthcoming duel, they read "like the confessions of a penitent monk."[104]

XXVIII

When Aaron Burr lay dying in a Staten Island hotel in 1836, at the age of eighty, a Reformed Dutch clergyman visited him several times. The man of God urged him to prepare to meet his maker and reminded Burr of his ancestry, his father the revered president of Princeton, his mother the daughter of the great Jonathan Edwards. Burr seemed moved, but when the minister tried to discuss the duel with Hamilton, Burr remarked he was "provoked to that encounter" and would say nothing else. To the minister's distress, Burr never asked to receive the sacrament of Holy Communion.

The last time the minister visited, Burr's pulse was "fluttering and erratic." The minister asked him if he believed in Jesus, his only hope of salvation. "On that subject," Burr said, "I am coy." The minister thought the colonel meant cautious, uncertain. But he found some hope in Burr's apparent willingness to let the clergyman pray for him.[105]

XXIX

Another view of Colonel Burr's later years comes from his last landlady, whom he charmed like most of the women in his life. One day, several visitors got into a political argument and began damning the contemporary crop of Jacksonian Democratic politicians, some of whom Burr was inclined to defend. The landlady saw that the colonel was upset and suggested they should all give some thought to the Robert Burns poem, "Address to the Unco Gude."

> Then gently scan your brother man
>> Still gentler sister woman;
> Tho' they may go a kennin wrang,
>> To step aside is human:
> One point must still be greatly dark,
>> The moving *why* they do it;
> And just as lamely can ye mark
>> How far perhaps they rue it.

Colonel Burr was deeply, keenly stirred. "*How* good," he said several times. "How *very* good."

A final recollection from the devoted landlady also illuminates Burr's tangled tragedy. She was given to fits of melancholy and sometimes wished she were dead. Burr always rebuked her and urged her to enjoy herself. During one particular patch of trouble, she cried: "Oh Colonel, how *shall* I get through this?"

"*Live* through it, my dear," Burr said.

The landlady refused to be solaced: "This will kill me, Colonel, I know I can not survive this."

"Well die then, Madame," Colonel Burr said. "But bless me, die *game.*"[106]

Notes

CHAPTER 1

1. Bleecker, Elizabeth DeHart [Mrs. Alexander L. McDonald]. Manuscript diary, 1799–1806. New York Public Library. Entry for Jan. 1, 1804: "A cloudy morning–about ten o'clock it began to rain–"

2. Anthony, Edward, and Sloane, Eric. *Mr. Daniels and The Grange.* New York, 1968: 72, 77. The property extended from 141st to 145th Street on the west side of Manhattan.

3. Syrett, Harold C. et al., eds. *The Papers of Alexander Hamilton* [hereafter *PAH*]. Vol. 25. New York, 27 vols., 1961–81: 52; Goebel, Julius. *The Law Practice of Alexander Hamilton.* Vol. 5. New York, 1964ff: 366, states his income as $13,000 in 1802, $9,570 in 1803, and $10,300 in 1797, the last previous year in which he practiced full time. Thereafter his duties as acting commander of the provisional army consumed much of his time for over two years (see below). Translating the value of 1804 dollars to modern amounts is a tricky business. In *How Much Is That in Real Money? An Historical Price Index for Use as a Deflator of Money Values in the Economy of the United States* (Worcester, MA: American Antiquarian Society, 1992), John J. McCusker suggests a multiple of twelve. I have used this as a general rule of thumb, but I am inclined to think it is conservative and have rounded my figures somewhat higher.

4. Cantor, Milton, ed. *Great Lives Observed: Hamilton.* Englewood Cliffs, NJ, 1971: 112. McDonald, Forrest, *Alexander Hamilton.* New York, 1979: 15.

5. Hendrickson, Robert. *Hamilton.* Vol. 2. New York, 1976: 556

6. Rossiter, Clinton. *The Grand Convention.* New York, 1966: 184–5; Hendrickson, *Hamilton*, Vol. 1, 479.

7. Flexner, James Thomas, *The Young Hamilton*, New York, 1978: 14. Scholars still debate whether Hamilton was born in 1755 or 1757. Harold Syrett, the editor of the Hamilton Papers, inclined to 1755. But he noted that in 1776, Hamilton described himself as 19 years old. That gives him a 1757 birthdate, which recent biographers, such as Flexner and Robert Hendrickson, prefer. See Syrett, Harold C. and Jean C. Cooke, eds, *Interview at Weekhawken, The Burr-Hamilton Duel as Told in the Original Documents,* Middletown CT, 1960: 35.

8. McDonald, *Alexander Hamilton,* 353.

9. *Historical Magazine,* 2: 193–204, has the best account of the duel, printing versions from both sides. Also see Stevens, William Oliver, *Pistols at Ten Paces.* Boston, 1940: 2–28.

10. Steinmetz, Andrew. *The Romance of Duelling*. London, 1868: 38, 90. Also see Freeman, Joanne B. "Duelling As Politics," *William and Mary Quarterly* 53 no. 2 (April 1996): 289–318.

11. Reilly, Robin. *William Pitt the Younger*. New York 1978: 358–59.

12. *PAH*, Vol. 25, 437; Hendrickson, *Hamilton*. Vol. 2, 536–37.

13. Adair, Douglass, *Fame and the Founding Fathers*. New York, 1974: 154. The quoted words are from a biography by Hamilton's son, John Church Hamilton.

14. *PAH*, Vol. 26, 70–71.

15. Anthony and Sloane, *Mr. Daniels and the Grange*, 77.

16. *PAH*, Vol. 25, 606–607, 613.

17. Adair, *Fame and the Founding Fathers*, 148.

18. Ibid., 155.

19. Thorne, R. G. *The House of Commons 1790–1820*. 5 vols., Vol 3. London, 1986: 441. Also see Phelan, Helene C. *The Man Who Owned the Pistols: John Barker Church and His Family*. Interlaken, NY, 1981: 10ff.

20. Ibid. (Phelan), 36ff. Also see Hendrickson, *Hamilton*, Vol. 1, 555–59.

21. *PAH* Vol. 21, 239, 259.

22. *PAH*, Vol. 21, 243–44.

23. Miller, John C. *Alexander Hamilton and the Growth of the New Nation*. New York, 1959: 465.

24. Talleyr and-Perigod, duc de, Charles Maurice Camille, *Etude sur la republique des Etats Unis d'Amerique*, New York, 1876, 192.

25. Hendrickson, *Hamilton*, Vol. 2, 324. In a memoir, Hamilton's son, James, recalled meeting Albert Gallatin, Jefferson's Secretary of the Treasury, in later years. Gallatin told him on Jefferson's orders he had scoured the books of the treasury trying to find something to pin on Hamilton. To Jefferson's manifest chagrin, Gallatin found nothing. (Hamilton, James H. *Reminiscences of Men and Events At Home and Abroad During Three Quarters of a Century*, New York, 1869, 23.

26. Tripp, Wendell. "Robert Troup: A Quest for Security in a Turbulent New Nation, 1775–1832" (unpub. Ph.D. diss., Columbia University, 1973): 198–99.

27. McDonald, *Alexander Hamilton*, 310. Also see Tripp, *Robert Troup*, 167.

28. *PAH*, Vol. 21, 78.

29. Adair, *Fame and the Founding Fathers*, 14–15.

30. Ibid., 15–16.

31. McDonald, *Alexander Hamilton*, 308–9.

32. Kline, Mary-Jo, ed., and Joanne Wood Ryan, assoc. ed. *Political Correspondence and Public Papers of Aaron Burr* [hereafter *PAB*] 2 vols, Princeton, NJ, 1983: 312. Lomask, Milton. *Aaron Burr*. 2 vols., Vol. 1. New York, 1979–1983: 209.

33. Berkeley, Edmund, and Dorothy Smith Berkeley, *John Beckley*. Philadelphia, 1973: 170; Miller, John C., *Alexander Hamilton*, 463–64.

34. Lomask, *Aaron Burr*, Vol. 1, 208–9.

35. Swiggett, Howard. *The Extraordinary Mr. Morris*. New York, 1952: 80.

36. *PAH*, Vol. 25, 544–45.

37. Ibid.

38. Swiggett, *Mr. Morris*, 363.

39. Morris, Anne Cary, ed. *Diary and Letters of Gouverneur Morris*. New York, 1888, vol. 2: 423.

40. Ibid., 423, 442–43.

41. *PAB*, 761–63.

42. Tripp, *Robert Troup*, 199.

43. Hamilton, *Intimate Life*, 205–6.

44. Howe, John R., Jr., "Republican Thought and Political Violence in the 1790s," *American Quarterly* 19 (Summer 1967): 147–165.

45. Hendrickson, *Hamilton*, Vol. 2, 476.

46. Ibid., 479.

47. Alexander, DeAlva S. *A Political History of the State of New York*. Vol. 1. New York, 1906–23: 89.

48. Hendrickson, *Hamilton*, Vol. 2, 500.

49. Goebel, Julius, ed. *The Law Practice of Alexander Hamilton*. Vol. 2. These categories are taken from the chapter headings in this volume.

50. *PAH*, Vol. 26, 346.

CHAPTER 2

1. Stokes, Isaac Newton Phelps. *The Iconography of Manhattan Island, 1498–1909*. Vol. 5. New York, 1915–28: 1356.

2. Adams, Henry. *The United States in 1800*. Ithaca, NY, 1974: 18.

3. Stokes, *Iconography*, 1356 Vol. 4, 163.

4. Brown, Henry Collins, ed. *Valentine's Manual*. New York, 1916–17: 40–41.

5. Lambert, John. *Travels through Canada and the United States of North America in the Years 1806, 1807, and 1808*. 2 vols, Vol. 2. 2nd ed. London, 1813: 49.

6. Anderson, Dr. Alexander. Diary. New York Historical Society. Entry for Jan. 1, 1797.

7. Lambert, *Travels*, 49.

8. Kaminski, John P. *George Clinton, Yeoman Politician of the New Republic*. Madison, WI, 1993: 220–26. Kaminski's view of Clinton is generally favorable but he admits his reputation was "badly tarnished" by this stolen election. James Madison and Thomas Jefferson, watching from the American Capitol, Philadelphia, were appalled and thought Clinton should resign.

9. McBain, Howard L. *De Witt Clinton and the Origin of the Spoils System in New York*. New York, 1907: 78–79.

10. Boyd, Julian P., et al., eds. *The Papers of Thomas Jefferson*. Princeton, NJ, 1950ff., 27 vols. Vol. 25: 14–16.

11. *PAH*, Vol. 11, 439.

12. McDonald, *Alexander Hamilton*, 265ff.

13. Peterson, Merrill D. *Thomas Jefferson and the New Nation*. New York, 1970: 571.

14. Ibid., 572–73. The final break was caused by Jefferson's nephew, Peter Carr, who wrote to Washington under a pseudonym, trying to inveigle a pro-Republican quote. In one of his last letters, Washington replied to a suggestion that he run for a third term in 1800, rejecting the idea and adding that he did not think he could win. Party politics was in control. The Republicans could "set up a broomstick and call it a true son of liberty and a democrat . . . and it will command their votes in toto." See Fitzpatrick, John C., ed. *Writings of George Washington*. 39 vols., Vol. 37. New York, 1925: 312–14.

15. Gordon, John Steele. *Hamilton's Blessing*. New York, 1997: 40.

16. Young, Alfred. *The Democratic Republicans in New York, The Origins, 1763–1797*. Chapel Hill, NC, 1967: 170, 176.

17. Keane, John. *Tom Paine: A Political Life*. London, 1995: 492–93. In 1804, the sixty-six-year-old Paine was detained at his New Rochelle farm until the end of February by a crippling attack of gout.

18. Ibid., 389–98.

19. Ibid., 429–33.

20. Ibid., 462, 468.

21. *New-York Evening Post*, Jan. 5, 1804.

22. Durey, Michael. "Thomas Paine's Apostles: Radical emigres and the triumph of Jeffersonian Republicanism," *William and Mary Quarterly*, 3rd series (44), 1987: 661–88.

23. Cunningham, Noble E., Jr. *The United States in 1800: Henry Adams Revisited*, Charlottesville, VA, 1988: 580.

24. Hamilton, *Intimate Life*, 235.

25. Schachner, Nathan. *Alexander Hamilton*. New York, 1946: 183.

26. Cunningham, *The Process of Government Under Jefferson*, Princeton, N.J., 1978: 500.

27. *Richmond Recorder*, Nov. 17, 1802.

28. Levy, Leonard W., ed. *Freeom of the Press from Zenger to Jefferson*. New York, 1966: 364. Preceding this letter, Levy printed a baker's dozen letters and statements from Jefferson, roundly upholding the importance of a free press. With Jefferson, Levy wryly noted, it was necessary to distinguish the rhetoric from the reality ("The Special Case of Thomas Jefferson," 327ff).

29. Hatcher, William B. *Edward Livingston, Jeffersonian Republican and Jacksonian Democrat*. Baton Rouge, LA, 1940: 92ff.

30. *New-York Evening Post* (April 20, 1804) gives the figure as $10,000. Other sources go as high as $15,000.

31. Bobbe, Dorothie De Bear. *DeWitt Clinton*. New York, 1933: 108.

32. Rock, Howard B. *Artisans of the New Republic*. New York, 1979: 230.

33. Brown, Everett S., ed. *William Plumer's Memorandum of Proceedings in the U.S. Senate, 1803–07*. New York, 1969 (reprint): 90.

34. McBain, *DeWitt Clinton and the Origin of the Spoils System in New York*. 152–55.

35. Brown, *Plumer's Memorandum*, 26.

36. Orth, Samuel P. *Five American Politicians*. 1906, New York, 1974 (reprint), 90.

37. Hanyan, Craig R. "DeWitt Clinton, Years of Moulding, 1768–1807" (unpub. Ph.D. thesis, Harvard University, 1964): 283–84.

38. *PAH*, Vol. 26: Pickering, 171; Wilkinson, 173; Truxtun, 179–180.

CHAPTER 3

1. *New-York Evening Post*, Jan. 2, 1804.

2. Hartfield, Clara Virginia. "Contemporary American Opinion of Napoleon" (unpub. Ph.D. diss., Johns Hopkins University, 1925), 23–24.

3. Ibid., 29.

4. Ibid., 41–42.

5. Ibid., 65.

6. Ibid., 62, 65

7. Ibid., 65.

8. Ibid., 66.

9. *PAH*, Vol. 26, 179–80.

10. Fischer, David Hackett. *The Revolution of American Conservatism*. New York, 1965: 137, 135.

11. Nevins, Allan. *The Evening Post*. New York, 1922: 47.

12. Freeman, *Duelling as Politics*, 301 (note); Stokes, *Iconography*, Vol. 5, 1352.

13. Jackson, Kenneth T., ed. *Encyclopedia of New York City*. New Haven, 1995: 1191.

14. Stegeman, John F., and Caty, Janet A. *The Life of Catherine Littlefield Greene*. Providence, RI, 1977: 95–96ff.

15. Magrath, C. Peter. *Yazoo, Law and Politics in the Young Republic*. New York, 1967: 3.

16. Ibid., 44–49.

17. *New-York Evening Post*, Jan. 3, 1804. Also see Ellis, Richard E. *The Jeffersonian Crisis, Courts and Politics in the Young Republic*. New York, 1971: 122–70, for the struggle over legal reform in Kentucky and Pennsylvania.

18. *PAH*, Vol. 26, 83.

19. *New-York Evening Post*, Jan. 2, 1804.

20. Hartfield, *Contemporary American Opinion of Napoleon*, 79.

21. *New-York Evening Post*, Jan. 14, 1804.

22. O'Brien, Conor Cruise. *The Long Affair*. Chicago, 1996: 253.

23. Peabody, James B. *John Adams, A Biography in His Own Words*. New York, 1973: 364.

24. Ibid., 364.

25. Cunningham, E. M., ed. *Correspondence between the Hon. John Adams and the Late Wm Cunningham Beginning in 1803 and Ending in 1812*. Boston, 1823: 184–85.

26. Ford, Worthington Chauncey, ed. *Statesman and Friend, Correspondence of John Adams with Benjamin Waterhouse, 1784–1822*. Boston, 1927: 65.

27. Cooke, Jacob E., ed., *Alexander Hamilton, a Profile*. New York, 1967: 226.

28. Hamilton, John C. *Life of Alexander Hamilton*. New York, 1840: 297 (letter to James Duane).

29. Boyd, Julian P. *Number 7, Alexander Hamilton's Secret Attempts to Control American Foreign Policy.* Princeton, NJ, 1964. Boyd, editor of the *Papers of Thomas Jefferson*, compiled this book as an anti-Hamilton broadside worthy of Jefferson himself. Boyd condemned Hamilton's "calculating and continuing use of deception" in sabotaging Jefferson's policies and eventually driving him from Washington's cabinet. Not everyone agrees with this narrow interpretation.

30. Hendrickson, *Hamilton,* Vol. 2, 483.

31. Cooke, Jacob E. *Alexander Hamilton: A Profile.* New York, 1967: 200.

32. *PAH,* Vol. 2, 406, 347–48.

33. Ibid., Vol. 26, 13.

34. Rock, *Artisans of the New Republic,* 30, 50–51.

35. *PAH,* Vol. 25, 587.

36. Govan, Thomas P. "The Rich, The Well Born and Alexander Hamilton," *Mississippi Historical Review,* 36 (1949–50): 678.

37. *New-York Evening Post,* Jan. 9, 1804.

38. Ibid., Jan. 10, 1804.

39. Cantor, *Great Lives Observed: Hamilton,* 108.

40. *PAH,* Vol. 25, 170.

41. Cunningham, Noble E., Jr. *The Process of Government Under Jefferson,* 247.

CHAPTER 4

1. Brown, *Plumer's Memorandum,* 74.

2. Davis, Matthew L. *The Memoirs of Aaron Burr.* Vol. 1. New York, 1836–37: 182.

3. *PAB,* 599.

4. Andrews, Wayne, ed. "Gallatin's Last Days As Recorded by James Waddel Alexander." *New York Historical Society Quarterly* (Jan. 1953): 66.

5. Davis, *Memoirs,* Vol. 1, 90–9.1

6. Ibid., 182.

7. Lomask, *Aaron Burr,* Vol. 1, 194.

8. *PAB,* 280.

9. One eyewitness described Alston as "short and rather thick in stature," with thick black hair, a swarthy complexion and "a formidable pair of whiskers that covered a great part of his face and nearly met at the chin" (Lomask, Vol. 1, 284).

10. Anthony, Katherine. *Dolley Madison, Her Life and Times.* New York, 1949: 158.

11. King, Charles R., ed. *Life and Correspondence of Rufus King.* Vol. 3. New York, 1895: 459.

12. Van Doren, Carl, ed. *Correspondence of Aaron Burr and His Daughter, Theodosia.* New York, 1929, 131.

13. *PAB,* 580.

14. Ibid., 579.

15. Ibid., 599.

16. Davis, *Memoirs*, Vol. 1, 178.

17. Lomask, *Aaron Burr*, Vol. 1, 55–63.

18. Davis, *Memoirs*, Vol. 1, 22; Lomask, *Aaron Burr*, Vol. 1, 215–16.

19. Wandell, Samuel, and Meade Minnegerode. *Aaron Burr*. New York, 1925, Vol. 1: 180–81; Lomask, *Aaron Burr*, 219–21; *PAB*, 410.

20. *PAB*, 423.

21. Rock, *Artisans of the New Republic*, 30.

22. Lomask, *Aaron Burr*, 244.

23. Parmet, Herbert S., and Marie B. Hecht. *Aaron Burr: Portrait of an Ambitious Man*. New York, 1967: 150.

24. *PAB*, 425; Lomask, *Aaron Burr*, 250.

25. *PAB*, 68.

26. *PAB*, 740.

27. Cunningham, *The United States in 1800*. 47–48.

28. *American Citizen*, Jan. 11, 1804.

29. Parmet and Hecht, *Aaron Burr*, 165.

30. *PAH*, Vol. 25, 257.

31. Ibid.

32. Ibid., 271–272.

33. Ibid., 290.

34. Ibid., 294–98.

35. Ibid., 323.

36. Ibid., 319.

37. *PAB*, 289ff, 740.

38. *PAH*, Vol. 22, 227, 234.

39. *PAB*, 70.

40. Davis, *Memoirs of Aaron Burr*, Vol. 2, 175.

41. Lomask, *Aaron Burr*, 174.

42. *PAH*, Vol. 12, 480–81, 543–44, 567–69.

43. *PAB*, 485.

44. Ibid., 487; *PAH*, Vol. 25, 345.

CHAPTER 5

1. Friedenberg, Daniel M. *Life, Liberty and the Pursuit of Land*. Buffalo, NY, 1992: 345.

2. Young, James Sterling. *The Washington Community, 1800–1828*. New York, 1966: 21–23.

3. Ibid., 26.

4. Wood, Gordon, ed. *The Rising Glory of America*. New York, 1971: 126 (narrative of Charles William Janson, *The Stranger in America*).

5. Young, *The Washington Community*, 88ff.

6. Ibid., 93.

7. Hanyan, *DeWitt Clinton*, 266.

8. Cooke, Jacob E., ed. *The Federalist*. Middletown, CT, 1961: 173.

9. Young, *The Washington Community*, 46.

10. Davis, Richard Beale, ed. *Jeffersonian America, Notes on the United States of America Collected in the Years 1805–6–7 and 11–12 by Sir Augustus John Foster Bart*. San Marino, CA, 1954: 10.

11. Ibid., 9.

12. Smith, James Morton, ed. *The Republic of Letters, The Correspondence between Thomas Jefferson and James Madison, 1776–1826*. 3 vols. Vol. 2. New York, 1995: 389–91.

13. Young, *The Democratic-Republicans in New York*, 170, 176.

14. Lester, Malcolm. *Anthony Merry Redivivus*. Charlottesville, VA, 1978,: 30–35.

15. Ibid., 33.

16. Hartfield, *Contemporary American Opinion of Napoleon*, 121.

17. Ellis, *The Jeffersonian Crisis*, 20.

18. Ibid., 20.

19. Ibid., 23.

20. Ibid., 38.

21. *PAB*, 659–60.

22. Lomask, *Aaron Burr*, 310.

23. Ellis, *The Jeffersonian Crisis*, 50.

24. Ibid., 52.

25. Malone, Dumas. *Jefferson the President, First Term, 1801–1805*, Boston, 1970: 442; *Jefferson the President, Second Term, 1805–1809*, Boston, 1974: 497–503.

26. Alexander, *A Political History of the State of New York*, 179.

27. *PAB*, 160–63.

28. Alexander, *A Political History of the State of New York*, 179.

29. *PAH*, Vol. 25, 558–59.

30. Lomask, *Aaron Burr*, Vol. 1, 315.

31. Parmet and Hecht, *Aaron Burr*, 185. Also see Lomask, *Aaron Burr*, Vol. 1, 317.

32. Ibid., 188. Also see *PAB*, 489–90.

33. Parmet and Hecht, *Aaron Burr*, 184.

34. Lomask, *Aaron Burr*, Vol. 1, 319–20.

35. Wandell and Minnegerode, *Aaron Burr*, Vol. 1, 245–46; Lomask, *Aaron Burr*, Vol. 1, 322; Stokes, Ed, *The Iconography of Manhattan Island*, Vol 5, 1404.

36. Hendrickson, *Hamilton*, Vol. 2, 601.

37. Bergh, Albert Ellery. *The Writings of Thomas Jefferson*. Vol. 1. Washington, D.C., 1903–4: 442–43

38. Kline, Mary Jo, et al., eds. *Papers of Aaron Burr*. Series I, Reel 5 (correspondence): Letter from Thomas Jefferson, Jan. 15, 1804.

39. Van Doren, *Correspondence of Aaron Burr and His Daughter, Theodosia*, 144.

40. Ibid., 147.

41. Ibid., 147.

42. Lamar, Glenn J. "Military Growth and Career of Jerome Bonaparte 1800–1814" (unpub. Ph.D. diss., Florida State University, 1994): 24.

43. Van Doren, ed. *Correspondence of Aaron Burr and His Daughter Theodosia*, 148

44. Ibid, 147–8

CHAPTER 6

1. Ellis, *The Jeffersonian Crisis*, 75.

2. Ibid., 72.

3. *PAB*, 823.

4. Ibid., 817.

5. Ibid., 452.

6. Ibid., 815–16.

7. Davis, *Memoirs*, Vol. 2, 265.

8. *PAB*, 812.

9. Ibid., 818.

10. Skolnik, Richard, comp. *1803: Jefferson's Decision*. New York, 1969: 171.

11. Malone, Dumas. *Jefferson the President, First Term*. Boston, 1970: 328.

12. Skolnick, *Jefferson's Decision*, 184.

13. Malone. *Jefferson the President*, 332.

14. Ibid., 337.

15. *New-York Evening Post*, Nov. 5, 1803.

16. Abernethy, Thomas P. *The Burr Conspiracy*. New York, 1954: 12.

17. *PAB*, 720.

18. Scanlon, James E. "A Sudden Conceit, Jefferson and the Louisiana Bill of 1804," *Louisiana History* (9)1968: 139–62.

19. Malone, *Jefferson The President, First Term*, 329. Also see Scanlan, *A Sudden Conceit*, 148–49, for attacks on the bill by Congressman Matthew Lyon and other Jeffersonians.

20. Brown, *Plumer's Memorandum*, 119.

21. Malone, *Jefferson the President, First Term*, 329.

22. *PAB*, 818.

23. Gates and Seaton, eds. *Annals of the Congress of the United States*, 8th Congress, Oct. 17, 1803-Mar. 3, 1805. Washington, D.C., 1849: 233.

24. Skolnick, *Jefferson's Decision*, 189.

25. Brown, *Plumer's Memorandum*, 123.

26. Knudson, Jerry W. "Newspaper Reaction to the Louisiana Purchase," *Missouri Historical Review* (Oct. 1953): 207.

27. *PAB*, 827.

28. Brown, *Plumer's Memorandum*, 110.

29. Ibid., 141; *PAB*, 826.

30. Ibid., 117.

31. Ibid., 517–18. Plumer recorded this incident some years after it occurred.

32. McDonald, *Alexander Hamilton*, 251.

33. Sharp, James Roger. *American Politics in the Early Republic*. New Haven, 1993: 251.

34. Prentiss, Hervey Putnam. *Timothy Pickering as the Leader of New England Federalism, 1800–1815*. Salem, Mass, 1934. Reprinted from The Essex Institute Historical Collections, January and April 1933 and April 1934. Salem, MA, 1934: 17.

35. Skolnick, *Jefferson's Decision*, 86.

CHAPTER 7

1. Davis, *Memoirs of Aaron Burr*, Vol. 2, 268.

2. Ibid., 271–72.

3. *PAB*, 819–22 (excerpt from Jefferson's *Anas*).

4. Ibid., 298, 301.

5. Ibid., 436.

6. Ibid., 825.

7. Ellis, *The Jeffersonian Crisis*, 162–69.

8. *PAB*, 822.

9. Dangerfield, George D. *Chancellor Robert R. Livingston of New York*. New York, 1960: 377–79. Dangerfield recounts Livingston's attempt to take credit, and Monroe's disarming statement that his success was "altogether owing to . . . the President."

10. Hanyan, *DeWitt Clinton*, 309.

11. Davis, *Memoirs of Aaron Burr*, Vol. 2, 277.

12. *PAB*, 831; Hanyan, *DeWitt Clinton*, 314.

13. Parmet and Hecht, *Aaron Burr*, 195–96. See also Kaminski, *George Clinton*, 272. Lansing later claimed the Clintons wanted him to appoint DeWitt chancellor.

14. *PAB*, 831.

15. *PAH*, Vol. 26, 187 (note), cites the *New-York Evening Post* of Feb. 21, 1804.

16. Parmet and Hecht, *Aaron Burr*, 195.

17. *PAB*, 842–43.

CHAPTER 8

1. Goebel, *The Law Practice of Alexander Hamilton*, Vol. 1, 784–85.

2. Durey, Michael. *"With The Hammer of Truth"—James Thomson Callender and America's Early National Heroes*. Charlottesville, VA, 1990: 165–66.

3. Ford, Worthington Chauncey, ed. *Thomas Jefferson and James Thomson Callender*. Brooklyn Historical Printing Club pamphlet reprinted from New England Historical and Genealogical Register, 1896–7: 19. See also Goebel, *The Law Practice of Alexander Hamilton*. Vol. 1, 778.

4. *The Wasp*, Aug. 23, 1802.

5. *The Wasp*, Jan. 26, 1803.

6. Hamilton, *Intimate Life*, 270.

7. Horton, John Theodore, *James Kent, A Study in Conservatism.* New York, 1939: 151.

8. Ibid., 151 (note 85).

9. Goebel, *Law Practice of Alexander Hamilton*, Vol. 1, 794–806.

10. Ibid., 833ff.

11. Goebel, *Law Practice of Alexander Hamilton*, Vol. 2, 843.

12. Hendrickson, *Hamilton*, Vol. 2, 616.

13. *PAH*, Vol. 26, 190.

14. *New-York Evening Post*, Feb. 23, 1804.

15. *PAH*, Vol. 26, 191.

16. *PAH*, Vol. 26, 192.

17. Ernst, Robert. *Rufus King, American Federalist.* Chapel Hill, NC, 1968: 275.

18. *PAH*, Vol. 26, 195.

19. Hendrickson, *Hamilton*, Vol. 2, 606.

20. *PAH*, Vol. 26, 196–97.

21. Ibid., 198.

22. Ibid., 198–99.

23. Ibid., 209–10.

24. Ibid., 211.

25. Ibid., 208.

26. Miller, *Alexander Hamilton & the Growth of a New Nation*, 569–70.

CHAPTER 9

1. Ellis, *The Jeffersonian Crisis*, 72.

2. *PAB*, 847–49.

3. Ellis, *The Jeffersonian Crisis*, 73.

4. *PAB*, 849; Brown, ed. *Plumer's Memorandum*, 147–77. See also *Annals of Congress*, 303ff. In a show of impartiality, the Randolph Committee exonerated Hamilton's friend Judge Richard Peters, who had been accused of complicity with Chase.

5. *PAB*, 852.

6. Ibid., 852; Hanyan, *DeWitt Clinton*, 327.

7. *PAB*, 852.

8. Lomask, *Aaron Burr*, Vol. 1, 346.

9. Wandell and Minnegerode, *Aaron Burr*, Vol. 1, 258.

10. Prentiss, *Timothy Pickering as the Leader of New England Federalism*, p. 11 (note).

11. Ibid., 25.

12. Ibid., 54.

13. Lomask, *Aaron Burr*, Vol. 1, 210ff.

14. *PAB*, 840–41. For Granger's claims, see Magrath, *Yazoo*, 38.

15. Adams, Henry. *History of the United States during the Administrations of Jefferson and Madison.* Vol. 2. New York, 1931: 179.

16. Ibid., 180–81.
17. *PAB*, 862–63.
18. Adams, *History*, 189.

CHAPTER 10

1. *PAB*, 832.
2. Ibid., 833.
3. Ibid.
4. Ibid., 834.
5. Ibid., 833–34.
6. Ibid., 834.
7. *American Citizen*, Jan. 4, 1804.
8. *New-York Evening Post*, Feb. 25, 1804.
9. *American Citizen*, Jan. 9, 1804.
10. Ibid., Jan. 6, 1804.
11. Ibid.
12. Ibid., Jan. 7, 1804.
13. Ibid., Mar. 2, 1804.
14. Ibid.
15. Ibid., Mar. 5, 1804.
16. Ibid.
17. *PAB*, 835.
18. *American Citizen*, Mar. 22, 1804.
19. Lomask, *Aaron Burr*, Vol. 1, 343.
20. *PAB*, 831–32. Also see *PAH*, Vol. 26, 104.
21. *New-York Evening Post*, Apr. 14, 1804.
22. Stokes, *Iconography*, Vol. 5, 1420.
23. Parmet and Hecht, *Aaron Burr,* 197–98; *American Citizen*, Mar. 30, 1804.
24. Ibid., Mar. 6, 1804.
25. *New-York Evening Post*, Apr. 17, 1804.
26. *PAB*, 800.
27. Ibid.
28. Ibid., 866.
29. Hendrickson, *Hamilton*, Vol. 2, 506–7.
30. Ibid., 621.

CHAPTER 11

1. *PAB*, 865.
2. *American Citizen*, 25–26.
3. Ibid.

4. Parmet and Hecht, *Aaron Burr*, 197.

5. *PAB*, 866–67.

6. *American Citizen*, Apr. 5, 1804.

7. *PAB*, 852.

8. *American Citizen*, Apr. 6, 1804.

9. *American Citizen*, Apr. 19, 1804.

10. *New-York Evening Post*, Apr. 20, 1804.

11. Davis, *Memoirs of Aaron Burr*, Vol. 2, 282–83.

12. Ibid., 282.

13. Ibid., 283.

14. *American Citizen*, Apr. 20, 1804.

15. Ibid.

16. Ibid., Apr. 23, 1804.

17. Ibid., Apr. 28, 1804.

18. *PAB*, 842.

19. Davis, *Memoirs of Aaron Burr*, Vol. 2, 283–85.

20. *New-York Evening Post*, Apr. 25, 1804.

21. Syrett, Donald C., and Jean G. Cooke, eds. *Interview in Weehawken.* Middleton, CT, 1960: 48.

22. *New-York Evening Post*, Apr. 26, 1804.

23. *American Citizen*, Apr. 27, 1804.

24. Parmet and Hecht, *Aaron Burr,* 201 (citing *New-York Evening Post*, Apr. 30, 1804).

25. Kent, William. *Memoirs and Letters of James Kent.* Boston, 1898: 120–21.

CHAPTER 12

1. Schom, Alan. *Napoleon Bonaparte.* New York, 1997: 323. See also Marshall-Cornwall, Sir James. *Napoleon.* Princeton, 1967: 118.

2. Schom, *Bonaparte*, 326–27.

3. Bryant, Arthur. *Years of Victory.* New York, 1945: 63.

4. Lloyd, Lady Mary, ed. *New Letters of Napoleon I.* New York, 1897: 22.

5. Marshall-Cornwall, *Napoleon*, 119.

6. Schom, *Bonaparte*, 314–15.

7. Bryant, *Years of Victory*, 50.

8. Oman, Carola. *Napoleon at the Channel.* New York, 1942: 98–111.

9. Bryant, *Years of Victory,* 53–54.

10. Oman, *Napoleon*, 141.

11. Ibid., 167–68.

12. Marshall-Cornwall, *Napoleon,* 119; *New-York Evening Post*, Feb. 3, 1804.

13. Cronin, Vincent. *Napoleon Bonaparte: An Intimate Biography.* New York, 1971: 141ff.

14. Ibid., 241–44.

15. Ibid., 243.

16. Brant, Irving. *James Madison*. Vol. 4. Indianapolis, 1941–53: 180–82, 188–99.

17. Jacobs, James Ripley. *Tarnished Warrior* (Biography of James Wilkinson). New York, 1938: 204–5.

18. Ibid., 204.

19. *PAB*, 868.

20. Adams, Henry. *Life of Albert Gallatin*. New York, 1880: 323.

21. Jacobs, *Tarnished Warrior,* 203.

22. *PAB*, 720–22.

23. Jacobs, *Tarnished Warrior,* 205–7.

24. Ibid., 199.

25. Ibid., 195.

26. Malone, *Jefferson the President, First Term*, 386.

27. Ibid., 383.

28. Ibid., 410.

29. Ibid., 415.

30. Peterson, Merrill D. *Thomas Jefferson and the New Nation*. New York, 1970: 790.

31. Brodie, Fawn. *Thomas Jefferson: An Intimate History*. New York, 1974: 382.

32. Ibid., 383.

33. Goebel, *Law Practice of Alexander Hamilton* Vol I, 844–45.

CHAPTER 13

1. *American Citizen*, Apr. 30, 1804.

2. Ibid., May 4, 1804.

3. Ibid., May 5, 1894.

4. Ibid., May 7, 1804.

5. Davis, *Memoirs of Aaron Burr*, Vol. 2, 285. Most biographers have translated Burr's French comment as "so much the better." But it seems more likely that he meant "It's just as well" or "That's that." Larousse *Grand Dictionaire* (1993 ed.) illustrates the usage of *tant mieux* thus: "il est parti et c'est tant mieux [he has left and it's just as well]."

6. *New-York Evening Post*, May 3, 1804.

7. Ibid., May 2, 1804.

8. *American Citizen*, May 8, 1804.

9. Ibid., May 10, 1804.

10. Ibid., May 18, 1804.

11. Ibid., May 19, 1804.

12. Parmet and Hecht, *Aaron Burr*, 201.

13. *PAB*, 867–68.

14. *Papers of Aaron Burr* (microfilm ed.). Series 1, reel 5.

15. Parmet and Hecht, *Aaron Burr*, 244.

16. *Papers of Aaron Burr* (microfilm ed.). Series 1, reel 5.

17. Davis, *Memoirs of Aaron Burr,* Vol. 2, 288.

18. Ibid., 287.

CHAPTER 14

1. Kent, William. *Memoirs and Letters of James Kent.* 327.

2. Ibid., 143.

3. Ibid.

4. Hendrickson, *Hamilton,* Vol. 2, 625.

5. *PAH,* Vol. 26, 215.

6. Ibid., 221ff.

7. Ibid., 217.

8. Hartfield, *Contemporary American Opinion of Napoléon,* 146.

9. Ibid., 145.

10. Ibid.

11. *DeWitt Clinton Letterbook.* Special Collections, Columbia University, letter of May 10 to Captain Livingston, commandant at Fort Jay.

12. Stokes, *The Iconography of Manhattan Island.* Vol. 5, 1422.

13. Goebel, *Law Practice of Alexander Hamilton,* Vol. 1, 845.

14. *American Citizen,* June 4, 1804.

15. Ibid.

16. Davis, *Memoirs of Aaron Burr*, Vol. 2, 289.

17. Ibid., 289. The author consulted Robert B. Daroff, M.D., Professor of Neurology at Case Western Reserve School of Medicine, an internationally recognized expert on migraine and other headache disorders, for this diagnosis.

18. *PAB,* 871.

19. Ibid., 870.

20. Ibid.

21. Cowan, Helen I. *Charles Williamson, Genesee Promoter—Friend of Anglo-American Rapprochement.* Rochester, NY, 1941: 223. Williamson also wanted Pulteney and his associates to pay another $490,621.93 to cover the agency's outstanding debts.

22. Ibid, 270

CHAPTER 15

1. Van Doren, *Correspondence of Aaron Burr and Theodosia,* 164.

2. *PAB,* 877.

3. Syrett and Cooke, *Interview in Weekhawken,* 43. [also *PAH* 242–43.]

4. Reader's Press, comp. *The Cries of New York.* New York, 1931: 33, 43.

5. *PAH,* Vol. 26, 147–48.

6. Syrett and Cooke, *Interview in Weekhawken,* 52–54.

7. Ibid., 58–59.

8. Ibid., 57–58.

9. Ibid., 62.

10. Ibid., 67.

11. Ibid., 68–69.

12. Davis, *Memoirs of Aaron Burr,* Vol. 2, 289–90.

13. Syrett and Cooke, *Interview in Weekhawken*, 83.

14. Ibid., 97–98.

CHAPTER 16

1. Syrett and Cooke, *Interview in Weehawken*, 99–102.

2. Adams, *Documents Relating to New England Federalism*, 169.

3. Ibid.

4. Ibid., 170.

5. Ernst, *Rufus King*, 282–83.

6. Davis, *Memoirs of Aaron Burr*, Vol. 2, 292.

7. Adair, *Fame and the Founding Fathers*, 291.

8. Syrett and Cooke, *Interview in Weehawken*, 111.

9. Cowan, *Charles Willliamson*, 17.

10. *PAH*, Vol., 26, 292. For Adams quote, see Nagel, Paul C. *Descent from Glory*, New York, 1983: 60.

11. *PAH*, Vol. 26, 310.

12. Ibid., 310–11.

13. Hendrickson, *Hamilton*, Vol. 2, 636–37.

14. Hamilton, *Intimate Life of Alexander Hamilton*, 414, for the expenses. His 1804 income is from Goebel, *The Law Practice of Alexander Hamilton*, Vol. 5, 366.

15. *New-York Evening Post*, Jan. 7, 1804.

16. U.S. Bicentennial Society. 1976 announcement of reproductions of the pistols used in the duel. Merrill Lindsay, arms consultant.

17. Tripp, *Robert Troup*, 199.

18. Syrett and Cooke, *Interview in Weehawken,* 132–33.

19. *PAH*, Vol. 26, 309.

20. Davis, *Memoirs of Aaron Burr*, 325–26.

21. Ibid., 322–23.

CHAPTER 17

1. *PAH*, 26, 60.

2. Steinmetz, *The Romance of Duelling*, 81–84.

3. *PAH*, Vol. 26, 341.

4. *PAH*, Vol. 26, 317; 347.

5. Ibid., 317.

6. Ibid., 315–16.

7. Ibid., 347.

8. Ibid., 341.

9. Ibid., 347.

10. Ibid., 312.

11. *Pendleton Papers*. New York Historical Society. Pendleton to Rufus King, July 12, 1804.

12. Morris, *Diary and Letters of Gouveneur Morris*, Vol 2, 455–56.

13. Ibid., 458.

14. PAH, Vol XXVI, 347.

CHAPTER 18

1. Morris, *Diary and Letters of Gouverneur Morris*, 456–57.

2. *PAH*, Vol. 26, 316.

3. *PAB*, 884.

4. *American Citizen*, July 13, 1804.

5. *PAH*, Vol. 26, 322–24.

6. Morris, *Diary and Letters of Gouverneur Morris*, 457–58.

7. Ibid., 458.

8. Ibid.

9. *PAH*, Vol. 26, 333–34.

10. Ibid., 319.

11. Wandell and Minnigerode, *Aaron Burr*, 300.

12. Ibid. 300–301.

13. *New-York Evening Post*, July 20, 1804.

14. Parton, James. *The Life and Times of Aaron Burr*. New York, 1858: 359.

15. Hendrickson, *Hamilton*, Vol. 2, 639.

16. Davis, *Memoirs of Aaron Burr*, Vol. 2, 327.

17. *PAB*, 885.

18. Ibid., 887.

19. Ibid., 335.

20. Ibid., 338.

21. Hirsch, Felix E. "The Bard Family," *Columbia University Quarterly* (Oct. 1941): 236.

22. Parton, *The Life and Times of Aaron Burr*, Vol. 1. 366–68.

23. Wandell and Minnigerode, *Aaron Burr*, 306.

24. *PAB*, 890.

25. Wandell and Minnigerode, *Aaron Burr*, Vol. 1, 306.

26. Parton, *The Life and Times of Aaron Burr*, 369.

27. Hay, Thomas Robson. "Charles Williamson and the Burr Conspiracy," *Journal of Southern History* 2 (1936): 184.

28. *PAB*, 890.

29. Wandell and Minnigerode, *Aaron Burr,* Vol. 1, 307.

30. Malone, *Jefferson the President, First Term,* 357.

31. East, Robert A., and Josephine Mayer. "Settlement of Alexander Hamilton's Debts," *New York History* (Oct. 1937): 382.

32. Hendrickson, *Hamilton,* Vol. 2, 661.

33. *PAH*, Vol. 26, 319–20.

34. Parton, *The Life and Times of Aaron Burr,* 369.

35. *PAB*, 890.

36. Ibid., 891–92.

AFTERWARD

1. Freeman, *Duelling as Politics*, 301.

2. *PAB*, 891.

3. Ibid., 894.

4. Wandell and Minnigerode, *Aaron Burr*, Vol. 1, 302–3.

5. Lomask, *Aaron Burr*, Vol. 1, 356.

6. Wandell and Minnigerode, *Aaron Burr*, Vol. 1, 306.

7. *PAB*, 643.

8. Parmet and Hecht, *Aaron Burr*, 223.

9. *PAB*, 896.

10. Lomask, *Aaron Burr,* 361, citing Plumer's Memorandum.

11. Malone, *Jefferson the President, First Term,* 433.

12. *PAB*, 898–99.

13. Ibid., 899.

14. Abernethy, *The Burr Conspiracy*, 21–22.

15. Fruchtman, Jack Jr. *Thomas Paine: Apostle of Freedom.* New York, 1994: 413.

16. Stevens, *Pistols at Ten Paces*, 161.

17. Hendrickson, *Hamilton,* Vol. 2, 659.

18. Ibid., 661.

19. Mitchell, *Alexander Hamilton*, Vol. 2, 550–55.

20. Tripp, *Robert Troup*, 199, 322.

21. Lomask, *Aaron Burr*, 365; Parmet and Hecht, *Aaron Burr,* 226–27.

22. Baker, Leonard. *John Marshall, A Life in Law.* New York, 1974: 424.

23. Ibid., 425.

24. Ibid., 432.

25. Ibid., 429.

26. Ellis, *The Jeffersonian Crisis*, 74.

27. Baker, *John Marshall*, 470–471.

28. *PAB*, 861–62.

29. Baker, *John Marshall*, 427.

30. Ibid., 435.

31. Ibid., 433, 435.

32. Malone, *Jefferson the President, First Term*, 479.

33. Baker, *John Marshall*, 437.

34. Lomask, *Aaron Burr*, 367.

35. Baker, *John Marshall*, 437.

36. Richard Ellis, in *The Jeffersonian Crisis*, suggests that John Randolph did his cause no good by violently opposing an attempt to compensate the Yazoo claimants a few days before the trial began, further alienating himself from the moderate wing of the Republican party and antagonizing Republican senators who may have favored a settlement. Ellis also argues, unconvincingly in my opinion, that Jefferson had changed his mind about Chase's impeachment and had sent signals in his usual covert style that he no longer supported the move—which he had initiated.

37. Lomask, *Aaron Burr*, 362.

38. *PAB*, 912–16.

39. Ibid., 910.

40. Ibid., 912.

41. Ibid., 911.

42. Ibid., 908–9.

43. Ibid., 902.

44. Davis, *Memoirs of Aaron Burr*, Vol 2, 365

45. Malone, *Jefferson the President, Second Term*, 5.

46. Malone, *Jefferson the President, Second Term*, 359–60.

47. *PAB*, 923–24.

48. Ibid., 927–30.

49. Ibid., 941–42.

50. Lomask, *Aaron Burr*, Vol. 2, 81.

51. *PAB*, 944–45. For some reason, Burr raised his request to 110,000 pounds—as if he were charging the British interest for the delay.

52. Ibid., 953–54.

53. Ibid., 972–73.

54. Hay, Thomas R. "Charles Williamson and the Burr Conspiracy," *Journal of Southern History* (2)1936: 199 (note).

55. Parmet and Hecht, *Aaron Burr*, 248.

56. *PAB*, 962.

57. Ibid., 968.

58. Abernethy, *The Burr Conspiracy*, 42.

59. Hay, *Charles Williamson and the Burr Conspiracy*, 200. Swartout and Colonel William Stephens Smith threw in their adventurous lot with General Francisco de

Miranda, a Venezuelan-born soldier who attempted to liberate his country from Spain with disastrous consequences for all concerned.

60. *PAB*, 973–80; Parmet and Hecht, *Aaron Burr*, 270.

61. Baker, *John Marshall*, 462–3.

62. Robertson, David. *Reports of the Trials of Colonel Aaron Burr taken in short hand by David Robertson.* Vol. 1. Philadelphia, 1808: 4–5.

63. Wandell and Minnigerode, *Aaron Burr*, 180. Also see Baker, *John Marshall*, 464.

64. Malone, *Jefferson the President, Second Term*, 303.

65. Wandell, *Aaron Burr*, 181. Also see Abernethy, *The Burr Conspiracy*, 232.

66. Baker, *John Marshall*, 465; *Papers of John Marshall*, Vol. 7, 17.

67. Lomask, *Aaron Burr*, Vol. 2, 233.

68. Abernethy, *The Burr Conspiracy*, 234–35.

69. Parmet and Hecht, *Aaron Burr*, 288.

70. Abernethy, *The Burr Conspiracy*, 235; Baker, *John Marshall*, 471–72.

71. Baker, 477; Malone, *Jefferson the President, Second Term*, 314.

72. Malone, 312; Baker, 477.

73. Baker, *John Marshall*, 483. Also see Johnson, Herbert A., et al., eds. *The Papers of John Marshall*. Vol. 3. Chapel Hill, NC, 1974–98: 37–50. See note on page 50 for the "wished" and "expected" remark.

74. Lomask, *Aaron Burr*, Vol. 2, 208.

75. Malone, *Jefferson the President, Second Term*, 329; Baker, *John Marshall*, 489.

76. Abernethy, *The Burr Conspiracy*, 240–41.

77. Ibid., 240. Also see *PAB*, 1038.

78. Parmet and Hecht, *Aaron Burr*, 294.

79. Ibid., 295.

80. Lomask, *Aaron Burr*, Vol. 2, 261–62.

81. Baker, *John Marshall*, 501; Lomask, *Aaron Burr*, Vol 2, 267–69.

82. Baker, *Marshall*, 507–9.

83. Lomask, *Aaron Burr*, Vol. 2, 279–80; Baker, *John Marshall*, 513–15.

84. Lomask, *Burr*, 281; *Papers of John Marshall*, Vol. 7, 115.

85. Baker, *John Marshall*, 514.

86. Ibid., 517.

87. Malone, *Jefferson the President, Second Term*, 366–67.

88. Stevens, *Pistols at Ten Paces*, 43.

89. Mushkat, Jerome. "Matthew Livingston Davis and the Political Legacy of Aaron Burr," *The New York Historical Society Quarterly* (April 1975): 134.

90. Parmet and Hecht, *Aaron Burr*, 309.

91. Nevins, Allan. *The Evening Post.* New York, 1922: 42.

92. *PAB*, 1103–4.

93. Ibid., 1133, 1145.

94. Van Doren, ed., *Correspondence of Aaron Burr and His Daughter Theodosia*, 348.

95. Smith, James Morton, ed. *The Republic of Letters, The Correspondence between Thomas Jefferson and James Madison.* New York, 1995: 1682.

96. Young, *The Washington Community*, 184.

97. Nevins, *The Evening Post*, 54.

98. Smith, *The Republic of Letters*, 1732.

99. *PAB*, 1165–66.

100. Ibid., 1169.

101. Sakolski, Aaron Morton. *The Great American Land Bubble.* New York, 1932: 223–24, 226, 229.

102. Hendrickson, *Hamilton*, Vol. 2, 657.

103. Webb, James. "The Fateful Encounter," *American Heritage* (Aug. 1975): 83.

104. Ibid., 93.

105. Parton, *Life and Times of Aaron Burr*, 679–81.

106. Ibid., 674–75.

Index